A WRITER'S REFERENCE

A WRITER'S REFERENCE

Fourth Edition

Diana Hacker

Prince George's Community College

BEDFORD/ST. MARTIN'S   BOSTON ◆ NEW YORK

For Bedford/St. Martin's

Developmental Editor: Michelle McSweeney
Production Editor: Heidi L. Hood
Production Supervisor: Joe Ford
Marketing Manager: Karen Melton
Editorial Assistant: Katherine A. Gilbert
Production Assistant: Deborah Baker
Copyeditor: Barbara G. Flanagan
Text Design: Claire Seng-Niemoeller
Cover Design: Hannus Design Associates
Composition: Monotype Composition
Printing and Binding: RR Donnelley & Sons Company

President: Charles H. Christensen
Editorial Director: Joan E. Feinberg
Director of Editing, Design, and Production: Marcia Cohen
Managing Editor: Elizabeth M. Schaaf

Library of Congress Catalog Card Number: 98–85193

For information, write: Bedford/St. Martin's, 75 Arlington Street, Boston, MA 02116   (617-399-4000)

ISBN: 0–312–40161–2

ACKNOWLEDGMENTS

Nelson W. Aldrich, Jr., from *Old Money: The Mythology of America's Upper Class.* Copyright ©1988 by Nelson W. Aldrich, Jr. Published by Alfred A. Knopf, Inc.

The American Heritage Dictionary of the English Language, from the entry "regard." Copyright ©1996 by Houghton Mifflin Company. Reprinted by permission from *The American Heritage Dictionary of the English Language,* Third Edition.

Acknowledgments and copyrights are continued at the back of the book on pages 423–24, which constitute an extension of the copyright page.

How to use this book

A *Writer's Reference* has been carefully designed to save you time. As you can see, the book lies flat, making it easy to consult while you are revising and editing a draft. And the book's twelve section dividers will lead you—in most cases very quickly—to the information you need.

Here are brief descriptions of the book's major reference aids, followed by several tutorials that give you hands-on experience using the book.

The menu system

The main menu inside the front cover displays the book's contents as briefly and simply as possible. Each of the twelve sections in the main menu leads you to a color-coded tabbed divider, on the back of which you will find a more detailed menu.

Let's say you have a question about the proper use of commas between items in a series. Your first step is to scan the main menu, where you will find the comma listed as the first item under section P (Punctuation). Next flip the book open to the red tabbed divider marked P. Now consult the detailed menu for the precise subsection (P1-c) and the exact page number.

The index

If you aren't sure what topic to choose from the main menu, consult the index at the back of the book. For example, you may not realize that the issue of whether to use *is* or *are* is a matter of subject-verb agreement (G1 on the main menu). In that case, simply look up *"is* versus *are"* in the index and you will be directed to the exact pages you need.

The Glossary of Usage

When in doubt about the correct use of a particular word (such as *affect* and *effect, among* and *between,* or *hopefully*), flip to section W1 and consult the alphabetically arranged glossary for the word in question. If the word you are looking for isn't in the Glossary of Usage, try the index instead. For example, you won't find an entry for *"I* versus *me"* in the glossary because the issue is too complicated for a short glossary entry. The index, however, will take you straight to the pages you need.

The directories to documentation models

When you are writing a research paper, there is no need to memorize all of the technical details about handling citations or constructing a list of the works you have cited. Instead, you can rely on one of the book's directories to documentation models. If you are using the Modern Language Association (MLA) system of documentation, flip the book open to the tabbed section marked M to find the appropriate directory. If you are using the American Psychological Association (APA) or the *Chicago* system, flip to the tabbed section marked A.

List of ESL boxes

If you are a nonnative speaker of English, you will find most of the ESL (English as a second language) advice in the tabbed section marked T (for ESL Trouble Spots). Other ESL advice appears in boxed ESL notes throughout *A Writer's Reference.* For quick reference, a list of these ESL notes is given near the end of the book, after the index and before the revision symbols.

Revision symbols

Some instructors mark student papers with the codes given on the main menu or detailed menus, such as E1 or G3-c. If your instructor uses standard revision symbols instead, consult the list on the very last page of the book, right before the endpapers.

Detailed menu (inside the back cover)

A menu more detailed than the main menu appears inside the back cover.

Tutorials

The following tutorials will give you practice using the book's menu system, the index, the Glossary of Usage, and the directory to the MLA documentation models. Answers to all tutorials appear on pages xii–xiv.

TUTORIAL 1   Using the menu system

Each of the following "rules" violates the principle it expresses. Using the menu system, find the section in *A Writer's Reference* that explains the principle. Then fix the problem. Examples:

> *has*
> A verb ~~have~~ to agree with its subject. *G1*
> ^

> *Tutors in*
> ~~In~~ the writing center, ~~they~~ say that vague pronoun reference is
> ^
> unacceptable. *G3-b*

1. Each pronoun must agree with their antecedent.
2. About sentence fragments. You should avoid them.
3. Its important to use apostrophe's correctly.
4. Watch out for *-ed* endings that have been drop from verbs.
5. Discriminate careful between adjectives and adverbs.
6. Be alert for irregular verbs that have came to you in the wrong form.
7. If your sentence begins with a long introductory word group use a comma to separate the word group from the rest of the sentence.
8. Don't write a run-on sentence, you must connect independent clauses with a comma and a coordinating conjunction or with a semicolon.
9. A writer must be careful not to shift your point of view.
10. When dangling, watch your modifiers.

TUTORIAL 2   Using the index

Assume that you have written the following sentences and want to know the answers to the questions in brackets. Use the index at the back of the book to locate the information you need, and edit the sentences if necessary.

1. Each of the candidates have agreed to participate in tonight's debate. [Does the subject *Each* agree with *have* or with *has*?]
2. We had intended to go surfing but spent most of our vacation lying on the beach. [Should I use *lying* or *laying*?]
3. We only looked at two houses before buying the house of our dreams. [Is *only* in the right place?]
4. In Saudi Arabia it is considered ill mannered for you to accept a gift. [Is it okay to use *you* to mean "anyone in general"?]
5. Joanne picked up several bottles of Vermont maple syrup for her sister and me. [Should I write *for her sister and I*?]

TUTORIAL 3   Using the menu system or the index

Imagine that you are in the following situations. Using either the menu system or the index, find the information you need.

1. You are Ray Farley, a community college student who has been out of high school for ten years. You recall learning to punctuate items in a series by putting a comma between all items except the last two. In your college readings, however, you have noticed that most writers use a comma between all items. You're curious about the current rule. What does *A Writer's Reference* tell you?
2. You are Maria Sanchez, an honors student working in your university's writing center. Mike Lee, who speaks English as a second language, has come to you for help. He is working on a rough draft that contains a number of problems involving the use of articles (*a, an,* and *the*). You know how to use articles, but you aren't able to explain the rather complicated rules on their correct use. Which section of *A Writer's Reference* will you and Mike Lee consult?
3. You are John Pell, engaged to marry Jane Dalton. In a note to Jane's parents, you have written, "Thank you for giving Jane and myself such a generous contribution toward our honeymoon trip to Hawaii." You wonder if you should write "Jane and I" or "Jane and me" instead. What does *A Writer's Reference* tell you?
4. You are Selena Young, a supervisor of interns at a housing agency. Two of your interns, Jake Gilliam and Susan Green, have writing problems involving -*s* endings on verbs. Gilliam tends to drop -*s* endings; Green tends to add them where they don't belong. You suspect that both problems stem from nonstandard dialects spoken at home.

   Susan and Jake are in danger of losing their jobs because your boss thinks that anyone who writes "the tenant refuse" or "the landlords agrees" is beyond hope. You disagree. Susan and Jake are more intelligent than your boss supposes, and they have asked for your help. Where in *A Writer's Reference* can they find the rules they need?

5. You are Joe Thompson, a first-year college student. Your friend Samantha, who has completed two years of college, seems to enjoy correcting your English. Just yesterday she corrected your sentence "I felt badly about her death" to "I felt bad about her death." You're sure you've heard many educated persons, including professors, say "I felt badly." Upon consulting *A Writer's Reference,* what do you discover?

TUTORIAL 4   Using the Glossary of Usage

Consult the Glossary of Usage (section W1) to see if the italicized words are used correctly. Then edit any sentences containing incorrect usage. Example:

> *an*
> The pediatrician gave my daughter ~~a~~ injection for her allergy.

1. The *amount* of horses a Comanche warrior had in his possession indicated the wealth of his family.
2. This afternoon I plan to *lie* out in the sun and work on a tan.
3. That is the most *unique* floral arrangement I have ever seen.
4. Changing attitudes *toward* alcohol have *effected* the beer industry.
5. Jenny *should of* known better than to attempt that dive.
6. Everyone in our office is *enthused* about this project.
7. George and Pat are selling *there* house because now that *their* children are grown, *their* planning to move to Arizona.
8. Most sleds are pulled by no *fewer* than two dogs and no more than ten.
9. It is *man's* nature to think wisely and act foolishly.
10. Dr. Newman and *myself* have agreed to arrange the party.

TUTORIAL 5   Using the directory to MLA works cited models

Assume that you have written a short research paper on the growth of gambling operations on Indian reservations. You have cited the following sources in your paper, using MLA documentation, and you are ready to type your list of works cited. Flip the book open to the tabbed section marked M and use the MLA directory to locate the appropriate works cited models. Then write a correct entry for each source and arrange the entries in a properly formatted list of works cited. *Note:* Do not number the entries in a list of works cited.

A book by Bruce E. Johansen entitled *Life and Death in Mohawk Country.* The book was published in Golden, Colorado, in 1993 by North American Press.

An e-mail about casinos on reservations in the Northeast, sent to you by Helen Codoga on April 10, 1998. The subject line reads "Gambling on Reservations."

An article by Eric Schine entitled "First Gambling, Then a Bank: California Has Reservations," from the weekly magazine *Business Week*. The article appears on page 47 of the September 9, 1996, issue of the magazine.

An article by Sam Ridgebear entitled "Guilty Hands: Traditionalism and the Indian Gaming Industry" from the online journal *Many Voices: American Indian Students Journal*. The article appears in volume 1, issue 1, of this journal in 1995, and there is no pagination. You accessed the article through the Internet on April 2, 1998, at the following address: <http://thecity.sfsu.edu/users/BANN/journal/guiltyhands.html>.

A journal article by Mary H. Cooper entitled "Native Americans' Future: Do U.S. Policies Block Opportunities for Progress?" The article appears on pages 603 to 619 of *CQ Researcher*, which is paginated by volume. The volume number is 6 and the year is 1996.

An article by James Dao entitled "Gambling Proponents See Indian Casinos as Alternative." The article was published on January 30, 1997, and it appears on page B2 of the late edition of the *New York Times*.

An article by Kenan Pollack entitled "Mashantucket Pequots: A Tribe That's Raking It In," available on *U.S. News Online* at the address <http://www.usnews.com/usnews/issue/gambleb8.htm>. No page numbers are given, and there is no information available about the print version of the article, but the online version of the article was last updated on February 17, 1998. You accessed the article on May 1, 1998.

Answers to Tutorial 1

1. Each pronoun must agree with its antecedent. (G3-a)
2. You should avoid sentence fragments. (G5)
3. It's important to use apostrophes correctly. (P5-c and P5-e)
4. Watch out for *-ed* endings that have been dropped from verbs. (G2-d)
5. Discriminate carefully between adjectives and adverbs. (G4)
6. Be alert for irregular verbs that have come to you in the wrong form. (G2-a)
7. If your sentence begins with a long introductory word group, use a comma to separate the word group from the rest of the sentence. (P1-b)
8. Don't write a run-on sentence; you must connect independent clauses with a comma and a coordinating conjunction or with a semicolon. (G6)

9. A writer must be careful not to shift his or her [*not* their] point of view. *Or* Writers must be careful not to shift their point of view. (E4-a)
10. Watch out for dangling modifiers. (E3-e)

Answers to Tutorial 2

1. The index entry "each" mentions that the word is singular, so you might not need to look further to realize that *has* [not *have*] is correct. The first page reference leads you to section G1-e, which explains in more detail why *has* is correct.
2. The index entry "*lie, lay*" takes you to the Glossary of Usage and to section G2-b, where you will learn that *lying* (meaning "reclining or resting on a surface") is correct.
3. Look up "*only*" and you will be directed to section E3-a, which explains that limiting modifiers such as *only* should be placed before the words they modify. The sentence should read *We looked at only two houses before buying the house of our dreams.*
4. Looking up "*you,* inappropriate use of" leads you to the Glossary of Usage and section G3-b, both of which explain that *you* should not be used to mean "anyone in general." You can revise the sentence by using *a person* or *one* instead of *you,* or you can restructure the sentence completely: *In Saudi Arabia, accepting a gift is considered ill mannered.*
5. The index entries "*I* versus *me*" and "*me* versus *I*" take you to section G3-c, which explains why *me* is correct.

Answers to Tutorial 3

1. Section P1-c notes that although usage varies, most experts advise using a comma between all items in a series—to prevent possible misreadings or ambiguities. To find this section, Ray Farley would probably use the menu system.
2. Maria Sanchez and Mike Lee would consult section T1, on articles. This section is easy to locate on the main menu.
3. Section G3-c explains why "Jane and me" is correct. To find section G3-c, John Pell could use the menu system if he knew to look under "Problems with pronouns." Otherwise, he could look up "*I* versus *me*" in the index. Pell could also look up "*myself*" in the index or he could consult the Glossary of Usage, where a cross-reference would direct him to section G3-c.
4. Selena Young's employees could turn to sections G1 and G2-c for help. Young could use the menu system to find these sections if she knew to look under "Subject-verb agreement" or "Other problems with verbs." If she wasn't sure about the grammatical terminology, she could look up "*-s,* as verb ending" or "Verbs, *-s* form of" in the index.

5. Section G4-b explains why "I felt bad about her death" is correct. To find section G4-b, Joe Thompson could use the menu system if he knew that *bad* versus *badly* is a choice between an adjective and an adverb. Otherwise he could look up *"bad, badly"* in the index or the Glossary of Usage.

Answers to Tutorial 4

1. The *number* of horses a Comanche warrior had in his possession indicated the wealth of his family.
2. Correct
3. That is the most *unusual* floral arrangement I have ever seen.
4. Changing attitudes *toward* alcohol have *affected* the beer industry.
5. Jenny *should have* known better than to attempt that dive.
6. Everyone in our office is *enthusiastic* about this project.
7. George and Pat are selling *their* house because now that *their* children are grown, *they're* planning to move to Arizona.
8. Correct
9. It is *human* nature to think wisely and act foolishly.
10. Dr. Newman and *I* have agreed to arrange the party.

Answers to Tutorial 5

Codoga, Helen. "Gambling on Reservations." E-mail to the author. 10 Apr. 1998.

Cooper, Mary H. "Native Americans' Future: Do U.S. Policies Block Opportunities for Progress?" CQ Researcher 6 (1996): 603-19.

Dao, James. "Gambling Proponents See Indian Casinos as Alternative." New York Times 30 Jan. 1997, late ed.: B2.

Johansen, Bruce E. Life and Death in Mohawk Country. Golden, CO: North American, 1993.

Pollack, Kenan. "Mashantucket Pequots: A Tribe That's Raking It In." U.S. News Online 17 Feb. 1998. 1 May 1998 <http://www.usnews.com/usnews/issue/gambleb8.htm>.

Ridgebear, Sam. "Guilty Hands: Traditionalism and the Indian Gaming Industry." Many Voices: American Indian Students Journal 1.1 (1995). 2 Apr. 1998 <http://thecity.sfsu.edu/users/BANN/journal/ guiltyhands.html>.

Schine, Eric. "First Gambling, Then a Bank: California Has Reservations." Business Week 9 Sept. 1996: 47.

Preface for instructors

When Bedford and I invented the quick-reference format—with its main menu, tabbed dividers, and lie-flat binding—ten years ago, we had no idea that *A Writer's Reference* would become so popular (or so widely imitated). My hopes were more modest. I hoped that the format and the title would send a clear message: *A Writer's Reference* is meant to be consulted as needed; it is not a set of grammar lessons to be studied in a vacuum. I also hoped that the book would support and promote modern pedagogy, which places students' own texts at the center of writing instruction. These hopes have been realized: Instructors across the country tell me that their students can and do use the book on their own, keeping it flipped open next to their computers.

In preparing the fourth edition, I have been guided not just by my own classroom experience but by the experiences of instructors from all over the country. In more than two hundred reviews and questionnaires and in visits to college campuses, I have learned much about the way composition is being taught at all levels of instruction. Much has changed in the four years since the third edition was published, and the fourth edition reflects those changes. Here, briefly, is what's new.

Designed for faster reference

A new four-color design provides visual appeal, but it does more. Judicious use of color makes the fourth edition even faster to consult than previous editions. Here is how the colors have been used.

Color-coded main menu and tabbed dividers. Now multi-colored, the main menu points unmistakably to teal, red, and black sets of tabbed dividers, making it even easier for students to flip to the section they need.

Four-color page design, still uncluttered. Rules and hand-edited sentences continue to be highlighted in a single color (now red) so that students can scan for quick answers, reading as much or as little of the text as they need. Charts and boxes now appear consistently in teal and beige, making them easy to find and, just as important, easy to skip.

More visuals throughout. More charts highlight key material, and icons now draw attention to ESL boxes and new grammar checker boxes. Throughout the research sections, students will encounter fewer stretches of unbroken text and more visuals, including screen shots illustrating Internet searches.

Written for today's researchers

Research writing has changed dramatically since the publication of the third edition. Although the latest printing of the third edition brought the book into the electronic age, the fourth edition goes even further. In addition, the fourth edition provides a more thorough survey of the research process.

Updated coverage of researching online. Technology has transformed the entire process of research both in the library and on the rapidly changing Internet. The research section now reflects those changes, offering advice on conducting searches, previewing and evaluating both print and electronic sources, and managing information (without plagiarizing) in the electronic age.

More on planning, drafting, and revising a research paper. Coverage now includes choosing an appropriate research question, forming a tentative thesis, sketching an outline, drafting an introduction with a revised thesis, providing organizational cues, and finding an appropriate voice. At the end of the section there are two checklists for revision, one for global matters and the other for proper handling of sources.

MLA, APA, and Chicago documentation. New to this edition is coverage of *Chicago*-style footnotes or endnotes and bibliography, illustrated with sample pages. The MLA and APA sections have been updated for both print and electronic sources, and each style is illustrated with a full sample paper. A new MLA paper draws on both traditional and Internet sources.

Updated for the electronic age

In addition to its new material on electronic research, the fourth edition takes into account other technological changes that have occurred since publication of the third edition.

Fifty grammar checker boxes. New to this edition are fifty boxes that show students just what current grammar checkers can do — and what they can't do. To discover the capabilities and limits of current grammar checkers, I have run a large bank of exercise sentences (many containing errors), along with some student drafts, through four grammar checker programs. The results, summarized in screened boxes with computer icons throughout the book, show that grammar checkers can help with some but by no means all of the typical problems in a draft.

E-mail and Web pages. The section on document design now provides advice on the rhetoric and etiquette of e-mail and gives tips on designing effective Web pages.

A CD-ROM version of the handbook, with interactive exercises. An *Electronic Writer's Reference* covers all of the topics in the print equivalent, but I have rewritten each section to take advantage of the computer medium. By using pop-up boxes (including charts, definitions, lists, notes, and extra examples), I have kept the on-screen text to a manageable size and minimized the need for scrolling. Students access the text through clickable menus or a searchable index, and they can go deeper into the text, as needed, by clicking on boldface terms or underlined hyperlinks. In addition, students can bookmark sections for future reference. The software also provides a customizable list of Internet sources, with direct links to useful Web sites.

Exercise sets, accessible from menus or from the text itself, are practice lessons that students can use on their own. I have written more than a thousand pop-up boxes that let students know immediately whether their answer is right or wrong and, depending on the choice they made, give them a customized explanation. Students are therefore learning as they go along — not just showing what they knew before they began the exercise. Most exercises are scorable, and students can print out their work. Some exercises, those that deal with rhetorical issues, are not scorable; for these exercises, students are given one or two suggested revisions instead of a strictly wrong or right answer.

Expanded in just a few key places

Reviewers of the third edition asked me not to expand *A Writer's Reference* too much, so I have worked to keep the book as lean as possible. Apart from fuller coverage of research writing and technology, the only major addition that reviewers suggested was a section on argument. Reviewers also wanted slightly expanded coverage of ESL matters.

A section on argument. Using a process approach, a new section on argument shows students how to construct an argument that will have some hope of persuading readers who do not already agree with their views. Students are advised to keep an open mind, to weigh competing arguments using a critical assessment of the evidence, and to build common ground with readers by focusing on shared values. A sample argument paper appears at the end of the section.

More help for ESL students. Coverage of articles, sentence structure problems, and prepositions has been expanded. In addition, there are more ESL boxes throughout the text, and these boxes are now highlighted with icons.

An expanded ancillary package

To make *A Writer's Reference* more useful for both students and instructors, the publisher has improved the package of resources accompanying the handbook.

An Electronic Writer's Reference (available on CD-ROM and 3½″ disks for Windows® and Macintosh™)

Bedford/St. Martin's *Web Site* <http://www.bedfordstmartins.com>

Research and Documentation in the Electronic Age, Second Edition (also available online at <http://www.bedfordstmartins.com/hacker/resdoc>)

Exercises to Accompany A WRITER'S REFERENCE (with Answer Key)

Developmental Exercises to Accompany A WRITER'S REFERENCE (with Answer Key)

The ESL Workbook: Text and Exercises

The Bedford Bibliography for Teachers of Writing, Fourth Edition (also available online at <http://www.bedfordstmartins.com/bib>)

Acknowledgments

No author can possibly anticipate the many ways in which a variety of students might respond to a text: Where might students be confused? How much explanation is enough? What is too intimidating? Do the examples appeal to a range of students? Are they free of stereotypes? To help me answer such questions, more than two hundred professors from over one hundred and fifty colleges and universities contributed their useful insights based on their varied experiences in the classroom.

For their many helpful suggestions, I would like to thank an unusually perceptive group of reviewers:

Donna Ashcroft, Northland Pioneer College
Cynthia Bates, University of California, Davis
Larry Behrens, University of California, Santa Barbara
Valerie Belew, Nashville State Technical College
Kathleen Bottaro, Manchester Community–Technical College
Jennifer Brachfeld, Florida Atlantic University
Alice Brand, State University of New York at Brockport
Pamela Buass, University of Mobile
Cheryl Cassidy, Eastern Michigan University
David Chapman, Samford University
Virginia Crane, California State University at Los Angeles
Nancy Cross, Walla Walla College
Pamela Cross, The Richard Stockton College of New Jersey
Marcia Curtis, University of Massachusetts at Amherst
Genie Davis, University of Alabama
Elaine Delvecchio, Norwalk Community College
Cathy Powers Dice, University of Memphis
Carolyn Engdahl, Quinsigamond Community College
John Evans, Kennesaw State College
Ruth Fairchild, Ridgewater College
Ben Feigert, University of Texas
Deborah Fleming, Ashland University
Allison Fraiberg, University of Redlands
Donald Fucci, Ramapo College
Sarah Garnes, Ohio State University
Margaret Graham, Iowa State University
Kevin Griffith, Capital University
Paul Heilker, Virginia Polytechnic Institute and State
    University
Avis Hewitt, Calvin College
Eric Hoffman, American University

Sandra Howland, University of Massachusetts at Boston
Michael Hricik, Westmoreland Community College
Ronald Israel, San Diego Mesa College
Dana Jeanette, American University
Kathleen Kelly, Northeastern University
Matthew Leone, Colgate University
Leon Linderoth, Lake Superior State University
James Livingston, Northern Michigan University
Philip Luther, University of Cincinnati, Raymond Walters
    College
Emory Maiden, Appalachia State University
Renée Major, Louisiana State University
Angela Maloy, Muskegon Community College
Margaret Marshall, University of Pittsburgh
Anne Maxham-Kastrinos, Washington State University
Lawrence Milbourn, El Paso Community College
Meg Morgan, University of North Carolina
Bill Murdick, California University of Pennsylvania
Linda Myers, Texas Tech University
John O'Brien, Normandale Community College
Carolyn O'Hearn, Pittsburg State University
Tamara Olaivar, University of Florida, Gainesville
Beverly Palmer, Pomona College
Beth Paulson, California State University at Los Angeles
Phoebe Reeves, University of San Francisco
Mary Jo Reiff, Youngstown State University
Shirley Rose, Purdue University
Connie Rothwell, University of North Carolina
Cheryl Ruggiero, Virginia Polytechnic Institute and State
    University
Richard Sanzbacher, Embry-Riddle Aeronautical
    University
Jeff Schiff, Columbia College
Elizabeth Siler, Washington State University
Sydney Sowers, University of Alabama
Virginia Story, Western Maryland College
Will Tomory, Southwestern Michigan College
Ginger Utley, Utah State University
Wendy Wenner, Grand Valley State University
Caroll Wilson, Raritan Valley Community College

For helping me see the strengths and deficiencies of the third edition, thanks go to the many instructors who took the time to answer a detailed questionnaire:

Kenneth Albola, University of the Pacific; Gwendoly Alley, Ventura College; Olivia V. Anderson, East Los Angeles College; Jennifer Annick, Loyola Marymount University; Dorothy Augustine, Chapman University; Mary Balestraci, Northeastern University; Mary E. Barr, Fairleigh Dickinson University; Audrey Becker, Oakland University; Faith Benedetti, Bradford College; Kathryn Benzel, University of Nebraska; Kathye S. Bergin, College of the Mainland; Art Berman, Rochester Institute of Technology; F. H. Bottone, Monsignor Donovan High School; Karla Brown, Hawkeye Community College; Mary Burns, University of San Francisco; Jamie M. Burton, Northeastern University; Roseann Cacciola, Saddleback College; Robert S. Caim, West Virginia University at Parkersburg; Ann Campbell, Emory University; Michael Castro, Lindenwood University; Angier Brock Caudle, Virginia Commonwealth University; Brandon Cesmat, California State University, San Marcos; Dianne C. Check, University of Texas; Caroline Cherry, Eastern College; Darren Chiang-Schultheiss, Fullerton College; Elisabeth Cobb, Chapman University; Lola Coleman, Radford University; John Cool, Biola University; Marvin Cox, Boise State University; Marsha Daigle-Williamson, Spring Arbor College; Sarah Dangelantonio, Franklin Pierce College; Elizabeth Davidson, Passaic County Community College; Frances S. Davidson, Mercer County Community College; Mary L. De Nys, George Mason University; Evelyn Diaz, Queens College; Cathy Powers Dice, University of Memphis; C. B. Dodson, University of North Carolina at Wilmington; Kerry Dolan, University of San Francisco; Jeanine Eberhardt, North City Center; J. C. Ellefson, Champlain College; Carolyn Engdahl, Quinsigamond Community College; Mary E. Farry, Ashland High School; Sally Fitzgerald, Chabot College; Lynn Forkos, Community College of Southern Nevada; Kathy Frederickson, Quinsigamond Community College; Loris D. Galford, McNeese State University; Johanna Gedaka, Holy Family College; Mikhail Gershovich, Northeastern University; Lynn Gingrass, University of Colorado; Gwen J. Goodey, Yakima Valley Community College; Sandra Goodling, Messiah College; Rev. Anthony R. Grasso, King's College; Stuart Greene, University of Notre Dame; Jeanne Grinnan, State University of New York at Brockport; Andrew Grobman, Northeastern University; Mia Grogan, La Salle University; George Hammerbacher, King's College; Kenton Harsch, University of Hawaii at Mânoa; Michael Haselkorn, Bentley College; Bruce Henderson, Fullerton College; Avis Hewitt, Calvin College; Matthew Higgs, Northeastern University; Jen Hill, Cornell University; Mark Hochberg, Juniata College; Janis Butler Holm, Ohio University; David Honick, Bentley College; James W. Hood, Mars Hill College;

Judy Isaksen, Eckerd College; Fred Rue Jacobs, Bakersfield College; Emily R. Jensen, Lycoming College; Pamela Katzir, Florida International University; Sr. Mary Hubert Kealy, Immaculata College; Suzanne Keen, Washington & Lee University; Tina M. Kelleher, Johns Hopkins University; Carol B. Kenyon, Roberts Wesleyan College; Carol F. Kessler, Pennsylvania State University; Margaret J. King, Thomas Jefferson University; Susanne Klingenstein, Massachusetts Institute of Technology; Achim Kopp, Mercer University; Carla Kungl, Case Western Reserve University; Meredith Kurz, California State University at Northridge; M. D. Lauterbach, Community College of Aurora; Erin Laux, University of Nebraska; Robert M. Luscher, University of Nebraska; William J. Macauley, Jr., Indiana University of Pennsylvania; Sandra MacPherson, Ohio State University; Arnold A. Markley, Pennsylvania State University; Doris G. Marquit, University of Minnesota; Tom Marshall, University of California at Santa Cruz; Sylvia A. Martin, Black Hawk College; Erin McCormack, Middlesex Community College; William A. McGuire, University of San Francisco; Darlene D. Mettler, Wesleyan College; Taimi Metzler, University of Colorado; Jane Mills, Santa Rosa Junior College; Dorothy Minor, Tulsa Community College; Clyde Moneyhur, Youngstown State University; Gretchen Flesher Moon, Gustavus Adolphus College; Elizabeth Nist, Anoka-Ramsey Community College; Sr. Patricia Nome, College of Mt. St. Vincent; Tom O'Conner, Cape Cod Community College; Elizabeth Parker, Nashville State Technical Institute; Claire Peckosh, Truman State University; Barbara M. Pope, Chabot College; Monte Prater, Tulsa Community College; Alan Price, Pennsylvania State University; Katharine Purcell, Lander University; J. Andrea Ragab, Fresno City College; Diane M. Reisdorfer, Anoka-Ramsey Community College; Elaine Richardson, University of Minnesota; David Ripper, Everett Community College; Marjorie Roemer, Rhode Island College; Sally Romotsky, California State University at Fullerton; John Ruden, Sacramento City College; Jack Ryan, Gettysburg College; Amy St. Jean, Kent State University; Mary Ann Samyn, Oakland University; Andrew Schneider, The New School for Social Research; David Schwartz, University of Michigan; Mary Etta Scott, Avila College; Deborah Shaller, Towson University; Susan Siferd, Western Michigan University; Eileen Smith, Shasta College; Kathryn Wooten Sobel, Indiana University; Nancy Sorkin, Philadelphia College of Textiles and Science; Pauline Spatafora, La Guardia Community College; Claudia Stanger, Fullerton College; Scott Stankey, Anoka-Ramsey Community College; Rita Sturm, Santa Fe Community College; Kevin B. Sullivan, Northeastern University; Mary McCaslin Thompson, Anoka-Ramsey Community College; Richard Thompson, Canisius College; David Tobin, Niagara County Community College; Tamara Trujillo, Fullerton College; L. P. Van Buskirk, Cornell University; David Vela, Dominican College; Jane Verner, Western Washington University; Michael Vivian, Los Angeles Valley College; R. Waller, Florida International University; Shelia M. Walsh, Northeastern University; Carl Waluconis, Seattle Central Community College; Karen Warren, Gavilan College; Karen V. Waters, Marymount University; A. P. Weisman, Hamilton College; Stephen Wilhite, Long Beach City College; Judy Worman, Dartmouth College; Christine Wright, University of Georgia.

I am indebted to the students whose essays appear in this edition—John Garcia, Andrew Knutson, and Karen Shaw—for giving me permission to use their work and to adapt it for pedagogical purposes. My thanks also go to the following students for permission to use their paragraphs: Robert Diaz, Connie Haley, Kathleen Lewis, Julie Reardon, Margaret Smith, Margaret Stack, and David Warren.

Thanks also go to Bill Peirce, who contributed to the research and argument sections, and to Barbara Flanagan, Lloyd Shaw, and Barbara Fister, who helped me update the research and documentation sections.

Several talented editors have contributed to the book. Michelle McSweeney has been a first-rate developmental editor: tactful, savvy, and good-humored. Her knowledge of computers and the Internet proved invaluable as we worked to bring the fourth edition into the electronic age. Copyeditor Barbara Flanagan has once again brought grace and consistency to the final manuscript; her keen eye has saved me from many a blunder. Katherine Gilbert conducted an extensive review program, and she and Jeannine Thibodeau handled other matters too numerous to mention. Arthur Johnson tested early versions of *An Electronic Writer's Reference* with meticulous attention to detail.

Book editor Heidi Hood has expertly steered the book through production under impossible deadlines with the help of Deborah Baker; managing editor Elizabeth Schaaf has once again orchestrated the production of the book with her usual unflappable calm; and Joe Ford and Pat Ollague have ably guided the book through the manufacturing process. Award-winning designer Claire Seng-Niemoeller has created a new four-color design that enlivens the book while preserving the clean, uncluttered pages featuring hand-edited sentences.

As always, I am grateful to publisher Chuck Christensen for his bold vision and his wise and expert counsel and to editorial director Joan Feinberg for teaching me to write handbooks in the first place and for supporting me with such loyalty over the years.

Finally, a note of thanks goes to my mother, Georgianna Tarvin, and to Joseph and Marian Hacker, Robert Hacker, Greg Tarvin, Betty Renshaw, Bill Fry, Bill Mullinix, Joyce Neff, Christine McMahon, Anne King, Wanda Van Goor, Bill Peirce, Lloyd Shaw, Mary Stevenson, Kate Miller, Jessica Webner, Joan Naake, Melinda Kramer, the Dougherty family, Robbie Wallin, and Austin Nichols for their support and encouragement; and to the many students over the years who have taught me that errors, a natural byproduct of the writing process, are simply problems waiting to be solved.

Diana Hacker
Prince George's Community College

C

Composing
and Revising

C

Composing and Revising

Since it's not possible to think about everything all at once, most experienced writers handle a piece of writing in stages. Roughly speaking, those stages are planning, drafting, and revising. You should generally move from planning to drafting to revising, but be prepared to circle back to earlier stages whenever the need arises.

C1

Planning

C1-a Assess the writing situation.

Begin by taking a look at the writing situation in which you find yourself. The key elements of the writing situation include your subject, the sources of information available to you, your purpose, your audience, and constraints such as length, document design, review sessions, and deadlines.

It is unlikely that you will make final decisions about all of these matters until later in the writing process—after a first draft, for example. Nevertheless, you can save yourself time by thinking about as many of them as possible in advance. For a quick checklist, see pages 4–5.

ESL

What counts as good writing varies from culture to culture and even among groups within cultures. In some situations, you will need to become familiar with the writing styles—such as direct or indirect, personal or impersonal, plain or embellished—that are valued by the culture or discourse community for which you are writing.

C1-b Experiment with techniques for exploring ideas.

Instead of just plunging into a first draft, experiment with one or more techniques for exploring your subject—perhaps listing, clustering, asking questions, freewriting, annotating texts, browsing the Internet, or simply talking and listening. Whatever technique you turn to, the goal is the same: to generate a wealth of ideas. At this early stage of the writing process, you should aim for quantity, not necessarily quality, of ideas. If an idea proves to be off the point, trivial, or too far-fetched, you can always throw it out later.

Checklist for assessing the writing situation

SUBJECT

— Has a subject (or a range of possible subjects) been given to you, or are you free to choose your own?

— Why is your subject worth writing about?

— How broadly can you cover the subject? Do you need to narrow it to a more specific topic (because of length restrictions, for instance)?

— How detailed should your coverage be?

SOURCES OF INFORMATION

— Where will your information come from: Personal experience? Direct observation? Interviews? Questionnaires? Reading? The Internet?

— If your information comes from reading or the Internet, what sort of documentation is required?

PURPOSE

— Why are you writing: To inform readers? To persuade them? To entertain them? To call them to action? Some combination of these?

AUDIENCE

— Who are your readers?

— How well informed are your readers about the subject? What do you want them to learn about the subject?

— How interested and attentive are they likely to be? Will they resist any of your ideas?

— What is your relationship to them: Employee to supervisor? Citizen to citizen? Expert to novice? Scholar to scholar?

— How much time are they willing to spend reading?

— How sophisticated are they as readers? Do they have large vocabularies? Can they follow long and complex sentences?

LENGTH AND DOCUMENT DESIGN

— Are you working within any length specifications? If not, what length seems appropriate, given your subject, your purpose, and your audience?

— Must you use a particular design for your document? If so, do you have guidelines or examples that you can consult? (See also D.)

REVIEWERS AND DEADLINES

—Who will be reviewing your draft in progress: Your instructor? A writing center tutor? Your classmates? A friend? Someone in your family?

—What are your deadlines? How much time will you need to allow for the various stages of writing, including typing and proofreading the final draft?

Listing

You might begin by simply listing ideas, putting them down in the order in which they occur to you — a technique sometimes known as "brainstorming." Here, for example, is a list one writer jotted down:

The Phillips Collection

Washington, D.C.

1612 21st Street, close to Mass. Ave.

near Dupont Circle, in an interesting neighborhood

hard to find a parking space; better to take subway

elegant red brick townhouse, once home of Duncan and Marjorie Phillips (art collectors)

turned into a museum in 1918

facade reminds me of a bygone era — teas and debutante balls

free concerts on Sundays

mostly Impressionists, Postimpressionists, and modern masters

Renoir's *Luncheon of the Boating Party* — warm and joyful — you can almost smell the breeze off the Seine and hear the hum of conversation

you can wander through small rooms filled with paintings by Van Gogh, Degas, Cézanne, Bonnard, and Klee the Rothko room, with huge color paintings—pulsating, sensuous reds, yellows, blues, greens

the new wing—no more bygone era—clean and uncluttered lines appropriate for modern masters like Picasso, Pollock, Dalí, and Braque

a walled garden

The ideas appear here in the order in which they first occurred to the writer. Later she felt free to rearrange them, to cluster them under general categories, to delete some, and to add others. In other words, she treated her initial list as a source of ideas and a springboard to new ideas, not as a formal outline.

Clustering

Unlike listing, the technique of clustering highlights relationships among ideas. To cluster ideas, write your topic in the center of a sheet of paper, draw a circle around it, and surround that circle with related ideas connected to it with lines. If some of the satellite ideas lead to more specific clusters, write them down as well. The writer of the following cluster diagram was exploring ideas for an essay on home uses for computers.

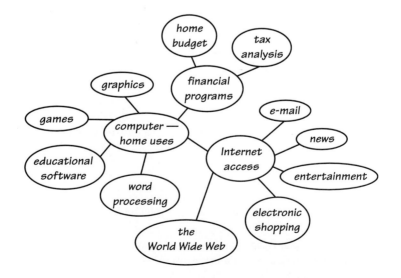

Asking questions

By asking relevant questions, you can generate many ideas—and you can make sure that you have adequately surveyed your subject. When gathering material for a story, journalists routinely ask themselves Who? What? When? Where? Why? and How? In addition to helping journalists get started, these questions ensure that they will not overlook an important fact: the date of a prospective summit meeting, for example, or the exact location of a burglary.

Whenever you are writing about events, whether current or historical, the journalist's questions are one way to get started. One student, whose subject was the reaction in 1915 to D. W. Griffith's silent film *The Birth of a Nation,* began exploring her topic with this set of questions:

> *Who* objected to the film?
>
> *What* were the objections?
>
> *When* were the protests first voiced?
>
> *Where* were protests most strongly expressed?
>
> *Why* did protesters object to the film?
>
> *How* did protesters make their views known?

In the academic world, scholars often generate ideas with specific questions related to their discipline: one set of questions for analyzing short stories, another for evaluating experiments in social psychology, still another for reporting field experiences in anthropology. If you are writing in a particular discipline, try to discover the questions that scholars typically explore. These are frequently presented in textbooks as checklists.

Freewriting

In its purest form, freewriting is simply nonstop writing. You set aside ten minutes or so and write whatever comes to you, without pausing to think about word choice, spelling, or even meaning. If you get stuck, you can write about being stuck, but you should keep your pencil moving. The point is to loosen up, relax, and see what happens. Even if nothing much happens, you have lost only ten minutes. It's more likely, though, that something interesting will emerge on paper—perhaps an eloquent sentence, an honest expression of feeling, or a line of thought worth exploring.

Annotating texts

When you write about reading, one of the best ways to explore ideas is to mark up the text—on the pages themselves if you own the work, on photocopies if you don't. Here, for example, are two paragraphs from an essay by philosopher Michael Tooley as one student annotated them.

But the subject has been discussed.

I guess he's for legalizing drugs. Why doesn't he say so?

Why is the American policy debate not focused more intensely on the relative merits or demerits of our current approach to drugs and of possible alternatives to it? The lack of discussion of this issue is rather striking, given that America has the most serious drug problem in the world, that alternatives to a prohibitionist approach are under serious consideration in other countries, and that the grounds for reconsidering our current approach are, I shall argue, so weighty. . . .

True? How is he defining "drug problem"?

Biased language?

I want to turn in detail to perhaps the two most important reasons for reconsidering our current drug policy: first, the difficulty of providing any adequate justification for the restrictions that prohibitive laws place on people's liberty; and second, the enormous social and personal costs associated with a prohibitionist approach.

Aren't there important aspects of the subject that he's ignoring?

This first reason seems off the point. Is it really worth half of our attention?

The Internet

The Internet is a rich source of information that is fast and convenient to use, although its sheer magnitude can be overwhelming. A good way to begin exploring your subject on the Internet is to browse a subject directory such as Argus Clearinghouse or to type keywords into a search engine such as Yahoo! (see p. 60 for the addresses). For more detailed advice on using the Internet to research a subject, see R1-d. For advice on evaluating Internet sources, see R2-a and R2-b. For advice on documenting Internet sources, see M or A.

Talking and listening

The early stages of the writing process need not be lonely. Many writers begin a writing project by brainstorming ideas in a group, debating a point with friends, or engaging in conversation with a professor. Others turn to themselves for company—by talking non-stop into a tape recorder.

If your computer is equipped with a modem, you can "virtually converse" by exchanging ideas through e-mail, by joining an Internet chat group, or by following a listserv discussion. If you are part of a networked classroom, you may be encouraged to exchange ideas with your classmates and instructor in an electronic workshop.

Talking can be a good way to get to know your audience. If you're planning to write a narrative, for instance, you can test its dramatic effect on a group of friends. Or if you hope to advance a certain argument, you can try it out on listeners who hold a different view.

As you have no doubt discovered, conversation can deepen and refine your ideas before you even begin to set them down on paper. Our first thoughts are not necessarily our wisest thoughts; by talking and listening to others we can all stretch our potential as thinkers and as writers.

C1-c Settle on a tentative focus.

As you explore your subject, you will begin to see possible ways to focus your material. At this point, try to settle on a tentative central idea. The more complex your subject, the more your initial central idea will change as your drafts evolve.

For many types of writing, the central idea can be asserted in one sentence, a generalization preparing readers for the supporting details that will follow. Such a sentence, which often appears in the opening paragraph, is called a *thesis* (see C2-a). A successful thesis—like the following, all taken from articles in *Smithsonian* magazine—points both the writer and the reader in a definite direction:

> Much maligned and the subject of unwarranted fears, most bats are harmless and highly beneficial.

> Geometric forms known as fractals may have a profound effect on how we view the world, not only in art and film but in many branches of science and technology, from astronomy to economics to predicting the weather.

> Aside from his more famous identities as colonel of the Rough Riders and President of the United States, Theodore Roosevelt was a lifelong professional man of letters.

The thesis sentence usually contains a key word or controlling idea that limits its focus. The preceding sentences, for example, prepare for essays that focus on the *beneficial* aspects of bats, the *effect* of fractals on how we view the world, and Roosevelt's identity as a writer, or *man of letters.*

It's a good idea to formulate a thesis early in the writing process, perhaps by jotting it on scratch paper, by putting it at the head of a rough outline, or by attempting to write an introductory paragraph that includes the thesis. Your tentative thesis will probably be less graceful than the thesis you include in the final version of your essay. Here, for example, is one student's early effort:

> Although they both play percussion instruments, drummers and percussionists are very different.

The thesis that appeared in the final draft of the student's paper was more polished.

> Two types of musicians play percussion instruments—drummers and percussionists—and they are as different as Quiet Riot and the New York Philharmonic.

Don't worry too soon about the exact wording of your thesis, however, because your main point may change as you refine your ideas. For a more detailed discussion of the thesis, see C2-a.

C1-d Sketch a tentative plan.

Once you have generated some ideas and formulated a tentative thesis, you may want to sketch an informal outline. Informal outlines can take many forms. Perhaps the most common is simply the thesis followed by a list of major supporting ideas.

> Hawaii is losing its cultural identity.
>
> —pure-blooded Hawaiians increasingly rare
> —native language diluted
> —natives forced off ancestral lands
> —little emphasis on native culture in schools
> —customs exaggerated and distorted by tourism

Clustering diagrams, often used to generate ideas, can also serve as rough outlines (see p. 6). And if you began by jotting down a list of ideas (see p. 5), you may be able to turn the list into a rough outline by crossing out some ideas, adding others, and numbering the ideas to create a logical order.

Planning with headings

When writing a relatively long college paper or business document, consider using headings to guide readers. In addition to helping readers follow the organization of your final draft, headings can be a powerful planning tool, especially if you are working on a computer. You can type in your tentative thesis and then experiment with possible headings; once you have settled on the headings that work best, you can begin typing in chunks of text beneath each heading. Here, for example, is what one student typed into his computer when planning a long history paper. The headings, written in the form of questions, are centered.

```
Although we will never know whether Nathan Bedford
Forrest directly ordered the massacre of Union troops
at Fort Pillow, evidence strongly suggests that he
was responsible for it.

                What happened at Fort Pillow?
            Why do the killings qualify as a massacre?
                Did Forrest order the massacre?
            Did the men have reason to think Forrest
                      wanted a massacre?
```

For more detailed advice about using headings, see D1-b. For a paper that uses headings, see M5.

When to use a formal outline

Early in the writing process, rough outlines have certain advantages over their more formal counterparts: They can be produced more quickly, they are more obviously tentative, and they can be revised more easily should the need arise. However, a formal outline may be useful later in the writing process, after you have written a rough draft, especially if your subject matter is complex.

The following formal outline brought order to a difficult subject, methods for limiting and disposing of nuclear waste. Notice that the student's thesis is an important part of the outline. Everything else in the outline supports it, directly or indirectly.

Thesis: Although various methods for limiting or disposing of nuclear waste have been proposed, each has its drawbacks.

I. Limiting nuclear waste: partitioning and transmutation
   A. The process is complex and costly.
   B. Radiation exposure to nuclear workers would increase.

II. Antarctic ice sheet disposal
   A. Our understanding of ice sheets is too limited.
   B. An international treaty prohibits disposal in Antarctica.

III. Outer space disposal
   A. The risk of an accident and resulting worldwide disaster is great.
   B. The cost is prohibitive.
   C. The method would be unpopular at home and abroad.

IV. Seabed disposal
   A. Scientists have not yet solved technical difficulties.
   B. We do not fully understand the impact of such disposal on the ocean's ecology.

V. Deep underground disposal
   A. There is much pressure against the plan from citizens who do not want their states to become nuclear dumps.
   B. Geologists disagree about the safest disposal sites.

In constructing a formal outline, keep the following guidelines in mind:

1. Put the thesis at the top.
2. Use parallel grammatical structure for ideas at the same level of generality. (See E1.)
3. Use sentences unless phrases are clear.
4. Use the conventional system of numbers and letters for the levels of generality:

   I.
      A.
      B.
         1.
         2.
            a.
            b.
               (1)
               (2)
                  (a)
                  (b)
   II.

5. Always use at least two subdivisions for a category.
6. Limit the number of major sections in the outline; if the list of roman numerals grows too long, find some way of clustering the items into a few major categories with more subcategories.
7. Be flexible. Treat your outline as a tentative plan that may need to be adjusted as your drafts evolve.

C2

Drafting

As you rough out an initial draft, keep your planning materials — lists, diagrams, outlines, and so on — close at hand. In addition to helping you get started, such notes and blueprints will encourage you to keep moving. Writing tends to flow better when it is drafted relatively quickly, without many starts and stops.

For most kinds of writing, an introduction announces a main idea, several body paragraphs develop it, and a conclusion drives it home. You can begin drafting, however, at any point. For example, if you find it difficult to introduce a paper that you have not yet written, you can draft the body first and save the introduction for later.

C2-a For most types of writing, draft an introduction that includes a thesis.

For most writing tasks, your introduction will be a paragraph of 50 to 150 words. Perhaps the most common strategy is to open the paragraph with a few sentences that engage the reader and to conclude it with a statement of the essay's main point. The sentence stating the main point is called a *thesis*. (See C1-c.) In the following examples, the thesis has been italicized.

> To the Australian aborigines, the Dreamtime was the time of creation. It was then that the creatures of the earth, including man, came into being. There are many legends about that mystical period, but unfortunately, the koala does not fare too well in any of them. *Slow-witted though it is in life, the koala is generally depicted in myth and folklore as a trickster and a thief.*
> —Roger Caras, "What's a Koala?"

When I was sixteen, I married and moved to a small town to live. My new husband nervously showed me the house he had rented. It was after dark when we arrived there, and I remember wondering why he seemed so apprehensive about my reaction to the house. I thought the place seemed shabby but potentially cozy and quite livable inside. The morning sun revealed the reason for his anxiety by exposing the squalor outdoors. Up to that point, my contact with any reality but that of my own middle-class childhood had come from books. *The next four years in a small Iowa town taught me that reading about poverty is a lot different from living with it.*
— Julie Reardon, student

Ideally, the sentences leading to the thesis should hook the reader, perhaps with one of the following:

a startling statistic or unusual fact

a vivid example

a description

a paradoxical statement

a quotation or bit of dialogue

a question

an analogy

a joke or an anecdote

Such hooks are particularly important when you cannot assume your reader's interest in the subject. Hooks are less necessary in scholarly essays and other writing aimed at readers with a professional interest in the subject.

Although the thesis frequently appears at the end of the introduction, it can just as easily appear at the beginning. Much work-related writing, in which a straightforward approach is most effective, commonly begins with the thesis.

Flex-time scheduling, which has proved its effectiveness at the Library of Congress, should be introduced on a trial basis at the main branch of the Montgomery County Public Library. By offering flexible work hours, the library can boost employee morale, cut down on absenteeism, and expand its hours of operation.
— David Warren, library employee

For some types of writing, it may be difficult or impossible to express the central idea in a thesis sentence; or it may be unwise or unnecessary to put a thesis sentence in the essay itself. A personal narrative, for example, may have a focus too subtle to be distilled in a single sentence, and such a sentence might ruin the story. Strictly informative writing, like that found in many business memos, may be difficult to summarize in a thesis. In such instances, do not try to force the central idea into a thesis sentence. Instead, think in terms of an overriding purpose, which may or may not be stated directly.

Characteristics of an effective thesis

An effective thesis should be a generalization, not a fact; it should be limited, not too broad; and it should be sharply focused, not too vague.

Because a thesis must prepare readers for facts and details, it cannot itself be a fact. It must always be a generalization demanding proof or further development.

> TOO FACTUAL   The polygraph was developed by Dr. John A. Larson in 1921.
>
> REVISED   Because the polygraph has not been proved reliable, even under the most controlled conditions, its use by employers should be banned.

Although a thesis must be a generalization, it must not be *too* general. You will need to narrow the focus of any thesis that you cannot adequately develop in the space allowed. Unless you were writing a book or a very long research paper, the following thesis would be too broad.

> TOO BROAD   Many drugs are now being used successfully to treat mental illnesses.

You would need to restrict the thesis, perhaps like this:

> REVISED   Despite its risks and side effects, Prozac is an effective treatment for depression.

Finally, a thesis should be sharply focused, not too vague. Beware of any thesis containing a fuzzy, hard-to-define word such as *interesting, good,* or *disgusting.*

> TOO VAGUE   Many of the songs played on station WXQP are disgusting.

The word *disgusting* is needlessly vague. To sharpen the focus of this thesis, the writer should be more specific.

> **REVISED**   Of the songs played on station WXQP, all too many depict sex crudely, sanction the beating or rape of women, or foster gang violence.

In the process of making a too-vague thesis more precise, you may find yourself outlining the major sections of your paper, as in the preceding example, which prepares readers for a three-part criticism of the songs played on WXQP. This technique, known as *blueprinting,* helps readers know exactly what to expect as they read on. It also helps you, the writer, control the shape of your essay.

ESL   If you come from a culture that prefers an indirect approach in writing, you may feel that asserting a thesis early in an essay sounds unrefined or even rude. In the United States, however, a direct approach is usually appreciated; when you state your point as directly as possible, you show that you value your reader's time.

C2-b   Draft the body.

Before drafting the body of an essay, think carefully about your thesis statement. What does the thesis promise readers? Try to keep this focus in mind.

It's a good idea to have a plan in mind as well. If you have sketched out a preliminary plan, try to block out your paragraphs accordingly. If you do not have a plan, you would be wise to pause a moment and sketch one (see C1-d). Of course it is also possible to begin without a plan—assuming you are prepared to treat your first attempt as a "discovery draft" that will almost certainly be tossed (or radically rewritten) once you discover what you really want to say.

For more advice about paragraphs and paragraphing, see C4.

C2-c   Draft a conclusion.

The conclusion should echo your main idea, without dully repeating it. Often the concluding paragraph can be relatively short.

In addition to echoing your main idea, a conclusion might summarize your main point, pose a question for future study, offer advice, or propose a course of action. To end an essay detailing the social skills required of a bartender, one writer concludes with some advice:

> If someone were to approach me one day looking for the secret to running a good bar, I suppose I would offer the following advice: Get your customers to pour out their ideas at a greater rate than you pour out the liquor. You will both win in the end.
> —Kathleen Lewis, student

To make the conclusion memorable, consider including a detail, example, or image from the introduction to bring readers full circle; a quotation or bit of dialogue; an anecdote; or a humorous, witty, or ironic comment.

Whatever concluding strategy you choose, avoid introducing new ideas at the end of an essay. Also avoid apologies and other limp, indeterminate endings. You should end crisply, preferably on a positive note.

C3

Revising

For the experienced writer, revising is rarely a one-step process. Global matters generally receive attention first—the focus, organization, paragraphing, content, and overall strategy. Improvements in sentence structure, word choice, grammar, punctuation, and mechanics come later. (See pp. 22–23 for examples.)

C3-a   Make global revisions.

Global revisions address the larger elements of writing. Usually they affect chunks of text longer than a sentence, and frequently they can be quite dramatic. Whole paragraphs might be dropped, others added. Material once stretched over two or three paragraphs might be condensed into one. Entire sections might be rearranged. Even the content may change dramatically, for the process of revising stimulates thought.

Checklist for global revision

PURPOSE AND AUDIENCE

— Does the draft accomplish its purpose—to inform readers, to persuade them, to entertain them, to call them to action (or some combination of these)?

— Is the draft appropriate for its audience? Does it take into consideration the audience's knowledge of the subject, level of interest in the subject, and possible attitudes toward the subject? Is the reading level appropriate?

FOCUS

— Do the introduction and conclusion focus clearly on the main point? Is the thesis clear enough? (If there is no thesis, is there a good reason for omitting one?)

— Are any ideas obviously off the point?

ORGANIZATION AND PARAGRAPHING

— Does the writer give readers enough organizational cues (such as topic sentences or headings)?

— Are ideas ordered effectively?

— Does the paragraphing make sense?

— Are any paragraphs too long or too short for easy reading?

CONTENT

— Is the supporting material persuasive?

— Which ideas need further development?

— Are the parts proportioned sensibly? Do major ideas receive enough attention?

— Where might material be deleted?

Many of us resist global revisions because we find it difficult to distance ourselves from a draft. We tend to review our work from our own, not from our audience's, perspective.

To distance yourself from a draft, put it aside for a while, preferably overnight or even longer. When you return to it, try to play the role of your audience as you read. If possible, enlist the help of reviewers—persons willing to play the role of audience for you. Ask your reviewers to focus on the larger issues of writing, not on the fine points. The checklist on page 18 may help them get started.

NOTE: When working on a computer, print out a hard copy so that you can read the draft as a whole rather than screen by screen. A computer screen focuses your attention on small chunks of text rather than the whole; a printout allows you to look at the entire paper when thinking about what global revisions to make.

Once you have decided what global revisions may be needed, the computer, of course, is an excellent tool. In fact, because the computer saves time, it encourages you to experiment with global revisions. Should you combine two paragraphs? Would your conclusion make a good introduction? Might several paragraphs be rearranged for greater impact? Will the addition of boldface headings improve readability? With little risk, you can explore the possibilities. When a revision misfires, it is easy to restore your original draft.

C3-b Revise and edit sentences.

Most of the rest of this book offers advice on revising sentences for style and clarity and on editing them for grammar, punctuation, and mechanics. The process of revising and editing sentences should ordinarily occur right on the pages of a draft.

> Finally ~~we decided~~ *deciding* that perhaps our dream needed
>
> ~~some~~ prompting, ~~and~~ we visited a fertility doctor and
>
> began the expensive, time-consuming round of proce-
>
> dures that held out ~~the~~ *some* promise of ~~fulfilling our~~
>
> ~~dream. All this was~~ *our dream's fulfillment. Our efforts, however, were* to no avail~~.~~*/* ~~and as~~ *As* we approached
>
> the sixth year of our marriage, we ~~had reached the~~ *could no longer*
>
> ~~point where we couldn't~~ even discuss our childlessness
>
> without becoming very depressed. We questioned why
>
> this had happened to us~~.~~*/* Why had we been singled out
>
> for ~~this~~ *such a* major disappointment?

The original paragraph was flawed by wordiness and an excessive reliance on structures connected with *and*. Such problems can be addressed through any number of acceptable revisions. The first sentence, for example, could have been changed like this:

```
    Finally we decided that perhaps our dream needed
                   After visiting                    we
~~some~~ prompting /, ~~and we visited~~ a fertility doctor, ~~and~~
              ^                                         ^

    began the expensive, time ⁀consuming round of proce-
              promised hope      ^
    dures that ~~held out the promise~~ of fulfilling our
               ^
    dream.
```

Though some writers might argue about the effectiveness of these improvements compared with the previous revision, most would agree that both revisions are better than the original.

Some of the paragraph's improvements involve less choice and are less open to debate. For example, the hyphen in *time-consuming* is necessary, and the question mark in the next-to-last sentence on page 19 must be changed to a period.

As it details the various rules for revising and editing sentences, *A Writer's Reference* suggests when an improvement is simply one among several possibilities and when it is more strictly a matter of right and wrong.

NOTE: Some writers handle most sentence-level revisions directly at the computer, experimenting on screen with a variety of possible improvements. Other writers prefer to print out a hard copy of the draft, mark it up, and then return to the computer.

Software tools

Software can provide help with sentence-level revisions. Most word processing programs have spell checkers that will catch many but not all spelling errors, and some have thesauruses to help with word choice.

Most programs are equipped with grammar checkers (sometimes called "style checkers" or "text analyzers"). When using a grammar checker, you need to be aware of what this tool can — and cannot — do. Grammar checkers are fairly good at flagging wordy sentences, jargon, slang, clichés, and passive verbs. But such matters represent only a small fraction of the sentence-level problems in a typical draft. Because so many problems—such as faulty parallelism, mixed constructions, and misplaced modifiers—lack mathematical precision, they slip right past the grammar checker. You should not assume, therefore, that once you have run your draft through a grammar checker, your grammar problems are over.

Throughout this book, you will find grammar checker advice linked to specific problems. For example, in section W3 you will learn that grammar checkers can flag most but not all passive verbs and that they flag passive constructions whether or not they are appropriate. In section G6 you will learn that grammar checkers flag some run-ons, miss others, and tell you that some sentences may be run-ons when in fact they are not.

The grammar checker advice is based on a large sample of correct and incorrect sentences that were run through four widely used grammar checker programs. For more details, see page xv of the preface.

C3-c Proofread the final manuscript.

After revising and editing, you are ready to prepare the final manuscript. (See M4 for guidelines.) At this point, make sure to allow yourself enough time for proofreading—the final and most important step in manuscript preparation.

Proofreading is a special kind of reading: a slow and methodical search for misspellings, typographical mistakes, and omitted words or word endings. Such errors can be difficult to spot in your own work because you may read what you intended to write, not what is actually on the page. To fight this tendency, try proofreading out loud, articulating each word as it is actually written. You might also try proofreading your sentences in reverse order, a strategy that takes your attention away from the meanings you intended and forces you to think about small surface features instead.

Although proofreading may be dull, it is crucial. Errors strewn throughout an essay are distracting and annoying. If the writer doesn't care about this piece of writing, thinks the reader, why should I? A carefully proofread essay, on the other hand, sends a positive message: It shows that you value your writing and respect your readers.

EXAMPLE OF GLOBAL REVISIONS

Sports on TV--A Win or a Loss?

Team sports are as much a part of Americain life as Mom and apple pie, and they have a good tendency to bring people together. They encourage team members to cooperate with one another, they also create shared enthusiasm among fans. Thanks to television, this togetherness now seems available to nearly all of us at the flick of a switch. We do not have to buy tickets, and travel to a stadium, to see the World Series or the Super Bowl, these games are on television. We can enjoy the game in the comfort of our own living room. ~~After Thanksgiving or Christmas dinner, the whole family may gather around the TV set to watch football together.~~ It would appear that television has done us a great service. But is this really the case? *Although television does make sports more accessible, it also creates a distance between the sport and the fans and between athletes and the teams they play for.*

The advantage of television is that it provides sports fans with greater convenience.

[insert]

We can see more games than if we had to attend each one in person, and we can follow greater varieties of sports.

EXAMPLE OF SENTENCE-LEVEL REVISIONS

Televised
Sports ~~on TV~~ -A Win or a Loss?

Team sports, ~~are~~ as much a part of American life
tend
as Mom and apple pie, ~~and they have a good tendency~~ to
us
bring ~~people~~ together. They encourage team members to
and
cooperate with one another, they ~~also~~ create shared
Because of
enthusiasm among fans. ~~Thanks to~~ television, this

togetherness now seems available ~~to nearly all of us~~

at the flick of a switch. ~~It would appear that television~~

~~has done us a great service.~~ But is this really
makes
the case? Although television ~~does make~~ sports more

accessible, it also creates a distance between the
their
sport and the fans and between athletes and ~~the~~ teams.

~~they play for.~~

The advantage of television is that it provides

sports fans with greater convenience. We do not have

to buy tickets/ and travel to a stadium/ to see the
but
World Series or the Super Bowl/ ~~these games are on~~
any
~~television. We~~ can enjoy ~~the~~ game in the comfort of
rooms
our own living ~~room.~~ We can see more games than if we

had to attend each one in person, and we can follow
a   *variety*
greater ~~varieties~~ of sports.

C4

Paragraphs

Except for special-purpose paragraphs, such as introductions and conclusions (see C2-a and C2-c), paragraphs are clusters of information supporting an essay's main point (or advancing a story's action). Aim for paragraphs that are clearly focused, well developed, organized, coherent, and neither too long nor too short for easy reading.

C4-a   Focus on a main point.

A paragraph should be unified around a main point. The point should be clear to readers, and all sentences in the paragraph must relate to it.

Stating the main point in a topic sentence

As a rule, state the main point of a paragraph in a topic sentence — a one-sentence summary that tells readers what to expect as they read on. Usually the topic sentence comes first:

> *Nearly all living creatures manage some form of communication.* The dance patterns of bees in their hive help to point the way to distant flower fields or announce successful foraging. Male stickleback fish regularly swim upside-down to indicate outrage in a courtship contest. Male deer and lemurs mark territorial ownership by rubbing their own body secretions on boundary stones or trees. Everyone has seen a frightened dog put his tail between his legs and run in panic. We, too, use gestures, expressions, postures, and movement to give our words point.
> —Olivia Vlahos, *Human Beginnings*

Although the topic sentence usually comes first, sometimes it follows a transitional sentence linking the paragraph to earlier material, and occasionally it is withheld until the end of the paragraph. And at times a topic sentence is not needed: if a paragraph continues developing an idea clearly introduced in an earlier paragraph, if the details of the paragraph unmistakably suggest its main point, or if the paragraph appears in a narrative of events where generalizations might interrupt the flow of the story.

Sticking to the point

Sentences that do not support the topic sentence destroy the unity of a paragraph. If the paragraph is otherwise well focused, such offending sentences can simply be deleted or perhaps moved elsewhere. In the following paragraph describing the inadequate facilities in a high school, the information about the word processing instructor (in italics) is clearly off the point.

> As the result of tax cuts, the educational facilities of Lincoln High School have reached an all-time low. Some of the books date back to 1985 and have long since shed their covers. The lack of lab equipment makes it necessary for four to five students to work at one table, with most watching rather than performing experiments. The few computers in working order must share one dot matrix printer. *Also, the word processing instructor left to have a baby at the beginning of the semester, and most of the students don't like the substitute.* As for the furniture, many of the upright chairs have become recliners, and the desk legs are so unbalanced that they play seesaw on the floor.

Sometimes the cure for a disunified paragraph is not as simple as deleting or moving material. Writers often wander into uncharted territory because they cannot think of enough evidence to support a topic sentence. Feeling that it is too soon to break into a new paragraph, they move on to new ideas for which they have not prepared the reader. When this happens, the writer is faced with a choice: Either find more evidence to support the topic sentence or adjust the topic sentence to mesh with the evidence that is available.

C4-b Develop the main point.

Though an occasional short paragraph is fine, particularly if it functions as a transition or emphasizes a point, a series of brief paragraphs suggests inadequate development. How much development is enough? That varies, depending on the writer's purpose and audience.

For example, when she wrote a paragraph attempting to convince readers that it is impossible to lose fat quickly, health columnist Jane Brody knew that she would have to present a great deal of evidence because many dieters want to believe the opposite. She did *not* write:

> When you think about it, it's impossible to lose—as many diets suggest—10 pounds of *fat* in ten days, even on a total fast. Even a moderately active person cannot lose so much weight so fast. A less active person hasn't a prayer.

This three-sentence paragraph is too skimpy to be convincing. But the paragraph that Brody in fact wrote contains enough evidence to convince even skeptical readers.

> When you think about it, it's impossible to lose—as many diets suggest—10 pounds of *fat* in ten days, even on a total fast. A pound of body fat represents 3,500 calories. To lose 1 pound of fat, you must expend 3,500 more calories than you consume. Let's say you weigh 170 pounds and, as a moderately active person, you burn 2,500 calories a day. If your diet contains only 1,500 calories, you'd have an energy deficit of 1,000 calories a day. In a week's time that would add up to a 7,000-calorie deficit, or 2 pounds of real fat. In ten days, the accumulated deficit would represent nearly 3 pounds of lost body fat. Even if you ate nothing at all for ten days and maintained your usual level of activity, your caloric deficit would add up to 25,000 calories. . . . At 3,500 calories per pound of fat, that's still only 7 pounds of lost fat.
> —Jane Brody, *Jane Brody's Nutrition Book*

C4-c Choose a suitable pattern of organization.

Although paragraphs may be patterned in an almost infinite number of ways, certain patterns of organization occur frequently, either alone or in combination: examples and illustrations, narration, description, process, comparison and contrast, analogy, cause and effect, classification and division, and definition. There is nothing particularly magical about these patterns (sometimes called *methods of development*). They simply reflect some of the ways in which we think.

Examples and illustrations

Examples, perhaps the most common pattern of organization, are appropriate whenever the reader might be tempted to ask, "For example?"

> Normally my parents abided scrupulously by "The Budget," but several times a year Dad would dip into his battered, black

strongbox and splurge on some irrational, totally satisfying luxury. Once he bought over a hundred comic books at a flea market, doled out to us thereafter at the tantalizing rate of two a week. He always got a whole flat of pansies, Mom's favorite flower, for us to give her on Mother's Day. One day a boy stopped at our house selling fifty-cent raffle tickets on a sailboat and Dad bought every ticket the boy had left—three books' worth.
                                                    —Connie Hailey, student

Illustrations are extended examples, frequently presented in story form.

Part of Harriet Tubman's strategy of conducting was, as in all battle-field operations, the knowledge of how and when to retreat. Numerous allusions have been made to her moves when she suspected that she was in danger. When she feared the party was closely pursued, she would take it for a time on a train southward bound. No one seeing Negroes going in this direction would for an instant suppose them to be fugitives. Once on her return she was at a railway station. She saw some men reading a poster and she heard one of them reading it aloud. It was a description of her, offering a reward for her capture. She took a southbound train to avert suspicion. At another time when Harriet heard men talking about her, she pretended to read a book which she carried. One man remarked, "This cannot be the woman. The one we want can't read or write." Harriet devoutly hoped the book was right side up.
                                                    —Earl Conrad, *Harriet Tubman*

Narration

A paragraph of narration tells a story or part of a story. The following paragraph, from Jane Goodall's *In the Shadow of Man,* recounts one of the author's experiences in the African wild.

One evening when I was wading in the shallows of the lake to pass a rocky outcrop, I suddenly stopped dead as I saw the sinuous black body of a snake in the water. It was all of six feet long, and from the slight hood and the dark stripes at the back of the neck I knew it to be a Storm's water cobra—a deadly reptile for the bite of which there was, at that time, no serum. As I stared at it an incoming wave gently deposited part of its body on one of my feet. I remained motionless, not even breathing, until the wave rolled back into the lake, drawing the snake with it. Then I leaped out of the water as fast as I could, my heart hammering.
                                                    — Jane Goodall, *In the Shadow of Man*

Description

A descriptive paragraph sketches a portrait of a person, place, or thing by using concrete and specific details that appeal to one or more senses—sight, sound, smell, taste, and touch. Consider, for example, the following description of the grasshopper invasions that devastated the midwestern landscape in the late 1860s.

> They came like dive bombers out of the west. They came by the millions with the rustle of their wings roaring overhead. They came in waves, like the rolls of the sea, descending with a terrifying speed, breaking now and again like a mighty surf. They came with the force of a williwaw and they formed a huge, ominous, dark brown cloud that eclipsed the sun. They dipped and touched earth, hitting objects and people like hailstones. But they were not hail. These were live demons. They popped, snapped, crackled, and roared. They were dark brown, an inch or longer in length, plump in the middle and tapered at the ends. They had transparent wings, slender legs, and two black eyes that flashed with a fierce intelligence.
>
> —Eugene Boe, "Pioneers to Eternity"

Process

A process paragraph is structured in chronological order. A writer may choose this pattern either to describe how something is made or done or to explain to readers, step by step, how to do something. The following paragraph explains how to perform a "roll cast," a popular fly fishing technique.

> Begin by taking up a suitable stance, with one foot slightly in front of the other and the rod pointing down the line. Then begin a smooth, steady draw, raising your rod hand to just above shoulder height and lifting the rod to the 10:30 or 11:00 position. This steady draw allows a loop of line to form between the rod top and the water. While the line is still moving, raise the rod slightly, then punch it rapidly forward and down. The rod is now flexed and under maximum compression, and the line follows its path, bellying out slightly behind you and coming off the water close to your feet. As you power the rod down through the 3:00 position, the belly of the line will roll forward. Follow through smoothly so that the line unfolds and straightens above the water.
>
> —*The Dorling Kindersley Encyclopedia of Fishing*

Comparison and contrast

To compare two subjects is to draw attention to their similarities, although the word *compare* also has a broader meaning that includes a consideration of differences. To contrast is to focus only on differences.

Whether a paragraph stresses similarities or differences, it may be patterned in one of two ways. The two subjects may be presented one at a time, as in the following paragraph of contrast.

> So Grant and Lee were in complete contrast, representing two diametrically opposed elements in American life. Grant was the modern man emerging; beyond him, ready to come on the stage, was the great age of steel and machinery, of crowded cities and a restless burgeoning vitality. Lee might have ridden down from the old age of chivalry, lance in hand, silken banner fluttering over his head. Each man was the perfect champion of his cause, drawing both his strengths and weaknesses from the people he led.
> —Bruce Catton, "Grant and Lee: A Study in Contrasts"

Or a paragraph may proceed point by point, treating two subjects together, one aspect at a time. The following paragraph uses the point-by-point method to contrast the writer's experiences in an American high school and an Irish convent.

> Strangely enough, instead of being academically inferior to my American high school, the Irish convent was superior. In my class at home, *Love Story* was considered pretty heavy reading, so imagine my surprise at finding Irish students who could recite passages from *War and Peace*. In high school we complained about having to study *Romeo and Juliet* in one semester, whereas in Ireland we simultaneously studied *Macbeth* and Dickens's *Hard Times,* in addition to writing a composition a day in English class. In high school, I didn't even begin algebra until the ninth grade, while at the convent seventh graders (or their Irish equivalent) were doing calculus and trigonometry.   —Margaret Stack, student

Analogy

Analogies draw comparisons between items that appear to have little in common. In the following paragraph, physician Lewis Thomas draws an analogy between the behavior of ants and that of humans.

Ants are so much like human beings as to be an embarrassment. They farm fungi, raise aphids as livestock, launch armies into wars, use chemical sprays to alarm and confuse enemies, capture slaves. The families of weaver ants engage in child labor, holding their larvae like shuttles to spin out the thread that sews the leaves together for their fungus gardens. They exchange information ceaselessly. They do everything but watch television.

—Lewis Thomas, "On Societies as Organisms"

Cause and effect

A paragraph may move from cause to effects or from an effect to its causes. The topic sentence in the following paragraph mentions an effect; the rest of the paragraph lists several causes.

The fantastic water clarity of the Mount Gambier sinkholes results from several factors. The holes are fed from aquifers holding rainwater that fell decades—even centuries—ago, and that has been filtered through miles of limestone. The high level of calcium that limestone adds causes the silty detritus from dead plants and animals to cling together and settle quickly to the bottom. Abundant bottom vegetation in the shallow sinkholes also helps bind the silt. And the rapid turnover of water prohibits stagnation.

—Hillary Hauser, "Exploring a Sunken Realm in Australia"

Classification and division

Classification is the grouping of items into categories according to some consistent principle. The following paragraph classifies species of electric fish.

Scientists sort electric fishes into three categories. The first comprises the strongly electric species like the marine electric rays or the freshwater African electric catfish and South American electric eel. Known since the dawn of history, these deliver a punch strong enough to stun a human. In recent years, biologists have focused on a second category: weakly electric fish in the South American and African rivers that use tiny voltages for communication and navigation. The third group contains sharks, nonelectric rays, and catfish, which do not emit a field but possess sensors that enable them to detect the minute amounts of electricity that leak out of other organisms.

—Anne Rudloe and Jack Rudloe, "Electric Warfare: The Fish That Kill with Thunderbolts"

Division takes one item and divides it into parts. As with classification, division should be made according to some consistent principle. The following paragraph describes the components that make up a baseball.

> Like the game itself, a baseball is composed of many layers. One of the delicious joys of childhood is to take apart a baseball and examine the wonders within. You begin by removing the red cotton thread and peeling off the leather cover—which comes from the hide of a Holstein cow and has been tanned, cut, printed, and punched with holes. Beneath the cover is a thin layer of cotton string, followed by several hundred yards of woolen yarn, which make up the bulk of the ball. Slice into the rubber and you'll find the ball's heart—a cork core. The cork is from Portugal, the rubber from southeast Asia, the covers are American, and the balls are assembled in Costa Rica.   —Dan Gutman, *The Way Baseball Works*

Definition

A definition puts a word or concept into a general class and then provides enough details to distinguish it from other members in the same class. In the following paragraph, the writer defines envy as a special kind of desire.

> Envy is so integral and so painful a part of what animates human behavior in market societies that many people have forgotten the full meaning of the word, simplifying it into one of the synonyms of desire. It is that, which may be why it flourishes in market societies: democracies of desire, they might be called, with money for ballots, stuffing permitted. But envy is more or less than desire. It begins with the almost frantic sense of emptiness inside oneself, as if the pump of one's heart were sucking on air. One has to be blind to perceive the emptiness, of course, but that's just what envy is, a selective blindness. *Invidia,* Latin for envy, translates as "nonsight," and Dante had the envious plodding along under cloaks of lead, their eyes sewn shut with leaden wire. What they are blind to is what they have, God-given and humanly nurtured, in themselves.   —Nelson W. Aldrich, Jr., *Old Money*

C4-d Make paragraphs coherent.

When sentences and paragraphs flow from one to another without discernible bumps, gaps, or shifts, they are said to be coherent. Coherence can be improved by strengthening the various ties between old information and new. A number of techniques for strengthening those ties are detailed in this section.

Linking ideas clearly

Readers expect to learn a paragraph's main point in a topic sentence early in the paragraph. Then, as they move into the body of the paragraph, they expect to encounter specific facts, details, or examples that support the topic sentence — either directly or indirectly. Consider the following paragraph, in which all of the sentences following the topic sentence directly support it.

> A passenger list of the early years of the Orient Express would read like a *Who's Who of the World,* from art to politics. Sarah Bernhardt and her Italian counterpart Eleonora Duse used the train to thrill the stages of Europe. For musicians there were Toscanini and Mahler. Dancers Nijinsky and Pavlova were there, while lesser performers like Harry Houdini and the girls of the Ziegfeld Follies also rode the rails. Violinists were allowed to practice on the train, and occasionally one might see trapeze artists hanging like bats from the baggage racks.
> — Barnaby Conrad III, "Train of Kings"

If a sentence does not support the topic sentence directly, readers expect it to support another sentence in the paragraph. The following paragraph begins with a topic sentence. The italicized sentences are direct supports, and the rest of the sentences are indirect supports.

> Though the open-space classroom works for many children, it is not practical for my son, David. *First, David is hyperactive.* When he was placed in an open-space classroom, he became distracted and confused. He was tempted to watch the movement going on around him instead of concentrating on his own work. *Second, David has a tendency to transpose letters and numbers, a tendency that can be overcome only by individual attention from the instructor.* In the open classroom he was moved from teacher to teacher, with each one responsible for a different subject. No single teacher worked with David long enough to diagnose the problem, let alone help him with it. *Finally, David is not a highly motivated learner.* In the open classroom, he was graded "at his own level," not by criteria for a certain grade. He could receive a B in reading and still be a grade level behind, because he was doing satisfactory work "at his own level."   — Margaret Smith, student

Repeating key words

Repetition of key words is an important technique for gaining coherence. To prevent repetitions from becoming dull, you can use variations of the key word (*hike, hiker, hiking*), pronouns referring to the word (*gamblers . . . they*), and synonyms (*run, spring, race, dash*). In the following paragraph describing plots among indentured servants in the seventeenth century, historian Richard Hofstadter binds sentences together by repeating the key word *plots* and echoing it with variations (italicized).

> *Plots* hatched by several servants to run away together occurred mostly in the plantation colonies, and the few recorded servant *uprisings* were entirely limited to those colonies. Virginia had been forced from its very earliest years to take stringent steps against *mutinous plots,* and severe punishments for *such behavior* were recorded. Most servant *plots* occurred in the seventeenth century: a contemplated *uprising* was nipped in the bud in York County in 1661; apparently led by some left-wing offshoots of the *Great Rebellion,* servants *plotted* an *insurrection* in Gloucester County in 1663, and four leaders were condemned and executed; some discontented servants apparently joined *Bacon's Rebellion* in the 1670's. In the 1680's, the planters became newly apprehensive of discontent among the servants "owing to their great necessities and want of clothes," and it was feared that they would *rise up* and *plunder* the storehouses and ships; in 1682 there were plant-cutting *riots* in which servants and laborers, as well as some planters, took part.   —Richard Hofstadter, *America at 1750*

Using parallel structures

Parallel structures are frequently used within sentences to underscore the similarity of ideas (see E1). They may also be used to bind together a series of sentences expressing similar information. In the following passage describing folk beliefs, anthropologist Margaret Mead presents similar information in parallel grammatical form.

> Actually, almost every day, even in the most sophisticated home, something is likely to happen that evokes the memory of some old folk belief. The salt spills. A knife falls to the floor. Your nose tickles. Then perhaps, with a slightly embarrassed smile, the person who spilled the salt tosses a pinch over his left shoulder. Or someone recites the old rhyme "Knife falls, gentleman calls." Or as you rub your nose you think, That means a letter. I wonder who's writing?   —Margaret Mead, "New Superstitions for Old"

Maintaining consistency

Coherence suffers whenever a draft shifts confusingly from one point of view to another (for example, from *I* to *you* or from *anyone* to *they*). Coherence also suffers when a draft shifts without reason from one verb tense to another (for example, from *swam* to *swims*). For advice on avoiding shifts, see E4.

Providing transitions

Certain words and phrases signal connections between ideas, connections that might otherwise be missed. Frequently used transitions are included in the chart on page 35.

Skilled writers use transitional expressions with care, making sure, for example, not to use a *consequently* when an *also* would be more precise. They are also careful to select transitions with an appropriate tone, perhaps preferring *so* to *thus* in an informal piece, *in summary* to *in short* for a scholarly essay.

In the following paragraph, taken from an argument that dinosaurs had the "'right-sized' brains for reptiles of their body size," biologist Stephen Jay Gould uses transitions (italicized) with skill:

> I don't wish to deny that the flattened, minuscule head of the large bodied "Stegosaurus" houses little brain from our subjective, top-heavy perspective, *but* I do wish to assert that we should not expect more of the beast. *First of all,* large animals have relatively smaller brains than related, small animals. The correlation of brain size with body size among kindred animals (all reptiles, all mammals, *for example*) is remarkably regular. *As* we move from small to large animals, from mice to elephants *or* small lizards to Komodo dragons, brain size increases, *but* not so fast as body size. *In other words,* bodies grow faster than brains, *and* large animals have low ratios of brain weight to body weight. *In fact,* brains grow only about two-thirds as fast as bodies. *Since* we have no reason to believe that large animals are consistently stupider than their smaller relatives, we must conclude that large animals require relatively less brain to do as well as smaller animals. *If* we do not recognize this relationship, we are likely to underestimate the mental power of very large animals, dinosaurs in particular.
>
> —Stephen Jay Gould,
> "Were Dinosaurs Dumb?"

Common transitions

TO SHOW ADDITION

and, also, besides, further, furthermore, in addition, more-over, next, too, first, second

TO GIVE EXAMPLES

for example, for instance, to illustrate, in fact, specifically

TO COMPARE

also, in the same manner, similarly, likewise

TO CONTRAST

but, however, on the other hand, in contrast, nevertheless, still, even though, on the contrary, yet, although

TO SUMMARIZE OR CONCLUDE

in other words, in short, in summary, in conclusion, to sum up, that is, therefore

TO SHOW TIME

after, as, before, next, during, later, finally, meanwhile, then, when, while, immediately

TO SHOW PLACE OR DIRECTION

above, below, beyond, farther on, nearby, opposite, close, to the left

TO INDICATE LOGICAL RELATIONSHIP

if, so, therefore, consequently, thus, as a result, for this reason, since

C4-e If necessary, adjust paragraph length.

Most readers feel comfortable reading paragraphs that range between one hundred and two hundred words. Shorter paragraphs force too much starting and stopping, and longer ones strain the reader's attention span. There are exceptions to this guideline, however. Paragraphs longer than two hundred words frequently appear in scholarly writing, where they suggest seriousness and depth. Paragraphs shorter than one hundred words occur in newspapers because of narrow columns; in informal essays to quicken the pace; in business letters, where readers routinely skim for main ideas; and in e-mail for ease of reading on the computer screen.

In an essay, the first and last paragraphs will ordinarily be the introduction and conclusion. These special-purpose paragraphs are likely to be shorter than the paragraphs in the body of the essay. Typically, the body paragraphs will follow the essay's outline: one paragraph per point in short essays, a group of paragraphs per point in longer ones. Some ideas require more development than others, however, so it is best to be flexible. If an idea stretches to a length unreasonable for a paragraph, you should divide the paragraph, even if you have presented comparable points in the essay in single paragraphs.

Paragraph breaks are not always made for strictly logical reasons. Writers use them for all of the following reasons.

REASONS FOR BEGINNING A NEW PARAGRAPH

—to mark off the introduction and the conclusion

—to signal a shift to a new idea

—to indicate an important shift in time or place

—to emphasize a point (by placing it at the beginning or the end, not in the middle, of a paragraph)

—to highlight a contrast

—to signal a change of speakers (in dialogue)

—to provide readers with a needed pause

—to break up text that looks too dense

Beware of using too many short, choppy paragraphs, however. Readers want to see how your ideas connect, and they become irritated when you break their momentum by forcing them to pause every few sentences. Here are some reasons you might have for combining some of the paragraphs in a rough draft.

REASONS FOR COMBINING PARAGRAPHS

—to clarify the essay's organization

—to connect closely related ideas

—to bind together text that looks too choppy

C5

Arguments

In argumentative writing, you take a stand on a debatable issue. The issue being debated might be a matter of public policy: Should religious groups be allowed to meet on school property? What is the least dangerous way to dispose of nuclear waste? Should a state enact laws rationing medical care? On such questions, reasonable persons can disagree.

Reasonable men and women also disagree about many scholarly issues. Psychologists debate the validity of behaviorism; historians interpret the causes of the Civil War quite differently; biologists conduct genetic experiments to challenge the conclusions of other researchers.

Your goal in argumentative writing is to change the way your readers think about a subject or to convince them to take an action that they might not otherwise be inclined to take. Do not assume that your audience already agrees with you; instead, envision skeptical readers who will make up their minds after listening to all sides of the debate.

C5-a Plan a strategy.

Planning a strategy for an argumentative essay is much like planning a debate for a speech class. A good way to begin is to list your arguments and the opposing arguments and then consider the likely impact of these arguments on your audience. If the opposing arguments look very powerful, you may want to rethink your position. By modifying your initial position—perhaps by claiming less or by proposing a less radical solution to a problem—you may have a greater chance of persuading readers to change their views.

Listing your arguments

Let's say that your tentative purpose (which may change as you think about your audience or modify your own ideas) is to argue in favor of lowering the legal drinking age from twenty-one to eighteen. Here is a list of possible arguments in favor of this point of view.

—Society treats eighteen-year-olds as mature for most purposes.

—They can vote.

—They can go away to college.

—At eighteen, men must register with Selective Service and be available for a possible draft.

—Age is not necessarily an indication of maturity.

—The current drinking age is unfair, since many older Americans were allowed to drink at eighteen.

—An unrealistic drinking age is almost impossible to enforce, and it breeds disrespect for the law.

—In European countries that allow eighteen-year-olds to drink, there is less irresponsible teenage drinking than in our country.

Listing the opposing viewpoints

The next step is to list the key arguments of those who hold opposing views. Here are some possible arguments *against* lowering the drinking age to eighteen.

—Teenage drinking frequently leads to drunk driving, which in turn leads to many deaths.

—Teenage drinking sometimes leads to date rape and gang violence.

—Alcoholism is a serious problem in our society, and a delayed drinking age can help prevent it.

—If the legal age were eighteen, many fifteen- and sixteen-year-olds would find a way to purchase alcohol illegally.

If possible, you should talk to someone who disagrees with your view or read some articles that are critical of your position. By familiarizing yourself with opposing viewpoints, you can be reasonably sure you have not overlooked an important argument that might be used against you.

Considering your audience

Once you have listed the major arguments on both (or all) sides, think realistically about the impact they are likely to have on your intended audience. If your audience is the voting-age population in the United States, for example, consider how you might assess some of the arguments of each side of the drinking age question.

Looking at your list, you would see that your audience, which includes many older Americans, might not be impressed by the suggestion that age is no sign of maturity or by the argument that because eighteen-year-olds are old enough to attend college they should be allowed to drink. You would decide to emphasize your other arguments instead. Americans who remember a time when young men were drafted, for example, might be persuaded that it is unfair to ask a man to die for his country but not allow him to drink. And anyone who has heard of Prohibition might be moved by the argument that an unrealistic drinking regulation can breed disrespect for the law.

As for the opposing arguments, clearly the first one on the list is the most powerful. Statistics show that drunk driving by teenagers causes much carnage on our highways and that teenagers themselves are frequently the victims. To have any hope of convincing your audience, you would need to take this argument very seriously; it would be almost impossible to argue successfully that reducing highway deaths is not important.

Rethinking your position

After exploring all sides of an argument, you may decide to modify your initial position. Maybe your first thoughts about the issue were oversimplified, too extreme, or mistaken in some other respect. Or maybe, after thinking more about your readers, you see little hope of persuading them of the truth or wisdom of your position.

If you were writing about the drinking age, for example, you might decide to modify your position in light of your audience. To have a better chance of convincing the audience, you could argue that eighteen-year-olds *in the military* should be allowed to drink. Or you could argue that eighteen-year-olds should be allowed to drink beer and wine, not hard alcohol. Or you could link your proposal to new tough laws against drunk driving.

C5-b   Frame a thesis and sketch an outline.

A thesis is a sentence that expresses the main point of an essay. (See C2-a.) In argumentative writing, your thesis should clearly state your position on the issue you have chosen to write about.

Let's say your issue is the high insurance rates that most companies set for young male drivers. After thinking carefully about your own views, the opposing arguments, and your audience (the general public), you might state your position like this:

> Although young males as a group have poor driving records, insurance companies should not be allowed to set high rates for any drivers who have maintained a good safety record during their first two years after obtaining a license.

Notice that this is a debatable point, one about which reasonable persons can disagree. It is not merely a fact (for example, that companies do set higher rates for young males). Nor is it a statement of belief (for example, that differing rates are always unfair). Neither facts nor beliefs can be substantiated by reasons, so they cannot serve as a thesis for an argument.

Once you have framed a thesis, try to state your major arguments, preferably in sentence form. Together, your thesis and your arguments will give you a rough outline of your essay, as in the following example:

> Thesis: Although young males as a group have poor driving records, insurance companies should not be allowed to set high rates for any drivers who have maintained a good safety record during their first two years after obtaining a license.

—The current policy of insurance companies is unfair.
  —It is unfair to evaluate an individual driver on the basis of group statistics.
  —Group statistics are used to justify higher rates for young males but usually not for other groups.

—Insurance companies could institute a more equitable policy at little expense.
  —Companies could charge higher rates for all newly licensed drivers (no matter their age or sex), in effect putting them on probation for a period such as two years.
  —Companies could keep individual records on all drivers and set rates yearly according to those records; the rates would apply to all drivers following the two-year probationary period.
  —With computer databases, records could be maintained at a reasonable cost.

Some of the sentences in your rough outline might become topic sentences of paragraphs in your final essay. (See C4-a.)

C5-c Draft an introduction that states your position without alienating readers.

In argumentative writing, your introduction should state your position on an issue in a clear thesis sentence (see C2-a and C5-b), and it should do this without needlessly alienating the audience whom you hope to convince. Where possible, try to establish common ground with readers who may not be in initial agreement with your views.

One way to establish common ground with readers who disagree with your position is to show that you share common values. If your subject is school prayer, for instance, you might show that even though you oppose allowing prayer in schools, you believe in the value of prayer. The writer of the following introduction successfully used this strategy.

> Although the Supreme Court has ruled against prayer in public schools on First Amendment grounds, many people still feel that prayers should be allowed. These people, most of whom hold strong religious beliefs, are well intentioned. What they fail to realize is that the Supreme Court decision, although it was made on legal grounds, makes good sense on religious grounds as well. Prayer is too important to be trusted to our public schools.
> —Kevin Smith, student

Because Smith takes into consideration the values of those who disagree with him, readers are likely to approach his essay with an open mind.

C5-d Support each argument with specific evidence.

When presenting the arguments for your position, you will of course need to back them up with evidence: facts, statistics, examples and illustrations, expert opinion, and so on.

If any of your evidence is based on reading, you will need to document your sources. Documentation gives credit to your sources and shows readers how to track down a source in case they want to assess its credibility or explore the issue further. (See R5-a.)

Using facts and statistics

A fact is something that is known with certainty because it has been objectively verified: The capital of Wyoming is Cheyenne. Carbon has an atomic weight of 12. John F. Kennedy was assassinated on November 22, 1963. Statistics are collections of numerical facts: More than three-quarters of U.S. households currently own a VCR. North America holds only 4 percent of the world's proven oil reserves; together, Iraq, Kuwait, and Saudi Arabia own 44 percent.

Most arguments are supported at least to some extent by facts and statistics. For example, Andrew Knutson, the student who wrote the argument paper on pages 46–48, gathered a few facts and statistics from two printed sources and one Internet source. When he used a statistic from one of these sources, he documented it with an MLA (Modern Language Association) citation in parentheses, like this:

> Currently the responsibility of educating about 75% of undocumented children is borne by just a few states—California, New York, Texas, and Florida (Edmondson 1).

Knutson got this statistic from an article by Brad Edmondson. The parenthetical citation at the end of the sentence names the author of the source and gives the page number. Complete information about the source appears in a works cited list at the end of the paper (see p. 48). (See M1 and M2 for more detailed information about citing sources.)

Some objective sources for statistics are *Statistical Abstract of the United States, American Statistics Index,* and *Statistical Yearbook.*

Using examples and anecdotes

Examples and anecdotes (illustrative stories) alone rarely prove a point, but when used in combination with other forms of evidence, they flesh out an argument and bring it to life. For example, in a research essay written for a psychology class, Karen Shaw used several examples from a variety of sources to show that apes are capable of using language creatively (see A1-d).

Citing expert opinion

Although they are no substitute for careful reasoning of your own, the views of an expert can contribute to the force of your argument.

When you rely on expert opinion, you should be certain that your source is, in fact, an expert in the field you are covering. In some cases you may need to provide an explanation of what makes your source an expert. Use particular caution when gathering research from online sources (see R2-b).

If you include expert testimony in your paper, you must document your sources. You can summarize or paraphrase the expert's opinion or you can quote the expert's exact words. For important advice on appropriate use of written sources, see R5.

C5-e Anticipate objections; refute opposing arguments.

Readers who already agree with you need no convincing, although a well-argued case for their own point of view is always welcome. But indifferent and skeptical readers may resist your arguments because they have minds of their own. To give up a position that seems reasonable, a reader has to see that there is an even more reasonable one. In addition to presenting your own case, therefore, you should review the opposing arguments and explain what you think is wrong with them.

There is no best place in an essay to deal with the opposition. Often it is useful to summarize the opposing position early in your essay. After stating your thesis but before developing your own arguments, you might have a paragraph beginning *Critics of this view argue that.* . . . But sometimes a better plan is to anticipate objections as you develop your case paragraph by paragraph. Wherever you decide to deal with opposing arguments, do your best to refute them. Show that those who oppose you are not as persuasive as they claim because their arguments are flawed or because your arguments to the contrary have greater weight.

C5-f Establish common ground.

As you refute opposing arguments, try to establish common ground with readers who are not in initial agreement with your views. If you can show that you share your readers' values, they may be able to switch to your position without giving up what they feel is important.

For example, to persuade people opposed to shooting deer that hunting is necessary, a state wildlife commission would have to show that it too cares about preserving deer and does not want them to die needlessly. Having established these values in common, the commission might be able to persuade critics that a carefully controlled hunting season is good for the deer population because it prevents starvation caused by overpopulation.

People believe that intelligence and decency support their side of an argument. To change sides, they must continue to feel intelligent and decent. Otherwise they will persist in their opposition.

C5-g Avoid common mistakes in reasoning.

Certain errors in reasoning occur frequently enough to deserve special attention. In both your reading and your writing, you will want to be alert to certain mistakes in reasoning known as *logical fallacies*. Some common fallacies are included in the following chart.

Common logical fallacies

HASTY GENERALIZATION

A generalization based on insufficient or unrepresentative evidence.

> Deaths from drug overdoses in Metropolis have doubled in the past three years. Therefore, more Americans than ever are dying from drug abuse.

NON SEQUITUR (DOES NOT FOLLOW)

A conclusion that does not follow logically from preceding statements or that is based on irrelevant data.

> Mary loves children, so she will make an excellent elementary school teacher.

FALSE ANALOGY

The assumption that because two things are alike in some respects, they are alike in others.

> If we put humans on the moon, we should be able to find a cure for the common cold.

EITHER . . . OR FALLACY

The suggestion that only two alternatives exist when in fact there are more.

> Either learn how to program a computer or you won't be able to get a decent job after college.

FALSE CAUSE (*POST HOC*)

The assumption that because one event follows another, the first is the cause of the second.

> Since Governor Smith took office, unemployment for minorities in the state has decreased by 7 percent. Governor Smith should be applauded for reducing unemployment among minorities.

CIRCULAR REASONING

An argument in which the writer, instead of supplying evidence, simply restates the point in other language.

> Students should not be allowed to park in lots now reserved for faculty because those lots should be for faculty only.

BANDWAGON APPEAL

A claim that an idea should be accepted because a large number of people favor it or believe it is true.

> Everyone knows that smoking marijuana is physically addictive and psychologically harmful.

ARGUMENT TO THE PERSON (*AD HOMINEM*)

An attack on the person proposing an argument rather than on the argument itself.

> Senator Jones was a conscientious objector during the Vietnam War, so his proposal to limit military spending has no merit.

RED HERRING

An argument that focuses on an irrelevant issue to distract attention from the real issue.

> ### Common logical fallacies (continued)
>
> Reporters are out to get the president, so it's no wonder we are hearing rumors about all of these scandals.
>
> **BIASED LANGUAGE**
>
> Words with strong positive or negative connotations.
>
> Those narrow-minded, do-gooder environmentalists care more about trees than they do about people.

SAMPLE ARGUMENT PAPER

In the following paper, student Andrew Knutson argues that Americans should continue to educate the children of illegal immigrants. As you read the paper, notice that Knutson is careful to establish common ground with readers who may hold a different view. Notice too that he attempts to refute the opposing arguments before laying out his own arguments.

In writing the paper, Knutson consulted two written sources and one Internet source. When he quotes from or uses statistics from a source, he cites the source with an MLA (Modern Language Association) in-text citation. Citations in the paper refer readers to the list of works cited at the end of the paper. (See M1 and M2 for detailed advice on citing sources.)

Why Educate the Children of

Illegal Immigrants?

Immigration laws have been a subject of debate throughout American history, especially in states such as California and Texas, where immigrant populations are high. Recently, some citizens have been questioning whether we should continue to educate the children of illegal immigrants. While this issue is steeped in emotional controversy, we must not allow divisive "us against them" rhetoric to cloud our thinking. Yes, educating undocumented immigrants costs us, but not educating them would cost us much more.

Thesis states writer's position on the issue.

Those who propose barring the children of illegal immigrants from our schools have understandable worries. They
worry that their state taxes will rise as undocumented
children crowd their school systems. They worry about the
crowding itself, given the loss of quality education that
comes with large class sizes. They worry that school resources will be deflected from their children because of
the linguistic and social problems that many of the newcom-
ers face. And finally, they worry that even more illegal
immigrants will cross our borders because of the lure of
free education.

The writer
establishes
common
ground.

This last worry is probably unfounded. It is unlikely
that many parents are crossing the borders solely to educate their children. More likely, they are in desperate
need of work, economic opportunity, and possibly political
asylum. As Charles Wheeler of the National Immigration Law
Center asserts, "There is no evidence that access to federal programs acts as a magnet to foreigners or that further restrictions would discourage illegal immigrants"
(qtd. in Public Agenda Foundation).

The writer refutes
an opposing view.

The other concerns are more legitimate, but they
can be addressed by less drastic measures than barring
children from schools. Currently the responsibility of educating about 75% of undocumented children is borne by just
a few states--California, New York, Texas, and Florida
(Edmondson 1). One way to help these and other states is to
have the federal government pick up the cost of educating
undocumented children, with enough funds to alleviate the
overcrowded classrooms that cause parents such concern.
Such cost shifting could have a significant benefit, for if
the federal government had to pay, it might work harder to
stem the tide of illegal immigrants.

Statistic is
documented with
an MLA in-text
citation.

So far, attempts to bar undocumented children from
public schools have failed. In the 1982 case of Plyler v.
Doe, the Supreme Court ruled on the issue. In a 5-4 decision, it overturned a Texas law that allowed schools to
deny education to illegal immigrants as a means of "preserving financial resources, protecting the state from an
influx of illegal immigrants, and maintaining high quality
education for resident children" (McCarthy 128). The Court

Discussion of a legal
precedent puts the
issue in context.

considered these issues but concluded that in the long
run the costs of educating immigrant children would pale
in comparison to the costs--both to the children and to
society--of not educating them.

It isn't hard to figure out what the costs of not edu-

*The writer supplies
examples of the
costs to children
and to society.*

cating these children would be. The costs to innocent children are obvious: loss of the opportunity to learn English,
to understand American culture and history, to socialize
with other children in a structured environment, and to
grow up to be successful, responsible adults.

The costs to society as a whole are fairly obvious as
well. That is why we work so hard to promote literacy and
prevent students from dropping out of school. An uneducated
populace is dangerous to the fabric of society, contribut-
ing to social problems such as vandalism and crime, an
underground economy, gang warfare, teenage pregnancy, sub-
stance abuse, and infectious and transmissible diseases.
The health issue alone makes it worth our while to educate
the children of undocumented immigrants, for when children
are in school, we can make sure they are inoculated properly and can teach them the facts about health and disease.

*The conclusion
drives home the
writer's point.*

Do we really want thousands of uneducated children
growing up on the streets, where we have little control
over them? Surely not. The lure of the streets is powerful
enough already. Only by inviting all children into safe and
nurturing and intellectually engaging schools can we combat
that power. Our efforts will be well worth the cost.

[NEW PAGE]

*Works cited page
follows MLA style*

Works Cited

Edmondson, Brad. "Life without Illegal Immigrants."
    American Demographics May 1996:1.

McCarthy, Martha M. "Immigrants in Public Schools: Legal
    Issues." Educational Horizons 71 (1993): 128-30.

Public Agenda Foundation. "Exploiting Fears." Admission
    Decisions: Should Immigration Be Restricted? 7 Oct.
    1996. Project Vote Smart. 9 Jan. 1997 <http://
    www.vote-smart.org/issues/Immigration/chap2/
    imm2itx.html>.

R

Research
Writing

R

Research Writing

Most college assignments ask you to pose a question worth exploring, to read widely in search of possible answers, to interpret what you read, to draw reasoned conclusions, and to support those conclusions with valid and well-documented evidence.

Admittedly, the process takes time: time for researching and time for drafting, revising, and documenting the paper in the style recommended by your instructor (see the tabbed dividers marked M and A). Before beginning a research project, you should set a realistic schedule of deadlines. For example, one student constructed the following schedule for a paper assigned on October 1 and due October 31.

SCHEDULE	FINISHED BY
1. Take the college's library tour and get familiar with computer search tools.	October 2
2. Pose a research question and plan a search strategy.	3
3. Find sources.	5
4. Read and take notes.	10
5. Decide on a tentative thesis and outline.	11
6. Draft the paper.	16
7. Visit the writing center to get help with ideas for revision.	17
8. Do further research if necessary.	20
9. Revise the paper.	25
10. Prepare a list of works cited.	26
11. Type and proofread the final draft.	28

Notice that this student has budgeted more than a week for drafting and revising the paper. It's easy to spend too much of your available time gathering sources; make sure you allow a significant portion of your schedule for drafting and editing your work.

R1

Conducting research

R1-a Pose possible questions worth exploring.

Working within the guidelines of your assignment, pose a few questions that seem worth researching. Here, for example, are some preliminary questions jotted down by students who were asked to write about a significant political or scholarly issue.

—Can a government-regulated rating system for television shows curb children's exposure to violent programming?

—Which geological formations are the safest repositories for nuclear waste?

—Will a ban on human cloning threaten important medical research?

—What was Marcus Garvey's contribution to the fight for racial equality?

—How can governments and zoos help preserve China's endangered panda?

—Why was amateur archaeologist Heinrich Schliemann such a controversial figure in his own time?

As you formulate possible questions, make sure that they are appropriate lines of inquiry for a research paper. Choose questions that are narrow (not too broad), challenging (not too bland), and grounded (not too speculative).

Choosing a narrow question

If your initial question is too broad, given the length of the paper you plan to write, look for ways to restrict your focus. Here, for example, is how two students narrowed their initial questions.

TOO BROAD
—What are the hazards of fad diets?

—Is the military seriously addressing the problem of sexual harassment?

NARROWER
—What are the hazards of liquid diets?

—To what extent has the army addressed the problem of sexual harassment since the Aberdeen scandal?

Choosing a challenging question

Your research paper will be more interesting to both you and your audience if you base it on an intellectually challenging line of inquiry. Avoid bland questions that fail to provoke thought or engage readers in a debate.

TOO BLAND
—What is obsessive-compulsive disorder?

—Where is wind energy being used?

CHALLENGING
—What treatments for obsessive-compulsive disorder show the most promise?

—Does investing in wind energy make economic sense?

You may well need to address a bland question in the course of answering a more challenging one. For example, if you were writing about promising treatments for obsessive-compulsive disorder, you would no doubt answer the question "What is obsessive-compulsive disorder?" at some point in your paper. It would be a mistake, however, to use the bland question as the focus for the whole paper.

Choosing a grounded question

Finally, you will want to make sure that your research question is grounded, not too speculative. Although speculative questions—such as those that address philosophical, ethical, or religious issues—are worth asking and may receive some attention in a research paper, they are inappropriate central questions. The central argument of a research paper should be grounded in evidence; it should not be based entirely on beliefs.

TOO SPECULATIVE
—Is capital punishment moral?

—What is the difference between a just and an unjust law?

GROUNDED
—Does capital punishment deter crime?

—Should we adjust our laws so that penalties for possession of powdered cocaine and crack cocaine are comparable?

R1-b Map out a search strategy.

A search strategy is a systematic system for tracking down sources. To create a search strategy appropriate for your research question, ask yourself two questions:

—What kinds of resources should I draw on?

—In what order should I conduct my search?

Appropriate resources

Before you start your search, consider what information you will need and where you are likely to find it (see the chart of possible resources on p. 55). If your research question addresses a historical issue, for example, you might look at reference works, books, scholarly articles (in print or online), and primary sources such as speeches. If your question addresses a current political issue, however, you might turn to magazine and newspaper articles, Web sites, government documents, discussion groups on the Internet, and possibly opinion surveys that you conduct yourself. With very current issues, books are not useful because by the time a book is published, it is already dated.

In addition to considering the currency of your proposed topic, take a careful look at your assignment. Most college assignments require you to seek out scholarly sources that challenge your intellect: books by authors who are experts in their field, specialized reference works (not just general encyclopedias), and articles in scholarly or technical journals (not just popular magazines). When in doubt about the kinds of sources you are expected to consult, check with your instructor.

Order of search

Often a good search strategy moves from sources that give you an overview of your subject to those that supply you with more specialized information. Some general reading will familiarize you with the ways in which scholars or debaters are framing issues related to your topic. Once you understand the intellectual or social context of your topic, you will be prepared to focus your search more narrowly.

R1-c Track down relevant library sources.

If you have not already done so, explore your library to find out what it offers. Most libraries provide maps and handouts that describe their services; many conduct orientation programs or offer tours or workshops. In addition, librarians can save you time by helping you define what you're looking for and then telling you where to find it.

Resources to consider when creating a search strategy

LIBRARY RESOURCES

— General and specialized reference works
— Books
— Articles in scholarly journals
— Articles in magazines and newspapers
— Government documents
— Primary sources such as diaries and letters
— Audiovisual materials

INTERNET RESOURCES

— Web sites
— Reference works
— Electronic texts (books, poems, and so on)
— Government documents
— News articles
— Newsgroups and listservs
— MUD's and MOO's
— E-mail

FIELD RESEARCH

— Interviews
— Opinion surveys
— Discussion groups
— Literature from organizations
— Observations and experiments

Most of the searching you do at the library will take place at computer terminals with specific functions. Some terminals are for accessing the computerized book catalog, others contain CD-ROM databases of periodicals, and still others serve as gateways to the Internet.

NOTE: Many libraries make their catalogs available on the Internet, so you can search a library's holdings remotely. This does not necessarily mean that you will be able to access materials from your remote computer, but you will be able to see what is available before you visit the library.

Reference works

For some topics, you may want to begin your search by consulting general or specialized reference works. Check with a reference librarian to see which works are available in electronic format.

GENERAL REFERENCE WORKS General reference works include encyclopedias, biographical references, atlases, almanacs, and unabridged dictionaries. Here are just a few frequently used general references that you might want to consider.

> *Encyclopedia Americana*
>
> *The National Geographic Atlas of the World*
>
> *The New Encyclopædia Britannica*
>
> *The Oxford English Dictionary*
>
> *Webster's New Biographical Dictionary*
>
> *World Almanac and Book of Facts*

For other titles, consult the computer catalog or check with a reference librarian.

NOTE: Although general encyclopedias are often a good place to learn background information about your topic, do not draw upon them in your final paper. Most instructors expect you to rely on more specialized sources.

SPECIALIZED REFERENCE WORKS Many specialized works are available: *Encyclopedia of the Environment, Contemporary Artists, The Historical and Cultural Atlas of African Americans, Almanac of American Politics, Anchor Bible Dictionary,* and so on. Some libraries provide handouts that list their specialized reference works, organized by academic discipline. If your library doesn't, ask a reference librarian for suggestions.

NOTE: A Bedford/St. Martin's Web site, *Research and Documentation in the Electronic Age,* lists many specialized reference works. If a work is available on the Web, the Bedford/St. Martin's site links you directly to the source. The address is <http://www.bedfordstmartins.com/hacker/resdoc>.

Books

Most libraries now use computer catalogs that allow you to search for books and often other materials—such as government documents and audiovisuals—at a computer terminal. While computer catalogs vary widely from library to library, most are easy to use, and a reference librarian will be available to help you if you get stuck. Most catalogs allow you to search for materials by subject, by author, or by title. The screens at the bottom of this page illustrate a subject search.

COMPUTER CATALOG SCREEN 1: LIST OF MATERIALS

```
PUMAS                        5    ITEMS
  1 Lawrence R D 192                        NU  SNELL  STACKS  1990
     The white puma : a novel              QL 795.P85L38  1990

  2 Shaw harley g                           NU  SNELL  STACKS  1989
     Soul among lions : the cougar as peaceful adv  QL 737.C23S52  1989

  3 Tinsley Jim Bob                         NU  SNELL  STACKS  1987
     The Puma : legendary lion of the Americas   QL 737.C2T5x  1987

  4                                         NU  SNELL  STACKS  1973
     Mountain lion social organization in the Idaho  QL 1.W54  no35

  5 Young Stanley Paul                      NU  SNELL  STACKS  1964
     The puma, mysterious American cat. Part I: Hist QL 737.C2Y56  1964

ALL ITEMS HAVE BEEN DISPLAYED..
Enter <Line number(s)> To Display Full Records (Number + B for Brief)
<Q>uit for New Search █
```

COMPUTER CATALOG SCREEN 2: DETAILS FOR A BOOK

```
-----------------------------------NU Libraries------------
AUTHOR(s):      Tinsley, Jim Bob.
TITLE(s):       The Puma : legendary lion of the Americas /  Jim Bob
                   Tinsley.
                1st ed.

                El Paso, Tex. : Texas Western Press, University of Texas
                   at El Paso,   c1987.
                142 p, : ill. ; 29 cm.
                Includes index.
                Bibliography: p. [127]-136.

OTHER ENTRIES:  Pumas.

Format:         statedoc

LOCN:   SNELL STACKS    STATUS: Not checked out --
CALL #: QL 737.C2T5x 1987

----3 of 5--------------------------NU Libraries------------
<R>epeat this display, <Q>uit,
<X> for Express,   <H> for Search History,   ? for Help   > █
```

The most common type of searching is by subject. Searching the catalog by subject involves the use of keywords or subject headings, which prompt the computer to retrieve information about relevant books and other source materials. If your search results in too few or too many finds (or "hits"), try refining your search by using one of the techniques listed in the chart on page 62.

Once you have narrowed your search to a list of relevant sources, you can usually command the computer to print out bibliographic information for a source, along with its call number. The call number is the book's address on the library shelf.

Periodicals

Periodicals are publications issued at regular intervals, such as magazines, newspapers, and scholarly or technical journals. To track down useful articles, consult a periodical index. Periodical indexes vary widely in their format and coverage, so you may wish to check with a reference librarian to find the resources that best suit your needs.

TYPES OF PERIODICAL INDEXES   Periodical indexes are usually available in both print and electronic formats. Most libraries now have a wide selection of electronic databases, either on CD-ROM's or through online subscription services. Be aware, however, that most electronic databases don't date back as far as the print versions do, so you may need to search print indexes for historical topics.

Some periodical indexes, such as *InfoTrac* and *Readers' Guide to Periodical Literature,* focus on popular periodicals and cover a wide range of subjects and publications. More specialized indexes, such as *Religion Index* and *Communication Abstracts,* focus on technical and scholarly journals in particular subject areas.

Periodical indexes also vary in the amount of information they provide. Some indexes contain only article titles and publication information, many include abstracts that summarize the articles, and a few contain the full text of the articles they list.

SEARCHING PERIODICAL INDEXES   You search for periodical articles in an electronic database just as you look for books in the library's computer catalog—by author, title, or subject keywords. Bibliographic records appear on the screen, and if further information is available (such as an abstract or the complete text), you can retrieve it by selecting the article you want. The following is an example of a periodical index screen.

PERIODICAL INDEX SCREEN: DETAILS FOR AN ARTICLE

---

1 RGA
   AUTHOR: Robinson, Jerome B.
   TITLE: Cat in the ballot box (California voters to decide on resumption
      of cougar hunting)
   SOURCE: Field & Stream (ISSN:8755-8580) v 100 p 30+ March '96
   CONTAINS: illustration(s)

SUBJECTS COVERED:
Puma attacks
Puma hunting
Game laws/California
ABSTRACT: For more than two decades, the California Department of Fish and
Game has been prohibited by law from taking measures to limit a mountain lion
population that has clearly overgrown its natural range and is expanding into
urban areas. Mountain lions usually eat deer, but in locations where deer
populations have become sparse, they have been forced to find new food
sources. Consequently, lions are killing livestock, cats, dogs, and even people.
Now California voters are being asked to decide if the "hands off" mountain
lion policy should continue. If voters pass a proposed referendum, the Fish
and Game Department could reintroduce limited sport hunting as a means of
controlling mountain lion populations.

If you are looking for periodical articles that appeared before the mid-1980s, you may need to turn to a print index. Like computer indexes, print indexes usually allow you to search by author, by title, or by subject.

Once you have found article titles that seem relevant to your topic, you will need to track down the periodicals that contain the actual articles. Most libraries provide either a print or an electronic listing of the periodicals they own. The listing tells you how each periodical has been preserved: on microfilm or microfiche, in bound volumes, or in unbound files. It also tells you which publication years the library owns.

CAUTION: Be careful not to confuse abstracts, which summarize articles, with actual articles.

Other library resources

Your library may have rare and unpublished manuscripts in a special collection. Holdings might also include government documents;

records, tapes, and CD's; films and videos; and drawings, paintings, engravings, and slides.

If your research topic is especially complex or unusual, you may need greater resources than your library offers. In such a case, talk to a librarian about interlibrary loan, a process in which one library borrows materials from another. This procedure can take a week or more, so be sure to allow yourself plenty of time.

R1-d Track down relevant Internet sources.

Some of your research will probably take place on the Internet, a vast network of computers that can communicate with one another. When you are logged on to the Internet—often by using a browser such as Netscape Navigator or Microsoft Internet Explorer—you have access to countless online sources. The most common way to locate relevant online sources is to use the Internet search tools described in this section.

CAUTION: Because the Internet lacks quality control, be sure to evaluate online sources with special care (see R2).

Search engines

Millions of Internet sites are cataloged by search engines each day, so online searching can be a daunting process. To maximize your search efforts, consider your own needs and the specialties of the various search engines that are available.

SEARCHING BY CATEGORY Multilevel subject or topic directories arrange sites into manageable categories and allow you to find relevant sites without searching the entire Internet. (For an example, see the sample screens on page 61.) Subject directories can be stand-alone programs such as *Argus Clearinghouse* (<http://www.clearinghouse.net>), or they can be part of a search engine such as *Yahoo!* (<http://www.yahoo.com>).

The benefit of searching by category is that you are restricting your hits to those listed in the subject areas you think are most relevant, so you are less likely to be overwhelmed with possible sources. The downside of searching by category is that you may miss out on useful sites categorized under other subject headings or not included in the directory.

SCREEN 1: CHOOSING A CATEGORY

```
Yahoo! - Microsoft Internet Explorer                              _ 8 X
File  Edit  View  Go  Favorites  Help
Address: http://www.yahoo.com/
```

- **Arts and Humanities**
  Architecture, Photography, Literature...

- **Business and Economy [Xtra!]**
  Companies, Finance, Employment...

- **Computers and Internet [Xtra!]**
  Internet, WWW, Software, Multimedia...

- **Education**
  Universities, K-12, College Entrance...

- **Entertainment [Xtra!]**
  Cool Links, Movies, Music, Humor...

- **Government**
  Military, Politics [Xtra!], Law, Taxes...

- **Health [Xtra!]**
  Medicine, Drugs, Diseases, Fitness...

- **News and Media [Xtra!]**
  Current Events, Magazines, TV, Newspapers...

- **Recreation and Sports [Xtra!]**
  Sports, Games, Travel, Autos, Outdoors...

- **Reference**
  Libraries, Dictionaries, Phone Numbers...

- **Regional**
  Countries, Regions, U.S. States...

- **Science**
  CS, Biology, Astronomy, Engineering...

- **Social Science**
  Anthropology, Sociology, Economics...

- **Society and Culture**
  People, Environment, Religion...

SCREEN 2: SEARCHING A CATEGORY

```
Yahoo! - Society and Culture:Environment and ... - Microsoft Internet Explorer   _ 8 X
File  Edit  View  Go  Favorites  Help
Address: http://www.yahoo.com/Society_and_Culture/Environment_and_Nature/
```

Top:Society and Culture:Environment and Nature

| mountain lion | Search | Options |

⦿ Search all of Yahoo ○ Search only in **Environment and Nature**

- **Indices** *(22)*

- **Animal Rights@**
- **Business** *(8)*
- **Climate Change Policy** *(25)*
- **Companies@**
- **Conservation** *(228)* NEW!
- **Countries** *(38)*
- **Databases** *(15)*
- **Disasters** *(151)* NEW!
- **Ecology@**

- **Law** *(34)*
- **Mining Issues@**
- **Mountains** *(16)*
- **News and Media** *(89)* NEW!
- **Oil and Gas Issues@**
- **Online Resources** *(43)*
- **Organizations** *(373)* NEW!
- **Ozone Depletion** *(18)*
- **Parks@**

SEARCHING BY KEYWORD The amount of information returned by a simple keyword search, much of it irrelevant to your topic, can be overwhelming. To make the best use of your research time, spend a few minutes looking over the help screens or advanced search instructions on individual search engines. In addition, keep the following points in mind:

—Make your keywords as specific as possible.

—Check your spelling.

—Refine or broaden your search as needed (see the chart at the bottom of this page for common techniques).

See the screens on page 63 for a sample keyword search.

USING META SEARCH ENGINES Meta search engines such as *Dogpile* (<http://www.dogpile.com>) and *Metacrawler* (<http://www.metacrawler.com>) search multiple search engines at once. Meta search engines are useful tools for conducting a preliminary search to determine what types of online sources are available.

Refining keyword searches

Although command terms and characters vary among electronic databases and Internet search engines, some of the most commonly used functions are listed here.

—Use quotation marks around words that are part of a phrase: "Broadway musicals".

—Use AND to connect words that must appear in a document: Ireland AND peace. Some search engines require a plus sign instead: Ireland + peace.

—Use NOT in front of words that must not appear in a document: Titanic NOT movie. Some search engines require a minus sign instead: Titanic – movie.

—Use OR if only one of the terms must appear in a document: "mountain lion" OR cougar.

—Use an asterisk as a substitute for letters that might vary: "marine biolog*".

—Use parentheses to group a search expression and combine it with another: (cigarettes OR tobacco OR smok*) AND lawsuits.

SCREEN 1: ENTERING A KEYWORD

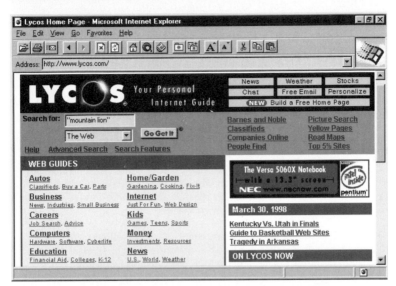

SCREEN 2: LIST OF HITS

Leading search engines and their specialties

ALTA VISTA <http://www.altavista.digital.com> *Alta Vista* is one of the most comprehensive search engines, so it is useful for finding obscure terms. This program allows you to restrict searches by date and to search only in particular fields—such as title, URL, or domain name (.com, .edu, and so on).

EXCITE <http://www.excite.com> *Excite* is good at ranking the probable relevance of a site, and it suggests sites that are similar to ones you found helpful.

HOT BOT <http://www.hotbot.com> The opening page of *Hot Bot* lets you customize your search. For example, it allows you to specify date restrictions, type of media desired, and domain names without having to go into an advanced search screen.

INFOSEEK <http://www.infoseek.com> *Infoseek* allows you to conduct a search on the results of a previous search. It also lets you search for terms only in a particular field, such as titles or URL's.

LYCOS <http://www.lycos.com> *Lycos* maintains a directory and searchable database of its top 5 percent rated sites. *Lycos* allows you to find sites similar to the ones you like best, and it offers advanced search features that allow you to set the relative importance of search parameters and choose the type of media desired.

YAHOO! <http://www.yahoo.com> *Yahoo!* has the most detailed subject directory of the leading search engines, so it is easy to click on a topic and see what's available. This program allows you to restrict a search by date.

One drawback of using meta search engines is that your research will probably result in a number of redundant hits. Another drawback is that you won't be able to take advantage of the specialized commands offered by the individual search engines.

Other online research tools

Because they search the entire Web, search engines are likely to return a number of irrelevant hits and possibly bury relevant ones. To conduct a more focused search, turn to other online resources such as virtual libraries, text databases and archives, government sites, and news sites.

SAMPLE VIRTUAL LIBRARY SCREEN

VIRTUAL LIBRARIES   Virtual libraries are excellent resources for finding online references and useful research sites; some even offer advice on writing and documenting research papers. Virtual libraries are usually organized like subject directories, with hierarchical categories. Here are some especially useful virtual libraries:

—*The Internet Public Library* <http://www.ipl.org>

—*Thor⁺: The Libraries of Purdue University* <http://thorplus.lib.purdue.edu/index.html>

—*The WWW Virtual Library* <http://vlib.stanford.edu/Overview.html>

—*The Library of Congress* <http://lcweb.loc.gov>

—*The Webliography: Internet Subject Guides* <http://www.lib.lsu.edu/weblio.html>

TEXT DATABASES AND ARCHIVES   A number of useful online databases and archives house the complete texts of selected works such as poems, books, and speeches. The materials in these sites are usually limited to older works because of copyright laws. The following online archives are impressive collections:

Useful online research sites

GENERAL REFERENCE SITES

—*Atlapedia Online* <http://www.atlapedia.com>

—*Britannica Online* <http://www.eb.com>

—*Encyclopedia Smithsonian* <http://www.si.edu/resource/faq>

DISCIPLINE-SPECIFIC SITES

—*Research and Documentation in the Electronic Age* (links to sites in a variety of academic disciplines) <http://www.bedfordstmartins.com/hacker/resdoc>

—*Bedford Links to Resources in Literature* <http://www.bedfordstmartins.com/litlinks>

—*Voice of the Shuttle: Web Page for Humanities Research* <http://humanitas.ucsb.edu>

—*H-net: Humanities and Social Sciences Online* <http://h-net2.msu.edu>

—*Social Science Information Gateway* <http://sosig.esrc.bris.ac.uk>

—*Stanford Encyclopedia of Philosophy* <http://plato.stanford.edu>

—"Famous Paintings Exhibition," *WebMuseum* <http://sunsite.unc.edu/wm/paint>

—*Perseus Project* <http://www.perseus.tufts.edu>

—*Bedford/St. Martin's Links to History Resources* <http://www.bedfordstmartins.com/history/historylinks.html>

—*Newsweek International Business Resource Center* <http://www.newsweek-int.com>

—*Science Online* <http://www.sciencemag.org>

—*Windows to the Universe* <http://www.windows.umich.edu>

SITES FOR EVALUATING SOURCES

—"Checklist for Evaluating Web Sites," *Canisius College Library & Internet* <http://www.canisius.edu/canhp/canlib/webcrit.htm>

—"Evaluating Web Sites: Criteria and Tools," *Olin Kroch Uris Libraries* <http://www.library.cornell.edu/okuref/research/webeval.html>

—"Evaluating Internet Information," *Internet Navigator* <http://sol.slcc.edu/lr/navigator/discovery/eval.html>

—*Electronic Text Center—University of Virginia Library* <http://etext.lib.virginia.edu>

—*Project Bartleby Archive* <http://www.columbia.edu/acis/bartleby>

—*Project Gutenberg* <http://promo.net/pg>

GOVERNMENT SITES Many government agencies at every level provide online information services. Government-maintained sites include useful resources such as texts of laws, facts and statistics, government documents, and reference works. If your topic is a political issue, consider going to one of these sites:

—*U.S. Census Bureau: The Official Statistics* <http://www.census.gov>

—*Thomas: Legislative Information on the Internet* <http://thomas.loc.gov>

—*U.S. State & Local Gateway* <http://www.statelocal.gov>

—*U.S. Government Printing Office* <http://www.access.gpo.gov>

—*United Nations* <http://www.un.org>

NEWS SITES Many popular newspapers, magazines, and television networks have online sites that offer some of the most up-to-date information available on the Web. These online services, such as the following, often allow nonsubscribers or "guests" to search partial archives:

—*The New York Times on the Web* <http://www.nytimes.com>

—*The Washington Post* <http://www.washingtonpost.com>

—*U.S. News Online* <http://www.usnews.com/usnews/home.htm>

—*nationalgeographic.com* <http://www.nationalgeographic.com/main.html>

—*CNN Interactive* <http://www.cnn.com>

Online communications

The Internet offers several communications options for conducting your own field research. You might join a listserv, for example, to send and receive e-mail messages relevant to your topic. Or you may wish to search a particular newsgroup's postings. To find listservs and newsgroups related to your topic, go to one of these sites:

—Tile.Net <http://www.tile.net>

—Liszt <http://www.liszt.com>

—Deja News <http://www.dejanews.com>

In addition to listservs and newsgroups, you might log on to real-time discussion forums such as MUD's (multi-user dimensions) and MOO's (multi-user dimensions, object-oriented) to discuss your topic.

CAUTION: If you plan to use online communications to conduct field research, be aware that most of the people you contact will not be experts on your topic. Although you are more likely to find serious and worthwhile commentary in moderated listservs and scholarly discussion forums than in more freewheeling newsgroups, it is difficult to guarantee the credibility of anyone you "meet" online.

R2

Evaluating sources

R2-a   Select sources worth your attention.

By spending just an hour or two searching for information in the library or on the Internet, you can locate dozens of potential sources for your topic—far more than you will have time to read. Your challenge will be to select a reasonable number of sources that are worth your time and attention.

As you conduct a library or Internet search, be alert for clues that indicate whether a book or article or Web site is worth tracking down. Titles often suggest the relevance of a source, and dates will help you rule out sources too old for consideration. In addition, many electronic indexes contain abstracts—brief summaries of articles—that can help you choose which ones to look at. Even the language used in a title or abstract can be a clue; the language might tell you, for example, that a source is too technical, too sensationalized, or not scholarly enough for your purposes.

Once you have tracked down a source, preview it quickly to see how much of your attention, if any, it is worth. Techniques for previewing a book, an article, and a Web site are a bit different. Suggested techniques appear in the chart on page 69.

Previewing techniques

PREVIEWING A BOOK

— Scan the front and back covers for any information about the book's scope and its author's credentials.

— Glance through the table of contents, keeping your research question in mind.

— Skim the preface in search of a statement of the author's purposes.

— Using the index, look up a few words related to your research question.

— If a chapter seems useful, read its opening and closing paragraphs and skim any headings.

— Consider the author's style and approach. Does the style suggest enough intellectual depth for your purpose? Does the author seem to present ideas in an unbiased way?

PREVIEWING AN ARTICLE

— Consider the publication in which the article is printed. Is the publisher reputable? Who is the target audience of the publication? Might the publication be biased toward the target audience?

— For a magazine or journal article, look for an abstract or a statement of purpose at the beginning; also look for a summary at the end.

— For a newspaper article, focus on the headline and the opening sentences, known as the *lead*.

— Skim any headings and take a look at any charts, graphs, diagrams, or illustrations that might indicate the article's focus and scope.

PREVIEWING A WEB SITE

— Browse the home page. Do its contents and links seem relevant to your research question?

— Consider the reputation, credibility, and motive of the site's author. Is the site reputable enough to consider for further evaluation?

— Check to see if there is a note about when the site was last updated. For a current topic, some sites may be outdated.

R2-b Read with an open mind and a critical eye.

As you research your topic, keep an open mind. Do not let your personal beliefs prevent you from listening to new ideas and opposing viewpoints. Your research question—not a snap-judgment answer to the question—should guide your reading.

CAUTION: When researching on the Internet, it is easy to ignore views different from your own. Web pages that appeal to you will often link to other pages that support the same viewpoint. If your sources all seem to agree with you—and with one another—seek out opposing views and try to evaluate them with an open mind.

When you read with a critical eye, you are not necessarily judging an author's work harshly; you are simply examining its assumptions, assessing its evidence, and weighing its conclusions.

Distinguishing between primary and secondary sources

As you begin assessing the evidence in a text, consider whether you are reading a primary or a secondary source. Primary sources are original documents such as speeches, diaries, novels, legislative bills, laboratory studies, field research reports, and eyewitness accounts. Secondary sources are commentaries on primary sources.

Although a primary source is not necessarily more reliable than a secondary source, it has the advantage of being a firsthand account. Naturally, you can better evaluate what a secondary source says if you have first read any primary sources it discusses.

Being alert for signs of bias

Both in print and online, some publishers and authors are more objective than others. If you were exploring the conspiracy theories surrounding the Kennedy assassination, for example, you wouldn't look to a supermarket tabloid such as the *National Enquirer* for answers. You would rely instead on newspapers and magazines with a national reputation for fair and objective reporting. Even reputable publications, however, can be editorially biased. For example, *USA Today, National Review,* and *Ms.* are likely to interpret certain events quite differently. If you are uncertain of a particular publication's special interests, check *Magazines for Libraries* and *Book Review Digest.*

Like publishers, some authors are more objective than others. No authors are altogether objective, of course, since they are human beings with their own life experiences, values, and beliefs.

Evaluating all sources

CHECKING FOR SIGNS OF BIAS

—Do the author and publisher have reputations for accurate and balanced reporting?

—Does the author or publisher have political leanings or religious views that could affect objectivity?

—Is the author or publisher associated with a special-interest group, such as Greenpeace or the National Rifle Association, that might see only one side of an issue?

—How fairly does the author treat opposing views?

—Does the author's language show signs of bias?

ASSESSING AN ARGUMENT

—What is the author's central claim or thesis?

—How does the author support this claim—with relevant and sufficient evidence or with just a few anecdotes or emotional examples?

—Are statistics accurate? Have they been used fairly? (It is possible to "lie" with statistics by using them selectively or by omitting mathematical details.)

—Are any of the author's assumptions questionable?

—Does the author consider opposing arguments and refute them persuasively? (See C5-e.)

—Does the author fall prey to any logical fallacies? (See C5-g.)

But if you have reason to believe that an author is particularly biased, you will want to assess his or her arguments with special care. For a list of questions worth asking, see the chart on this page and the one on page 72.

Assessing the author's argument

In nearly all subjects worth writing about, there is some element of argument, so don't be surprised to encounter experts who disagree. When you find areas of disagreement, you will want to read your sources' arguments with special care, testing them with your own critical intelligence. Questions such as those in the charts on this and the next page can help you weigh the strengths and weaknesses of each author's argument.

Evaluating Web sources

AUTHORSHIP Can you determine the author of the site? When you are on an internal page of a site, the author may not be named. To find out who wrote the material or what group sponsored the site, try going to the home page.

CREDIBILITY Is the author of the site knowledgeable and credible? Does the site offer links to the author's home page, résumé, or e-mail address?

OBJECTIVITY Who, if anyone, sponsors the site? Note that a site's domain name often specifies the type of group hosting the site: commercial (.com), educational (.edu), nonprofit (.org), governmental (.gov), military (.mil), or network (.net).

AUDIENCE AND PURPOSE Who is the intended audience of the site? Why is the information available: to argue a position? to sell a product? to inform readers?

DOCUMENTATION On the Internet, traditional methods of documentation are often replaced with links to original sources. Whenever possible, check out a linked source to confirm its authority.

QUALITY OF PRESENTATION Consider the design and navigation of the site. Is it well laid out and easy to use? Do its links work, and are they up-to-date and relevant? Is the material well written and relatively free of errors?

R3

Managing information

R3-a Maintain a working bibliography.

Keep a record of any sources that you decide to consult. You will need this record, called a *working bibliography,* when you compile the list of works cited that will appear at the end of your paper. (See pp. 359–60 for an example.) The working bibliography will contain more sources than you'll actually use and put in your list of works cited.

Information for a working bibliography

FOR BOOKS

—Call number

—All authors; any editors or translators

—Title and subtitle

—Edition (if not the first)

—Publication information: city, publishing company, and date

FOR PERIODICAL ARTICLES

—All authors of the article

—Title and subtitle of the article

—Title of the magazine, journal, or newspaper

—Date and page numbers

—Volume and issue numbers, if relevant

FOR INTERNET SOURCES

—All authors, editors, compilers, or translators of the text

—Title and subtitle of the material you want to use (if available) and title of the longer work (if applicable)

—Publication information for any print version of the source

—Title of the site or discussion list name

—Author, editor, or compiler of the Web site or online database

—Date of publication (or latest update) if available

—Any page or paragraph numbers

—Name of any organization or institution sponsoring or associated with the site

—Date you visited the site

—URL (address of the site) or other information needed to access the site

CAUTION: Punctuation, spelling, and sometimes even capitalization must be exact to access Internet sites. To ensure accuracy, you may wish to cut and paste the address from your browser into a computer file.

NOTE: For the exact bibliographic format to be used in the final paper, see M2.

Traditionally, researchers recorded bibliographic information about sources on 3″ × 5″ cards that they sorted alphabetically before typing their list of works cited. Today, however, most researchers save time by printing out bibliographic information from the library's computer catalog and periodical indexes or from the Internet. Although this printed bibliographic information will not appear in the exact form required for entries in the list of works cited, it will usually contain all the information you need to create the list. That information is given in the chart on page 73.

R3-b As you read, manage information systematically.

With a systematic method for managing information, you will save yourself time. In addition, a systematic method will help you remember later, when you are drafting your paper, just which words and phrases belong to your sources and which are your own. This is a crucial matter, for if any exact language from your sources finds its way into your final draft without quotation marks and proper documentation, you will be guilty of plagiarism, a serious academic offense. (See R3-c and R5-b.)

Working with photocopies and printouts

Most libraries provide photocopy machines so that you can copy pages from reference books and magazine articles and other sources that can't be removed from the library. In addition, many computer indexes now allow you to print full texts of articles. You can also print out texts from the Internet.

Working with photocopies and other "hard copy" has several advantages. It saves you time spent in the library. It allows you to highlight key passages, perhaps even color-coding the highlighted passages to reflect divisions in your outline. And you can annotate the text with notes in the margins and get a head start on the process of taking notes. (See p. 75 for an example.) Finally, working with hard copy reduces the chances of unintentional plagiarism (see R3-c), since you will be able to compare your use of a source in your paper with the actual source, not just with your notes.

When researching on the Internet, you will probably find it easier to print out pages of text to work from rather than to take notes from a computer screen. In addition, it is useful to keep a hard copy of sources found on the Internet because a source may not be accessible at a future date. Be sure that your printed materi-

SAMPLE INTERNET ANNOTATED PRINTOUT

California Mountain Lion Page   http://www.sierraclub.org/chapters/ca/mountain-lion/

California Mountain Lion Page

California Wildlife Protection Coalition

Is this site sponsored by the Sierra Club?

Prop. 197 defeated. Thanks everyone!

Note: These web pages were written to help defeat Prop. 197 last March 1996. For up to date information on Mountain Lions, please see the Mountain Lion Foundation's web page at http://www.mtn-lion.org
- DEA 12/96.

Lobbyists from the Gun Owners of California, National Rifle Association (NRA) and Safari Club rammed Senate Bill 28 through the legislature. It appeared on the March ballot as Proposition 197, but was defeated. Without collecting a single voter signature, and hiding behind a disinguous concern for public safety, trophy hunters convinced the politicians to delete the protections for cougars that were set into law directly by the citizens of California. They are exploiting people's concerns about public safety so they can hang mountain lions over their mantelpieces.

very strong language!

But not all supporters were gun-toting "trophy hunters."

If you blow all the smoke away, the bottom line is that Proposition 197 was a special interest trophy hunting measure, NOT a public safety measure.

may be true; proposition is difficult to read.

Current law allows the killing of any mountain lion that poses a threat to people. It also incorporates Department of Fish and Game (DFG) regulations that specifically allow trained state personnel to kill (or authorize others to kill) any and all lions that damage livestock, domestic animals, or other private property.

argues that current law is sufficient -- but is it?

But DFG won't do their job to provide public safety. Official testimony at legislative hearings and an internal DFG memo reveal that the Department has deliberately ignored the occasions when mountain lions posed a threat. Now, the media stories that have resulted from DFG's inaction are being used to bolster a campaign to restore trophy hunting. DFG's motivation? The Department obtains much of its funding from selling licenses to trophy hunters, and relies heavily on legislative lobbying by special interest groups like NRA for their annual budget.

Is this true? Look for proof in linked pages. Also, look for DFG view. Is there a DFG-sponsored site?

    Mountain Lion Background Information
    Trophy Hunting of Mountain Lions: A History of Deception
    Mountain Lions and **Public Safety**
    Full text of Proposition 197 (defeated)

Other sources say that current law makes it hard for DFG to do their job.

1 of 2   03/19/98 17:28:34

---

als include the site's URL, the date of access, and the full title of the site so you can include them in your list of works cited. (See above for an example of a printout from the Internet.)

NOTE: Libraries and computer labs may have restrictions on downloading and printing files. Check with a librarian or lab director to find out what options are available to you.

Using computer files

Computer files are a useful alternative to traditional note cards, especially if you prefer to type rather than to handwrite your notes. Once you have a sense of the natural subdivisions of your topic, you can create a file for each one.

For a paper on mountain lions, John Garcia created files with these labels: endangered, resurgence, attacks on humans, California propositions, and wildlife management. Working mainly with photocopied articles, Garcia typed notes into each of these files. (Garcia's paper appears in M5.)

CAUTION: Although you can download information from the Internet into your computer files and patch parts of it into your own work, be extremely careful. Some researchers have plagiarized their sources unintentionally because they lost track of which words came from a source and which were their own. To prevent unintentional plagiarism, put quotation marks around any text that you have patched into your own work, and make sure to introduce the quoted text with a signal phrase naming the author. (See R6-a.)

R3-c As you take notes, avoid unintentional plagiarism.

You will discover that it is amazingly easy to borrow too much language from a source as you take notes. Do not allow this to happen. You are guilty of the academic offense known as *plagiarism* if you half-copy the author's sentences—either by mixing the author's phrases with your own without using quotation marks or by plugging your synonyms into the author's sentence structure. (For examples of this kind of plagiarism, see R5-b.)

To prevent unintentional borrowing, resist the temptation to look at the source as you take notes—except when you are quoting. Keep the source close by so you can check for accuracy, but don't try to put ideas in your own words with the source's sentences in front of you.

There are three kinds of note taking: summarizing, paraphrasing, and quoting. As you take notes, be sure to include exact page references, since you will need the page numbers later if you use the information in your paper.

Summarizing without plagiarizing

A summary condenses information, perhaps reducing a chapter to a short paragraph or a paragraph to a single sentence. A summary should be written in your own words; if you use phrases from the source, put them in quotation marks.

Here is a passage from an original source read by John Garcia in researching a paper on mountain lions. Following the passage is Garcia's summary of the source.

ORIGINAL SOURCE

In some respects, the increasing frequency of mountain lion encounters in California has as much to do with a growing *human* population as it does with rising mountain lion numbers. The scenic solitude of the western ranges is prime cougar habitat, and it is falling swiftly to the developer's spade. Meanwhile, with their ideal habitat already at its carrying capacity, mountain lions are forcing younger cats into less suitable terrain, including residential areas. Add that cougars have generally grown bolder under a lengthy ban on their being hunted, and an unsettling scenario begins to emerge.
—Rychnovsky, "Clawing into Controversy," p. 40

SUMMARY

```
Source: Rychnovsky, "Clawing into Controversy" (40)
Encounters between mountain lions and humans are on the
rise in California because increasing numbers of lions are
competing for a shrinking habitat. As the lions' wild habitat
shrinks, older lions force younger lions into residential
areas. These lions have lost some of their fear of humans
because of a ban on hunting.
```

Paraphrasing without plagiarizing

Like a summary, a paraphrase is written in your own words; but whereas a summary reports significant information in fewer words than the source, a paraphrase retells the information in roughly the same number of words. If you retain occasional choice phrases from the source, use quotation marks so you'll know later which phrases are your own.

As you read the following paraphrase of the original source on page 77, notice that the language is significantly different from that in the original.

PARAPHRASE

Source: Rychnovsky, "Clawing into Controversy" (40)
Californians are encountering mountain lions more frequently because increasing numbers of humans and a rising population of lions are competing for the same territory. Humans have moved into mountainous regions once dominated by the lions, and the wild habitat that is left cannot sustain the current lion population. Therefore, the older lions are forcing younger lions out of the wilderness and into residential areas. And because of a ban on hunting, these younger lions have become bolder--less fearful of encounters with humans.

Using quotation marks to avoid plagiarizing

A quotation consists of the exact words from a source. In your notes, put all quoted material in quotation marks; do not trust yourself to remember later which words, phrases, and passages you have quoted and which are your own. When you quote, be sure to copy the words of your source exactly, including punctuation and capitalization. In the following example, John Garcia quotes from the original source on page 77.

QUOTATION

Source: Rychnovsky, "Clawing into Controversy" (40)
Because the mountain lions' natural habitat can no longer sustain the population, older lions "are forcing younger cats into less suitable terrain, including residential areas" (40).

R4

Planning and drafting

R4-a Form a tentative thesis and sketch a rough outline.

Before you begin writing, you should decide on a tentative thesis and construct a preliminary outline. Remain flexible, however, because you may need to revise your approach later. Writing about a subject is a way of learning about it; as you write, your understanding of your subject will almost certainly deepen.

Tentative thesis

Once you have read a variety of sources and considered all sides of your issue, you are ready to form a tentative thesis: a one-sentence (or occasionally a two-sentence) statement of your central idea. (See also C2-a and R4-b.) The thesis expresses not just your opinion, but your informed, reasoned judgment.

In a research paper, your thesis will answer the central research question that you posed earlier (see R1-a). Here, for example, is John Garcia's research question and his tentative thesis statement. (For Garcia's final thesis, see pp. 80–81.)

RESEARCH QUESTION

Because of increasing numbers of mountain lion attacks on humans, should Californians reconsider their laws protecting the lions?

TENTATIVE THESIS

Because the mountain lion is not endangered in California and because attacks on humans are increasing, California should lift its ban on hunting and thinning the lion population.

Rough outline

Before committing yourself to a detailed outline, create a rough outline consisting of your thesis and your key ideas supporting the thesis. For his outline, John Garcia used phrases similar to the titles of the computer files into which he typed his notes.

> Thesis: Because the mountain lion is not endangered in California and because attacks on humans are increasing, California should lift its ban on hunting and thinning the lion population.
> —The once-endangered mountain lion
> —Resurgence of the mountain lion
> —Human attacks on the rise
> —The 1996 California referendum
> —Wildlife management: a reasonable solution

R4-b Include your thesis in the introduction.

Readers are accustomed to seeing the thesis statement—the paper's main point—at the end of the first or second paragraph. The advantage of putting it in the first paragraph is that readers can immediately grasp your purpose. The advantage of delaying the thesis until the second paragraph is that you can provide a fuller context for your point.

As you draft your introduction, you may change your preliminary thesis, either because you have refined (or even changed) your main point or because new wording fits more smoothly into the context you have provided for it. For example, John Garcia decided that although he was in favor of wildlife management, he opposed sport hunting. His revised thesis reflects this refined view.

TENTATIVE THESIS

> Because the mountain lion is not endangered in California and because attacks on humans are increasing, California should lift its ban on hunting and thinning the lion population.

FINAL THESIS

> When California politicians revisit the mountain lion question, they should frame the issue in a new way. A

```
future proposition should retain the ban on sport hunt-
ing but allow the Department of Fish and Game to con-
trol the population.
```

In addition to stating your thesis and establishing a context for it, an introduction should hook readers. Sometimes you can connect your topic to something recently in the news or bring readers up to date about changing ideas. Other strategies are to pose a puzzling problem or to open with a startling statistic. John Garcia's paper begins like this: "On April 23, 1994, as Barbara Schoener was jogging in the Sierra foothills of California, she was pounced on from behind by a mountain lion."

R4-c Provide organizational cues.

Even if you are working with a good outline, your paper will appear disorganized unless you provide organizational cues: topic sentences, transitions between major sections of the paper, and perhaps headings. (See C4-a, C4-d, and D1-b.)

John Garcia uses headings to help readers follow his organization (see M5). Some of the annotations in the margins of Garcia's paper call attention to these and other organizational cues.

R4-d Draft the paper in an appropriate voice.

A chatty, breezy voice is usually not welcome in academic papers, but neither is a stuffy, pretentious style or a timid, unsure one.

TOO CHATTY	The cougar is a lean, mean killing machine.
BETTER	The cougar is so strong, fast, and agile that it can bring down prey five or six times its size.
TOO STUFFY	It has been determined that mountain lion onslaughts on humans are ascending exponentially.
BETTER	Statistics show that mountain lion attacks on humans are increasing at a dramatic rate.
TOO TIMID	Although I am no expert, it seems to me that state laws should treat the mountain lion just like any other species that is not endangered.
BETTER	State laws should treat the mountain lion just like any other species that is not endangered.

R5

Citing sources; avoiding plagiarism

R5-a Use a consistent system for citing sources.

In a research paper, you will be drawing on the work of other writers, and you must document their contributions by citing your sources. You must include a citation when you quote from a source, when you summarize or paraphrase a source, and when you borrow facts and ideas from a source that are not common knowledge. (See also R5-b.)

The various academic disciplines use their own editorial styles for citing sources. Most English professors prefer the Modern Language Association's system of in-text citations, the system used in examples throughout sections R5 and R6. Here, very briefly, is how an MLA in-text citation usually works:

1. The source is introduced by a signal phrase that names its author.
2. The material being cited is followed by a page number in parentheses.
3. At the end of the paper, a list of works cited (arranged alphabetically according to the authors' last names) gives complete publication information about the source.

IN-TEXT CITATION

As lion authority John Seidensticker remarks, "The boldness displayed by mountain lions just doesn't square with the shy, retiring behavior familiar to those of us who have studied these animals" (177).

ENTRY IN THE LIST OF WORKS CITED

Seidensticker, John. "Mountain Lions Don't Stalk People: True or False?" Audubon Feb. 1992: 113-22.

Handling an MLA citation is not always this simple. For a detailed discussion of possible variations, see M1.

If your instructor has asked you to use the American Psychological Association (APA) style of in-text citation, consult A1. If your instructor prefers *Chicago*-style footnotes or endnotes, consult A2. For a list of style manuals used in a variety of disciplines, see A3.

R5-b Avoid plagiarism.

Your research paper is a collaboration between you and your sources. To be fair and ethical, you must acknowledge your debt to the writers of these sources. If you don't, you are guilty of plagiarism, a serious academic offense.

Three different acts are considered plagiarism: (1) failing to cite quotations and borrowed ideas, (2) failing to enclose borrowed language in quotation marks, and (3) failing to put summaries and paraphrases in your own words.

Citing quotations and borrowed ideas

You must of course document all direct quotations. You must also cite any ideas borrowed from a source: paraphrases of sentences, summaries of paragraphs or chapters, statistics and little-known facts, and tables, graphs, or diagrams.

The only exception is common knowledge—information that your readers could find in any number of general sources because it is commonly known. For example, the current population of the United States is common knowledge in such fields as sociology and economics; Freud's theory of the unconscious is common knowledge in the field of psychology.

As a rule, when you have seen certain information repeatedly in your reading, you don't need to cite it. However, when information has appeared in only one or two sources or when it is controversial, you should cite it. If a topic is new to you and you are not sure what is considered common knowledge or what is controversial, ask someone with expertise. When in doubt, cite the source.

Enclosing borrowed language in quotation marks

To indicate that you are using a source's exact phrases or sentences, you must enclose them in quotation marks unless they have been set off from the text by indenting. (See pp. 89–90.) To omit the quotation marks is to claim—falsely—that the language is your own. Such an omission is plagiarism even if you have cited the source.

ORIGINAL SOURCE

Early colonists viewed the lion as a threat to livestock, as a competitor for the New World's abundant game, and most importantly, as the personification of the savage and godless wilderness they meant to cleanse and civilize. —Kevin Hansen, *Cougar,* p. 1

PLAGIARISM

Early colonists took a dim view of the lion. According to Kevin Hansen, they saw it as a threat to livestock, as a competitor for the New World's abundant game, and most importantly, as the personification of the savage and godless wilderness they meant to cleanse and civilize (1).

BORROWED LANGUAGE IN QUOTATION MARKS

Early colonists took a dim view of the lion. According to Kevin Hansen, they saw it "as a threat to livestock, as a competitor for the New World's abundant game, and most importantly, as the personification of the savage and godless wilderness they meant to cleanse and civilize" (1).

Putting summaries and paraphrases in your own words

When you summarize or paraphrase, you must restate the source's meaning using your own language. (See also R3-c.) In the example at the top of page 85, the paraphrase is plagiarized—even though the source is cited—because too much of its language is borrowed from the source. The underlined strings of words have been copied word-for-word (without quotation marks). In addition, the writer has closely followed the sentence structure of the original source, merely plugging in some synonyms (*children* for *minors, brutally* for *severely,* and *assault* for *attack*).

ORIGINAL SOURCE

The park [Caspers Wilderness Park] was closed to minors in 1992 after the family of a girl severely mauled there in 1986 won a suit against the county. The award of $2.1 million for the mountain lion attack on Laura Small, who was 5 at the time, was later reduced to $1.5 million.

—Reyes and Messina, "More Warning Signs," p. B1

PLAGIARISM: UNACCEPTABLE BORROWING

Reyes and Messina report that Caspers Wilderness Park was closed to children in 1992 after the family of a girl brutally mauled there in 1986 sued the county. The family was ultimately awarded $1.5 million for the mountain lion assault on Laura Small, who was 5 at the time (B1).

To avoid plagiarizing an author's language, set the source aside, write from memory, and consult the source later to check for accuracy. This strategy prevents you from being captivated by the words on the page.

TWO ACCEPTABLE PARAPHRASES

Reyes and Messina report that in 1992 Caspers Wilderness Park was placed off-limits to minors because of an incident that had occurred there some years earlier. In 1986, a five-year-old, Laura Small, was mauled by a mountain lion and seriously injured. Her family sued the county and eventually won a settlement of $1.5 million (B1).

In 1992, officials banned minors from Caspers Wilderness Park. Reyes and Messina explain that park officials took this measure after a mountain lion attack on a child led to a lawsuit. The child, five-year-old Laura Small, had been severely mauled by a lion in 1986, and her parents sued the county. Eventually they received an award of $1.5 million (B1).

R6

Integrating information from sources

With practice, you will learn to integrate information from sources (quotations, summaries, paraphrases, and facts) smoothly into your own text.

R6-a Use signal phrases to introduce quotations; limit your use of quotations.

Using signal phrases

Readers need to move from your own words to the words of a source without feeling a jolt. Avoid dropping quotations into the text without warning. Instead, provide clear signal phrases, usually including the author's name, to prepare readers for a quotation.

DROPPED QUOTATION

California law prevents the killing of mountain lions except for specific lions that have been proved to be a threat to humans or livestock. "Fish and Game is even blocked from keeping mountain lions from killing the endangered desert bighorn sheep" (Perry B4).

QUOTATION WITH SIGNAL PHRASE

California law prevents the killing of mountain lions except for specific lions that have been proved to be a threat to humans or livestock. Tony Perry points out that, ironically, "Fish and Game is even blocked from keeping mountain lions from killing the endangered desert bighorn sheep" (B4).

To avoid monotony, try to vary both the language and the placement of your signal phrases. The models in the chart on page 87 suggest a range of possibilities.

When your signal phrase includes a verb, choose one that is appropriate in the context. Is your source arguing a point, making an observation, reporting a fact, drawing a conclusion, refuting an argument, or stating a belief? By choosing an appropriate verb, you can make your source's stance clear. See the chart on page 87 for a list of verbs commonly used in signal phrases.

Limiting your use of quotations

Although it is tempting to insert many long quotations in your paper and to use your own words only for connecting passages, do not quote excessively. It is almost impossible to integrate numerous long quotations smoothly into your own text.

Varying signal phrases

MODEL SIGNAL PHRASES

In the words of lion researcher Maurice Hornocker, " . . . "

As Kevin Hansen has noted, " . . . "

Karen McCall and Jim Dutcher point out that " . . . "

" . . . , " claims CLAW spokesperson Stephani Cruickshank.

" . . . , " writes Rychnovsky, " . . . "

California politician Tim Leslie offers an odd argument for this view:

Jerome Robinson answers these objections with the following analysis:

VERBS IN SIGNAL PHRASES

acknowledges	comments	endorses	reasons
adds	compares	grants	refutes
admits	confirms	illustrates	rejects
agrees	contends	implies	reports
argues	declares	insists	responds
asserts	denies	notes	suggests
believes	disputes	observes	thinks
claims	emphasizes	points out	writes

Except for the following legitimate uses of quotations, use your own words to summarize and paraphrase your sources and to explain your own ideas.

WHEN TO USE QUOTATIONS

—When language is especially vivid or expressive

—When exact wording is needed for technical accuracy

—When it is important to let the debaters of an issue explain their positions in their own words

—When the words of an important authority lend weight to an argument

—When the language of a source is the topic of your discussion (as in an analysis or interpretation)

It is not always necessary to quote full sentences from a source. To reduce your reliance on the words of others, you can often integrate a phrase from a source into your own sentence structure.

> Uncommon as lion sightings may be, they are highly publicized. As George Laycock points out, a lion sighting in southern California "can push Pope, President, or the Los Angeles Dodgers off the front page" (88).

> In the early 1900s, western author Zane Grey wrote that a Navajo hunting guide refused to participate in a mountain lion hunt "because that would be tantamount to hunting a deity" (Hansen 56).

Using the ellipsis mark and brackets

Two useful marks of punctuation, the ellipsis mark and brackets, allow you to keep quoted material to a minimum and to integrate it smoothly into your text.

THE ELLIPSIS MARK   To condense a quoted passage, you can use the ellipsis mark (three periods, with spaces between) to indicate that you have omitted words. What remains must be grammatically complete.

MLA now recommends putting brackets around ellipsis dots. These brackets make clear that the ellipsis dots do not appear in the original work you are quoting. You may wish to check with your instructor before following this new MLA guideline. If you are using a citation style other than MLA (such as APA), do not use brackets around ellipsis dots.

> Mountain lions are attracted to areas populated by deer. As Kevin Hansen explains, "Deer are the lion's primary prey [. . .] and deer must be present in sufficient numbers in the lion's habitat for the cat to survive" (21).

On the rare occasions when you want to omit one or more full sentences, use a period before the three ellipsis dots.

> Michael Milstein, a former ranger for the National Park
> Service, reports that the eastern cougar "is probably
> already extinct. [. . .] Though rare reports of sightings
> still surface, a recent search by the U.S. Fish and
> Wildlife Service failed to turn up any sightings" (20).

Ordinarily, do not use an ellipsis mark at the beginning or at the end of a quotation. Your readers will understand that the quoted material is taken from a longer passage, so such marks are not necessary. The only exception occurs when words at the end of the final quoted sentence have been dropped. In such cases, put bracketed ellipsis dots before the closing quotation mark and parenthetical reference: [. . .]" (103).

Obviously you should not use an ellipsis mark to distort the meaning of your source.

BRACKETS Brackets (square parentheses) allow you to insert words of your own into quoted material. You can insert words in brackets to clarify matters or to keep a sentence grammatical in your context.

> According to Tony Perry of the Los Angeles Times, "The
> mountain lion [in California] has never been in danger
> of extinction, not even during the 56 years (1907-1963)
> when several rural counties in California tried to
> eradicate lions by paying bounties to hunters" (B4).

The writer has added "in California" in brackets to make the context of Perry's claim clear: Perry is writing about California lions, not about lions in states (such as Florida) where the lion has faced extinction.

Setting off long quotations

When you quote more than four typed lines of prose or more than three lines of poetry, set off the quotation by indenting it one inch (or ten spaces) from the left margin. Use the normal right margin and do not single-space.

Long quotations should be introduced by an informative sentence, usually followed by a colon. Quotation marks are unnecessary because the indented format tells readers that the words are taken directly from the source.

Lion researcher Maurice Hornocker offers some practical advice to hikers:

> Visitors to lion habitat should carry a big stick and make noise as they hike to let the animal know they are approaching. Lions are intimidated by height, so if a cougar is sighted in the area, parents should put their children on their shoulders. If attacked, a person should not run, nor should he play dead. Stand firm, fight back, and yell--most people who have resisted attack have successfully fought off the lion. (60)

Notice that at the end of an indented quotation the parenthetical citation goes outside the final period. (When a quotation runs in to your text, the opposite is true. See the sample citation on p. 82.)

R6-b　Use signal phrases to introduce most summaries and paraphrases.

Introduce most summaries and paraphrases with a signal phrase that names the author and places the material in context. Readers will then understand that everything between the signal phrase and the parenthetical citation summarizes or paraphrases the cited source.

Without the signal phrase (underlined) in the following example, readers might think that only the last sentence is being cited, when in fact most of the paragraph is based on the source.

For much of this century, the U.S. government has encouraged the extermination of mountain lions and other wild animals. Sketching a brief history, Kevin Hansen tell us that in 1915 Congress appropriated funds to wipe out animals that were attacking cattle, and the U.S. Biological Survey hired hunters and trappers to accomplish the mission. Then, in 1931, the government stepped up its efforts with the passage of the Animal Damage Control Act, nicknamed "All Dead Critters" by its critics. Between 1937 and 1970, reports Hansen, over seven thousand mountain lions were killed by Animal Damage Control (57).

R6-c With statistics and other facts, a signal phrase may not be needed.

When you are citing a statistic or other specific fact, a signal phrase is often not necessary. In most cases, readers will understand that the citation refers to the statistic or fact (not the whole paragraph).

Even road kill statistics confirm the dramatic increase in California lions. In the 1970s only one or two lions were killed on state highways, but twenty-five to thirty were killed in 1989 alone (Turback 74).

There is nothing wrong, however, with using a signal phrase to introduce a statistic or other fact.

Gary Turback points out that even road kill statistics confirm the dramatic increase in California lions. In the 1970s, he says, only one or two lions were killed on California highways, but twenty-five to thirty were killed in 1989 alone (74).

Reviewing a research paper: Global revisions

FOCUS

—Is the thesis stated clearly enough? Is it placed where readers will notice it?

—Does each paragraph support the thesis?

ORGANIZATION

—Can readers follow the organization? Would headings help?

—Do topic sentences signal new ideas? Do transitions help readers move from one major group of paragraphs to another?

—Are ideas presented in a logical order?

CONTENT

—Is the supporting material persuasive? Are the arguments strong enough to stand up to arguments of those who disagree with the thesis?

—Are the parts proportioned sensibly? Do the major ideas receive enough attention?

—Is the draft concise—free of irrelevant, unimportant, or repetitious material?

STYLE

—Is the voice appropriate—not too chatty, too stuffy, or too timid?

—Are the sentences clear, emphatic, and varied?

Reviewing a research paper: Use of sources

USE OF QUOTATIONS

— Is quoted material enclosed within quotation marks (unless it has been set off from the text)? (See R5-b.)

— Is quoted language word-for-word accurate? If not, do brackets or ellipsis marks indicate the changes or omissions? (See pp. 88–89.)

— Does a clear signal phrase (usually naming the author) prepare readers for each quotation? (See R6-a.)

— Does a parenthetical citation follow each quotation? (See R5-a.)

USE OF SUMMARIES AND PARAPHRASES

— Are summaries and paraphrases free of plagiarized wording (not copied or half-copied from the source)? (See R5-b.)

— Are summaries and paraphrases documented with parenthetical citations? (See R5-a.)

— Do readers know where the material being cited begins? In other words, does a signal phrase mark the beginning of the cited material unless the context makes clear exactly what is being cited? (See R6-b.)

USE OF STATISTICS AND OTHER FACTS

— Are statistics and facts (other than common knowledge) documented with parenthetical citations? (See R5-a.)

— If there is no signal phrase, will readers understand exactly which facts are being cited? (See R6-c.)

R7

Revising your draft

When you are revising any paper, it is a good idea to concentrate first on global elements—focus, organization, content, and audience appeal—and then turn to matters of style and correctness. (See C4.) With a research paper, this strategy is especially important because reviewing your use of quotations and other source material requires considerable attention to detail.

On pages 92–93 is a two-part chart for reviewing the draft of a research paper: one part on global revision, the other on proper handling of sources.

E

Effective
Sentences

E

Effective Sentences

E1

Parallelism

If two or more ideas are parallel, they are easier to grasp when expressed in parallel grammatical form. Single words should be balanced with single words, phrases with phrases, clauses with clauses.

A kiss can be a comma, a question mark, or an exclamation point.
—Mistinguett

This novel is not to be tossed lightly aside, but to be hurled with great force.
—Dorothy Parker

In matters of principle, stand like a rock; in matters of taste, swim with the current.
—Thomas Jefferson

> GRAMMAR CHECKERS do not flag faulty parallelism. Because computer programs have no way of assessing whether two or more ideas are parallel in meaning, they fail to catch the faulty parallelism in sentences such as this: *In my high school, boys were either jocks, preppies, or studied constantly.*

E1-a Balance parallel ideas in a series.

Readers expect items in a series to appear in parallel grammatical form. When one or more of the items violate readers' expectations, a sentence will be needlessly awkward.

► Abused children commonly exhibit one or more of the following

symptoms: withdrawal, rebelliousness, restlessness, and *depression.*
~~they are depressed.~~
^

The revision presents all of the items as nouns.

▶ Hooked on romance novels, I learned that there is nothing more
important than being rich, looking good, and ~~to have~~ a good
              having
                                                ^
time.

The revision uses *-ing* forms for all items in the series.

▶ After assuring us that he was sober, Sam drove down the middle
                                went through
of the road, ran one red light, and two stop signs before a police
                                       ^
officer pulled him over.

The revision adds a verb to make the three items parallel: *drove . . . ,
ran . . . , went through. . . .*

NOTE: In headings and lists, aim for as much parallelism as the
content allows. See D1-b and D1-c.

E1-b   Balance parallel ideas presented as pairs.

When pairing ideas, underscore their connection by expressing
them in similar grammatical form. Paired ideas are usually connected in one of these ways:

— with a coordinating conjunction such as *and, but,* or *or*

— with a pair of correlative conjunctions such as *either . . . or* or
not only . . . but also

— with a word introducing a comparison, usually *than* or *as*

Parallel ideas linked with coordinating conjunctions

Coordinating conjunctions (*and, but, or, nor, for, so,* and *yet*) link
ideas of equal importance. When those ideas are closely parallel in
content, they should be expressed in parallel grammatical form.

▶ At Lincoln High School, vandalism can result in suspension
         expulsion
or even ~~being expelled~~ from school.
      ^

The revision balances the nouns *suspension* and *expulsion*.

▶ Many states are reducing property taxes for homeowners and
extending
~~extend~~ financial aid in the form of tax credits to renters.
^

The revision balances the *-ing* verb forms *reducing* and *extending*.

Parallel ideas linked with correlative conjunctions

Correlative conjunctions come in pairs: *either . . . or, neither . . . nor, not only . . . but also, both . . . and, whether . . . or.* Make sure that the grammatical structure following the second half of the pair is the same as that following the first half.

▶ Thomas Edison was not only a prolific inventor but also ~~was~~ a

successful entrepreneur.

The words *a prolific inventor* follow *not only,* so *a successful entrepreneur* should follow *but also.* Repeating *was* creates an unbalanced effect.

to
▶ I was advised either to change my flight or take the train.
^

To change my flight, which follows *either,* should be balanced with *to take the train,* which follows *or.*

Comparisons linked with than *or* as

In comparisons linked with *than* or *as,* the elements being compared should be expressed in parallel grammatical structure.

to ground
▶ It is easier to speak in abstractions than ~~grounding~~ one's thoughts
^
in reality.

▶ Mother could not persuade me that giving is as much a joy as
receiving.
~~to receive.~~
^

To speak in abstractions is balanced with *to ground one's thoughts in reality. Giving* is balanced with *receiving.*

NOTE: Comparisons should also be logical and complete. See E2-c.

E1-c Repeat function words to clarify parallels.

Function words such as prepositions (*by, to*) and subordinating conjunctions (*that, because*) signal the grammatical nature of the word groups to follow. Although they can sometimes be omitted, include them whenever they signal parallel structures that might otherwise be missed by readers.

> ▶ **In an attempt to break their bad habit, many smokers try**
> *to*
> **switching to a brand they find distasteful or ⌃ a low tar and nicotine**
>
> **cigarette.**

In the original sentence the prepositional phrase was too complex for easy reading. The repetition of the preposition *to* prevents readers from losing their way.

E2

Needed words

Do not omit words necessary for grammatical or logical completeness. Readers need to see at a glance how the parts of a sentence are connected.

Languages sometimes differ in the need for certain words. In particular, be alert for missing articles, verbs, subjects, or expletives. See **ESL** T1, T2-e and T3-a.

GRAMMAR CHECKERS do not flag the vast majority of missing words. They can, however, catch some missing verbs (see G2-e). Although they can flag some missing articles (*a, an,* and *the*), they often suggest that an article is missing when in fact it is not. (See also T1.)

E2-a Add words needed to complete compound structures.

In compound structures, words are often omitted for economy: *Tom is a man who means what he says and [who] says what he means.* Such omissions are perfectly acceptable as long as the omitted word is common to both parts of the compound structure.

If the shorter version defies grammar or idiom because an omitted word is not common to both parts of the compound structure, the word must be put back in.

▶ Some of the regulars are acquaintances whom we see at work or *who* live in our community.

The word *who* must be included because *whom live in our community* is not grammatically correct.

▶ I never have *accepted* and never will accept a bribe.

Have . . . accept is not grammatically correct.

▶ Many of these tribes in the South Pacific still believe *in* and live by ancient laws.

Believe . . . by is not idiomatic English.

E2-b Add the word *that* if there is any danger of misreading without it.

If there is no danger of misreading, the word *that* may sometimes be omitted when it introduces a subordinate clause: *The value of a principle is the number of things [that] it will explain.* Occasionally, however, a sentence might be misread without *that.*

▶ From the family room Sarah saw *that* her favorite tree, which she had climbed so often as a child, was gone.

Sarah didn't see the tree; she saw that the tree was gone.

E2-c Add words needed to make comparisons logical and complete.

Comparisons should be made between like items. To compare unlike items is illogical and distracting.

▶ Henry preferred the restaurants in Pittsburgh to ^*those in* Philadelphia.

Restaurants must be compared with restaurants.

▶ ~~The graduation rate of our~~ ^*Our* student athletes ~~is higher~~ ^*graduate at a higher rate* than the rest of the student population.

A rate cannot be logically compared to a population. The writer could revise the sentence by inserting *that of* after *than,* but the preceding revision is more concise.

▶ Some say that Ella Fitzgerald's renditions of Cole Porter's songs are better than any other ~~singer.~~ ^*singer's.*

Ella Fitzgerald's renditions cannot be logically compared to a singer. The revision uses the possessive form *singer's,* with the word *renditions* being implied.

Sometimes the word *other* must be inserted to make a comparison logical.

▶ Jupiter is larger than any ^*other* planet in our solar system.

Jupiter cannot be larger than itself.

Sometimes the word *as* must be inserted to make a comparison grammatically correct.

▶ Our nursing graduates are as skilled, ^*as* if not more skilled than, those of any other state college.

The construction *as skilled . . . than* is not grammatical.

Comparisons should be complete enough so that readers will understand what is being compared.

INCOMPLETE   Brand X is less salty.

COMPLETE   Brand X is less salty than Brand Y.

Also, you should leave no ambiguity about meaning. In the following sentence, two interpretations are possible.

AMBIGUOUS   Mr. Kelly helped me more than Sam.

CLEAR   Mr. Kelly helped me more than he helped Sam.

CLEAR   Mr. Kelly helped me more than Sam did.

E2-d   Add the articles *a, an,* and *the* where necessary for grammatical completeness.

Articles are sometimes omitted in recipes and other instructions that are meant to be followed while they are being read. Such omissions are inappropriate, however, in nearly all other forms of writing, whether formal or informal.

> ► Blood can be drawn only by ̂*a* doctor or by ̂*an* authorized person
> *the* ̂ who has been trained in ̂procedure.

It is not always necessary to repeat articles with paired items: *We bought a computer and printer.* However, if one of the items requires *a* and the other requires *an,* both articles must be included.

> ► We bought a computer and ̂*an* ink-jet printer.

Articles can cause special problems for speakers of English as a second language. See T1.

ESL

E3

Problems with modifiers

Modifiers, whether they are single words, phrases, or clauses, should point clearly to the words they modify. As a rule, related words should be kept together.

 GRAMMAR CHECKERS can flag split infinitives, such as *to carefully and thoroughly sift* (E3-d). However, they don't alert you to other problems with modifiers, including danglers like this one: *When a young man, my mother enrolled me in tap dance classes, hoping I would become the next Gregory Hines.*

E3-a   Put limiting modifiers in front of the words they modify.

Limiting modifiers such as *only, even, almost, nearly,* and *just* should appear in front of a verb only if they modify the verb: *At first I couldn't even touch my toes.* If they limit the meaning of some other word in the sentence, they should be placed in front of that word.

▶ Lasers ~~only~~ destroy the *only* target, leaving the surrounding healthy tissue intact.

▶ Our team didn't ~~even~~ score *even* once.

The limiting modifier *not* is frequently misplaced, suggesting a meaning the writer did not intend.

▶ *Not all* ~~All~~ wicker is ~~not~~ antique.

The original version means that no wicker is antique. The revision makes the writer's real meaning clear.

E3-b Place phrases and clauses so that readers can see at a glance what they modify.

Although phrases and clauses can appear at some distance from the words they modify, make sure that your meaning is clear. When phrases or clauses are oddly placed, absurd misreadings can result.

MISPLACED   The king returned to the clinic where he had under-
             gone heart surgery in 1992 in a limousine sent by the
             White House.

REVISED   Traveling in a limousine sent by the White House, the
             king returned to the clinic where he had undergone
             heart surgery in 1992.

The king did not undergo heart surgery in a limousine. The revision corrects this false impression.

► *On the walls*
  ~~There~~ are many pictures of comedians who have performed at

  Gavin's. ~~on the walls.~~

The comedians weren't performing on the walls; the pictures were on the walls.

►   *150-pound,*
  The robber was described as a six-foot-tall man with a mustache.

  ~~weighing 150 pounds.~~

The robber, not the mustache, weighed 150 pounds.

Occasionally the placement of a modifier leads to an ambiguity, in which case two revisions will be possible, depending on the writer's intended meaning.

AMBIGUOUS   The exchange students we met for coffee occasionally
             questioned us about our latest slang.

CLEAR   The exchange students we occasionally met for coffee
             questioned us about our latest slang.

CLEAR   The exchange students we met for coffee questioned
             us occasionally about our latest slang.

In the original version, it was not clear whether the meeting or the questioning happened occasionally. The revisions eliminate the ambiguity.

E3-c Move awkwardly placed modifiers.

As a rule, a sentence should flow from subject to verb to object, without lengthy detours along the way. When a long adverbial element separates a subject from its verb, a verb from its object, or a helping verb from its main verb, the result is usually awkward.

>   *A*   *Hong Kong*
> ▶ ~~Hong Kong,~~ ⱥfter more than 150 years of British rule, ^was
>
> transferred back to Chinese control in 1997.

There is no reason to separate the subject *Hong Kong* from the verb *was transferred* with a long phrase.

EXCEPTION: Occasionally a writer may choose to delay a verb or an object to create suspense. In the following passage, for example, Robert Mueller inserts the *after* phrase between the subject *women* and the verb *walk* to heighten the dramatic effect.

> I asked a Burmese why women, after centuries of following their men, now walk ahead. He said there were many unexploded land mines since the war.   —Robert Mueller

ESL

English does not allow an adverb to appear between a verb and its object. See T3-e.

>   *easily.*
> ▶ Yolanda lifted ~~easily~~ the fifty-pound weight/^

E3-d Do not split infinitives needlessly.

An infinitive consists of *to* plus a verb: *to think, to breathe, to dance.* When a modifier appears between its two parts, an infinitive is said to be "split": *to carefully balance.* If a split infinitive is obviously awkward, it should be revised.

>   *If possible, patients*
> ▶ ~~Patients~~ should try to ~~if possible~~ avoid going up and down stairs.
>   ^

Usage varies when a split infinitive is less awkward than the preceding one. To be on the safe side, however, you should not split infinitives, especially in formal writing.

▶ Our chief financial officer ordered the publicity department to
    ~~significantly~~ reduce its budget.

> *significantly.*

When a split infinitive is more natural and less awkward than alternative phrasing, most readers find it acceptable: *We decided to actually enforce the law* is a perfectly natural construction in English. *We decided actually to enforce the law* is not.

E3-e Repair dangling modifiers.

A dangling modifier fails to refer logically to any word in the sentence. Dangling modifiers are easy to repair, but they can be hard to recognize, especially in your own writing.

Recognizing dangling modifiers

Dangling modifiers are usually word groups (such as verbal phrases) that suggest but do not name an actor. When a sentence opens with such a modifier, readers expect the subject of the next clause to name the actor. If it doesn't, the modifier dangles.

> *When the driver opened*

▶ ~~Opening~~ the window to let out a huge bumblebee, the car

accidentally swerved into an oncoming car.

The car didn't open the window; the driver did.

> *women have often been denied*

▶ After completing seminary training, ~~women's~~ access to the pulpit.

~~has often been denied.~~

The women (not their access to the pulpit) complete the training.

The following sentences illustrate four common kinds of dangling modifiers.

DANGLING   *Deciding to join the navy,* the recruiter enthusiastically pumped Joe's hand. [Participial phrase]

DANGLING   *Upon entering the doctor's office,* a skeleton caught my attention. [Preposition followed by a gerund phrase]

Checking for dangling modifiers

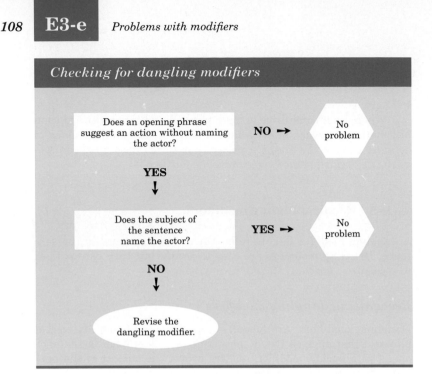

DANGLING   *To please the children,* some fireworks were set off a
day early. [Infinitive phrase]

DANGLING   *Though only sixteen,* UCLA accepted Martha's application. [Elliptical clause with an understood subject and
verb]

These dangling modifiers falsely suggest that the recruiter decided
to join the navy, that the skeleton entered the doctor's office, that
the fireworks intended to please the children, and that UCLA is
sixteen years old.

Repairing dangling modifiers

To repair a dangling modifier, you can revise the sentence in one of
two ways:

1. name the actor in the subject of the sentence, or
2. name the actor in the modifier.

Depending on your sentence, one of these revision strategies may be more appropriate than the other.

ACTOR NAMED IN SUBJECT

I noticed
► Upon entering the doctor's office, a skeleton. ~~caught my attention.~~

we set off
► To please the children, some fireworks ~~were set off~~ a day early.

ACTOR NAMED IN MODIFIER

When Joe decided
► ~~Deciding~~ to join the navy, the recruiter enthusiastically pumped
his
~~Joe's~~ hand.

Martha was   *her*
► Though only sixteen, UCLA accepted ~~Martha's~~ application.

NOTE: You cannot repair a dangling modifier just by moving it. Consider, for example, the sentence about the skeleton. If you put the modifier at the end of the sentence (*A skeleton caught my attention upon entering the doctor's office*), you are still suggesting— absurdly, of course—that the skeleton entered the office. The only way to avoid the problem is to put the word *I* in the sentence, either as the subject or in the modifier.

I noticed
► Upon entering the doctor's office, a skeleton. ~~caught my attention.~~

As I entered
► ~~Upon entering~~ the doctor's office, a skeleton caught my attention.

E4

Shifts

GRAMMAR CHECKERS do not flag the shifts discussed in this section: shifts in point of view; shifts in verb tense, mood, or voice; and shifts between direct and indirect questions or quotations. Even the most obvious errors such as this one will slip right past most grammar checkers: *My three-year-old fell into the pool and to my surprise she swims to the shallow end.*

E4-a Make the point of view consistent.

The point of view of a piece of writing is the perspective from which it is written: first person (*I* or *we*), second person (*you*), or third person (*he/she/it/one* or *they*). The *I* (or *we*) point of view, which emphasizes the writer, is a good choice for informal letters and writing based primarily on personal experience. The *you* point of view, which emphasizes the reader, works well for giving advice or explaining how to do something. The third-person point of view, which emphasizes the subject, is appropriate in formal academic and professional writing.

Writers who are having difficulty settling on an appropriate point of view sometimes shift confusingly from one to another. The solution is to choose a suitable perspective and then stay with it.

▶ One week our class met in a junkyard to practice rescuing a

victim trapped in a wrecked car. We learned to dismantle the car
                        We   *our*   *our*
with the essential tools. ~~You~~ were graded on ~~your~~ speed and ~~your~~

skill in extricating the victim.

The writer should have stayed with the *we* point of view. *You* is inappropriate because the writer is not addressing the reader directly. *You* should not be used in a vague sense meaning *anyone*. (See G3-b.)

    You
▶ ~~Everyone~~ should purchase a lift ticket unless you plan to spend

most of your time walking or crawling up a steep hill.

Here *you* is an appropriate choice, since the writer is giving advice directly to readers.

Shifts from the third-person singular to the third-person plural are especially common.

    Police officers are
▶ ~~A police officer is~~ often criticized for always being there when

they aren't needed and never being there when they are.

The writer shifted from the third-person singular (*police officer*) to the third-person plural (*they*). (See also G3-a.)

E4-b Maintain consistent verb tenses.

Consistent verb tenses clearly establish the time of the actions being described. When a passage begins in one tense and then shifts without warning and for no reason to another, readers are distracted and confused.

▶ There was no way I could fight the current. Just as I was losing
    jumped   *swam*
hope, a stranger ~~jumps~~ off a passing boat and ~~swims~~ toward me.
           ^   ^

Writers often shift verb tenses when writing about literature. The literary convention is to describe fictional events consistently in the present tense. (See G2-f.)

▶ The scarlet letter is a punishment sternly placed on Hester's
                                        is
breast by the community, and yet it ~~was~~ an extremely fanciful and
                                     ^
imaginative product of Hester's own needlework.

E4-c Make verbs consistent in mood and voice.

Unnecessary shifts in the mood of a verb can be as distracting as needless shifts in tense. There are three moods in English: the indicative, used for facts, opinions, and questions; the imperative, used for orders or advice; and the subjunctive, used for wishes or conditions contrary to fact (see G2-g).

The following passage shifts confusingly from the indicative to the imperative mood.

▶ The officers advised against allowing access to our homes without
                            They also suggested that we
proper identification. ~~Also,~~ alert neighbors to vacation schedules.
                    ^

Since the writer's purpose was to report the officers' advice, the revision puts both sentences in the indicative.

The voice of a verb may be either active (with the subject doing the action) or passive (with the subject receiving the action). (See G2-h.) If a writer shifts without warning from one to the other, readers may be left wondering why.

> lists
> ► When the tickets are ready, the travel agent notifies the client/,
>
> e   files
> **E**ach ticket ~~is then listed~~ on a daily register form, and a copy of
> ^   ^
> the itinerary. ~~is filed.~~
> ^

The original version began in the active voice (*agent notifies*) and then switched to the passive (*ticket is listed . . . copy is filed*). Because the active voice is clearer and more direct, the writer put all the verbs in the active voice.

E4-d Avoid sudden shifts from indirect to direct questions or quotations.

An indirect question reports a question without asking it: *We asked whether we could take a swim.* A direct question asks directly: *Can we take a swim?* Sudden shifts from indirect to direct questions are awkward.

> ► I wonder whether the sister knew about the theft and, if so,
> *whether she reported*
> ~~did she report~~ it to the police.
> ^

The revision poses both questions indirectly. The writer could also ask both questions directly: *Did the sister know about the theft and, if so, did she report it to the police?*

An indirect quotation reports someone's words without quoting word for word: *Anna said that she is a Virgo.* A direct quotation presents someone's exact words, set off with quotation marks: *Anna said, "I am a Virgo."* Unannounced shifts from indirect to direct quotations are distracting and confusing.

> *asked me not to*
> ► Mother said that she would be late for dinner and ~~please do not~~
> *came*   ^
> leave for choir practice until Dad ~~comes~~ home from his dentist
> ^
>
> appointment.

The revision reports all of the mother's words. The writer could also quote directly: *Mother said, "I will be late for dinner. Please do not leave for choir practice until Dad comes home. . . ."*

E5

Mixed constructions

A mixed construction contains elements that do not sensibly fit together. The mismatch may be a matter of grammar or of logic.

> GRAMMAR CHECKERS can flag *is when, is where,* and *reason . . . is because* constructions (E5-c), but they fail to identify nearly all other mixed constructions, including sentences as tangled as this one: *Depending on the number and strength of drinks, the amount of time that has passed, and one's body weight determines the concentration of alcohol in the blood.*

E5-a Untangle the grammatical structure.

Once you head into a sentence, your choices are limited by the range of grammatical patterns in English. (See B2 and B3.) You cannot begin with one grammatical plan and switch without warning to another.

MIXED   For most drivers who have a blood alcohol level of .05 percent double their risk of causing an accident.

REVISED   For most drivers who have a blood alcohol level of .05 percent, the risk of causing an accident is doubled.

REVISED   Most drivers who have a blood alcohol level of .05 percent double their risk of causing an accident.

The writer began with a long prepositional phrase that was destined to be a modifier but then tried to press it into service as the subject of the sentence. This cannot be done. If the sentence is to begin with the prepositional phrase, the writer must finish the sentence with a subject and verb (*risk . . . is doubled*). The writer who wishes to stay with the original verb (*double*) must head into the sentence another way (*Most drivers . . .*).

> *Being*
> ~~When an employee is~~ promoted without warning can be
> ^
> alarming.

The adverb clause *When an employee is promoted without warning* cannot serve as the subject of the sentence. The revision replaces the adverb clause with a gerund phrase, a word group that can function as the subject. (See B3-b and B3-e.)

> Although many pre-Columbian peoples achieved a high level
>
> of civilization, ~~but~~ they were unfamiliar with the wheel.

The *Although* clause is subordinate, so it cannot be linked to an independent clause with the coordinating conjunction *but.* (If you speak English as a second language, see also T3-d.)

Occasionally a mixed construction is so tangled that it defies grammatical analysis. When this happens, back away from the sentence, rethink what you want to say, and then say it again as clearly as you can.

MIXED   In the whole-word method children learn to recognize entire words rather than by the phonics method in which they learn to sound out letters and groups of letters.

REVISED   The whole-word method teaches children to recognize entire words; the phonics method teaches them to sound out letters and groups of letters.

ESL

English does not allow double subjects, nor does it allow an object or adverb to be repeated in an adjective clause. See T3-b and T3-c.

> ▶ The squirrel that came down our chimney ~~it~~ did much
>
>   damage.

> ▶ Hearing screams, Serena ran over to the pool that her
>
>   daughter was swimming in ~~it~~.
>   ^

E5-b Straighten out the logical connections.

The subject and the predicate should make sense together. When they don't, the error is known as *faulty predication.*

▶ Reluctantly we decided that ~~Tiffany's welfare~~ would not be safe

     Tiffany
     ^

living with her mother.

Tiffany, not her welfare, would not be safe.

▶ Under the revised plan, the elderly~~, who now receive a double~~

     double personal exemption for the
     ^

~~personal exemption,~~ will be abolished.

The exemption, not the elderly, will be abolished.

An appositive and the noun to which it refers should be logically equivalent. When they are not, the error is known as *faulty apposition.*

▶ ~~The tax accountant,~~ a very lucrative field, requires intelligence,

  Tax accounting,
  ^

patience, and attention to detail.

The tax accountant is a person, not a field.

E5-c Avoid *is when, is where,* and *reason . . . is because* constructions.

In formal English many readers object to *is when, is where,* and *reason . . . is because* constructions on either logical or grammatical grounds.

▶ Anorexia nervosa is ~~where people,~~ believing they are too fat, diet

     a disorder suffered by people who,
     ^

to the point of starvation.

Anorexia nervosa is a disorder, not a place.

▶ ~~The reason~~ I was late ~~is~~ because my motorcycle broke down.

The writer might have replaced the word *because* with *that,* but the preceding revision is more concise.

E6

Coordination and subordination

When combining ideas in one sentence, use coordination to create equal emphasis and use subordination to create unequal emphasis.

> GRAMMAR CHECKERS do not catch the problems with coordination and subordination discussed in this section. Not surprisingly, computer programs have no way of sensing the relative importance of ideas.

Coordination

Coordination draws equal attention to two or more ideas. To coordinate words or phrases, join them with a coordinating conjunction (*and, but, or, nor, for, so, yet*). To coordinate independent clauses (word groups that can stand alone as sentences), join them with a comma and a coordinating conjunction or with a semicolon. The semicolon is often accompanied by a conjunctive adverb such as *therefore, moreover,* or *however.*

Grandmother lost her sight, but her hearing sharpened.

Grandmother lost her sight; however, her hearing sharpened.

Subordination

To give unequal emphasis to two or more ideas, express the major idea in an independent clause and place any minor ideas in subordinate clauses or phrases. (See B3.) Subordinate clauses, which cannot stand alone, typically begin with one of the following subordinating conjunctions or relative pronouns.

after	if	until	while
although	since	when	who
as	that	where	whom
because	though	whether	whose
before	unless	which	

Deciding which idea to emphasize is not simply a matter of right and wrong. Consider the two ideas about Grandmother's sight and hearing.

Grandmother lost her sight. Her hearing sharpened.

If your purpose is to stress your grandmother's acute hearing rather than her blindness, subordinate the idea concerning her blindness.

As Grandmother lost her sight, her hearing sharpened.

To focus on your grandmother's blindness, subordinate the idea concerning her hearing.

Though her hearing sharpened, Grandmother gradually lost her sight.

E6-a Combine choppy sentences.

Short sentences demand attention, so they should be used primarily for emphasis. Too many short sentences, one after the other, create a choppy style.

If an idea is not important enough to deserve its own sentence, try combining it with a sentence close by. Put any minor ideas in subordinate structures such as phrases or subordinate clauses.

CHOPPY   The huts vary in height. They measure from ten to fifteen feet in diameter. They contain no modern conveniences.

IMPROVED   The huts, which vary in height and measure from ten to fifteen feet in diameter, contain no modern conveniences.

Three sentences have become one, with minor ideas expressed in a subordinate clause beginning with *which.*

▶ The Chesapeake and Ohio Canal, is a 184-mile waterway constructed in the 1800s, It was a major source of transportation for goods during the Civil War.

A minor idea is now expressed in an appositive phrase (*a 184-mile waterway constructed in the 1800s*). (See B3-c.)

▶ ~~Sister Consilio was~~ $\overset{E}{e}$nveloped in a black robe with only her face
and hands visible~~/,~~ $\overset{Sister\ Consilio}{\underset{\wedge}{\sim}She}$ was an imposing figure.

A minor idea is now expressed in a participial phrase beginning with
Enveloped. (See B3-b.)

▶ My sister owes much of her recovery to a bodybuilding program**/**
$\overset{that\ she}{\underset{\wedge}{She}}$ began ~~the program~~ three years ago.

A minor idea is now expressed in an adjective clause beginning with
that. (See B3-e.)

▶ $\overset{When\ my}{\underset{\wedge}{My}}$ son asked his great-grandmother if she had been a slave**/,**
$\overset{she}{\underset{\wedge}{She}}$ became very angry.

A minor idea is now expressed in an adverb clause beginning with
When. (See B3-e.)

Although subordination is ordinarily the most effective technique for combining short, choppy sentences, coordination is appropriate when the ideas are equal in importance.

▶ The hospital decides when patients will sleep and wake~~/,~~ $\overset{}{\underset{\wedge}{It}}$ dictates
what and when they will eat~~/,~~ $\overset{and}{\underset{\wedge}{It}}$ tells them when they may be with
family and friends.

Three sentences have become one, with equivalent ideas expressed in a
coordinate series.

ESL

When combining sentences, do not repeat the subject of the sentence; also do not repeat an object or adverb in an adjective clause.
See T3-b and T3-c.

▶ The apartment that we moved into ~~it~~ needed many repairs.

▶ Tanya climbed into the tree house where the boys were

playing.~~there.~~

E6-b   Avoid ineffective coordination.

Coordinate structures are appropriate only when you intend to draw the reader's attention equally to two or more ideas: *Gregory praises loudly, and he criticizes softly.* If one idea is more important than another—or if a coordinating conjunction does not clearly signal the relation between the ideas—you should subordinate the lesser idea.

▶ *When my*
~~My~~ uncle noticed the frightened look on my face, ~~and~~ he told me
   ^

that the dentures in the glass were not real teeth.

The less important idea has become a subordinate clause beginning with *When.* (See B3-e.)

▶ These particles, ~~are~~ known as "stealth liposomes," ~~and they~~ can
                 ^

hide in the body for a long time without detection.

The less important idea has become a participial phrase beginning with *known.* (See B3-b.)

▶ *After four hours,*
~~Four hours went by, and~~ a rescue truck finally arrived, but by
   ^

that time the injured swimmer had been evacuated in a helicopter.

Three independent clauses were excessive. The least important idea has become a prepositional phrase. (See B3-a.)

E6-c   Do not subordinate major ideas.

If a sentence buries its major idea in a subordinate construction, readers are not likely to give it enough attention. Express the major idea in an independent clause and subordinate any minor ideas.

▶   *had polio as a child,*
   Lanie, who now walks with the help of braces/,~~had polio as a~~
             ^   ^

~~child.~~

The writer wanted to focus on Lanie's ability to walk, but the original sentence buried this idea in an adjective clause. The revision puts the major idea in an independent clause and tucks the less important idea into an adjective clause (*who had polio as a child*). (See B3-e.)

> As
> ▶ ^I was driving home from my new job, heading down New York
>
> Avenue, ~~when~~ my car suddenly overheated.

The revision puts the major idea—that the car overheated—in the independent clause and subordinates the other information. (See B3-e.)

E6-d Do not subordinate excessively.

In attempting to avoid short, choppy sentences, writers sometimes move to the opposite extreme, putting more subordinate ideas into a sentence than its structure can bear. If a sentence collapses of its own weight, occasionally it can be restructured. More often, however, such sentences must be divided.

> ▶ Our job is to stay between the stacker and the tie machine
>   *If they do,*
>   watching to see if the newspapers jam,~~in which case~~we pull the
>   ^
>   bundles off and stack them on a skid, because otherwise they
>
>   would back up in the stacker.

E7

Sentence variety

When a rough draft is filled with too many same-sounding sentences, try to inject some variety—as long as you can do so without sacrificing clarity or ease of reading.

GRAMMAR CHECKERS are of little help with sentence variety. It takes a human ear to know when and why sentence variety is needed.

    Some programs tell you when you have used the same word to open several sentences, but sometimes it is a good idea to do so—if you are trying to highlight parallel ideas, for example (see p. 33).

E7-a Use a variety of sentence structures.

A writer should not rely too heavily on simple sentences and compound sentences, for the effect tends to be both monotonous and choppy. (See E6-a and E6-b.) Too many complex sentences, however, can be equally monotonous. If your style tends to one or the other extreme, try to achieve a better mix of sentence types.

For a discussion of sentence types, see B4-a.

E7-b Use a variety of sentence openings.

Most sentences in English begin with the subject, move to the verb, and continue to an object, with modifiers tucked in along the way or put at the end. For the most part, such sentences are fine. Put too many of them in a row, however, and they become monotonous.

Adverbial modifiers, being easily movable, can often be inserted ahead of the subject. Such modifiers might be single words, phrases, or clauses.

> *Eventually a*
> ▶ A few drops of sap ~~eventually~~ began to trickle into the pail.
>   ^

> *Just as the sun was coming up, a*
> ▶ A pair of black ducks flew over the lake . ~~just as the sun was~~
>   ^   ^
>
> ~~coming up.~~

Participial phrases can frequently be moved to the beginning of a sentence without loss of clarity. (See B3-b.)

> *Tired of the struggle in Vietnam, many Americans*
> ▶ ~~Many Americans, tired of the struggle in Vietnam,~~ began to
>   ^
>
> sympathize with antiwar protesters.

>   *A*   *José and I*
> ▶ ~~José and I,~~ anticipating a peaceful evening, sat down at the
>   ^
>
> campfire to brew a cup of coffee.

CAUTION: When beginning a sentence with a participial phrase, make sure that the subject of the sentence names the person or thing described in the introductory phrase. If it doesn't, the phrase will dangle. (See E3-e.)

E7-c Try inverting sentences occasionally.

A sentence is inverted if it does not follow the normal subject-verb-object pattern. Many inversions sound artificial and should be avoided except in the most formal contexts. But if an inversion sounds natural, it can provide a welcome touch of variety.

▶ *Opposite the produce section is a*
~~A~~ refrigerated case of mouth-watering cheeses. ~~is opposite the~~
^   ^

~~produce section.~~

▶ *Set at the top two corners of the stage were huge*
~~Huge~~ lavender hearts outlined in bright white lights. ~~were set at~~
^   ^

~~the top two corners of the stage.~~

W

Word Choice

W

Word Choice

W1

Glossary of usage

This glossary includes words commonly confused (such as *accept* and *except*), words commonly misused (such as *hopefully*), and words that are nonstandard (such as *hisself*). It also lists colloquialisms and jargon. Colloquialisms are expressions that may be appropriate in informal speech but are inappropriate in formal writing. Jargon is needlessly technical or pretentious language that is inappropriate in most contexts. If an item is not listed here, consult the index. For irregular verbs (such as *sing, sang, sung*), see G2-a. For idiomatic use of prepositions, see W5-d.

> GRAMMAR CHECKERS can point out commonly confused words and suggest that you check your usage. It is up to you, however, to determine the correct word for your intended meaning.

a, an Use *an* before a vowel sound, *a* before a consonant sound: *an apple, a peach.* Problems sometimes arise with words beginning with *h.* If the *h* is silent, the word begins with a vowel sound, so use *an: an hour, an heir, an honest senator, an honorable deed.* If the *h* is pronounced, the word begins with a consonant sound, so use *a: a hospital, a hymn, a historian, a hotel.* When an abbreviation or acronym begins with a vowel sound, use *an: an EKG, an MRI, an AIDS patient.*

accept, except *Accept* is a verb meaning "to receive." *Except* is usually a preposition meaning "excluding." *I will accept all the packages except that one. Except* is also a verb meaning "to exclude." *Please except that item from the list.*

adapt, adopt *Adapt* means "to adjust or become accustomed"; it is usually followed by *to. Adopt* means "to take as one's own." *Our family adopted a Vietnamese orphan, who quickly adapted to his new surroundings.*

adverse, averse *Adverse* means "unfavorable." *Averse* means "opposed" or "reluctant"; it is usually followed by *to. I am averse to your proposal because it could have an adverse impact on the economy.*

advice, advise *Advice* is a noun, *advise* a verb: *We advise you to follow John's advice.*

affect, effect   *Affect* is usually a verb meaning "to influence." *Effect* is usually a noun meaning "result." *The drug did not affect the disease, and it had adverse side effects. Effect* can also be a verb meaning "to bring about." *Only the president can effect such a dramatic change.*

aggravate   *Aggravate* means "to make worse or more troublesome." *Overgrazing aggravated the soil erosion.* In formal writing, avoid the colloquial use of *aggravate* meaning "to annoy or irritate." *Her babbling annoyed* (not *aggravated*) *me.*

agree to, agree with   *Agree to* means "to give consent." *Agree with* means "to be in accord" or "to come to an understanding." *He agrees with me about the need for change, but he won't agree to my plan.*

ain't   *Ain't* is nonstandard. Use *am not, are not* (*aren't*), or *is not* (*isn't*). *I am not* (not *ain't*) *going home for spring break.*

all ready, already   *All ready* means "completely prepared." *Already* means "previously." *Susan was all ready for the concert, but her friends had already left.*

all right   *All right* is written as two words. *Alright* is nonstandard.

all together, altogether   *All together* means "everyone gathered." *Altogether* means "entirely." *We were not altogether certain that we could bring the family all together for the reunion.*

allude   To *allude* to something is to make an indirect reference to it. Do not use *allude* to mean "to refer directly." *In his lecture the professor referred* (not *alluded*) *to several pre-Socratic philosophers.*

allusion, illusion   An *allusion* is an indirect reference. An *illusion* is a misconception or false impression. *Did you catch my allusion to Shakespeare? Mirrors give the room an illusion of depth.*

a lot   *A lot* is two words. Do not write *alot. We have had a lot of rain this spring.* See also *lots, lots of.*

among, between   See *between, among.*

amongst   In American English, *among* is preferred.

amoral, immoral   *Amoral* means "neither moral nor immoral"; it also means "not caring about moral judgments." *Immoral* means "morally wrong." *Until recently, most business courses were taught from an amoral perspective. Murder is immoral.*

amount, number   Use *amount* with quantities that cannot be counted; use *number* with those that can. *This recipe calls for a large amount of sugar. We have a large number of toads in our garden.*

an   See *a, an.*

and etc.   *Et cetera* (*etc.*) means "and so forth"; therefore, *and etc.* is redundant. See also *etc.*

and/or Avoid the awkward construction *and/or* except in technical or legal documents.

angry at, angry with To write that one is *angry at* another person is nonstandard. Use *angry with* instead.

ante-, anti- The prefix *ante-* means "earlier" or "in front of"; the prefix *anti-* means "against" or "opposed to." *William Lloyd Garrison was one of the leaders of the antislavery movement during the antebellum period.* *Anti-* should be used with a hyphen when it is followed by a capital letter or a word beginning with *i*.

anxious *Anxious* means "worried" or "apprehensive." In formal writing, avoid using *anxious* to mean "eager." *We are eager* (not *anxious*) *to see your new house.*

anybody, anyone *Anybody* and *anyone* are singular. (See G1-e and G3-a.)

anymore Reserve the adverb *anymore* for negative contexts, where it means "any longer." *Moviegoers are rarely shocked anymore by profanity.* Do not use *anymore* in positive contexts. Use *now* or *nowadays* instead. *Interest rates are so low nowadays* (not *anymore*) *that more people can afford to buy homes.*

anyone See *anybody, anyone.*

anyone, any one *Anyone,* an indefinite pronoun, means "any person at all." *Any one,* the pronoun *one* preceded by the adjective *any,* refers to a particular person or thing in a group. *Anyone from Chicago may choose any one of the games on display.*

anyplace *Anyplace* is informal for *anywhere.* Avoid *anyplace* in formal writing.

anyways, anywheres *Anyways* and *anywheres* are nonstandard. Use *anyway* and *anywhere.*

as *As* is sometimes used to mean "because." But do not use it if there is any chance of ambiguity. *We canceled the picnic because* (not *as*) *it began raining. As* here could mean "because" or "when."

as, like See *like, as.*

as to *As to* is jargon for *about. He inquired about* (not *as to*) *the job.*

averse See *adverse, averse.*

awful The adjective *awful* means "awe-inspiring." Colloquially it is used to mean "terrible" or "bad." The adverb *awfully* is sometimes used in conversation as an intensifier meaning "very." In formal writing, avoid these colloquial uses. *I was very* (not *awfully*) *upset last night. Susan had a terrible* (not *an awful*) *time calming her nerves.*

awhile, a while   *Awhile* is an adverb; it can modify a verb, but it cannot be the object of a preposition such as *for.* The two-word form *a while* is a noun preceded by an article and therefore can be the object of a preposition. *Stay awhile. Stay for a while.*

back up, backup   *Back up* is a verb phrase. *Back up the car carefully. Be sure to back up your hard drive.* A *backup* is a duplicate of electronically stored data. *Keep your backup in a safe place. Backup* can also be used as an adjective. *I regularly create backup disks.*

bad, badly   *Bad* is an adjective, *badly* an adverb. (See G4-a and G4-b.) *They felt bad about being early and ruining the surprise. Her arm hurt badly after she slid headfirst into second base.*

being as, being that   *Being as* and *being that* are nonstandard expressions. Write *because* or *since* instead. *Because* (not *Being as*) *I slept late, I had to skip breakfast.*

beside, besides   *Beside* is a preposition meaning "at the side of" or "next to." *Annie Oakley slept with her gun beside her bed. Besides* is a preposition meaning "except" or "in addition to." *No one besides Terrie can have that ice cream. Besides* is also an adverb meaning "in addition." *I'm not hungry; besides, I don't like ice cream.*

between, among   Ordinarily, use *among* with three or more entities, *between* with two. *The prize was divided among several contestants. You have a choice between carrots and beans.*

bring, take   Use *bring* when an object is being transported toward you, *take* when it is being moved away. *Please bring me a glass of water. Please take these flowers to Mr. Scott.*

burst, bursted; bust, busted   *Burst* is an irregular verb meaning "to come open or fly apart suddenly or violently." Its principal parts are *burst, burst, burst.* The past-tense form *bursted* is nonstandard. *Bust* and *busted* are slang for *burst* and, along with *bursted,* should not be used in formal writing.

can, may   The distinction between *can* and *may* is fading, but many careful writers still observe it in formal writing. *Can* is traditionally reserved for ability, *may* for permission. *Can you ski down the advanced slope without falling? May I help you?*

capital, capitol   *Capital* refers to a city, *capitol* to a building where lawmakers meet. *Capital* also refers to wealth or resources. *The capitol has undergone extensive renovations. The residents of the state capital protested the development plans.*

censor, censure   *Censor* means "to remove or suppress material considered objectionable." *Censure* means "to criticize severely." *The library's new policy of censoring controversial books has been censured by the media.*

cite, site *Cite* means "to quote as an authority or example." *Site* is usually a noun meaning "a particular place." *He cited the zoning law in his argument against the proposed site of the gas station.* Locations on the Internet are usually referred to as *sites. The library's Web site improves every week.*

climactic, climatic *Climactic* is derived from *climax,* the point of greatest intensity in a series or progression of events. *Climatic* is derived from *climate* and refers to meteorological conditions. *The climactic period in the dinosaurs' reign was reached just before severe climatic conditions brought on an ice age.*

coarse, course *Coarse* means "crude" or "rough in texture." *The coarse weave of the wall hanging gave it a three-dimensional quality. Course* usually refers to a path, a playing field, or a unit of study; the expression *of course* means "certainly." *I plan to take a course in car repair this summer. Of course, you are welcome to join me.*

compare to, compare with *Compare to* means "to represent as similar." *She compared him to a wild stallion. Compare with* means "to examine the ways in which two things are similar." *The study compared the language ability of apes with that of dolphins.*

complement, compliment *Complement* is a verb meaning "to go with or complete" or a noun meaning "something that completes." *Compliment* as a verb means "to flatter"; as a noun it means "flattering remark." *Her skill at rushing the net complements his skill at volleying. Mother's flower arrangements receive many compliments.*

conscience, conscious *Conscience* is a noun meaning "moral principles." *Conscious* is an adjective meaning "aware or alert." *Let your conscience be your guide. Were you conscious of his love for you?*

continual, continuous *Continual* means "repeated regularly and frequently." *She grew weary of the continual telephone calls. Continuous* means "extended or prolonged without interruption." *The broken siren made a continuous wail.*

could care less *Could care less* is a nonstandard expression. Write *couldn't care less* instead. *He couldn't* (not *could*) *care less about his psychology final.*

could of *Could of* is nonstandard for *could have. We could have* (not *could of*) *had steak for dinner if we had been hungry.*

council, counsel A *council* is a deliberative body, and a *councilor* is a member of such a body. *Counsel* usually means "advice" and can also mean "lawyer"; *counselor* is one who gives advice or guidance. *The councilors met to draft the council's position paper. The pastor offered wise counsel to the troubled teenager.*

criteria *Criteria* is the plural of *criterion,* which means "a standard or rule or test on which a judgment or decision can be based." *The only criterion for the scholarship is ability.*

data *Data* is a plural noun technically meaning "facts or propositions." But *data* is increasingly being accepted as a singular noun. *The new data suggest* (or *suggests*) *that our theory is correct.* (The singular *datum* is rarely used.)

different from, different than Ordinarily, write *different from. Your sense of style is different from Jim's.* However, *different than* is acceptable to avoid an awkward construction. *Please let me know if your plans are different than* (to avoid *from what*) *they were six weeks ago.*

differ from, differ with *Differ from* means "to be unlike"; *differ with* means "to disagree." *She differed with me about the wording of the agreement. My approach to the problem differed from hers.*

disinterested, uninterested *Disinterested* means "impartial, objective"; *uninterested* means "not interested." *We sought the advice of a disinterested counselor to help us solve our problem. He was uninterested in anyone's opinion but his own.*

don't *Don't* is the contraction for *do not. I don't want any. Don't* should not be used as the contraction for *does not,* which is *doesn't. He doesn't* (not *don't*) *want any.* (See G2-c.)

double negative Standard English allows two negatives only if a positive meaning is intended. *The runners were not unhappy with their performance.* Double negatives used to emphasize negation are nonstandard. *Jack doesn't have to answer to anybody* (not *nobody*). (See G4-d.)

due to *Due to* is an adjective phrase and should not be used as a preposition meaning "because of." *The trip was canceled because of* (not *due to*) *lack of interest. Due to* is acceptable as a subject complement and usually follows a form of the verb *be. His success was due to hard work.*

each *Each* is singular. (See G1-e and G3-a.)

effect, affect See *affect, effect.*

e.g. In formal writing, replace the Latin abbreviation *e.g.* with its English equivalent: *for example* or *for instance.*

either *Either* is singular. (See G1-e and G3-a.) For *either . . . or* constructions, see G1-d and G3-a.

elicit, illicit *Elicit* is a verb meaning "to bring out" or "to evoke." *Illicit* is an adjective meaning "unlawful." *The reporter was unable to elicit any information from the police about illicit drug traffic.*

emigrate from, immigrate to *Emigrate* means "to leave one country or region to settle in another." *In 1900, my grandfather emigrated from Russia to escape the religious pogroms. Immigrate* means "to enter another country and reside there." *Many Mexicans immigrate to the United States to find work.*

eminent, imminent *Eminent* means "outstanding" or "distinguished." *We met an eminent professor of Greek history. Imminent* means "about to happen." *The announcement is imminent.*

enthused Many people object to the use of *enthused* as an adjective. Use *enthusiastic* instead. *The children were enthusiastic* (not *enthused*) *about going to the circus.*

etc. Avoid ending a list with *etc.* It is more emphatic to end with an example, and in most contexts readers will understand that the list is not exhaustive. When you don't wish to end with an example, *and so on* is more graceful than *etc.* See also *and etc.*

eventually, ultimately Often used interchangeably, *eventually* is the better choice to mean "at an unspecified time in the future" and *ultimately* is better to mean "the furthest possible extent or greatest extreme." *He knew that eventually he would complete his degree. The existentialist considered suicide the ultimately rational act.*

everybody, everyone *Everybody* and *everyone* are singular. (See G1-e and G3-a.)

everyone, every one *Everyone* is an indefinite pronoun. *Every one,* the pronoun *one* preceded by the adjective *every,* means "each individual or thing in a particular group." *Every one* is usually followed by *of. Everyone wanted to go. Every one of the missing books was found.*

except, accept See *accept, except.*

expect Avoid the colloquial use of *expect* meaning "to believe, think, or suppose." *I think* (not *expect*) *it will rain tonight.*

explicit, implicit *Explicit* means "expressed directly" or "clearly defined"; *implicit* means "implied, unstated." *I gave him explicit instructions not to go swimming. My mother's silence indicated her implicit approval.*

farther, further *Farther* usually describes distances. *Further* usually suggests quantity or degree. *Chicago is farther from Miami than I thought. You extended the curfew further than you should have.*

female, male The terms *female* and *male* are jargon when used to refer to specific people. *Two women* (not *females*) *and one man* (not *male*) *applied for the position.*

fewer, less *Fewer* refers to items that can be counted; *less* refers to general amounts. *Fewer people are living in the city. Please put less sugar in my tea.*

finalize *Finalize* is jargon meaning "to make final or complete." Use ordinary English instead. *The architect prepared final drawings* (not *finalized the drawings*).

firstly *Firstly* sounds pretentious, and it leads to the ungainly series *firstly, secondly, thirdly, fourthly,* and so on. Write *first, second, third* instead.

further See *farther, further.*

get *Get* has many colloquial uses. In formal writing, avoid using *get* to mean the following: "to evoke an emotional response" (*That music always gets to me*); "to annoy" (*After a while his sulking got to me*); "to take revenge on" (*I got back at him by leaving the room*); "to become" (*He got sick*); "to start or begin" (*Let's get going*). Avoid using *have got to* in place of *must*. *I must* (not *have got to*) *finish this paper tonight.*

good, well *Good* is an adjective, *well* an adverb. (See G4.) *He hasn't felt good about his game since he sprained his wrist last season. She performed well on the uneven parallel bars.*

hanged, hung *Hanged* is the past-tense and past-participle form of the verb *hang* meaning "to execute." *The prisoner was hanged at dawn. Hung* is the past-tense and past-participle form of the verb *hang* meaning "to fasten or suspend." *The stockings were hung by the chimney with care.*

hardly Avoid expressions such as *can't hardly* and *not hardly,* which are considered double negatives. *I can* (not *can't*) *hardly describe my elation at getting the job.* (See G4-d.)

has got, have got *Got* is unnecessary and awkward in such constructions. It should be dropped. *We have* (not *have got*) *three days to prepare for the opening.*

he At one time *he* was commonly used to mean "he or she." Today such usage is inappropriate. (See W4-e and G3-a.)

he/she, his/her In formal writing, use *he or she* or *his or her.* For alternatives to these wordy constructions, see W4-e and G3-a.

hisself *Hisself* is nonstandard. Use *himself.*

hopefully *Hopefully* means "in a hopeful manner." *We looked hopefully to the future.* Do not use *hopefully* in constructions such as the following: *Hopefully, your daughter will recover soon.* Indicate who is doing the hoping: *I hope that your daughter will recover soon.*

hung, hanged See *hanged, hung.*

i.e. In formal writing, replace the Latin abbreviation *i.e.* with its English equivalent: *that is.*

if, whether Use *if* to express a condition and *whether* to express alternatives. *If you go on a trip, whether it be to Nebraska or New Jersey, remember to bring traveler's checks.*

illusion, allusion See *allusion, illusion.*

immigrate, emigrate See *emigrate from, immigrate to.*

imminent, eminent See *eminent, imminent.*

immoral, amoral See *amoral, immoral.*

implement *Implement* is a pretentious way of saying "do," "carry out," or "accomplish." Use ordinary language instead. *We carried out* (not *implemented*) *the director's orders with some reluctance.*

imply, infer *Imply* means "to suggest or state indirectly"; *infer* means "to draw a conclusion." *John implied that he knew all about computers, but the interviewer inferred that John was inexperienced.*

in, into *In* indicates location or condition; *into* indicates movement or a change in condition. *They found the lost letters in a box after moving into the house.*

individual *Individual* is a pretentious substitute for *person. We invited a person* (not *an individual*) *from the audience to participate in the experiment.*

ingenious, ingenuous *Ingenious* means "clever." *Sarah's solution to the problem was ingenious. Ingenuous* means "naive" or "frank." *For a successful manager, Ed is surprisingly ingenuous.*

in regards to *In regards to* confuses two different phrases: *in regard to* and *as regards*. Use one or the other. *In regard to* (or *As regards*) *the contract, ignore the first clause.*

irregardless *Irregardless* is nonstandard. Use *regardless.*

is when, is where These mixed constructions are often incorrectly used in definitions. *A run-off election is a second election held to break a tie* (not *is when a second election breaks a tie*). (See E5-c.)

it is *It is* is nonstandard when used to mean "there is." *There is* (not *It is*) *a fly in my soup.*

its, it's *Its* is a possessive pronoun; *it's* is a contraction for *it is*. (See P5-c and P5-e.) *The dog licked its wound whenever its owner walked into the room. It's a perfect day to walk the twenty-mile trail.*

kind(s) *Kind* is singular and should be treated as such. Don't write *These kind of chairs are rare.* Write instead *This kind of chair is rare. Kinds* is plural and should be used only when you mean more than one kind. *These kinds of chairs are rare.*

kind of, sort of Avoid using *kind of* or *sort of* to mean "somewhat." *The movie was somewhat* (not *kind of*) *boring.* Do not put *a* after either phrase. *That kind of* (not *kind of a*) *salesclerk annoys me.*

lay, lie See *lie, lay.*

lead, led *Lead* is a noun referring to a metal. *Led* is the past tense of the verb *lead. He led me to the treasure.*

learn, teach *Learn* means "to gain knowledge"; *teach* means "to impart knowledge." *I must teach* (not *learn*) *my sister to read.*

leave, let *Leave* means "to exit." Avoid using it with the nonstandard meaning "to permit." *Let* (not *Leave*) *me help you with the dishes.*

less, fewer See *fewer, less.*

let, leave See *leave, let.*

liable *Liable* means "obligated" or "responsible." Do not use it to mean "likely." *You're likely* (not *liable*) *to trip if you don't tie your shoelaces.*

lie, lay *Lie* is an intransitive verb meaning "to recline or rest on a surface." Its principal parts are *lie, lay, lain. Lay* is a transitive verb meaning "to put or place." Its principal parts are *lay, laid, laid.* (See G2-b.)

like, as *Like* is a preposition, not a subordinating conjunction. It can be followed only by a noun or a noun phrase. *As* is a subordinating conjunction that introduces a subordinate clause. In casual speech you may say *She looks like she hasn't slept* or *You don't know her like I do.* But in formal writing, use *as. She looks as if she hasn't slept. You don't know her as I do.* (See prepositions and subordinating conjunctions, B1-f and B1-g.)

loose, lose *Loose* is an adjective meaning "not securely fastened." *Lose* is a verb meaning "to misplace" or "to not win." *Did you lose your only loose pair of work pants?*

lots, lots of *Lots* and *lots of* are colloquial substitutes for *many, much,* or *a lot.* Avoid using them in formal writing.

male, female See *female, male.*

mankind Avoid *mankind* whenever possible. It offends many readers because it excludes women. Use *humanity, humans, the human race,* or *humankind* instead. (See W4-e.)

may, can See *can, may.*

maybe, may be *Maybe* is an adverb meaning "possibly." *May be* is a verb phrase. *Maybe the sun will shine tomorrow. Tomorrow may be a brighter day.*

may of, might of *May of* and *might of* are nonstandard for *may have* and *might have. We may have* (not *may of*) *had too many cookies.*

media, medium *Media* is the plural of *medium. Of all the media that cover the Olympics, television is the medium that best captures the spectacle of the events.*

most *Most* is colloquial when used to mean "almost" and should be avoided. *Almost* (not *Most*) *everyone went to the parade.*

must of See *may of, might of.*

myself *Myself* is a reflexive or intensive pronoun. Reflexive: *I cut myself.* Intensive: *I will drive you myself.* Do not use *myself* in place of *I* or *me. He gave the flowers to Melinda and me* (not *myself*). (See also G3-c.)

neither *Neither* is singular. (See G1-e and G3-a.) For *neither . . . nor* constructions, see G1-d and G3-a.

none *None* is usually singular. (See G1-e.)

nowheres *Nowheres* is nonstandard for *nowhere.*

number See *amount, number.*

of Use the verb *have,* not the preposition *of,* after the verbs *could, should, would, may, might,* and *must. They must have* (not *of*) *left early.*

off of *Off* is sufficient. Omit *of. The ball rolled off* (not *off of*) *the table.*

OK, O.K., okay All three spellings are acceptable, but in formal speech and writing avoid these colloquial expressions for consent or approval.

parameters *Parameter* is a mathematical term that has become jargon for "fixed limit," "boundary," or "guideline." Use ordinary English instead. *The task force was asked to work within certain guidelines* (not *parameters*).

passed, past *Passed* is the past tense of the verb *pass. Mother passed me another slice of cake. Past* usually means "belonging to a former time" or "beyond a time or place." *Our past president spoke until past midnight. The hotel is just past the next intersection.*

percent, per cent, percentage *Percent* (also spelled *per cent*) is always used with a specific number. *Percentage* is used with a descriptive term such as *large* or *small,* not with a specific number. *The candidate won 80 percent of the primary vote. Only a small percentage of registered voters turned out for the election.*

phenomena *Phenomena* is the plural of *phenomenon,* which means "an observable occurrence or fact." *Strange phenomena occur at all hours of the night in that house, but last night's phenomenon was the strangest of all.*

plus *Plus* should not be used to join independent clauses. *This raincoat is dirty; moreover* (not *plus*), *it has a hole in it.*

precede, proceed *Precede* means "to come before." *Proceed* means "to go forward." *As we proceeded up the mountain path, we noticed fresh tracks in the mud, evidence that a group of hikers had preceded us.*

principal, principle *Principal* is a noun meaning "the head of a school or an organization" or "a sum of money." It is also an adjective meaning "most important." *Principle* is a noun meaning "a basic truth or law." *The principal expelled her for three principal reasons. We believe in the principle of equal justice for all.*

proceed, precede See *precede, proceed.*

quote, quotation *Quote* is a verb; *quotation* is a noun. Avoid using *quote* as a shortened form of *quotation. Her quotations* (not *quotes*) *from Shakespeare intrigued us.*

raise, rise *Raise* is a transitive verb meaning "to move or cause to move upward." It takes a direct object. *I raised the shades. Rise* is an intransitive verb meaning "to go up." It does not take a direct object. *Heat rises.*

real, really *Real* is an adjective; *really* is an adverb. *Real* is sometimes used informally as an adverb, but avoid this use in formal writing. *She was really* (not *real*) *angry.* (See G4-a.)

reason . . . is because Use *that* instead of *because. The reason I'm late is that* (not *because*) *my car broke down.* (See E5-a.)

reason why The expression *reason why* is redundant. *The reason* (not *The reason why*) *Jones lost the election is clear.*

relation, relationship *Relation* describes a connection between things. *Relationship* describes a connection between people. *There is a relation between poverty and infant mortality. Our business relationship has cooled over the years.*

respectfully, respectively *Respectfully* means "showing or marked by respect." *Respectively* means "each in the order given." *He respectfully submitted his opinion to the judge. John, Tom, and Larry were a butcher, a baker, and a lawyer, respectively.*

sensual, sensuous *Sensual* means "gratifying the physical senses," especially those associated with sexual pleasure. *Sensuous* means "pleasing to the senses," especially those involved in the experience of art, music, and nature. *The sensuous music and balmy air led the dancers to more sensual movements.*

set, sit *Set* is a transitive verb meaning "to put" or "to place." Its principal parts are *set, set, set. Sit* is an intransitive verb meaning "to be seated." Its principal parts are *sit, sat, sat. She set the dough in a warm corner of the kitchen. The cat sat in the warmest part of the room.*

shall, will *Shall* was once used as the helping verb with *I* or *we: I shall, we shall, you will, he/she/it will, they will.* Today, however, *will* is generally accepted even when the subject is *I* or *we.* The word *shall* occurs primarily in polite questions. (*Shall I find you a pillow?*) and in legalistic sentences suggesting duty or obligation (*The applicant shall file form 1080 by December 31*).

should of *Should of* is nonstandard for *should have. They should have* (not *should of*) *been home an hour ago.*

since Do not use *since* to mean "because" if there is any chance of ambiguity. *Because* (not *Since*) *we won the game, we have been celebrating with a pitcher of beer. Since* here could mean "because" or "from the time that."

sit, set See *set, sit.*

site, cite See *cite, site.*

somebody, someone *Somebody* and *someone* are singular. (See G1-e and G3-a.)

something *Something* is singular. (See G1-e.)

sometime, some time, sometimes *Sometime* is an adverb meaning "at an indefinite or unstated time." *Some time* is the adjective *some* modifying the noun *time* and is spelled as two words to mean "a period of time." *Sometimes* is an adverb meaning "at times, now and then." *I'll see you sometime soon. I haven't lived there for some time. Sometimes I run into him at the library.*

suppose to Write *supposed to.*

sure and *Sure and* is nonstandard for *sure to. We were all taught to be sure to* (not *and*) *look both ways before crossing a street.*

take, bring See *bring, take.*

than, then *Than* is a conjunction used in comparisons; *then* is an adverb denoting time. *That pizza is more than I can eat. Tom laughed, and then we recognized him.*

that See *who, which, that.*

that, which Many writers reserve *that* for restrictive clauses, *which* for nonrestrictive clauses. (See P1-e.)

theirselves *Theirselves* is nonstandard for *themselves. The two people were able to push the Volkswagon out of the way themselves* (not *theirselves*).

them The use of *them* in place of *those* is nonstandard. *Please send those* (not *them*) *flowers to the patient in room 220.*

then, than See *than, then.*

there, their, they're *There* is an adverb specifying place; it is also an expletive. Adverb: *Sylvia is lying there unconscious.* Expletive: *There are two plums left. Their* is a possessive pronoun. *Fred and Jane finally washed their car. They're* is a contraction of *they are. They're later than usual today.*

they The use of *they* to indicate possession is nonstandard. Use *their* instead. *Cindy and Sam decided to sell their* (not *they*) *1975 Corvette.*

this kind See *kind(s).*

to, too, two *To* is a preposition; *too* is an adverb; *two* is a number. *Too many of your shots slice to the left, but the last two were right on the mark.*

toward, towards *Toward* and *towards* are generally interchangeable, although *toward* is preferred in American English.

try and *Try and* is nonstandard for *try to. The teacher asked us all to try to* (not *and*) *write an original haiku.*

ultimately, eventually See *eventually, ultimately.*

unique Avoid expressions such as *most unique, more straight, less perfect, very round.* Either something is unique or it isn't. It is illogical to suggest degrees of uniqueness. (See G4-c.)

usage The noun *usage* should not be substituted for *use* when the meaning is "employment of." *The use* (not *usage*) *of computers dramatically increased the company's profits.*

use to Write *used to.*

utilize *Utilize* means "to make use of." It often sounds pretentious; in most cases, *use* is sufficient. *I used* (not *utilized*) *the best workers to get the job done fast.*

wait for, wait on *Wait for* means "to be in readiness for" or "await." *Wait on* means "to serve." *We're only waiting for* (not *waiting on*) *Ruth to take us to the game.*

ways *Ways* is colloquial when used to mean "distance." *The city is a long way* (not *ways*) *from here.*

weather, whether The noun *weather* refers to the state of the atmosphere. *Whether* is a conjunction referring to a choice between alternatives. *We wondered whether the weather would clear up in time for our picnic.*

well, good See *good, well.*

where Do not use *where* in place of *that. I heard that* (not *where*) *the crime rate is increasing.*

which See *that, which* and *who, which, that.*

while Avoid using *while* to mean "although" or "whereas" if there is any chance of ambiguity. *Although* (not *While*) *Gloria lost money in the slot machine, Tom won it at roulette.* Here *While* could mean either "although" or "at the same time that."

who, which, that Do not use *which* to refer to persons. Use *who* instead. *That,* though generally used to refer to things, may be used to refer to a group or class of people. *Fans wondered how an old man who* (not *that* or *which*) *walked with a limp could play football. The team that scores the most points in this game will win the tournament.*

who, whom *Who* is used for subjects and subject complements; *whom* is used for objects. (See G3-d.)

who's, whose *Who's* is a contraction of *who is; whose* is a possessive pronoun. *Who's ready for more popcorn? Whose coat is this?* (See P5-c and P5-e.)

will See *shall, will.*

would of *Would of* is nonstandard for *would have. She would have* (not *would of*) *had a chance to play if she had arrived on time.*

you In formal writing, avoid *you* in an indefinite sentence meaning "anyone." (See G3-b.) *Any spectator* (not *You*) *could tell by the way John caught the ball that his throw would be too late.*

your, you're *Your* is a possessive pronoun; *you're* is a contraction of *you are. Is that your new motorcycle? You're on the list of finalists.* (See P5-c and P5-e.)

W2

Wordy sentences

Long sentences are not necessarily wordy, nor are short sentences always concise. A sentence is wordy if its meaning can be conveyed in fewer words.

> GRAMMAR CHECKERS can flag some, but not all, wordy constructions. Most programs alert you to common redundancies, such as *true fact,* and empty or inflated phrases, such as *in my opinion* or *in order that.* In addition, they alert you to wordiness caused by passive verbs, such as *is determined* (see also W3). They are less helpful in identifying sentences with needlessly complex structures.

W2-a Eliminate redundancies.

Redundancies such as *cooperate together, close proximity, basic essentials,* and *true fact* are a common source of wordiness. There is no need to say the same thing twice.

► Black slaves were ~~portrayed or~~ stereotyped as lazy even though

they were the main labor force of the South.

> *works*

► Daniel ~~is now employed~~ at a private rehabilitation center ~~working~~
             ^

as a registered physical therapist.

Although modifiers ordinarily add meaning to the words they modify, occasionally they are redundant.

► Sylvia ~~very hurriedly~~ scribbled her name, address, and phone

number on the back of a greasy napkin.

► Joel was determined ~~in his mind~~ to lose weight.

W2-b Avoid unnecessary repetition of words.

Although words may be repeated deliberately, for effect, repetitions will seem awkward if they are clearly unnecessary. When a more concise version is possible, choose it.

► Our fifth patient, in room six, is ~~a~~ mentally ill ~~. patient.~~
                                                       ^

> *grow*

► The best teachers help each student to ~~become a better student~~
                                         ^

both academically and emotionally.

W2-c Cut empty or inflated phrases.

An empty phrase can be cut with little or no loss of meaning. Common examples are introductory word groups that apologize or hedge: *in my opinion, I think that, it seems that, one must admit that,* and so on.

> *O*

► ~~In my opinion,~~ ~~O~~ur current immigration policy is misguided on

several counts.

Inflated phrases can be reduced to a word or two without loss of meaning.

INFLATED	CONCISE
along the lines of	like
as a matter of fact	in fact
at all times	always
at the present time	now, currently
at this point in time	now, currently
because of the fact that	because
by means of	by
due to the fact that	because
for the purpose of	for
for the reason that	because
have the ability to	can, be able to
in order to	to
in spite of the fact that	although, though
in the event that	if
in the final analysis	finally
in the nature of	like
in the neighborhood of	about
until such time as	until

► We will file the appropriate papers ~~in the event that~~ we are

    if

unable to meet the deadline.

W2-d Simplify the structure.

If the structure of a sentence is needlessly indirect, try simplifying it. Look for opportunities to strengthen the verb.

► The financial analyst claimed that because of volatile market

conditions she could not ~~make an~~ estimate ~~of~~ the company's future

profits.

The verb *estimate* is more vigorous and more concise than *make an estimate of.*

The colorless verbs *is, are, was,* and *were* frequently generate excess words. (See also W3-a.)

► The administrative secretary ~~is responsible for monitoring~~

                            monitors and balances

~~and balancing~~ the budgets for travel, contract services, and

personnel.

The expletive constructions *there is* and *there are* (or *there was* and *there were*) can also generate excess words. The same is true of expletive constructions beginning with *it*.

▶ ~~There is~~ ^A^nother videotape ~~that~~ tells the story of Charles Darwin

   and introduces the theory of evolution.

▶ ~~It is important that~~ ^H^ikers ^must^ remain inside the park boundaries.

Finally, verbs in the passive voice may be needlessly indirect. When the active voice expresses your meaning as well, use it. (See also W3-b.)

▶ All too often, athletes with marginal academic skills ^our coaches have recruited^ . ~~have been recruited by our coaches.~~

W2-e   Reduce clauses to phrases, phrases to single words.

Word groups functioning as modifiers can often be made more compact. Look for any opportunities to reduce clauses to phrases or phrases to single words.

▶ We visited Monticello, ~~which was~~ the home of Thomas Jefferson.

▶ Susan's stylish pants, ~~made of leather,~~ ^leather^ were too warm for Miami.

W3

Active verbs

Active verbs express meaning more emphatically and vigorously than their weaker counterparts—forms of the verb *be* or verbs in the passive voice. Forms of the verb *be* (*be, am, is, are, was, were, being, been*) lack vigor because they convey no action. Verbs in the passive voice lack strength because their subjects receive the action instead of doing it (see B2-b).

Although the forms of *be* and passive verbs have legitimate uses, if an active verb can carry your meaning, use it.

BE VERB   A surge of power *was* responsible for the destruction of the coolant pumps.

PASSIVE   The coolant pumps *were destroyed* by a surge of power.

ACTIVE   A surge of power *destroyed* the coolant pumps.

Even among active verbs, some are more active—and therefore more vigorous and colorful—than others. Carefully selected verbs can energize a piece of writing.

▶ The goalie crouched low, ~~reached~~ out his stick, and ~~sent~~ the
    swept   *hooked*

rebound away from the mouth of the net.

W3-a   Replace *be* verbs that result in dull or wordy sentences.

Not every *be* verb needs replacing. The forms of *be* (*be, am, is, are, was, were, being, been*) work well when you want to link a subject to a noun that clearly renames it or to an adjective that describes it: *History is a bucket of ashes. Scoundrels are always sociable.* (See B2-b.) And when used as helping verbs before present participles (*is flying, are disappearing*) to express ongoing action, *be* verbs are fine: *Derrick was plowing the field when his wife went into labor.* (See G2-f.)

If using a *be* verb makes a sentence needlessly dull or wordy, however, consider replacing it. Often a phrase following the verb will contain a word (such as *violation*) that suggests a more vigorous, active alternative (*violate*).

▶ Burying nuclear waste in Antarctica would ~~be in violation of~~
                                                                    violate

an international treaty.

Violate is less wordy and more vigorous than *be in violation of.*

▶ Escaping into the world of drugs, I ~~was rebellious about~~ every
                                                       rebelled against

rule set down by my parents.

Rebelled against is more active than *was rebellious about.*

W3-b Use an active verb unless you have a good reason for choosing a passive verb.

In what is known as the active voice, the subject of the sentence does the action; in the passive voice, the subject receives the action. (See also B2-b.)

ACTIVE	Hernando *caught* the fly ball.
PASSIVE	The fly ball *was caught* by Hernando.

In passive sentences, the actor (in this case *Hernando*) frequently disappears from the sentence: *The fly ball was caught.*

In most cases, you will want to emphasize the actor, so you should use the active voice. To replace a passive verb with an active alternative, make the actor the subject of the sentence.

> Lightning struck the transformer,
> ▶ ~~The transformer was struck by lightning,~~ plunging us into
> ⌃
> darkness.

The active verb (*struck*) makes the point more forcefully than the passive verb (*was struck*).

The passive voice is appropriate if you wish to emphasize the receiver of the action or to minimize the importance of the actor.

APPROPRIATE PASSIVE	Many native Hawaiians *are forced* to leave their beautiful beaches to make room for hotels and condominiums.
APPROPRIATE PASSIVE	As the time for harvest approaches, the tobacco plants *are sprayed* with a chemical to retard the growth of suckers.

The writer of the first sentence wished to emphasize the receivers of the action, Hawaiians. The writer of the second sentence wished to focus on the tobacco plants, not on the people spraying them.

In much scientific writing, the passive voice properly puts the emphasis on the experiment or process being described, not on the researcher.

APPROPRIATE PASSIVE	The solution *was heated* to the boiling point, and then it was reduced in volume by 50 percent.

ESL

Some speakers of English as a second language avoid the passive voice even when it is appropriate. For advice on transforming an active-voice sentence to the passive, see B2-b.

GRAMMAR CHECKERS are fairly good at flagging passive verbs, such as *were given*. However, because passive verbs are sometimes appropriate, you—not the computer program—must decide whether to make a passive verb active.

W4

Appropriate language

Language is appropriate when it suits your subject, conforms to the needs of your audience, and blends naturally with your own voice.

W4-a Stay away from jargon.

Jargon is specialized language used among members of a trade, profession, or group. Use jargon only when readers will be familiar with it; even then, use it only when plain English will not do as well.

> JARGON For years the indigenous body politic of South Africa attempted to negotiate legal enfranchisement without result.

> REVISED For years the indigenous people of South Africa negotiated in vain for the right to vote.

Broadly defined, jargon includes puffed-up language designed more to impress readers than to inform them. Common examples in business, government, higher education, and the military are given in the following list, with plain English translations in parentheses.

ameliorate (improve)	impact on (affect)
commence (begin)	indicator (sign)
components (parts)	optimal (best, most favorable)
endeavor (try)	parameters (boundaries, limits)
exit (leave)	peruse (read, look over)
facilitate (help)	prior to (before)
factor (consideration, cause)	utilize (use)
finalize (finish)	viable (workable)

Sentences filled with jargon are hard to read, and they are often wordy as well.

▶ All ~~employees functioning in the capacity of~~ work-study students *must prove that they are currently enrolled.* ~~are required to give evidence of current enrollment.~~

▶ Mayor Summers will ~~commence~~ *begin* his term of office by ~~ameliorating~~ *improving* living conditions in ~~economically deprived zones.~~ *poor neighborhoods.*

W4-b Avoid pretentious language, most euphemisms, and "doublespeak."

Hoping to sound profound or poetic, some writers embroider their thoughts with large words and flowery phrases, language that in fact sounds pretentious. Pretentious language is so ornate and often so wordy that it obscures the thought that lies beneath.

▶ When our ~~progenitors reach their silver-haired and golden years,~~ *parents become old,* we frequently ~~ensepulcher~~ *bury* them in homes ~~for senescent beings~~ *old-age* as if they were already ~~among the deceased.~~ *dead.*

Euphemisms, nice-sounding words or phrases substituted for words thought to sound harsh or ugly, are sometimes appropriate. It is customary, for example, to say that a couple is "sleeping together" or that someone has "passed away." Most euphemisms, however, are needlessly evasive or even deceitful. Like pretentious language, they obscure the intended meaning.

EUPHEMISM	PLAIN ENGLISH
adult entertainment	pornography
preowned automobile	used car

EUPHEMISM	PLAIN ENGLISH
economically deprived	poor
selected out	fired
negative savings	debts
strategic withdrawal	retreat or defeat
revenue enhancers	taxes
chemical dependency	drug addiction
incendiary device	bomb
correctional facility	prison

The term *doublespeak,* coined by George Orwell in the novel *1984,* applies to any deliberately evasive or deceptive language, including euphemisms. Doublespeak is especially common in politics, where missiles are named "Peacekeepers," airplane crashes are termed "uncontrolled contact with the ground," and a military retreat is described as "tactical redeployment." Business also gives us its share of doublespeak. When the manufacturer of a pacemaker writes that its product "may result in adverse health consequences in pacemaker-dependent patients as a result of sudden 'no output' failure," it takes an alert reader to grasp the message: The pacemakers might suddenly stop functioning and cause a heart attack or even death.

> GRAMMAR CHECKERS can be helpful in identifying jargon and pretentious language. For example, they commonly advise against using words such as *utilize, finalize, facilitate,* and *effectuate.* You may find, however, that a program advises you to "simplify" language that is not jargon or pretentious language and may in fact be appropriate in academic writing.

W4-c In most contexts, avoid slang, regional expressions, and nonstandard English.

Slang is an informal and sometimes private vocabulary that expresses the solidarity of a group such as teenagers, rock musicians, or football fans; it is subject to more rapid change than standard English. For example, the slang teenagers use to express approval changes every few years; *cool, groovy, neat, wicked, awesome,* and *stylin'* have replaced one another within the last three decades. Sometimes slang becomes so widespread that it is accepted as standard vocabulary. *Jazz,* for example, started as slang but is now generally accepted to describe a style of music.

Although slang has a certain vitality, it is a code that not everyone understands, and it is very informal. Therefore, it is inappropriate in most written work.

▶ If we don't begin studying for the final, a whole semester's work ~~is~~ *will be wasted.*
~~going down the tubes.~~
  ^

  disgust you.
▶ The government's "filth" guidelines for food will ~~gross you out.~~
  ^

Regional expressions are common to a group in a geographical area. *Let's talk with the bark off* (for *Let's speak frankly*) is an expression in the southern United States, for example. Regional expressions have the same limitations as slang and are therefore inappropriate in most writing.

  turn on
▶ John was four blocks from the house before he remembered to ~~cut~~
  ^

the headlights. ~~on.~~
  ^

▶ I'm not ~~for~~ sure, but I think the dance has been postponed.

Standard English is the language used in all academic, business, and professional fields. Nonstandard English is spoken by people with a common regional or social heritage. Although nonstandard English may be appropriate when spoken within a close group, it is out of place in most formal and informal writing.

  has
▶ The counselor ~~have~~ so many problems in her own life that she
  doesn't ^
  ~~don't~~ know how to advise anyone else.
  ^

If you speak a nonstandard dialect, try to identify the ways in which your dialect differs from standard English. Look especially for the following features of nonstandard English, which commonly cause problems in writing:

Misuse of verb forms such as *began* and *begun* (See G2-a.)

Omission of *-s* endings on verbs (See G1-a and G2-c.)

Omission of *-ed* endings on verbs (See G2-d.)

Omission of necessary verbs (See G2-e.)

Double negatives (See G4-d.)

You might also scan the Glossary of Usage (W1), which alerts you to nonstandard words and expressions such as *ain't, could of, hisself, theirselves, them* (meaning "those"), *they* (meaning "their"), *it is* (meaning "there is"), and so on.

W4-d Choose an appropriate level of formality.

In deciding on a level of formality, consider both your subject and your audience. Does the subject demand a dignified treatment, or is a relaxed tone more suitable? Will the audience be put off if you assume too close a relationship with them, or might you alienate them by seeming too distant?

For most college and professional writing, some degree of formality is appropriate. In a letter applying for a job, for example, it is a mistake to sound too breezy and informal.

TOO INFORMAL	I'd like to get that receptionist's job you've got in the paper.
MORE FORMAL	I would like to apply for the receptionist's position listed in the *Peoria Journal Star.*

Informal writing is appropriate for private letters, business correspondence between close associates, articles in popular magazines, and personal narratives. In such writing, formal language can seem out of place.

▶ Once a pitcher for the Cincinnati Reds, Bob shared with me the
                                               began
  secrets of his trade. His lesson ~~commenced~~ with his famous curve
     which he threw   ^
  ball, ~~implemented~~ by tucking the little finger behind the ball
  ^   *revealed*
  instead of holding it straight out. Next he ~~elucidated~~ the mysteries
                                                   ^
  of the sucker pitch, a slow ball coming behind a fast windup.

GRAMMAR CHECKERS can flag slang and some informal language. Be aware, though, that they tend to be conservative on the matter of using contractions. If your ear tells you that a contraction such as *isn't* or *doesn't* strikes the right tone, stay with it.

W4-e Avoid sexist language.

Sexist language is language that stereotypes or demeans men or women, usually women. Using nonsexist language is a matter of courtesy—of respect for and sensitivity to the feelings of others.

Recognizing sexist language

Some sexist language is easy to recognize because it reflects genuine contempt for women: referring to a woman as a "broad," for example, or calling a lawyer a "lady lawyer," or saying in an advertisement, "If our new sports car were a lady, it would get its bottom pinched."

Other forms of sexist language are less blatant. The following practices, while they may not result from conscious sexism, reflect stereotypical thinking: referring to nurses as women and doctors as men, using different conventions when naming or identifying women and men, or assuming that all of one's readers are men.

STEREOTYPICAL LANGUAGE
After the nursing student graduates, *she* must face a difficult state board examination. [Not all nursing students are women.]

Running for city council are Jake Stein, an attorney, and *Mrs.* Cynthia Jones, a professor of English *and mother of three.* [The title *Mrs.* and the phrase *and mother of three* are irrelevant.]

Wives of senior government officials are required to report any gifts they receive that are valued at more than $100. [Not all senior government officials are men.]

Still other forms of sexist language result from outmoded traditions. The pronouns *he, him,* and *his,* for instance, were traditionally used to refer generically to persons of either sex.

GENERIC *HE* OR *HIS*
When a senior physician is harassed by managed care professionals, *he* may be tempted to leave the profession.

A journalist is stimulated by *his* deadline.

Today, however, such usage is widely viewed as sexist because it excludes women and encourages sex-role stereotyping—the view that men are somehow more suited than women to be doctors, journalists, and so on.

Like the pronouns *he, him,* and *his,* the nouns *man* and *men* were once used indefinitely to refer to persons of either sex. Current usage demands gender-neutral terms instead.

INAPPROPRIATE	APPROPRIATE
anchorman	anchor
businessman	business executive, businessperson
chairman	chairperson, moderator, chair, head
clergyman	member of the clergy, minister, pastor
congressman	member of Congress, representative, legislator
fireman	firefighter
forefathers	ancestors
foreman	supervisor
mailman	mail carrier, postal worker, letter carrier
mankind	people, humans
manpower	personnel
policeman	police officer
salesman	sales associate, sales representative
to man	to operate, to staff
weatherman	weather forecaster, meteorologist
workman	worker, laborer

GRAMMAR CHECKERS are good at flagging sexist words, such as *mankind,* but they may also flag words, such as *girl* and *woman,* when they aren't being used in a sexist manner. It's sexist to call a woman a girl or a doctor a woman doctor, but you don't need to avoid the words *girl* and *woman* entirely and replace them with needlessly abstract terms like *female* and *individual.* All in all, just use your common sense. It's usually easy to tell when a word is offensive — and when it is not.

Although grammar checkers can flag sexist words, they cannot flag other kinds of sexist language, such as inconsistent treatment of men and women.

Revising sexist language

When revising sexist language, be sparing in your use of the wordy constructions *he or she* and *his or her.* Although these constructions are fine in small doses, they become awkward when repeated throughout an essay. A better revision strategy, many writers have discovered, is to write in the plural; yet another strategy is to recast the sentence so that the problem does not arise.

ACCEPTABLE BUT WORDY

When a senior physician is harassed by managed care professionals, *he or she* may be tempted to leave the profession.

A journalist is stimulated by *his or her* deadline.

BETTER: USING THE PLURAL

When senior *physicians* are harassed by managed care professionals, *they* may be tempted to leave the profession.

Journalists are stimulated by *their* deadlines.

BETTER: RECASTING THE SENTENCE

When harassed by managed care professionals, *a senior physician*
may be tempted to leave the profession.

A journalist is stimulated by *a* deadline.

For more examples of these revision strategies, see G3-a.

W4-f Revise language that may offend groups of people.

Obviously it is impolite to use offensive terms such as *Polack* or
redneck, but offensive language can take more subtle forms. Because language evolves over time, names once thought acceptable
may become offensive. When describing groups of people, choose
names that the groups currently use to describe themselves.

▶ North Dakota takes its name from the ~~Indian~~ word meaning
_{Sioux}

"friend" or "ally."

▶ Many ~~Oriental~~ immigrants have recently settled in our small town.
_{Asian}

Negative stereotypes (such as "drives like a teenager" or "hag-
gard as an old crone") are of course offensive. But you should avoid
stereotyping a person or a group even if you believe your generalization to be positive.

▶ It was no surprise that Greer, ~~a Chinese American,~~ was selected
_{an excellent math and science student,}

for the honors chemistry program.

W5

Exact language

Two reference works will help you find words to express your meaning exactly: a good dictionary and a book of synonyms and antonyms such as *Roget's International Thesaurus* (see W6).

W5-a Select words with appropriate connotations.

In addition to their strict dictionary meanings (or *denotations*), words have *connotations,* emotional colorings that affect how readers respond to them. The word *steel* denotes "made of or resembling commercial iron that contains carbon," but it also calls up a cluster of images associated with steel, such as the sensation of touching it. These associations give the word its connotations—cold, smooth, unbending.

If the connotation of a word does not seem appropriate for your purpose, your audience, or your subject matter, you should change the word. When a more appropriate word does not come quickly to mind, consult a dictionary or a thesaurus. (See W6.)

> *slender*
> ► The model was ~~skinny~~ and fashionable.
> ⌃

The connotation of the word *skinny* is too negative.

> *sweat*
> ► As I covered the boats with marsh grass, the ~~perspiration~~ I had
> ⌃
> worked up evaporated in the wind, making the cold morning air
> even colder.

The term *perspiration* is too dainty for the context, which suggests vigorous exercise.

W5-b Prefer specific, concrete nouns.

Unlike general nouns, which refer to broad classes of things, specific nouns point to definite and particular items. *Film,* for example, names a general class, *science fiction film* names a narrower class, and *Jurassic Park* is more specific still.

Unlike abstract nouns, which refer to qualities and ideas (*justice, beauty, realism, dignity*), concrete nouns point to immediate, often sensate experience and to physical objects (*steeple, asphalt, lilac, stone, garlic*).

Specific, concrete nouns express meaning more vividly than general or abstract ones. Although general and abstract language is sometimes necessary to convey your meaning, ordinarily prefer specific, concrete alternatives.

▶ The senator spoke about the challenges of the future: problems *of famine, pollution, dwindling resources, and terrorism.* ~~concerning the environment and world peace.~~
   ^

Nouns such as *thing, area, factor,* and *individual* are especially dull and imprecise.

                                                               challenges.
▶ A career in transportation management offers many ~~things.~~
                                                           ^

                            experienced technician.
▶ Try pairing a trainee with an ~~individual with technical experience.~~
                                           ^

W5-c Do not misuse words.

If a word is not in your active vocabulary, you may find yourself misusing it, sometimes with embarrassing consequences. When in doubt, check the dictionary.

                   climbing
▶ The fans were ~~migrating~~ up the bleachers in search of good seats.
                  ^

                   permeated
▶ Drugs have so ~~diffused~~ our culture that they touch all segments of
                  ^
our society.

Be especially alert for misused word forms — using a noun such as *absence, significance,* or *persistence,* for example, when your meaning requires the adjective *absent, significant,* or *persistent.*

                            persistent
▶ Most dieters are not ~~persistence~~ enough to make a permanent
                         ^
change in their eating habits.

W5-d Use standard idioms.

Idioms are speech forms that follow no easily specified rules. The British say "Maria went *to hospital,*" an idiom strange to American ears, which are accustomed to hearing *the* in front of *hospital.* Native speakers of a language seldom have problems with idioms, but prepositions sometimes cause trouble, especially when they follow certain verbs and adjectives. When in doubt, consult a good desk dictionary: Look up the word preceding the troublesome preposition.

UNIDIOMATIC	IDIOMATIC
abide with (a decision)	abide by (a decision)
according with	according to
agree to (an idea)	agree with (an idea)
angry at (a person)	angry with (a person)
capable to	capable of
comply to	comply with
desirous to	desirous of
different than (a person or thing)	different from (a person or thing)
intend on doing	intend to do
off of	off
plan on doing	plan to do
preferable than	preferable to
prior than	prior to
superior than	superior to
sure and	sure to
try and	try to
type of a	type of

ESL

Because idioms follow no particular rules, you must learn them individually. You may find it helpful to keep a list of idioms that you frequently encounter in conversation and in reading.

GRAMMAR CHECKERS can flag some nonstandard idioms, such as *comply to.* However, to choose some idioms, such as *angry at* or *angry with,* you need to consider context.

W5-e Avoid clichés.

The pioneer who first announced that he had "slept like a log" no doubt amused his companions with a fresh and unlikely comparison. Today, however, that comparison is a cliché, a saying that has lost its dazzle from overuse. No longer can it surprise.

To see just how predictable clichés are, put your hand over the right-hand column below and then finish the phrases given on the left.

cool as a	cucumber
beat around	the bush
blind as a	bat
busy as a	bee, beaver
crystal	clear
dead as a	doornail
out of the frying pan and	into the fire
light as a	feather
like a bull	in a china shop
playing with	fire
nutty as a	fruitcake
selling like	hotcakes
starting out at the bottom	of the ladder
water under the	bridge
white as a	sheet, ghost
avoid clichés like the	plague

The cure for clichés is frequently simple: Just delete them. When this won't work, try adding some element of surprise. One woman, for example, who had written that she had butterflies in her stomach, revised her cliché like this:

> If all of the action in my stomach is caused by butterflies, there must be a horde of them, with horseshoes on.

The image of butterflies wearing horseshoes is fresh and unlikely, not dully predictable like the original cliché.

GRAMMAR CHECKERS are fairly good at flagging clichés such as *leave no stone unturned* or *selling like hotcakes,* but they tend not to suggest alternative expressions.

W5-f Use figures of speech with care.

A figure of speech is an expression that uses words imaginatively (rather than literally) to make abstract ideas concrete. Most often, figures of speech compare two seemingly unlike things to reveal surprising similarities.

In a *simile,* the writer makes the comparison explicitly, usually by introducing it with *like* or *as:* "By the time cotton had to be picked, grandfather's neck was as red as the clay he plowed." In a *metaphor,* the *like* or *as* is omitted, and the comparison is implied. For example, in the Old Testament Song of Solomon, a young woman compares the man she loves to a fruit tree: "With great delight I sat in his shadow, and his fruit was sweet to my taste."

Writers sometimes use figures of speech without thinking carefully about the images they evoke. This can result in a *mixed metaphor,* the combination of two or more images that don't make sense together.

▶ Crossing Utah's salt flats in his new Corvette, my father flew *at jet speed.* ~~under a full head of steam.~~
  ^

▶ Our office had decided to put all controversial issues on a back

  burner. ~~in a holding pattern.~~
   ^

W6

The dictionary and thesaurus

W6-a The dictionary

A good desk dictionary — such as *The American Heritage Dictionary of the English Language, The Random House College Dictionary,* or *Merriam-Webster's Collegiate* or *New World Dictionary of the American Language* — is an indispensable writer's aid.

A sample dictionary entry, taken from *The American Heritage Dictionary,* appears on page 159. Labels show where various kinds of information about a word can be found in that dictionary.

Spelling, word division, pronunciation

The main entry (*re·gard* in the sample entry) shows the correct spelling of the word. When there are two correct spellings of a word (as in *collectible, collectable,* for example), both are given, with the preferred spelling usually appearing first.

The main entry also shows how the word is divided into syllables. The dot between *re* and *gard* separates the word's two syllables. When a word is compound, the main entry shows how to write it: as one word (*crossroad*), as a hyphenated word (*cross-stitch*), or as two words (*cross section*).

The word's pronunciation is given just after the main entry. The accents indicate which syllables are stressed; the other marks are explained in the dictionary's pronunciation key.

Word endings and grammatical labels

When a word takes endings to indicate grammatical functions (called *inflections*), the endings are listed in boldface, as with *-garded, -garding,* and *-gards* in the sample entry.

Labels for the parts of speech and for other grammatical terms are abbreviated. The most commonly used abbreviations are these:

n.	noun	adj.	adjective
pl.	plural	adv.	adverb
sing.	singular	pron.	pronoun
v.	verb	prep.	preposition
tr.	transitive verb	conj.	conjunction
int.	intransitive verb	interj.	interjection

Meanings, word origin, synonyms, and antonyms

Each meaning for the word is given a number. Occasionally a word's use is illustrated in a quoted sentence.

Sometimes a word can be used as more than one part of speech (*regard,* for instance, can be used as either a verb or a noun). In such a case, all the meanings for one part of speech are given before all the meanings for another, as in the sample entry. The entry also gives idiomatic uses of the word.

The origin of the word, called its *etymology,* appears in brackets after all the meanings (in some dictionaries it appears before the meanings).

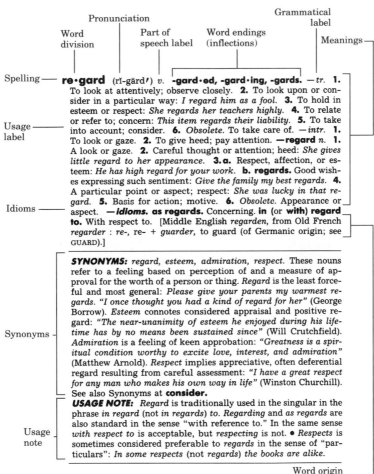

Pronunciation

Word division | Part of speech label | Word endings (inflections) | Grammatical label

Meanings

Spelling — **re·gard** (rǐ-gärd′) *v.* **-gard·ed, -gard·ing, -gards.** —*tr.* **1.** To look at attentively; observe closely. **2.** To look upon or consider in a particular way: *I regard him as a fool.* **3.** To hold in esteem or respect: *She regards her teachers highly.* **4.** To relate or refer to; concern: *This item regards their liability.* **5.** To take into account; consider. **6.** *Obsolete.* To take care of. —*intr.* **1.** To look or gaze. **2.** To give heed; pay attention. —**regard** *n.* **1.** A look or gaze. **2.** Careful thought or attention; heed: *She gives little regard to her appearance.* **3.a.** Respect, affection, or esteem: *He has high regard for your work.* **b. regards.** Good wishes expressing such sentiment: *Give the family my best regards.* **4.** A particular point or aspect; respect: *She was lucky in that regard.* **5.** Basis for action; motive. **6.** *Obsolete.* Appearance or aspect. —**idioms. as regards.** Concerning. **in** (or **with**) **regard to.** With respect to. [Middle English *regarden,* from Old French *regarder* : *re-,* re- + *guarder,* to guard (of Germanic origin; see GUARD).]

Usage label

Idioms

SYNONYMS: *regard, esteem, admiration, respect.* These nouns refer to a feeling based on perception of and a measure of approval for the worth of a person or thing. *Regard* is the least forceful and most general: *Please give your parents my warmest regards.* *"I once thought you had a kind of regard for her"* (George Borrow). *Esteem* connotes considered appraisal and positive regard: *"The near-unanimity of esteem he enjoyed during his lifetime has by no means been sustained since"* (Will Crutchfield). *Admiration* is a feeling of keen approbation: *"Greatness is a spiritual condition worthy to excite love, interest, and admiration"* (Matthew Arnold). *Respect* implies appreciative, often deferential regard resulting from careful assessment: *"I have a great respect for any man who makes his own way in life"* (Winston Churchill). See also Synonyms at **consider.**

Synonyms

USAGE NOTE: *Regard* is traditionally used in the singular in the phrase *in regard* (not *in regards*) *to. Regarding* and *as regards* are also standard in the sense *"*with reference to.*"* In the same sense *with respect to* is acceptable, but *respecting* is not. • *Respects* is sometimes considered preferable to *regards* in the sense of "particulars": *In some respects* (not *regards*) *the books are alike.*

Usage note

Word origin (etymology)

Synonyms, words similar in meaning to the main entry, are frequently listed. In the sample entry, the dictionary draws distinctions in meaning among the various synonyms. Antonyms, which do not appear in the sample entry, are words having a meaning opposite from that of the main entry.

Usage

Usage labels indicate when, where, or under what conditions a particular meaning for a word is appropriately used. Common labels are *informal* (or *colloquial*), *slang, nonstandard, dialect, obsolete, archaic, poetic,* and *British.* In the sample entry, two meanings of *regard* are labeled *obsolete* because they are no longer in use.

Dictionaries sometimes include usage notes as well. In the sample entry, the dictionary offers advice on several uses of *regard* not specifically covered by the meanings. Such advice is based on the opinions of many experts and on actual usage in current magazines, newspapers, and books.

W6-b The thesaurus

When you are looking for just the right word, you may want to consult a book of synonyms and antonyms such as *Roget's International Thesaurus* (or its software equivalent). In the back of *Roget's* is an index to the groups of synonyms that make up the bulk of the book. Look up the adjective *still,* for example, and you will find references to lists containing the words *dead, motionless, silent,* and *tranquil.* If *tranquil* is close to the word you have in mind, turn to its section in the front of the book. There you will find a long list of synonyms, including such words as *quiet, quiescent, reposeful, calm, pacific, halcyon, placid,* and *unruffled.* Unless your vocabulary is better than average, the list will contain words you've never heard of or with which you are only vaguely familiar. Whenever you are tempted to use one of these words, look it up in the dictionary first to avoid misusing it.

On discovering the thesaurus, many writers use it for the wrong reasons, so a word of caution is in order. Do not turn to a thesaurus in search of exotic, fancy words — such as *halcyon* — with which to embellish your essays. Look instead for words that express your meaning exactly. Most of the time these words will be familiar to both you and your readers. *Tranquil* was probably the word you were looking for all along.

Grammatical
Sentences

G

Grammatical Sentences

G1

Subject-verb agreement

Native speakers of standard English know by ear that *he talks, she has,* and *it doesn't* (not *he talk, she have,* and *it don't*) are standard subject-verb combinations. For such speakers, problems with subject-verb agreement arise only in certain tricky situations, which are detailed in G1-b to G1-k.

If you don't trust your ear—perhaps because you speak English as a second language, perhaps because you speak or hear nonstandard English in your community—you will need to learn the standard forms explained in G1-a. Even if you do trust your ear, take a quick look at G1-a to see what "subject-verb agreement" means.

> GRAMMAR CHECKERS attempt to flag faulty subject-verb agreement, but they have mixed success. They fail to flag many problems; in addition, they flag a number of correct sentences, usually because they have misidentified the subject, the verb—or both. For example, one program flagged the following correct sentence: *Nearly everyone on the panel favors the health care reform proposal.* The program identified the subject as *care* and the verb as *reform;* in fact, the subject is *everyone* and the verb is *favors.*

G1-a Consult this section for standard subject-verb combinations.

In the present tense, verbs agree with their subjects in number (singular or plural) and in person (first, second, or third). The present-tense ending *-s* (or *-es*) is used on a verb if its subject is third-person singular; otherwise the verb takes no ending. Consider, for example, the present-tense forms of the verb *love,* given at the beginning of the chart on page 166.

The verb *be* varies from this pattern; unlike any other verb, it has special forms in *both* the present and the past tense. These forms appear at the end of the chart on page 166.

If you aren't confident that you know the standard forms, use the charts on pages 166 and 167 as you proofread for subject-verb agreement. You may also want to take a look at G2-c, which discusses the matter of *-s* endings in some detail.

G1-b Make the verb agree with its subject, not with a word that comes between.

Word groups often come between the subject and the verb. Such word groups, usually modifying the subject, may contain a noun that at first appears to be the subject. By mentally stripping away such modifiers, you can isolate the noun that is in fact the subject.

The *samples* on the tray in the lab *need* testing.

▶ High levels of air pollution cause̸ damage to the respiratory tract.

The subject is *levels,* not *pollution.* Strip away the phrase *of air pollution* to hear the correct verb: *levels cause.*

▶ The slaughter of pandas for their pelts ~~have~~ *has* caused the panda population to decline drastically.

The subject is *slaughter,* not *pandas* or *pelts.*

NOTE: Phrases beginning with the prepositions *as well as, in addition to, accompanied by, together with,* and *along with* do not make a singular subject plural.

▶ The governor, as well as his press secretary, ~~were~~ *was* shot.

To emphasize that two people were shot, the writer could use *and* instead: *The governor and his press secretary were shot.*

G1-c Treat most subjects joined with *and* as plural.

A subject with two or more parts is said to be compound. If the parts are connected by *and,* the subject is nearly always plural.

Leon and Jan often *jog* together.

Subject-verb agreement at a glance

PRESENT-TENSE FORMS OF *LOVE*
(A TYPICAL VERB)

	SINGULAR		PLURAL	
FIRST PERSON	I	love	we	love
SECOND PERSON	you	love	you	love
THIRD PERSON	he/she/it	loves	they	love

PRESENT-TENSE FORMS OF *HAVE*

	SINGULAR		PLURAL	
FIRST PERSON	I	have	we	have
SECOND PERSON	you	have	you	have
THIRD PERSON	he/she/it	has	they	have

PRESENT-TENSE FORMS OF *DO*

	SINGULAR		PLURAL	
FIRST PERSON	I	do/don't	we	do/don't
SECOND PERSON	you	do/don't	you	do/don't
THIRD PERSON	he/she/it	does/doesn't	they	do/don't

PRESENT-TENSE AND PAST-TENSE
FORMS OF *BE*

	SINGULAR		PLURAL	
FIRST PERSON	I	am/was	we	are/were
SECOND PERSON	you	are/were	you	are/were
THIRD PERSON	he/she/it	is/was	they	are/were

> ▶ Jill's natural ability and her desire to help others ~~has~~ **have** led to a
>
> career in the ministry.

EXCEPTIONS: When the parts of the subject form a single unit or when they refer to the same person or thing, treat the subject as singular.

When to use the -s (or -es) form of a present-tense verb

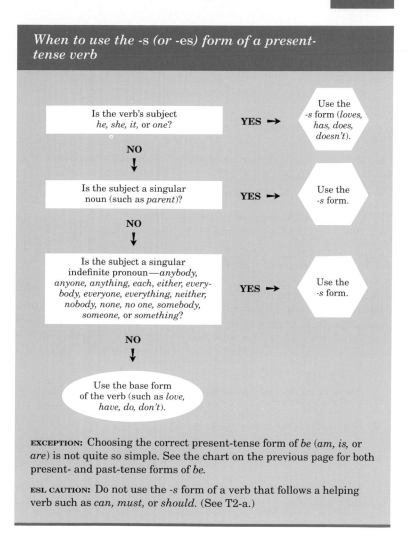

EXCEPTION: Choosing the correct present-tense form of *be* (*am, is,* or *are*) is not quite so simple. See the chart on the previous page for both present- and past-tense forms of *be*.

ESL CAUTION: Do not use the -*s* form of a verb that follows a helping verb such as *can, must,* or *should.* (See T2-a.)

Strawberries and cream was a last-minute addition to the menu.

Sue's friend and adviser was surprised by her decision.

When a compound subject is preceded by *each* or *every,* treat the subject as singular.

Each tree, shrub, and vine needs to be sprayed.

G1-d With subjects connected by *or* or *nor* (or by
either . . . or or *neither . . . nor*), make the verb agree with
the part of the subject nearer to the verb.

A driver's *license* or credit *card is* required.

A driver's *license* or two credit *cards are* required.

> *is*
▶ If a relative or neighbor ~~are~~ abusing a child, notify the police.

> *were*
▶ Neither the professor nor his assistants ~~was~~ able to solve the

mystery of the eerie glow in the laboratory.

G1-e Treat most indefinite pronouns as singular.

Indefinite pronouns refer to nonspecific persons or things. Even
though the following indefinite pronouns may seem to have plural
meanings, treat them as singular in formal English: *anybody, anyone, anything, each, either, everybody, everyone, everything, neither,
nobody, none, no one, somebody, someone, something.*

Everyone on the team *supports* the coach.

> *has*
▶ Each of the furrows ~~have~~ been seeded.

> *was*
▶ Everybody who signed up for the ski trip ~~were~~ taking lessons.

The indefinite pronouns *none* and *neither* are considered singular when used alone.

Three rooms are available; *none has* a private bath.

Neither is able to attend.

When these pronouns are followed by prepositional phrases with a
plural meaning, however, usage varies. Some experts insist on
treating the pronouns as singular, but many writers disagree. It is
safer to treat them as singular.

None of these trades *requires* a college education.

Neither of those pejoratives *fits* Professor Brady.

A few indefinite pronouns (*all, any, some*) may be singular or plural depending on the noun or pronoun they refer to.

Some of the *lemonade has* disappeared.

Some of the *rocks were* slippery.

G1-f Treat collective nouns as singular unless the meaning is clearly plural.

Collective nouns such as *jury, committee, audience, crowd, class, troop, family,* and *couple* name a class or a group. In American English, collective nouns are usually treated as singular: They emphasize the group as a unit. Occasionally, when there is some reason to draw attention to the individual members of the group, a collective noun may be treated as plural. (See also G3-a.)

SINGULAR   The *class respects* the teacher.

PLURAL   The *class are* debating among themselves.

To underscore the notion of individuality in the second sentence, many writers would add a clearly plural noun such as *members: The members of the class are debating among themselves.*

▶ The scout troop ~~meet~~ **meets** in our basement on Tuesdays.

The troop as a whole meets in the basement; there is no reason to draw attention to its individual members.

▶ A young couple ~~was~~ **were** arguing about politics while holding hands.

The meaning is clearly plural. Only individuals can argue and hold hands.

NOTE: The phrase *the number* is treated as singular, *a number* as plural.

SINGULAR *The number* of school-age children *is* declining.

PLURAL *A number* of children *are* attending the wedding.

NOTE: When units of measurement are used collectively, treat them as singular; when they refer to individual persons or things, treat them as plural.

SINGULAR *Three-fourths* of the pie *has* been eaten.

PLURAL *One-fourth* of the drivers *were* driving at least ten miles per hour over the speed limit.

G1-g Make the verb agree with its subject even when the subject follows the verb.

Verbs ordinarily follow subjects. When this normal order is reversed, it is easy to become confused. Sentences beginning with *There is* or *There are* (or *There was* or *There were*) are inverted; the subject follows the verb.

There *are* surprisingly few *children* in our neighborhood.

Occasionally you may decide to invert a sentence for variety or effect. When you do so, check to make sure that your subject and verb agree.

▶ Of particular concern ~~is~~ penicillin and tetracycline, antibiotics
   are

   often used by veterinarians to make animals more resistant to

   disease.

The subject *penicillin and tetracycline* is plural, so the verb must be *are*.

G1-h Make the verb agree with its subject, not with a subject complement.

One sentence pattern in English consists of a subject, a linking verb, and a subject complement: *Jack is an attorney.* (See B2-b.) Because the subject complement names or describes the subject, it is sometimes mistaken for the subject.

> *are*
> ► A tent and a sleeping bag ~~is~~ the required equipment.
> ^

> *Tent and bag* is the subject, not *equipment.*

> *is*
> ► A major force in today's economy ~~are~~ women—as earners,
> ^
>
> consumers, and investors.

> *Force* is the subject, not *women.* If the correct sentence seems awkward, you can make *women* the subject: *Women are a major force in today's economy. . . .*

G1-i *Who, which,* and *that* take verbs that agree with their antecedents.

Like most pronouns, the relative pronouns *who, which,* and *that* have antecedents, nouns or pronouns to which they refer. Relative pronouns used as subjects of subordinate clauses take verbs that agree with their antecedents. (See B3-e.)

> Take a *suit that travels* well.

Problems arise with the constructions *one of the* and *only one of the.* As a rule, treat *one of the* constructions as plural, *only one of the* constructions as singular.

> ► Our ability to use language is one of the things that sets us apart
>
> from animals.

> The antecedent of *that* is *things,* not *one.* Several things set us apart from animals.

▶ Carmen is the only one of the applicants who ~~have~~ the ability to
has

step into this position.

The antecedent of *who* is *one*, not *applicants*. Only one applicant has
the ability to step into the position.

G1-j Words such as *athletics, economics, mathematics, physics, statistics, measles,* and *news* are usually singular, despite their plural form.

▶ Statistics ~~are~~ among the most difficult courses in our program.
is

EXCEPTION: When they describe separate items rather than a collective body of knowledge, words such as *athletics, mathematics, physics,* and *statistics* are plural: *The statistics on school retention rates are impressive.*

G1-k Titles of works, company names, words mentioned as words, and gerund phrases are singular.

▶ *Lost Cities* ~~describe~~ the discoveries of many ancient
describes

civilizations.

▶ Delmonico Brothers ~~specialize~~ in organic produce and
specializes

additive-free meats.

▶ *Controlled substances* ~~are~~ a euphemism for illegal drugs.
is

A gerund phrase consists of an *-ing* verb form followed by any objects, complements, or modifiers (see B3-b). Treat gerund phrases as singular.

▶ Encountering busy signals ~~are~~ troublesome to our clients,
is

so we have hired two new switchboard operators.

G2

Other problems with verbs

The verb is the heart of the sentence, so it is important to get it right. Section G1 deals with the problem of subject-verb agreement. This section describes a number of other potential problems with verbs:

a. irregular verb forms (such as *drive, drove, driven*)
b. *lie* and *lay*
c. *-s* (or *-es*) endings on verbs
d. *-ed* endings on verbs
e. omitted verbs
f. tense
g. subjunctive mood
h. active versus passive voice

ESL

If English is not your native language, see also T2, Special Problems with Verbs.

G2-a   Choose standard English forms of irregular verbs.

Except for the verb *be,* all verbs in English have five forms. The following list gives the five forms and provides a sample sentence in which each might appear.

BASE FORM	Usually I (*walk, ride*).
PAST TENSE	Yesterday I (*walked, rode*).
PAST PARTICIPLE	I have (*walked, ridden*) many times before.
PRESENT PARTICIPLE	I am (*walking, riding*) right now.
-*S* FORM	He/she/it usually (*walks, rides*).

For regular verbs, such as *walk,* the past-tense and past-participle forms are the same (ending in *-ed* or *-d*), so there is no danger of confusion. This is not true, however, for irregular verbs such as *ride.* Writers sometimes confuse the past-tense and past-participle forms of irregular verbs, producing nonstandard sentences.

NONSTANDARD   Have you rode on the new subway?

STANDARD   Have you ridden on the new subway?

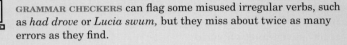

GRAMMAR CHECKERS can flag some misused irregular verbs, such as *had drove* or *Lucia swum,* but they miss about twice as many errors as they find.

Choosing standard English forms

The past-tense form, which expresses action that occurred entirely in the past, never has a helping verb. (For a complete list of helping verbs, see B1-c.) The past participle is used with a helping verb— either with *has, have,* or *had* to form one of the perfect tenses or with *be, am, is, are, was, were, being,* or *been* to form the passive voice.

PAST TENSE   Last July, we *went* to Paris.

PAST PARTICIPLE   We have *gone* to Paris twice.

When you aren't sure which verb form to choose (*went* or *gone, began* or *begun,* and so on), consult the list of common irregular verbs that starts on page 175. Choose the past-tense form if the verb in your sentence doesn't have a helping verb; use the past-participle form if it does.

▶ Yesterday we ~~seen~~ an unidentified flying object.
  saw

▶ The reality of the situation ~~sunk~~ in.
  sank

The past-tense forms *saw* and *sank* are required.

▶ The truck was apparently ~~stole~~ while the driver ate lunch.
  stolen

▶ The teacher asked Dwain if he had ~~did~~ his homework.
(done, inserted above "did")

Because of the helping verbs *was* and *had,* the past-participle forms *stolen* and *done* are required.

Common irregular verbs

When in doubt about the standard English forms of irregular verbs, consult the following list or look up the base form of the verb in the dictionary, which also lists any irregular forms. (If no additional forms are listed in the dictionary, the verb is regular, not irregular.)

BASE FORM	PAST TENSE	PAST PARTICIPLE
arise	arose	arisen
awake	awoke, awaked	awaked, awoke
be	was, were	been
beat	beat	beaten, beat
become	became	become
begin	began	begun
bend	bent	bent
bite	bit	bitten, bit
blow	blew	blown
break	broke	broken
bring	brought	brought
build	built	built
burst	burst	burst
buy	bought	bought
catch	caught	caught
choose	chose	chosen
cling	clung	clung
come	came	come
cost	cost	cost
deal	dealt	dealt
dig	dug	dug
dive	dived, dove	dived
do	did	done
drag	dragged	dragged
draw	drew	drawn
dream	dreamed, dreamt	dreamed, dreamt
drink	drank	drunk
drive	drove	driven
eat	ate	eaten
fall	fell	fallen
fight	fought	fought

BASE FORM	PAST TENSE	PAST PARTICIPLE
find	found	found
fly	flew	flown
forget	forgot	forgotten, forgot
freeze	froze	frozen
get	got	gotten, got
give	gave	given
go	went	gone
grow	grew	grown
hang (suspend)	hung	hung
hang (execute)	hanged	hanged
have	had	had
hear	heard	heard
hide	hid	hidden
hurt	hurt	hurt
keep	kept	kept
know	knew	known
lay (put)	laid	laid
lead	led	led
lend	lent	lent
let (allow)	let	let
lie (recline)	lay	lain
lose	lost	lost
make	made	made
prove	proved	proved, proven
read	read	read
ride	rode	ridden
ring	rang	rung
rise (get up)	rose	risen
run	ran	run
say	said	said
see	saw	seen
send	sent	sent
set (place)	set	set
shake	shook	shaken
shoot	shot	shot
shrink	shrank	shrunk, shrunken
sing	sang	sung
sink	sank	sunk
sit (be seated)	sat	sat
slay	slew	slain
sleep	slept	slept
speak	spoke	spoken
spin	spun	spun
spring	sprang	sprung
stand	stood	stood
steal	stole	stolen

BASE FORM	PAST TENSE	PAST PARTICIPLE
sting	stung	stung
strike	struck	struck, stricken
swear	swore	sworn
swim	swam	swum
swing	swung	swung
take	took	taken
teach	taught	taught
throw	threw	thrown
wake	woke, waked	waked, woken
wear	wore	worn
wring	wrung	wrung
write	wrote	written

G2-b Distinguish among the forms of *lie* and *lay*.

Writers and speakers frequently confuse the various forms of *lie* (meaning "to recline or rest on a surface") and *lay* (meaning "to put or place something"). *Lie* is an intransitive verb; it does not take a direct object: *The tax forms lie on the table.* The verb *lay* is transitive; it takes a direct object: *Please lay the tax forms on the table.* (See B2-b.)

In addition to confusing the meaning of *lie* and *lay*, writers and speakers are often unfamiliar with the standard English forms of these verbs.

BASE FORM	PAST TENSE	PAST PARTICIPLE	PRESENT PARTICIPLE
lie	lay	lain	lying
lay	laid	laid	laying

► Sue was so exhausted that she ~~laid~~ *lay* down for a nap.

The past-tense form of *lie* ("to recline") is *lay*.

► Mary ~~lay~~ *laid* the baby on my lap.

The past-tense form of *lay* ("to place") is *laid*.

► My grandmother's letters were ~~laying~~ *lying* in the corner of the chest.

The present participle of *lie* ("to rest on a surface") is *lying*.

G2-c Use *-s* (or *-es*) endings on present-tense verbs that have third-person singular subjects.

When the subject of a sentence is third-person singular, its verb takes an *-s* or *-es* ending in the present tense. (See also G1-a and the charts on pp. 166–67.)

	SINGULAR		PLURAL	
FIRST PERSON	I	know	we	know
SECOND PERSON	you	know	you	know
THIRD PERSON	he/she/it	knows	they	know
	child	knows	parents	know
	everyone	knows		

All singular nouns (such as *child*) and the pronouns *he, she,* and *it* are third-person singular; indefinite pronouns (such as *everyone*) are also third-person singular.

In nonstandard speech, the *-s* ending required by standard English is sometimes omitted.

>   *turns*   *dissolves*   *eats*
> ▶ Sulfur dioxide ~~turn~~ leaves yellow, ~~dissolve~~ marble, and ~~eat~~ away
>
> iron and steel.

The subject *sulfur dioxide* is third-person singular, so the verbs must end in *-s*.

CAUTION: Do not add the *-s* ending to the verb if the subject is not third-person singular.

> ▶ I prepare~~s~~ program specifications and logic diagrams.

> ▶ The dirt floors require~~s~~ continual sweeping.

The subject *I* is first-person singular. The subject *floors* is third-person plural.

In nonstandard speech, the *-s* verb form *has, does,* or *doesn't* is sometimes replaced with *have, do,* or *don't.* In standard English, use *has, does,* or *doesn't* with a third-person singular subject. (See also G1-a.)

> *has*
> This respected musician always ~~have~~ a message in his work.
>   ^

> *Does*
> ~~Do~~ she know the correct procedure for the experiment?
> ^

>   *doesn't*
> My uncle ~~don't~~ want to change jobs right now.
>   ^

GRAMMAR CHECKERS can catch some missing -*s* endings on verbs and some misused -*s* forms of the verb. Unfortunately, they flag quite a few correct sentences, so you need to know how to interpret what the programs tell you. (See the grammar checker advice on p. 164 for more detailed information.)

G2-d   Do not omit -*ed* endings on verbs.

Speakers who do not fully pronounce -*ed* endings sometimes omit them unintentionally in writing. Failure to pronounce -*ed* endings is common in many dialects and in informal speech even in standard English. In the following frequently used words and phrases, for example, the -*ed* ending is not always fully pronounced.

advised	developed	prejudiced	stereotyped
asked	fixed	pronounced	used to
concerned	frightened	supposed to	

When a verb is regular, both the past tense and the past participle are formed by adding -*ed* to the base form of the verb.

Past tense

Use an -*ed* or -*d* ending to express the past tense of regular verbs. The past tense is used when the action occurred entirely in the past.

>   *fixed*
> Over the weekend, Ed ~~fix~~ his brother's skateboard and tuned up
>   ^
> his mother's 1955 Thunderbird.

>   *advised*
> Last summer my counselor ~~advise~~ me to ask my family for help.
>   ^

Past participles

Past participles are used in three ways: (1) following *have, has,* or *had* to form one of the perfect tenses; (2) following *be, am, is, are, was, were, being,* or *been* to form the passive voice; and (3) as adjectives modifying nouns or pronouns. The perfect tenses are listed on page 182, and the passive voice is discussed in W3-b. For a discussion of participles functioning as adjectives, see B3-b.

▶ Robin has ~~ask~~ me to go to California with her.
    asked
    ^

Has asked is present perfect tense (*have* or *has* followed by a past participle).

▶ Though it is not a new phenomenon, domestic violence is ~~publicize~~
    publicized
    ^
more frequently than before.

Is publicized is in the passive voice (a form of *be* followed by a past participle).

▶ It took all of Daryl's strength to control the ~~frighten~~ horse.
    frightened
    ^

The past participle *frightened* functions as an adjective modifying the noun *horse.*

GRAMMAR CHECKERS can catch some missing *-ed* endings, but they tend to slip past as many as they catch. For example, although programs flagged *was accustom,* they ignored *has change* and *was pass.*

G2-e Do not omit needed verbs.

Although standard English allows some linking verbs and helping verbs to be contracted, at least in informal contexts, it does not allow them to be omitted.

Linking verbs, used to link subjects to subject complements, are frequently a form of *be: be, am, is, are, was, were, being, been.* (See B2-b.) Some of these forms may be contracted (*I'm, she's, we're*), but they should not be omitted altogether.

▶ Hassan a man who can defend himself.
    is
    ^

Helping verbs, used with main verbs, include forms of *be, do,* and *have* or the words *can, will, shall, could, would, should, may, might,* and *must.* (See B1-c.) Some helping verbs may be contracted (*he's leaving, we'll celebrate, they've been told*), but they should not be omitted altogether.

would
▶ Do you know someone who be good for the job?
ㅤㅤㅤㅤㅤㅤㅤㅤㅤ^

ESLㅤSpeakers of English as a second language sometimes have problems with omitted verbs and correct use of helping verbs. See T2-e and T2-a.

GRAMMAR CHECKERS are fairly good at flagging omitted verbs, but they do not catch all of them. For example, programs caught the missing verb in this sentence: *He always talking.* But in the following, more complicated sentence, they did not catch the missing verb: *We often don't know whether he angry or just talking.*

G2-f ㅤChoose the appropriate verb tense.

Tenses indicate the time of an action in relation to the time of the speaking or writing about that action.

The most common problem with tenses—shifting from one tense to another—is discussed in E4-b. Other problems with tenses are detailed in this section, after the following survey of tenses.

Survey of tenses

Tenses are classified as present, past, and future, with simple, perfect, and progressive forms for each.

The simple tenses indicate relatively simple time relations. The simple present tense is used primarily for actions occurring at the time of the speaking or for actions occurring regularly. The simple past tense is used for actions completed in the past. The simple future tense is used for actions that will occur in the future. In the tables on the following pages, the simple tenses are given for the regular verb *walk,* the irregular verb *ride,* and the highly irregular verb *be.*

SIMPLE PRESENT

SINGULAR		PLURAL	
I	walk, ride, am	we	walk, ride, are
you	walk, ride, are	you	walk, ride, are
he/she/it	walks, rides, is	they	walk, ride, are

SIMPLE PAST

SINGULAR		PLURAL	
I	walked, rode, was	we	walked, rode, were
you	walked, rode, were	you	walked, rode, were
he/she/it	walked, rode, was	they	walked, rode, were

SIMPLE FUTURE

I, you, he/she/it, we, they	will walk, ride, be

More complex time relations are indicated by the perfect tenses. A verb in one of the perfect tenses (a form of *have* plus the past participle) expresses an action that was or will be completed at the time of another action.

PRESENT PERFECT

I, you, we, they	have walked, ridden, been
he/she/it	has walked, ridden, been

PAST PERFECT

I, you, he/she/it, we, they	had walked, ridden, been

FUTURE PERFECT

I, you, he/she/it, we, they	will have walked, ridden, been

The simple and perfect tenses just discussed have progressive forms that describe actions in progress. A progressive verb consists of a form of *be* followed by a present participle.

PRESENT PROGRESSIVE

I	am walking, riding, being
he/she/it	is walking, riding, being
you, we, they	are walking, riding, being

PAST PROGRESSIVE

I, he/she/it	was walking, riding, being
you, we, they	were walking, riding, being

FUTURE PROGRESSIVE

I, you, he/she/it, we, they	will be walking, riding, being

PRESENT PERFECT PROGRESSIVE

I, you, we, they	have been walking, riding, being
he/she/it	has been walking, riding, being

PAST PERFECT PROGRESSIVE
I, you, he/she/it, we, they   had been walking, riding, being

FUTURE PERFECT PROGRESSIVE
I, you, he/she/it, we, they   will have been walking, riding, being

ESL

> The progressive forms are not normally used with mental activity
> verbs such as *believe*. See T2-a.

Special uses of the present tense

Use the present tense when expressing general truths, when writing about literature, and when quoting, summarizing, or paraphrasing an author's views.

General truths or scientific principles should appear in the present tense, unless such principles have been disproved.

▶ Italian astronomer Galileo taught that the earth ~~revolved~~ *revolves* around

the sun.

> Since Galileo's teaching has not been discredited, the verb should be in the present tense. The following sentence, however, is acceptable: *Ptolemy taught that the sun revolved around the earth.*

When writing about a work of literature, you may be tempted to use the past tense. The convention, however, is to describe fictional events in the present tense.

▶ In Masuji Ibuse's *Black Rain,* a child ~~reached~~ *reaches* for a pomegranate

in his mother's garden, and a moment later he ~~was~~ *is* dead, killed by

the blast of the atomic bomb.

When you are quoting, summarizing, or paraphrasing the author of a nonliterary work, use present-tense verbs such as *writes, reports, asserts,* and so on. (See page 87 for a more complete list.) This convention is usually followed even when the author is dead (unless a date or the context specifies the time of writing).

▶ Baron Bowan of Colwood ~~wrote~~ that a metaphysician is "one who
    writes

goes into a dark cellar at midnight without a light, looking for a

black cat that is not there."

EXCEPTION: When you are documenting a paper with the APA (American Psychological Association) style of in-text citations, which include a date after the author's name, use past-tense verbs such as *reported* or *demonstrated* or present perfect verbs such as *has reported* or *has demonstrated*.

> E. Wilson (1994) reported that positive reinforcement alone was a less effective teaching technique than a mixture of positive reinforcement and constructive criticism.

The past perfect tense

The past perfect tense consists of a past participle preceded by *had* (*had worked, had gone*). This tense is used for an action already completed by the time of another past action or for an action already completed at some specific past time.

> Everyone *had spoken* by the time I arrived.

> Everyone *had spoken* by 10:00 A.M.

Writers sometimes use the simple past tense when they should use the past perfect.

▶ We built our cabin high on a pine knoll, forty feet above an
                        had been
   abandoned quarry that ~~was~~ flooded in 1920 to create a lake.

> The building of the cabin and the flooding of the quarry both occurred in the past, but the flooding was completed before the time of building.

                                         had
▶ By the time we arrived at the party, the guest of honor left.

> The past perfect tense is needed because the action of leaving was completed at a specific past time (by the time we arrived).

Some writers tend to overuse the past perfect tense. Do not use the past perfect if two past actions occurred at the same time.

▶ When we arrived in Paris, Pauline ~~had~~ met us at the train station.

Sequence of tenses with infinitives and participles

An infinitive is the base form of a verb preceded by *to.* (See B3-b.) Use the present infinitive to show action at the same time as or later than the action of the verb in the sentence.

>   *raise*
> ▶ The club had hoped to ~~have raised~~ a thousand dollars by April 1.
>   ^

The action expressed in the infinitive (*to raise*) occurred later than the action of the sentence's verb (*had hoped*).

Use the perfect form of an infinitive (*to have* followed by the past participle) for an action occurring earlier than that of the verb in the sentence.

>   *have joined*
> ▶ Dan would like to ~~join~~ the navy, but he did not pass the physical.
>   ^

The liking occurs in the present; the joining would have occurred in the past.

Like the tense of an infinitive, the tense of a participle is also governed by the tense of the sentence's verb. Use the present participle (ending in *-ing*) for an action occurring at the same time as that of the sentence's verb.

Hiking the Appalachian Trail in early spring, we spotted many wildflowers.

Use the past participle (such as *given* or *helped*) or the present perfect participle (*having* plus the past participle) for an action occurring before that of the verb.

Discovered off the coast of Florida, the ship yielded many treasures.

Having worked her way through college, Lee graduated debt-free.

G2-g Use the subjunctive mood in the few contexts that require it.

There are three moods in English: the *indicative,* used for facts, opinions, and questions; the *imperative,* used for orders or advice; and the *subjunctive,* used in certain contexts to express wishes, requests, or conditions contrary to fact. Of these moods, the subjunctive is most likely to cause problems for writers.

Forms of the subjunctive

In the subjunctive mood, present-tense verbs do not change form to indicate the number and person of the subject (see G1-a). Instead, the subjunctive uses the base form of the verb (*be, drive, employ*) with all subjects.

It is important that you *be* [not *are*] prepared for the interview.

We asked that she *drive* [not *drives*] more slowly.

Also, in the subjunctive mood, there is only one past-tense form of *be: were* (never *was*).

If I *were* [not *was*] you, I'd proceed more cautiously.

Uses of the subjunctive

The subjunctive mood appears in only a few contexts: in contrary-to-fact clauses beginning with *if* or expressing a wish; in *that* clauses following verbs such as *ask, insist, recommend, request,* and *suggest;* and in certain set expressions.

IN CONTRARY-TO-FACT CLAUSES BEGINNING WITH *IF*   When a subordinate clause beginning with *if* expresses a condition contrary to fact, use the subjunctive mood.

> ▶ If I ~~was~~ a member of Congress, I would vote for that bill.
>   *were*

> ▶ We could be less cautious if Jake ~~was~~ more trustworthy.
>   *were*

The verbs in these sentences express conditions that do not exist: The writer is not a member of Congress, and Jake is not trustworthy.

Do not use the subjunctive mood in *if* clauses expressing conditions that exist or may exist.

If Marjorie *wins* the contest, she will leave for Barcelona in June.

IN CONTRARY-TO-FACT CLAUSES EXPRESSING A WISH   In formal English the subjunctive is used in clauses expressing a wish or desire; in informal speech, however, the indicative is more commonly used.

FORMAL   I wish that Dr. Kurtinitis *were* my professor.

INFORMAL   I wish that Dr. Kurtinitis *was* my professor.

IN *THAT* CLAUSES FOLLOWING VERBS SUCH AS *ASK, INSIST, RECOM-
MEND, REQUEST,* AND *SUGGEST*   Because requests have not yet become reality, they are expressed in the subjunctive mood.

> Professor Moore insists that her students ~~are~~ *be* on time.

> We recommend that Lambert ~~files~~ *file* form 1050 soon.

IN CERTAIN SET EXPRESSIONS   The subjunctive mood, once more
widely used in English, remains in certain set expressions: *be that
as it may, as it were, come rain or shine, far be it from me,* and so on.

GRAMMAR CHECKERS rarely flag problems with the subjunctive
mood. They may at times question your correct use of the subjunctive, since your correct use will seem to violate the rules of subject-
verb agreement (see G1). For example, one program suggested using
was instead of *were* in the following correct sentence: *This isn't my
dog; if it were, I would feed it.* Because the sentence describes a condition contrary to fact, the subjunctive form *were* is correct.

G2-h   Use the active voice unless you have a good reason for choosing the passive.

Transitive verbs (verbs that take a direct object) appear in either
the active or the passive voice. (See B2-b.) In the active voice, the
subject of the sentence does the action; in the passive, the subject
receives the action.

ACTIVE   The committee *reached* a decision.

PASSIVE   A decision *was reached* by the committee.

Active and passive verbs are both grammatically correct, but
active verbs are usually more effective because they are simpler
and more direct. For a full discussion of when to use active or passive verbs, see W3.

G3

Problems with pronouns

Pronouns are words that substitute for nouns (see B1-b). Four frequently encountered problems with pronouns are discussed in this section:

   a. pronoun-antecedent agreement (singular vs. plural)
   b. pronoun reference (clarity)
   c. pronoun case (personal pronouns such as *I* vs. *me, she* vs. *her*)
   d. pronoun case (*who* vs. *whom*)

For other problems with pronouns, consult the Glossary of Usage (W1).

G3-a   Make pronouns and antecedents agree.

The antecedent of a pronoun is the word the pronoun refers to. A pronoun and its antecedent agree when they are both singular or both plural.

   SINGULAR   The *doctor* finished *her* rounds.

   PLURAL   The *doctors* finished *their* rounds.

ESL

The pronouns *he, his, she, her, it,* and *its* must agree in gender (masculine, feminine, or neuter) with their antecedents, not with the words they modify.

   Jane visited *her* [not *his*] brother in Denver.

GRAMMAR CHECKERS usually miss pronoun-antecedent agreement problems. It takes a human eye to see that a singular noun, such as *logger,* does not agree with a plural pronoun, such as *their,* in a sentence like this: *The logger in the Northwest relies on the old forest growth for their living.*

Indefinite pronouns

Indefinite pronouns refer to nonspecific persons or things. Even though the following indefinite pronouns may seem to have plural meanings, treat them as singular in formal English: *anybody, anyone, anything, each, either, everybody, everyone, everything, neither, nobody, none, no one, somebody, someone, something.*

In this class *everyone* performs at *his or her* [not *their*] fitness level.

When a plural pronoun refers mistakenly to a singular indefinite pronoun, you can usually choose one of three options for revision.

1. Replace the plural pronoun with *he or she* (or *his or her*).
2. Make the antecedent plural.
3. Rewrite the sentence so that no problem of agreement arises.

▶ When someone has been drinking, ~~they are~~ more likely to speed.
                he or she is

▶ When ~~someone has~~ been drinking, they are more likely to speed.
  drivers have

▶ ~~When someone~~ has been drinking~~, they are~~ more likely to speed.
  Someone who   *is*

Because the *he or she* construction is wordy, often the second or third revision strategy is more effective.

NOTE: The traditional use of *he* (or *his*) to refer to persons of either sex is now widely considered sexist (see W4-e).

Generic nouns

A generic noun represents a typical member of a group, such as a typical student, or any member of a group, such as any lawyer. Although generic nouns may seem to have plural meanings, they are singular.

Every *runner* must train vigorously if *he or she* wants [not *they* want] to excel.

When a plural noun refers mistakenly to a generic noun, you will usually have the same three revision options as just mentioned for indefinite pronouns.

▶ A medical student must study hard if ~~they want~~ to succeed.
   he or she wants

▶ ~~A medical student~~ must study hard if they want to succeed.
   Medical students

▶ A medical student must study hard ~~if they want~~ to succeed.

Collective nouns

Collective nouns such as *jury, committee, audience, crowd, class, troop, family, team,* and *couple* name a class or group. If the group functions as a unit, treat the noun as singular; if the members of the group function individually, treat the noun as plural.

AS A UNIT   The planning *committee* granted *its* permission to build.

AS INDIVIDUALS   The *committee* put *their* signatures on the document.

When treating a collective noun as plural, many writers prefer to add a clearly plural antecedent such as *members* to the sentence: *The members of the committee put their signatures on the document.*

To some extent, you can choose whether to treat a collective noun as singular or plural depending on your meaning. Make sure, however, that you are consistent.

▶ The jury has reached ~~their~~ decision.
   its

The writer selected the verb *has* to match the singular noun *jury* (see G1-a), so for consistency the pronoun must be *its.*

Compound antecedents

Treat compound antecedents joined by *and* as plural.

Joanne and John moved to the mountains, where *they* built a log cabin.

With compound antecedents joined by *or* or *nor,* make the pronoun agree with the nearer antecedent.

Either *Bruce* or *James* should receive first prize for *his* sculpture.

Neither the *mouse* nor the *rats* could find *their* way through the maze.

NOTE: If one of the antecedents is singular and the other plural, as in the second example, put the plural one last to avoid awkwardness.

EXCEPTION: If one antecedent is male and the other female, do not follow the traditional rule. The sentence *Either Bruce or Anita should receive the blue ribbon for her sculpture* makes no sense. The best solution is to recast the sentence: *The blue ribbon for best sculpture should go to Bruce or Anita.*

G3-b Make pronoun references clear.

Pronouns substitute for nouns; they are a kind of shorthand. In a sentence like *After Andrew intercepted the ball, he kicked it as hard as he could,* the pronouns *he* and *it* substitute for the nouns *Andrew* and *ball.* The word a pronoun refers to is called its *antecedent.*

A pronoun should refer clearly to its antecedent. A pronoun's reference will be unclear if it is ambiguous, implied, vague, or indefinite.

GRAMMAR CHECKERS do not flag problems with faulty pronoun reference. Although a computer program can identify pronouns, it has no way of knowing which words, if any, they refer to. For example, grammar checkers miss the fact that the pronoun *it* has an ambiguous reference in the following sentence: *The thief stole the woman's purse and her car and then destroyed it.* Did the thief destroy the purse or the car? It takes human judgment to realize that readers might be confused.

Ambiguous reference

Ambiguous reference occurs when the pronoun could refer to two possible antecedents.

▶ When Gloria set ~~the pitcher~~ on the glass-topped table, ~~it~~ broke.
   it (above "the pitcher")   *the pitcher* (above "it")

▶ Tom told James ~~that he had~~ won the lottery.
   "You have ... *"*

What broke—the table or the pitcher? Who won the lottery—Tom or James? The revisions eliminate the ambiguity.

Implied reference

A pronoun must refer to a specific antecedent, not to a word that is implied but not present in the sentence.

▶ After braiding Ann's hair, Sue decorated ~~them~~ with ribbons.
   the braids

The pronoun *them* referred to Ann's braids (implied by the term *braiding*), but the word *braids* did not appear in the sentence.

Modifiers, such as possessives, cannot serve as antecedents. A modifier may strongly imply the noun that the pronoun might logically refer to, but it is not itself that noun.

▶ In ~~Euripides'~~ *Medea,* ~~he~~ describes the plight of a woman rejected
   Euripides

by her husband.

The pronoun *he* cannot refer logically to the possessive modifier *Euripides'*.

Broad reference of *this, that, which, and* it

For clarity, the pronouns *this, that, which,* and *it* should ordinarily refer to specific antecedents rather than to whole ideas or sentences. When a pronoun's reference is needlessly broad, either replace the pronoun with a noun or supply an antecedent to which the pronoun clearly refers.

▶ More and more often, we are finding ourselves victims of serious
   crimes. We learn to accept ~~this~~ with minor complaints.
   our fate

▶ Romeo and Juliet were both too young to have acquired much
    a fact
wisdom, which accounts for their rash actions.
    ^

Indefinite reference of they, it, *or* you

The pronoun *they* should refer to a specific antecedent. Do not use *they* to refer indefinitely to persons who have not been specifically mentioned.

▶ Sometimes a list of ways to save energy is included with the gas
                the gas company suggests
bill. For example, ~~they suggest~~ setting a moderate temperature for
        ^

the hot water heater.

The word *it* should not be used indefinitely in constructions such as "In the article it says that. . . ."

    The
▶ ~~In the~~ encyclopedia ~~it~~ states that male moths can smell female
  ^

moths from several miles away.

The pronoun *you* is appropriate when the writer is addressing the reader directly: *Once you have kneaded the dough, let it rise in a warm place.* Except in very informal contexts, however, the indefinite *you* (meaning "anyone in general") is inappropriate.

    one doesn't
▶ In Chad, ~~you don't~~ need much property to be considered well-off.
  ^

If the pronoun *one* seems stilted, the writer might recast the sentence, perhaps like this: *In Chad, a person doesn't need much property to be considered well-off.*

G3-c Distinguish between pronouns such as *I* and *me*.

The personal pronouns in the following chart change what is known as case form according to their grammatical function in a sentence. Pronouns functioning as subjects or subject complements appear in the *subjective* case; those functioning as objects appear in the *objective* case; and those functioning as possessives appear in the *possessive* case.

SUBJECTIVE CASE	OBJECTIVE CASE	POSSESSIVE CASE
I	me	my
we	us	our
you	you	your
he/she/it	him/her/it	his/her/its
they	them	their

This section explains the difference between the subjective and objective cases; then it alerts you to certain structures that may tempt you to choose the wrong pronoun. Finally, it describes a special use of possessive-case pronouns.

GRAMMAR CHECKERS can flag some incorrect pronouns and explain the rules for using *I* or *me, he* or *him, she* or *her, we* or *us,* and *they* or *them.* For example, grammar checkers correctly flagged *we* in the following sentence, suggesting that *us* should be used as the object of the preposition *for: I say it is time for we parents to revolt.*

You should not assume, however, that a computer program will catch all incorrect pronouns. For example, grammar checkers did not flag *more than I* in this sentence, where the writer's meaning requires *me: I get a little jealous that our dog likes my neighbor more than I.*

Subjective case

When a pronoun functions as a subject or a subject complement, it must be in the subjective case (*I, we, you, he/she/it, they*).

SUBJECT   Sylvia and *he* shared the award.

SUBJECT   Greg announced that the winners were Sylvia
COMPLEMENT   and *he.*

Subject complements—words following linking verbs that complete the meaning of the subject—frequently cause problems for writers, since we rarely hear the correct form in casual speech. (See B2-b.)

▶ During the Lindbergh trial, Bruno Hauptmann repeatedly denied
                           he.
   that the kidnapper was ~~him.~~
                         ^

If *kidnapper was he* seems too stilted, rewrite the sentence: *During the Lindbergh trial, Bruno Hauptmann repeatedly denied that he was the kidnapper.*

Objective case

When a pronoun functions as a direct object, an indirect object, or the object of a preposition, it must be in the objective case (*me, us, you, him/her/it, them*).

DIRECT OBJECT	Bruce found Tony and brought *him* home.
INDIRECT OBJECT	Alice gave *me* a surprise party.
OBJECT OF A PREPOSITION	Jessica wondered if the call was for *her.*

Compound word groups

When a subject or an object appears as part of a compound structure, you may occasionally become confused. To test for the correct pronoun, mentally strip away all of the compound word group except the pronoun in question.

▶ While diving for pearls, Ikiko and ~~her~~ *she* found a treasure chest full of gold bars.

Ikiko and she is the subject of the verb *found.* Strip away the words *Ikiko and* to test for the correct pronoun: *she found* (not *her found*).

▶ The most traumatic experience for her father and ~~I~~ *me* occurred long after her operation.

Me is the object of the preposition *for.* We would not say *the most traumatic experience for I.*

When in doubt about the correct pronoun, some writers try to evade the choice by using a reflexive pronoun such as *myself.* Such evasions are nonstandard, even though they are used by some educated persons.

▶ The Egyptian cab driver gave my husband and ~~myself~~ *me* some good tips on traveling in North Africa.

My husband and me is the indirect object of the verb *gave.* For correct uses of *myself,* see the Glossary of Usage (W1).

Appositives

Appositives are noun phrases that rename nouns or pronouns. A pronoun used as an appositive has the same function as the noun or pronoun it renames.

▶ The winners of the art competition, Patricia and ~~me,~~ *I,* will spend a

month studying fresco painting in Florence.

The appositive *Patricia and I* renames the subject *winners*.

▶ The reporter interviewed only two witnesses, the shopkeeper and ~~I.~~ *me.*

The appositive *the shopkeeper and me* renames the direct object *witnesses*.

We *or* us *before a noun*

When deciding whether *we* or *us* should precede a noun, choose the pronoun that would be appropriate if the noun were omitted.

▶ ~~Us~~ *We* tenants would rather fight than move.

▶ Management is shortchanging ~~we~~ *us* tenants.

No one would say *Us would rather fight than move* or *Management is shortchanging we.*

Comparisons with than *or* as

Sentence parts, usually verbs, are often omitted in comparisons beginning with *than* or *as*. To test for the correct pronoun, mentally complete the sentence.

▶ My husband is six years older than ~~me.~~ *I.*

I is the subject of the verb *am,* which is understood. If the correct English seems too formal, add the verb: *My husband is six years older than I am.*

▶ We respected no other candidate as much as ~~she.~~ *her.*

Her is the direct object of an understood verb: *We respected no other candidate as much as* [*we respected*] *her.*

Subjects of infinitives

An infinitive is the word *to* followed by the base form of a verb. Subjects of infinitives are an exception to the rule that subjects must be in the subjective case. Whenever an infinitive has a subject, the subject must be in the objective case.

> We expected Chris and ~~he~~ to win the doubles championship.
>   *him*
>   ^

Chris and him is the subject of the infinitive *to win*.

Possessive case to modify a gerund

If a pronoun modifies a gerund or a gerund phrase, it should appear in the possessive case (*my, our, your, his/her/its, their*). A gerund is a verb form ending in *-ing* that functions as a noun.

> The chances against ~~you~~ being hit by lightning are about two
>   *your*
>   ^
>
> million to one.

Your modifies the gerund phrase *being hit by lightning*.

Nouns as well as pronouns may modify gerunds. To form the possessive case of a noun, use an apostrophe and an *-s* (*a victim's suffering*) or just an apostrophe (*victims' suffering*). See P5-a.

> The old order in France paid a high price for the ~~aristocracy~~
>   *aristocracy's*
>   ^
>
> exploiting the lower classes.

The possessive noun *aristocracy's* modifies the gerund phrase *exploiting the lower classes*.

G3-d Distinguish between *who* and *whom*.

Who, a subjective-case pronoun, can be used only for subjects and subject complements. *Whom,* an objective-case pronoun, can be used only for objects. (For more about pronoun case, see G3-c.)

Who and *whom* are relative pronouns used to introduce subordinate clauses. (See B3-e.) They are also interrogative pronouns used to open questions.

GRAMMAR CHECKERS can flag some sentences with a misused *who* or *whom* and explain the nature of the error. For example, grammar checkers flagged the subjective-case pronoun *who* in the following sentence, suggesting correctly that the context calls for the objective-case pronoun *whom: One of the women who Martinez hired became the most successful lawyer in the agency.*

However, at times the programs skip past a misused *who* or *whom*, as they did with this sentence: *Now that you have studied with both musicians, whom in your opinion is the better teacher?* The programs could not tell that the objective-case pronoun *whom* functions as the subject of the verb *is.*

In subordinate clauses

The case of a relative pronoun in a subordinate clause is determined by its function *within the subordinate clause.*

▶ When medicine is scarce and expensive, physicians must give it to
whoever
~~whomever~~ has the best chance of surviving.

The writer selected the pronoun *whomever,* thinking that it was the object of the preposition *to.* However, the object of the preposition is the entire subordinate clause *whoever has the best chance of surviving.* The verb of the clause is *has,* and its subject is *whoever.* (See also B3-e.)

When it functions as an object in a subordinate clause, *whom* appears out of order, before both the subject and the verb. To choose the correct pronoun, you can mentally restructure the clause.

whom
▶ You will work with our senior engineers, ~~who~~ you will meet later.

Whom is the direct object of the verb of the subordinate clause, *will meet.* This becomes clear if you mentally restructure the clause: *you will meet whom.* (See also B3-e.)

whom
▶ The tutor ~~who~~ I was assigned to was very supportive.

Whom is the object of the preposition *to.* If the correct English seems too formal, drop *whom: The tutor I was assigned to. . . .*

NOTE: Ignore inserted expressions such as *they know* or *I think* when determining the case of a relative pronoun.

▶ All of the school bullies want to take on a big guy ~~whom~~ they
　　　　　　　　　　　　　　　　　　　　　　　　who
　　　　　　　　　　　　　　　　　　　　　　　　^

know will not hurt them.

Who is the subject of *will hurt,* not the object of *know.*

In questions

The case of an interrogative pronoun is determined by its function
within the question.

　　　Who
▶ ~~Whom~~ is responsible for creating that computer virus?
　　^

Who is the subject of the verb *is.*

When *whom* appears as an object in a question, it appears out
of order, before both the subject and the verb. To choose the correct
pronoun, you can mentally restructure the question.

　　　Whom
▶ ~~Who~~ did the Democratic Party nominate in 1976?
　　^

Whom is the direct object of the verb *did nominate.* This becomes clear
if you restructure the question: *The Democratic Party did nominate
whom in 1976?*

G4

Adjectives and adverbs

Adjectives modify nouns or pronouns; adverbs modify verbs, adjectives, or other adverbs. (See B1-d and B1-e.)

　　Many adverbs are formed by adding *-ly* to adjectives (*formal,
formally*). But don't assume that all words ending in *-ly* are adverbs
or that all adverbs end in *-ly.* Some adjectives end in *-ly* (*lovely,
friendly*) and some adverbs don't (*always, here, there*). When in
doubt, consult a dictionary.

ESL

> In English, adjectives are not pluralized to agree with the words
> they modify: *The red* [not *reds*] *roses were a wonderful surprise.*

GRAMMAR CHECKERS can flag a number of problems with adjectives and adverbs: some misuses of *bad* or *badly* and *good* or *well;* some double comparisons, such as *more meaner;* some absolute comparisons, such as *most unique;* and some double negatives, such as *can't hardly.* However, the programs slip past more problems than they find. Programs ignored errors like these: *could have been handled more professional* and *hadn't been bathed regular.*

G4-a Use adverbs, not adjectives, to modify verbs, adjectives, and adverbs.

When adverbs modify verbs (or verbals), they usually answer one of these questions: When? Where? How? Why? Under what conditions? How often? To what degree?

The incorrect use of adjectives in place of adverbs to modify verbs occurs primarily in casual or nonstandard speech.

▶ The manager must see that the office runs ~~smooth~~ and ~~efficient.~~
                                 smoothly   *efficiently.*

The incorrect use of the adjective *good* in place of the adverb *well* is especially common in casual and nonstandard speech.

▶ Marcia performed very ~~good~~ at her Drama Club audition.
                       well

NOTE: The word *well* is an adjective when it means "healthy," "satisfactory," or "fortunate": *I am very well, thank you. All is well. It is just as well.*

Adjectives are sometimes used incorrectly to modify adjectives or other adverbs.

▶ In the early 1970s, chances for survival of the bald eagle looked ~~real~~ slim.
   really

ESL

Placement of adjectives and adverbs can be a tricky matter for second-language speakers. See T3-e.

G4-b Use adjectives, not adverbs, as subject complements.

Adjectives ordinarily precede nouns, but they can also function as subject complements following linking verbs (see B2-b). When an adjective functions as a subject complement, it describes the subject.

> Justice is *blind.*

Problems can arise with verbs such as *smell, taste, look,* and *feel,* which may or may not be linking. If the word following one of these verbs describes the subject, use an adjective; if it modifies the verb, use an adverb.

ADJECTIVE The detective looked *cautious.*

ADVERB The detective looked *cautiously* for the fingerprints.

Linking verbs suggest states of being, not actions. For example, to look cautious suggests the state of being cautious, whereas to look cautiously is to perform an action in a cautious way.

▶ The lilacs in our backyard smell especially ~~sweetly~~ *sweet* this year.

▶ Lori looked ~~well~~ *good* in her new raincoat.

▶ All of us on the team felt ~~badly~~ *bad* about our performance.

The verbs *smell, looked,* and *felt* suggest states of being, not actions. Therefore, they should be followed by adjectives, not adverbs.

G4-c Use comparatives and superlatives with care.

Most adjectives and adverbs have three forms: the positive, the comparative, and the superlative.

POSITIVE	COMPARATIVE	SUPERLATIVE
soft	softer	softest
fast	faster	fastest
careful	more careful	most careful
bad	worse	worst
good	better	best

Comparative versus superlative

Use the comparative to compare two things, the superlative to compare three or more.

▶ Which of these two brands of toothpaste is ~~best?~~ *better?*

▶ Though Shaw and Jackson are impressive, Hobbs is the ~~more~~ *most* qualified of the three candidates running for mayor.

Form of comparatives and superlatives

To form comparatives and superlatives of most one- and two-syllable adjectives, use the endings *-er* and *-est: smooth, smoother, smoothest; easy, easier, easiest.* With longer adjectives, use *more* and *most: exciting, more exciting, most exciting.*

Some one-syllable adverbs take the endings *-er* and *-est (fast, faster, fastest),* but longer adverbs and all of those ending in *-ly* form the comparative and superlative with *more* and *most.*

The comparative and superlative forms of the following adjectives and adverbs are irregular: *good, better, best; bad, worse, worst; badly, worse, worst.*

▶ The Kirov was the ~~talentedest~~ *most talented* ballet company we had ever seen.

▶ Lloyd's luck couldn't have been ~~worser~~ *worse* than David's.

Double comparatives or superlatives

Do not use a double comparative (an *-er* ending and the word *more*) or a double superlative (an *-est* ending and the word *most*).

▶ All the polls indicated that Dewey was more ~~likelier~~ *likely* to win than Truman.

▶ Of all her family, Julia is the ~~most~~ happiest about the move.

Absolute concepts

Do not use comparatives or superlatives with absolute concepts such as *unique* or *perfect.* Either something is unique or it isn't. It is illogical to suggest that absolute concepts come in degrees.

►   That is the most ~~unique~~ wedding gown I have ever seen.
(unusual)

►   The painting would have been even more ~~priceless~~ had it been
(valuable)

signed.

G4-d   Avoid double negatives.

Standard English allows two negatives only if a positive meaning is intended: *The orchestra was not unhappy with its performance.* Double negatives used to emphasize negation are nonstandard.

Negative modifiers such as *never, no,* and *not* should not be paired with other negative modifiers or with negative words such as *neither, none, no one, nobody,* and *nothing.*

►   Management is not doing ~~nothing~~ to see that the trash is
(anything)

picked up.

►   George won't ~~never~~ forget that day.
(ever)

The modifiers *hardly, barely,* and *scarcely* are considered negatives in standard English, so they should not be used with negatives such as *not, no one,* or *never.*

►   Maxine is so weak she ~~can't~~ hardly climb stairs.
(can)

G5

Sentence fragments

A sentence fragment is a word group that pretends to be a sentence. Sentence fragments are easy to recognize when they appear out of context, like these:

> On the old wooden stool in the corner of my grandmother's kitchen.

> And immediately popped their flares and life vests.

When fragments appear next to related sentences, however, they are harder to spot.

> On that morning I sat in my usual spot. On the old wooden stool in the corner of my grandmother's kitchen.

> The pilots ejected from the burning plane, landing in the water not far from the ship. And immediately popped their flares and life vests.

GRAMMAR CHECKERS can flag as many as half of the sentence fragments in a sample; but that means, of course, that they miss half or more of them. If fragments are a serious problem for you, you will still need to proofread for them.

Sometimes you will get "false positives," sentences that have been flagged but are not fragments. For example, one program flagged this complete sentence as a possible fragment: *I bent down to crawl into the bunker.* When a program spots a possible fragment, you should check to see if it is really a fragment. You can do this by using the flow chart on page 205.

ESL   Unlike some languages, English does not allow omission of subjects (except in imperative sentences); nor does it allow omission of verbs. See T3-a and T2-e.

Recognizing sentence fragments

To be a sentence, a word group must consist of at least one full independent clause. An independent clause has a subject and a verb, and it either stands alone or could stand alone.

To test a word group for sentence completeness, use the flow chart on page 205. For example, by using the flow chart, you can see exactly why *On the old wooden stool in the corner of my grandmother's kitchen* is a fragment: It lacks both a subject and a verb. *And immediately popped their flares and life vests* is a fragment because it lacks a subject.

Repairing sentence fragments

You can repair most fragments in one of two ways: Either pull the fragment into a nearby sentence or turn the fragment into a sentence.

Test for sentence completeness

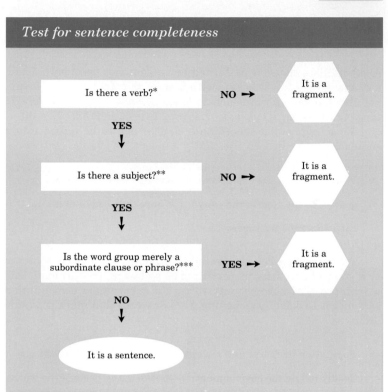

Is there a verb?*   **NO** ➜   It is a fragment.

YES ↓

Is there a subject?**   **NO** ➜   It is a fragment.

YES ↓

Is the word group merely a subordinate clause or phrase?***   **YES** ➜   It is a fragment.

NO ↓

It is a sentence.

*Do not mistake verbals for verbs. (See B3-b).
**The subject of a sentence may be *you,* understood. (See B2-a.)
***A sentence may open with a subordinate clause or phrase, but the sentence must also include an independent clause. (See B3.)

If you find any fragments, try one of these methods of revision:

1. Attach the fragment to a nearby sentence.
2. Turn the fragment into a sentence.

▶ On that morning I sat in my usual spot/. ~~On~~ ^on^ the old wooden stool

in the corner of my grandmother's kitchen.

▶ The pilots ejected from the burning plane, landing in the water not

far from the ship. ~~And~~ ^They^ immediately popped their flares and life vests.

G5-a Attach fragmented subordinate clauses or turn them into sentences.

A subordinate clause is patterned like a sentence, with both a subject and a verb, but it begins with a word that tells readers it cannot stand alone—a word such as *after, although, because, before, if, though, unless, until, when, where, who, which,* and *that.* (See B3-e.)

Most fragmented subordinate clauses beg to be pulled into a sentence nearby.

> ▶ With machetes, the explorers cut their way through the tall
>
> grasses to the edge of the canyon/. ~~Where~~ they began to lay out
> ^{where}
>
> their tapes for the survey.

If a fragmented clause cannot be attached to a nearby sentence or if you feel that attaching it would be awkward, try turning it into a sentence. The simplest way to turn a subordinate clause into a sentence is to delete the opening word or words that mark it as subordinate.

> ▶ Population increases and uncontrolled development are taking a
>
> deadly toll on the environment. ~~So that in~~ many parts of the world,
> ^{In}
>
> fragile ecosystems are collapsing.

G5-b Attach fragmented phrases or turn them into sentences.

Like subordinate clauses, phrases function within sentences as adjectives, as adverbs, or as nouns. They cannot stand alone. Fragmented phrases are often prepositional or verbal phrases; sometimes they are appositives, words or word groups that rename nouns or pronouns. (See B3-a, B3-b, and B3-c.)

Many fragmented phrases may simply be pulled into nearby sentences.

> ▶ The panther lay quite motionless behind the rock/. ~~Waiting~~
> ^{waiting}
>
> silently for its prey.

Waiting silently for its prey is a verbal phrase.

▶ Mary is suffering from agoraphobia/, $\overset{a}{\cancel{A}}$ fear of the outside

world.

A fear of the outside world is an appositive renaming the noun *agoraphobia*.

If a fragmented phrase cannot be pulled into a nearby sentence effectively, turn the phrase into a sentence. You may need to add a subject, a verb, or both.

▶ In the computer training session, Eugene explained how to install

our new software. $\overset{\text{He also taught us}}{\cancel{\text{Also}}}$ how to organize our files, connect to the

Internet, and back up our hard drives.

The word group beginning *Also how to organize* is a fragmented verbal phrase. The revision turns the fragment into a sentence by adding a subject and a verb. The word group beginning with *and* is part of a compound predicate.

G5-c Attach other fragmented word groups or turn them into sentences.

Other word groups that are commonly fragmented include parts of compound predicates, lists, and examples introduced by *such as, for example,* or similar expressions.

Parts of compound predicates

A predicate consists of a verb and its objects, complements, and modifiers (see B2-b). A compound predicate includes two or more predicates joined by a coordinating conjunction such as *and, but,* or *or.* Because the parts of a compound predicate share the same subject, they should appear in the same sentence.

▶ The woodpecker finch of the Galápagos Islands carefully selects a

twig of a certain size and shape/ $\overset{\text{and}}{\cancel{\text{And}}}$ then uses this tool to pry out

grubs from trees.

Notice that no comma appears between the parts of a compound predicate. (See P2-a.) The word group beginning with *and* is part of a compound predicate.

Lists

When a list is mistakenly fragmented, it can often be attached to a nearby sentence with a colon or a dash. (See P4-a and P7-d.)

▶ It has been said that there are only three indigenous American art

forms: Jazz, musical comedy, and soap opera.

Examples introduced by such as, for example, or similar expressions

Expressions that introduce examples (or explanations) can lead to unintentional fragments. Although you may begin a sentence with some of the following words or phrases, make sure that what you have written is a sentence, not a fragment.

also	especially	in addition	namely	that is
and	for example	like	or	
but	for instance	mainly	such as	

Sometimes fragmented examples can be attached to the preceding sentence.

▶ The South has produced some of our most distinguished twentieth-

century writers, ~~Such~~ *such* as Flannery O'Connor, Eudora Welty,

William Faulkner, Alice Walker, Tennessee Williams, and

Thomas Wolfe.

At times, however, it may be necessary to turn the fragment into a sentence.

▶ If Eric doesn't get his way, he goes into a fit of rage. For example,

he lies *opens*
~~lying~~ on the floor screaming or ~~opening~~ the cabinet doors and
slams
then ~~slamming~~ them shut.

The writer corrected this fragment by adding a subject—*he*—and substituting verbs—*lies, opens,* and *slams*—for the verbals *lying, opening,* and *slamming.*

G5-d Exception: Fragments may be used for special purposes.

Skilled writers occasionally use sentence fragments for the following special purposes.

FOR EMPHASIS	Following the dramatic Americanization of their children, even my parents grew more publicly confident. *Especially my mother.* —Richard Rodriguez
TO ANSWER A QUESTION	Are these new drug tests 100 percent reliable? *Not in the opinion of most experts.*
AS A TRANSITION	*And now the opposing arguments.*
EXCLAMATIONS	*Not again!*
IN ADVERTISING	*Fewer calories. Improved taste.*

Although fragments are sometimes appropriate, writers and readers do not always agree on when they are appropriate. Therefore you will find it safer to write in complete sentences.

G6

Run-on sentences

Run-on sentences are independent clauses that have not been joined correctly. An independent clause is a word group that can stand alone as a sentence. (See B4.) When two independent clauses appear in one sentence, they must be joined in one of these ways:

— with a comma and a coordinating conjunction (*and, but, or, nor, for, so, yet*)

— with a semicolon (or occasionally a colon or a dash)

Recognizing run-on sentences

There are two types of run-on sentences. When a writer puts no mark of punctuation and no coordinating conjunction between independent clauses, the result is called a *fused sentence.*

```
┌──────────────── INDEPENDENT CLAUSE ────────────────┐
```
FUSED   Gestures are a means of communication for everyone
```
┌──────────── INDEPENDENT CLAUSE ────────────┐
```
they are essential for the hearing-impaired.

A far more common type of run-on sentence is the *comma splice*—two or more independent clauses joined by a comma without a coordinating conjunction. In some comma splices, the comma appears alone.

COMMA   Gestures are a means of communication for everyone,
SPLICE   they are essential for the hearing-impaired.

In other comma splices, the comma is accompanied by a joining word that is *not* a coordinating conjunction. There are only seven coordinating conjunctions in English: *and, but, or, nor, for, so, yet.* Notice that all of these words are short—only two or three letters long. (See also G6-b.)

COMMA   Gestures are a means of communication for everyone,
SPLICE   however, they are essential for the hearing-impaired.

To review your writing for possible run-on sentences, use the chart on page 212.

GRAMMAR CHECKERS can flag only about 20 to 50 percent of the run-on sentences in a sample. The programs tend to be cautious, telling you that you "may have" a run-on sentence; you will almost certainly get a number of "false positives," sentences that have been flagged but are not run-ons. For example, a grammar checker flagged the following acceptable sentence as a possible run-on: *They believe that requiring gun owners to purchase a license is sufficient.*

If you have a problem with run-ons, you will need to proofread for them even after using a grammar checker. Also, if your program spots a "possible" run-on, you will need to check to see if it is in fact a run-on. You can do this by using the flow chart on page 212.

Revising run-on sentences

To revise a run-on sentence, you have four choices:

1. Use a comma and a coordinating conjunction (*and, but, or, nor, for, so, yet*).

                                                        but
▶ Gestures are a means of communication for everyone, they are
                                                      ^
essential for the hearing-impaired.

2. Use a semicolon (or, if appropriate, a colon or a dash). A semicolon may be used alone; it can also be accompanied by a transitional expression (see also G6-b and P3-b).

▶ Gestures are a means of communication for everyone/; they are

essential for the hearing-impaired.

▶ Gestures are a means of communication for everyone/ *; however,* they are

essential for the hearing-impaired.

3. Make the clauses into separate sentences.

▶ Gestures are a means of communication for everyone/. *T*hey are

essential for the hearing-impaired.

4. Restructure the sentence, perhaps by subordinating one of the clauses.

▶ *Although gestures* ~~Gestures~~ are a means of communication for everyone, they are

essential for the hearing-impaired.

One of these revision techniques will often work better than the others for a particular sentence. The fourth technique, the one requiring the most extensive revision, is frequently the most effective.

G6-a Consider separating the clauses with a comma and a coordinating conjunction.

There are seven coordinating conjunctions in English: *and, but, or, nor, for, so,* and *yet*. When a coordinating conjunction joins independent clauses, it must be preceded by a comma. (See P1-a.)

▶ The paramedic asked where I was hurt, *and* as soon as I motioned

toward my pain, he cut up the leg of my favorite pair of designer

jeans.

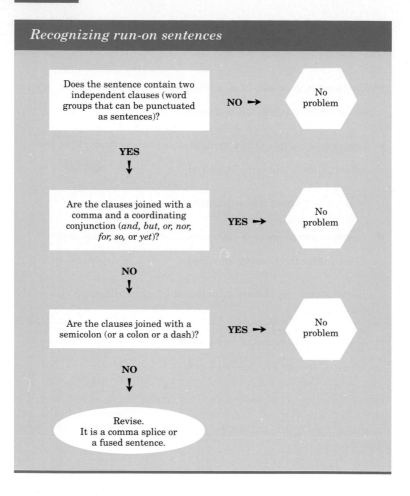

Recognizing run-on sentences

Does the sentence contain two independent clauses (word groups that can be punctuated as sentences)?

NO ➙ No problem

YES ↓

Are the clauses joined with a comma and a coordinating conjunction (*and, but, or, nor, for, so,* or *yet*)?

YES ➙ No problem

NO ↓

Are the clauses joined with a semicolon (or a colon or a dash)?

YES ➙ No problem

NO ↓

Revise.
It is a comma splice or a fused sentence.

▶ Many government officials privately admit that the polygraph is

　　　　　　　yet
unreliable, ~~however,~~ they continue to use it as a security measure.
　　　　　　　^

G6-b Consider separating the clauses with a semicolon (or, if appropriate, with a colon or a dash).

When the independent clauses are closely related and their relation is clear without a coordinating conjunction, a semicolon is an acceptable method of revision. (See P3-a.)

▶ Tragedy depicts the individual confronted with the fact of death$_\wedge\!/^{\!\!;}$ comedy depicts the adaptability and ongoing survival of human society.

A semicolon is required between independent clauses that have been linked with a transitional expression (see also P3-b).

TRANSITIONAL EXPRESSIONS

also	in addition	now
as a result	indeed	of course
besides	in fact	on the other hand
consequently	in other words	otherwise
finally	in the first place	similarly
for example	meanwhile	still
furthermore	moreover	then
hence	nevertheless	therefore
however	next	thus

▶ The timber wolf looks like a large German shepherd$_\wedge\!/^{\!\!;}$however, the wolf has longer legs, larger feet, and a wider head.

If the first independent clause introduces the second or if the second clause summarizes or explains the first, a colon or a dash may be an appropriate method of revision. (See P4-b and P7-d.) In formal writing, the colon is usually preferred to the dash.

▶ Nuclear waste is hazardous ~~this~~ $\overset{: \textit{This}}{\wedge}$ is an indisputable fact.

▶ The female black widow spider is often a widow of her own making$\overset{--}{/_\wedge}$she has been known to eat her partner after mating.

If the first independent clause introduces a quoted sentence, a colon is an appropriate method of revision.

▶ Carolyn Heilbrun has this to say about the future$\overset{:}{/_\wedge}$"Today's shocks are tomorrow's conventions."

G6-c Consider making the clauses into separate sentences.

▶ Why should we spend money on expensive space exploration./?
   We
   ~~we~~ have enough underfunded programs here on earth.

Since one independent clause is a question and the other is a statement, they should be separate sentences.

▶ I gave the necessary papers to the police officer./. *T*hen he said I

   would have to accompany him to the police station, where a

   counselor would talk with me and call my parents.

Because the second independent clause is quite long, a sensible revision is to use separate sentences.

NOTE: When two quoted independent clauses are divided by explanatory words, make each clause its own sentence.

▶ "It's always smart to learn from your mistakes," quipped my boss./.
   "It's
   "~~it's~~ even smarter to learn from the mistakes of others."

G6-d Consider restructuring the sentence, perhaps by subordinating one of the clauses.

If one of the independent clauses is less important than the other, try turning it into a subordinate clause or phrase. (See E6-a.)

▶ *Although many*
   ~~Many~~ scholars dismiss the abominable snowman of the Himalayas

   as a myth, others claim it may be a kind of ape.

▶ Of the many geysers in Yellowstone National Park, the most
   which
   famous is Old Faithful, ~~it~~ sometimes reaches 150 feet in height.

▶ Mary McLeod Bethune, ~~was~~ the seventeenth child of former

   slaves, ~~she~~ founded the National Council of Negro Women in 1935.

T

ESL Trouble
Spots

T

ESL Trouble Spots

This section of *A Writer's Reference* has a special audience: speakers of English as a second language (ESL) who have learned English but continue to have difficulty with a few trouble spots.

T1

Articles

Except for occasional difficulty in choosing between *a* and *an,* native speakers of English encounter few problems with articles. To speakers whose native language is not English, however, articles can prove troublesome, for the rules governing their use are surprisingly complex. This section summarizes those rules.

The articles a, an, *and* the

The indefinite articles *a* and *an* and the definite article *the* signal that a noun is about to appear. The noun may follow the article immediately, or modifiers may intervene (see B1-a and B1-d).

ART	N	ART		N
a sunset		an incredible sunset		

ART	N	ART		N
the table		the round pine table		

Other noun markers

Articles are not the only words used to mark nouns. Noun markers (sometimes called *determiners*) also include words such as the following, which identify or quantify nouns.

—possessive nouns, such as *Elena's*

—*my, your, his, her, its, our*

—*this, that, these, those*

—*all, any, each, either, every, few, many, more, most, much, neither, several, some*

—numbers: *one, two,* and so on

Usually an article is not used with another noun marker. Common exceptions include expressions such as *a few, the most,* and *all the.*

GRAMMAR CHECKERS can flag some missing or misused articles, pointing out, for example, that an article usually precedes a word such as *paintbrush* or *vehicle* or that the articles *a* and *an* are not usually used before a noncount noun such as *sugar* or *advice*.

However, the programs fail to flag many missing or misused articles. For example, in two paragraphs with eleven missing or misused articles, grammar checkers caught only two of the problems. The programs frequently suggest that an article is missing when it is not. For example, one program suggested that an article might be needed before *teacher* in this correct sentence: *My social studies teacher entered me in a public-speaking contest.*

T1-a Use *a* (or *an*) with singular count nouns whose specific identity is not known to the reader.

Count nouns refer to persons, places, or things that can be counted: *one girl, two girls; one city, three cities; one apple, four apples.* Noncount nouns refer to entities or abstractions that cannot be counted: *water, silver, air, furniture, patience, knowledge.* To see what nouns English categorizes as noncount nouns, refer to the chart on page 220 or consult an ESL dictionary such as the *Longman Dictionary of American English.*

If the specific identity of a singular count noun is not known to the reader—perhaps because it is being mentioned for the first time, perhaps because its specific identity is unknown even to the writer—the noun should be preceded by *a* or *an* unless it has been preceded by another noun marker. *A* (or *an*) usually means "one among many" but can also mean "any one."

▶ Mary Beth arrived in *a* limousine.

▶ We are looking for *an* apartment close to the lake.

NOTE: *A* is used before a consonant sound: *a banana, a tree, a picture, a hand, a happy child. An* is used before a vowel sound: *an eggplant, an occasion, an uncle, an hour, an honorable person.* Notice that words beginning with *h* can have either a consonant sound (*hand, happy*) or a vowel sound (*hour, honorable*). (See also W1.)

T1-b Do not use *a* (or *an*) with noncount nouns.

A (or *an*) is not used to mark noncount nouns. A noncount noun refers to an entity or an abstract concept that cannot be counted: *sugar, gold, honesty,* or *jewelry.* For a list of commonly used noncount nouns, see the chart on page 220.

▶ Claudia asked her mother for ~~an~~ advice.

If you want to express an approximate amount, you can often use one of the following quantifiers with a noncount noun.

QUANTIFIER	NONCOUNT NOUN
a great deal of	candy, courage
a little	salt, rain
any	sugar, homework
enough	bread, wood, money
less	meat, violence
little (*or* a little)	knowledge, time
more	coffee, information
much (*or* a lot of)	snow, pollution
plenty of	paper, lumber
some	tea, news, work

To express a more specific amount, you can often precede a noncount noun with a unit word that is typically associated with it. Here are some common combinations.

A OR *AN* + UNIT + *OF*	NONCOUNT NOUNS
a bottle of	water, vinegar
a carton of	ice cream, milk, yogurt
a head of	cabbage, lettuce
a loaf of	bread
a piece of	meat, furniture, advice
a pound of	butter, sugar
a quart of	milk, ice cream
a slice of	bread, bacon

CAUTION: Noncount nouns do not have plural forms, and they should not be used with numbers or words suggesting plurality (such as *several, many, a few, a couple of, a number of*).

▶ We need some information~~s~~ about rain forests.

▶ Do you have ~~many~~ *much* money with you?

Commonly used noncount nouns

FOOD AND DRINK

bacon, beef, bread, broccoli, butter, cabbage, candy, cauliflower, celery, cereal, cheese, chicken, chocolate, coffee, corn, cream, fish, flour, fruit, ice cream, lettuce, meat, milk, oil, pasta, rice, salt, spinach, sugar, tea, water, wine, yogurt

NONFOOD SUBSTANCES

air, cement, coal, dirt, gasoline, gold, paper, petroleum, plastic, rain, silver, snow, soap, steel, wood, wool

ABSTRACT NOUNS

advice, anger, beauty, confidence, courage, employment, fun, happiness, health, honesty, information, intelligence, knowledge, love, poverty, satisfaction, truth, wealth

OTHER

biology (and other areas of study), clothing, equipment, furniture, homework, jewelry, luggage, lumber, machinery, mail, money, news, poetry, pollution, research, scenery, traffic, transportation, violence, weather, work

NOTE: A few noncount nouns may also be used as count nouns, especially in informal English: *Bill loves chocolate; Bill offered me a chocolate. I'll have coffee; I'll have a coffee.*

T1-c   Use *the* with most nouns whose specific identity is known to the reader.

The definite article *the* is used with most nouns whose identity is known to the reader. (For exceptions, see T1-d.) Usually the identity will be clear to the reader for one of the following reasons:

—The noun has been previously mentioned.

—A phrase or clause following the noun restricts its identity.

—A superlative such as *best* or *most intelligent* makes the noun's identity specific.

—The noun describes a unique person, place, or thing.

—The context or situation makes the noun's identity clear.

► A truck loaded with dynamite cut in front of our van. When *the* truck
  ^
  skidded a few seconds later, we almost plowed into it.

The noun *truck* is preceded by *A* when it is first mentioned. When the noun is mentioned again, it is preceded by *the* since readers now know the specific truck being discussed.

► Bob warned me that *the* gun on the top shelf of the cupboard was
  ^
  loaded.

The phrase *on the top shelf of the cupboard* identifies the specific gun.

► Our petite daughter dated *the* tallest boy in her class.
  ^
The superlative *tallest* restricts the identity of the noun *boy.*

► During an eclipse, one should not look directly at *the* sun.
  ^
There is only one sun in our solar system, so its identity is clear.

► Please don't slam *the* door when you leave.
  ^
Both the speaker and the listener know which door is meant.

T1-d Do not use *the* with plural or noncount nouns meaning "all" or "in general"; do not use *the* with most singular proper nouns.

When a plural or a noncount noun means "all" or "in general," it is not marked with *the.*

► ~~The~~ *F* fountains are an expensive element of landscape design.

► In some parts of the world, ~~the~~ rice is preferred to all other grains.

As you probably know, proper nouns—which name specific people, places, or things—are capitalized. Although there are many exceptions, *the* is not used with most singular proper nouns, such as *Judge Ito, Spring Street,* and *Lake Huron.* However, *the* is used with plural proper nouns, such as *the United Nations, the Bahamas,* and *the Finger Lakes.*

The *with geographical names*

WHEN TO OMIT *THE*

streets, squares, parks	Ivy Street, Union Square, Denali National Park
cities, states, counties	Miami, Idaho, Bee County
most countries	Italy, Nigeria, China
continents	South America, Africa
bays, single lakes	Tampa Bay, Lake Geneva
single mountains, islands	Mount Everest, Crete

WHEN TO USE *THE*

united countries	the United States, the Republic of China
large regions, deserts	the East Coast, the Sahara
peninsulas	the Iberian Peninsula
oceans, seas, gulfs	the Pacific, the Dead Sea, the Persian Gulf
canals and rivers	the Panama Canal, the Amazon
mountain ranges	the Rocky Mountains, the Alps
groups of islands	the Solomon Islands

Geographical names create problems because there are so many exceptions to the rules. When in doubt, consult the chart on this page or ask a native speaker.

T2

Special problems with verbs

Both native and nonnative speakers of English encounter the following problems with verbs, which are treated elsewhere in this book:

problems with subject-verb agreement (G1)

misuse of verb forms (G2-a to G2-d)

problems with tense, mood, and voice (G2-f, G2-g, G2-h)

This section focuses on features of the English verb system that cause special difficulties for second-language speakers.

T2-a Match helping verbs and main verbs appropriately.

Only certain combinations of helping verbs and main verbs make sense in English. The correct combinations are discussed in this section, after the following review of helping verbs and main verbs.

Review of helping verbs and main verbs

Helping verbs always appear before main verbs. (See B1-c.)

> HV MV   HV   MV
> We will leave for the picnic at noon. Do you want a ride?

Some helping verbs—*have, do,* and *be*—change form to indicate tense; others, known as modals, do not.

FORMS OF *HAVE, DO,* AND *BE*
have, has, had
do, does, did
be, am, is, are, was, were, being, been

MODALS
can, could, may, might, must, shall, should, will, would
(*also* ought to)

Every main verb has five forms (except *be,* which has eight forms). The following list shows these forms for the regular verb *help* and the irregular verb *give.* (See G2-a for a list of common irregular verbs.)

BASE FORM	help, give
PAST TENSE	helped, gave
PAST PARTICIPLE	helped, given
PRESENT PARTICIPLE	helping, giving
-*S* FORM	helps, gives

Modal + base form

After the modals *can, could, may, might, must, shall, should, will,* and *would,* use the base form of the verb.

▶ My cousin will send̸s us photographs from her wedding.

> *speak*
> ▶ We could ~~spoke~~ Spanish when we were young.
> ^

CAUTION: Do not use *to* in front of a main verb that follows a modal. (*Ought to* is an exception.)

> ▶ Gina can ~~to~~ drive us home from the party if we miss the last
>
> subway train.

Do, does, *or* did + *base form*

After helping verbs that are a form of *do,* use the base form of the verb.

The helping verbs *do, does,* and *did* are used in three ways: (1) to express a negative meaning with the adverb *not* or *never,* (2) to ask a question, and (3) to emphasize a main verb used in a positive sense.

> ▶ Mariko does not want/any more dessert.

> *buy*
> ▶ Did Janice ~~bought~~ the gift for Katherine?
> ^

> *hope*
> ▶ We do ~~hoping~~ that you will come to Hernando's graduation party
> ^
> next Saturday night.

Have, has, *or* had + *past participle (perfect tenses)*

After the helping verb *have, has,* or *had,* use the past participle to form one of the perfect tenses. (See G2-f.) Past participles usually end in *-ed, -d, -en, -n,* or *-t.* (See G2-a.)

> *offered*
> ▶ On cold nights many churches in the city have ~~offer~~ shelter to the
> ^
> homeless.

> *spoken*
> ▶ An-Mei has not ~~speaking~~ Chinese since she was a child.
> ^

The helping verb *have* is sometimes preceded by a modal such as *will: By nightfall, we will have driven five hundred miles.* (See also perfect tenses, G2-f.)

Form of be + *present participle (progressive forms)*

After the helping verb *be, am, is, are, was, were,* or *been,* use the present participle (the *-ing* form of the verb) to express a continuing action. (See G2-f.)

▶ Carlos is ~~build~~ his house on a cliff overlooking the ocean.
  ^building^

▶ Uncle Roy was ~~driven~~ a brand-new red Corvette.
  ^driving^

The helping verb *be* must be preceded by a modal (*can, could, may, might, must, shall, should, will,* or *would*): *Edith will be going to Germany soon.* The helping verb *been* must be preceded by *have, has,* or *had: Andy has been studying English for five years.* (See also progressive forms, G2-f.)

CAUTION: Certain verbs are not normally used in the progressive sense in English. In general, these verbs express a state of being or mental activity, not a dynamic action. Common examples are *appear, believe, belong, contain, have, hear, know, like, need, see, seem, taste, think, understand,* and *want.*

▶ I ~~am wanting~~ to see August Wilson's *Fences* at Arena Stage.
  ^want^

Some of these verbs, however, have special uses in which progressive forms are normal (*We are thinking about going to the Bahamas*). You will need to make a note of exceptions as you encounter them.

Form of be + *past participle (passive voice)*

When a sentence is written in the passive voice, the subject receives the action instead of doing it (*Melissa was given a special award*).

To form the passive voice, use *am, is, are, was, were, being, be,* or *been* followed by a past participle (usually ending in *-ed, -d, -en, -n,* or *-t*). (See also W3-b.)

▶ *Bleak House* was ~~wrote~~ by Charles Dickens.
  ^written^

▶ The scientists were ~~honor~~ for their work with endangered
  ^honored^

species.

When the helping verb is *be, being,* or *been,* it must be preceded by another helping verb. *Be* must be preceded by a modal such as *will: Senator Dixon will be defeated. Being* must be preceded by *am, is, are, was,* or *were: The child was being teased. Been* must be preceded by *have, has,* or *had: I have been invited to a party.*

CAUTION: Although they may seem to have passive meanings, verbs such as *occur, happen, sleep, die,* and *fall* may not be used to form the passive voice because they are intransitive. Only transitive verbs, those that take direct objects, may be used to form the passive voice. (See transitive and intransitive verbs, B2-b.)

▶ The earthquake ~~was~~ occurred last Wednesday.

GRAMMAR CHECKERS can catch some mismatches of helping and main verbs. They can tell you, for example, that the base form of the verb should be used after certain helping verbs, such as *did* and *could,* in incorrect sentences like these: *Did you understood my question? Could Alan comes with us?*

Programs can also catch some, but not all, problems with main verbs following forms of *have* or *be.* For example, grammar checkers flagged *have spend,* explaining that the past participle *spent* is required, and they flagged *are expose,* suggesting that either *exposed* or *exposing* is required. However, programs failed to flag problems in many other sentences, such as these: *Sasha has change her major three times. The provisions of the contract were broke by both parties.*

T2-b In conditional sentences, choose verbs with care.

Conditional sentences state that one set of circumstances depends on whether another set of circumstances exists. Choosing verbs in such sentences can be tricky, partly because two clauses are involved: usually an *if* or a *when* or an *unless* clause and an independent clause.

Three kinds of conditional sentences are discussed in this section: factual, predictive, and speculative.

Factual

Factual conditional sentences express factual relationships. When such sentences express scientific truths, use the present tense in both clauses.

If water *cools* to 32°, it *freezes*.

When such sentences describe conditions that are habitually true, use the same tense in both clauses.

When Sue *bicycles* along the canal, her dog *runs* ahead of her.

Whenever the coach *asked* for help, I *volunteered*.

Predictive

Predictive conditional sentences are used to predict the future or to express future plans or possibilities. In such a sentence, an *if* or *unless* clause contains a present-tense verb; the verb in the independent clause usually consists of the modal *will, can, may, should,* or *might* followed by the base form of the verb.

If you *practice* regularly, your tennis game *will improve*.

We *will lose* our remaining wetlands unless we *act* now.

Speculative

Speculative conditional sentences are used for three purposes: (1) to speculate about unlikely possibilities in the present or future, (2) to speculate about events that did not happen in the past, and (3) to speculate about conditions that are contrary to fact. Each of these purposes requires its own combination of verbs.

UNLIKELY POSSIBILITIES Somewhat confusingly, English uses the past tense in an *if* clause to speculate about a possible but unlikely condition in the present or future. The verb in the independent clause consists of *would, could,* or *might* plus the base form of the verb.

If I *had* the time, I *would travel* to Senegal.

If Katya *studied* harder, she *could master* calculus.

In the *if* clause, the past-tense form *were* is used with subjects that would normally take *was: Even if I were* [not *was*] *invited, I wouldn't go to the picnic.* (See also G2-g.)

EVENTS THAT DID NOT HAPPEN English uses the past perfect tense in an *if* clause to speculate about an event that did not happen in the past or to speculate about a state of being that was unreal in the past. (See past perfect tense, G2-f.) The verb in the independent clause consists of *would have, could have,* or *might have* plus the past participle.

> If I *had saved* enough money, I *would have traveled* to Senegal last year.
>
> If Aunt Grace *had been* alive for your graduation, she *would have been* very proud.

CONDITIONS CONTRARY TO FACT   To speculate about conditions that are currently unreal or contrary to fact, English usually uses the past-tense verb *were* (never *was*) in an *if* clause. (See G2-g.) The verb in the independent clause consists of *would, could,* or *might* plus the base form of the verb.

> If Aunt Grace *were* alive today, she *would be* very proud of you.
>
> I *would make* children's issues a priority if I *were* the president.

 GRAMMAR CHECKERS do not flag problems with conditional sentences. The programs miss even obvious errors, such as this one: *Whenever I washed my car, it rains.*

T2-c   Become familiar with verbs that may be followed by gerunds or infinitives.

A gerund is a verb form that ends in *-ing* and is used as a noun: *sleeping, dreaming.* (See B3-b.) An infinitive is the base form of the verb preceded by the word *to: to sleep, to dream.* The word *to* is not a preposition in this use but an infinitive marker.

A few verbs may be followed by either a gerund or an infinitive; others may be followed by a gerund but not by an infinitive; still others may be followed by an infinitive (either directly or with a noun or pronoun intervening) but not by a gerund.

Verb + gerund or infinitive

The following commonly used verbs may be followed by a gerund or an infinitive, with little or no difference in meaning:

begin	continue	like	start
can't stand	hate	love	

I love *skiing.* I love *to ski.*

With a few verbs, however, the choice of a gerund or an infinitive changes the meaning dramatically:

forget	remember	stop	try

She stopped *speaking* to Lucia. [She no longer spoke to Lucia.]

She stopped *to speak* to Lucia. [She paused so that she could speak to Lucia.]

Verb + gerund

These verbs may be followed by a gerund but not by an infinitive:

admit	discuss	imagine	put off	risk
appreciate	enjoy	miss	quit	suggest
avoid	escape	postpone	recall	tolerate
deny	finish	practice	resist	

Bill enjoys *playing* [not *to play*] the piano.

Verb + infinitive

These verbs may be followed by an infinitive but not by a gerund:

agree	decide	manage	plan	wait
ask	expect	mean	pretend	want
beg	have	need	promise	wish
claim	hope	offer	refuse	

We plan *to visit* [not *visiting*] the Yucatán next week.

Verb + noun or pronoun + infinitive

With certain verbs in the active voice, a noun or pronoun must come between the verb and the infinitive that follows it. The noun or pronoun usually names a person who is affected by the action.

advise	command	have	persuade	tell
allow	convince	instruct	remind	urge
cause	encourage	order	require	warn

The class encouraged *Luis to tell* the story of his escape.

A few verbs may be followed either by an infinitive directly or by an infinitive preceded by a noun or pronoun.

| ask | expect | need | promise | want | would like |

We asked *to speak* to the congregation.

We asked *Rabbi Abrams to speak* to our congregation.

Verb + noun or pronoun + unmarked infinitive

An unmarked infinitive is an infinitive without *to*. A few verbs may be followed by a noun or pronoun and an unmarked (but not a marked) infinitive.

| have ("cause") | let ("allow") | make ("force") |

Please let *me pay* [not *to pay*] for the tickets.

GRAMMAR CHECKERS can flag some, but not all, problems with gerunds and infinitives following verbs. For example, programs flagged many sentences with misused infinitives, such as these: *Have you finished to weed the garden? Chris enjoys to play tennis.* Programs were less successful at flagging sentences with misused present participles, skipping past incorrect sentences like this one: *We want traveling to Hawaii next spring.*

T2-d Use two-word verbs correctly.

Many verbs in English consist of a verb followed by a preposition or an adverb known as a *particle* (see B1-c). A two-word verb (also known as a *phrasal verb*) often expresses an idiomatic meaning that cannot be understood literally. Consider the verbs in the following sentences, for example.

We *ran across* Dr. Magnotto on the way to the bookstore.

Calvin *dropped in* on his adviser this morning.

Regina told me to *look* her *up* when I got to Seattle.

As you probably know, *ran across* means "encountered," *dropped in* means "paid an unexpected visit," and *look up* means "visit." When you were first learning English, however, these two-word verbs must have suggested strange meanings. When in doubt about the meaning of a two-word verb, consult the dictionary.

Some two-word verbs are intransitive; they do not take direct objects. (See B2-b.)

This morning I *got up* at dawn.

Transitive two-word verbs (those that take direct objects) have particles that are either separable or inseparable. Separable particles may be separated from the verb by the direct object.

Lucinda *called* the wedding *off.*

When the direct object is a noun, a separable particle may also follow the verb immediately.

At the last minute, Lucinda *called off* the wedding.

When the direct object is a pronoun, however, the particle must be separated from the verb.

Why was there no wedding? Lucinda *called* it *off* [not *called off* it].

Inseparable particles must follow the verb immediately. A direct object cannot come between the verb and the particle.

The police will *look into* the matter [not *look* the matter *into*].

T2-e Do not omit needed verbs.

Some languages allow the omission of the verb when the meaning is clear without it; English does not.

► Jim *is* exceptionally intelligent.

► Many streets in San Francisco *are* very steep.

T3

Sentence structure

T3-a Do not omit subjects or the expletive *there* or *it.*

English requires a subject for all sentences except imperatives, in which the subject *you* is understood (*Give to the poor*). (See B2-a.) If your native language allows the omission of an explicit subject in other sentences or clauses, be especially alert to this requirement in English.

▶   *I have*
   ~~Have~~ a large collection of baseball cards.
   ^

▶   *she*
   Your aunt is very energetic; seems young for her age.
                         ^

When the subject has been moved from its normal position before the verb, English sometimes requires an expletive (*there* or *it*) at the beginning of the sentence or clause. (See B2-a.) *There* is used at the beginning of a sentence or clause that draws the reader's (or listener's) attention to the location or existence of something.

▶   *There is*
   ~~Is~~ an apple in the refrigerator.
   ^

▶   *there*
   As you know, are many religious sects in India.
               ^

Notice that the verb agrees with the subject that follows it: *apple is, sects are.* (See G1-g.)

   In one of its uses, the word *it* functions as an expletive, to call attention to a subject following the verb.

▶   *It is*
   ~~Is~~ healthy to eat fruit and grains.
   ^

▶   *It is*
   ~~Is~~ clear that we must change our approach.
   ^

The subjects of these sentences are *to eat fruit and grains* (an infinitive phrase) and *that we must change our approach* (a noun clause). (See B3-b and B3-e.)

   As you probably know, the word *it* is also used as the subject of sentences describing the weather or temperature, stating the time, indicating distance, or suggesting an environmental fact.

It is raining in the valley, and it is snowing in the mountains.

In July, it is very hot in Arizona.

It is 9:15 A.M.

It is three hundred miles to Chicago.

It gets noisy in our dorm on weekends.

GRAMMAR CHECKERS can flag some sentences with a missing expletive (*there* or *it*), but they often misdiagnose the problem, suggesting that if a sentence opens with a word such as *Is* or *Are,* it may need a question mark at the end. Consider this sentence, which grammar checkers flagged: *Are two grocery stores on Elm Street.* Clearly, the sentence doesn't need a question mark. What it needs is an expletive: *There are two grocery stores on Elm Street.*

T3-b Do not repeat the subject of a sentence.

English does not allow a subject to be repeated in its own clause.

▶   The doctor she advised me to cut down on salt.

The pronoun *she* repeats the subject *doctor.*

The subject of a sentence should not be repeated even if a word group intervenes between the subject and the verb.

▶   The car that had been stolen it was found.

The pronoun *it* repeats the subject *car.*

T3-c Do not repeat an object or an adverb in an adjective clause.

In some languages, an object or an adverb is repeated later in the adjective clause in which it appears; in English such repetitions are not allowed. Adjective clauses begin with relative pronouns (*who, whom, whose, which, that*) or relative adverbs (*when, where*), and these words always serve a grammatical function within the clauses they introduce. (See B3-e.) Another word in the clause cannot also serve that same grammatical function.

When a relative pronoun functions as the object of a verb or the object of a preposition, do not add another word with the same function later in the clause.

▶ The puppy ran after the car that we were riding in. ~~it.~~
                                                      ^

The relative pronoun *that* is the object of the preposition *in,* so the object *it* is not allowed.

Even when the relative pronoun has been omitted, do not add another word with its same function.

▶ The puppy ran after the car we were riding in. ~~it.~~
                                                  ^

The relative pronoun *that* is understood even though it is not present in the sentence.

Like a relative pronoun, a relative adverb should not be echoed later in its clause.

▶ The place where I work ~~there~~ is one hour from the city.

The adverb *there* should not echo the relative adverb *where.*

GRAMMAR CHECKERS can flag certain sentences with repeated subjects or objects, but they misdiagnose the problem as two independent clauses incorrectly joined. For example, programs flagged this sentence: *The roses that they brought home they cost three dollars each.* The sentence does not have two independent clauses incorrectly joined. The problem with the sentence is that *they* repeats the subject *roses.*

T3-d Avoid mixed constructions beginning with *although* or *because.*

In English, using both *although* and *but* (or *however*) to link two word groups results in a mixed construction, which consists of sentence parts that don't go together (see E5-a). Using both *because* and *so* (or *therefore*) results in the same problem.

If you want to retain the subordinating conjunction *although* or *because*, drop the other linking word.

▶ Although the sales figures look impressive, ~~but~~ the company is

losing money.

▶ Because finance laws are not always enforced, ~~therefore~~ investing

in the former Soviet Union can be very risky.

If you want to retain the coordinating conjunction (*but, so*) or the transitional expression (*however, therefore*), drop *although* or *because*.

▶ ~~Although~~ $\overset{T}{t}$he sales figures look impressive, but the company is

losing money.

> When the coordinating conjunction *but* links independent clauses (word groups that can stand alone), it is preceded by a comma. (See P1-a.)

▶ ~~Because~~ $\overset{F}{f}$inance laws are not always enforced$\overset{;}{\underset{\wedge}{,}}$ therefore$\underset{\wedge}{,}$ investing

in the former Soviet Union can be very risky.

> When the transitional expression *therefore* appears between independent clauses, it is preceded by a semicolon and usually followed by a comma. (See P3-b.)

T3-e Place adjectives and adverbs with care.

Adjectives modify nouns or pronouns; adverbs modify verbs, adjectives, or other adverbs (see B1-d, B1-e). Both native and nonnative speakers encounter problems in the use of adjectives and adverbs (see G4). For nonnative speakers, the placement of adjectives and adverbs can also be troublesome.

Placement of adjectives

No doubt you have already learned that in English adjectives usually precede the nouns they modify and that they may also appear following linking verbs. (See B1-d and B2-b.)

Usual order of cumulative adjectives

ARTICLE OR OTHER NOUN MARKER

a, an, the, her, Joe's, two, many, some

EVALUATIVE WORD

attractive, dedicated, delicious, ugly, disgusting

SIZE

large, enormous, small, little

LENGTH OR SHAPE

long, short, round, square

AGE

new, old, young, antique

COLOR

yellow, blue, crimson

NATIONALITY

French, Peruvian, Vietnamese

RELIGION

Catholic, Protestant, Jewish, Muslim

MATERIAL

silver, walnut, wool, marble

NOUN/ADJECTIVE

tree (as in *tree house*), kitchen (as in *kitchen table*)

THE NOUN MODIFIED

house, sweater, bicycle, bread, woman, priest

Janine wore a *new* necklace. Janine's necklace was *new.*

When adjectives pile up in front of a noun, however, you may sometimes have difficulty arranging them. English is quite particular about the order of cumulative adjectives, those not separated by commas. (See P2-d.)

> Janine was wearing *a beautiful antique silver* necklace [not *a silver antique beautiful* necklace].

The chart on page 236 shows the order in which cumulative adjectives ordinarily appear in front of the noun they modify. This list is only a guide; don't be surprised if you encounter exceptions.

Placement of adverbs

Adverbs modifying verbs appear in various positions: at the beginning or end of the sentence, before or after the verb, or between a helping verb and its main verb.

> *Slowly,* we drove along the rain-slick road.

> Mother wrapped the gift *carefully.*

> Martin *always* wins our tennis matches.

> Christina is *rarely* late for our lunch dates.

> My daughter has *often* spoken of you.

An adverb may not, however, be placed between a verb and its direct object.

> carefully
> ▶ Mother wrapped ~~carefully~~ the gift.
>   ^

The adverb *carefully* may be placed at the beginning or at the end of this sentence or before the verb. It cannot appear after the verb because the verb is followed by the direct object *the gift.*

GRAMMAR CHECKERS do not flag problems with the placement of adjectives and adverbs. They can, however, flag a few other problems with adjectives and adverbs. See the grammar checker advice on page 200.

T4

Other trouble spots

T4-a Distinguish between present participles and past participles used as adjectives.

Both present and past participles may be used as adjectives. The present participle always ends in *-ing*. Past participles usually end in *-ed, -d, -en, -n,* or *-t*. (See G2-a.)

PRESENT PARTICIPLES   confusing, speaking

PAST PARTICIPLES   confused, spoken

Participles used as adjectives can precede the nouns they modify; they can also follow linking verbs, in which case they describe the subject of the sentence. (See B2-b.)

It was a *depressing* movie. Jim was a *depressed* young man.

The essay was *confusing*. The student was *confused*.

A present participle should describe a person or thing causing or stimulating an experience; a past participle should describe a person or thing undergoing an experience.

The lecturer was *boring* [not *bored*].

The audience was *bored* [not *boring*].

In the first example, the lecturer is causing boredom, not experiencing it. In the second example, the audience is experiencing boredom, not causing it.

The participles that cause the most trouble for nonnative speakers are those describing mental states:

annoying/annoyed	exhausting/exhausted
boring/bored	fascinating/fascinated
confusing/confused	frightening/frightened
depressing/depressed	satisfying/satisfied
exciting/excited	surprising/surprised

When you come across these words in your drafts, check to see that you have used them correctly.

GRAMMAR CHECKERS do not flag problems with present and past participles used as adjectives. Not surprisingly, the programs have no way of knowing the meaning a writer intends. For example, both of the following sentences could be correct, depending on the writer's meaning: *My roommate was annoying. My roommate was annoyed.*

T4-b Become familiar with common prepositions that show time and place.

The most frequently used prepositions in English are *at, by, for, from, in, of, on, to,* and *with.* Each of these prepositions has a variety of uses that must be learned gradually, in context.

Prepositions that indicate time and place can be difficult to master because the differences among them are subtle and idiomatic. The chart on page 240 limits itself to four troublesome prepositions that show time and place: *at, on, in,* and *by.*

Not every possible use is listed in the chart, so don't be surprised when you encounter exceptions and idiomatic uses that you must learn one at a time. For example, in English we ride *in* a car but *on* a bus, train, or subway. And when we fly *on* (not *in*) a plane, we are not sitting on top of the plane.

GRAMMAR CHECKERS are of little or no help with prepositions showing time and place. The conventions of preposition use do not have the kind of mathematical precision that a computer program requires.

At, on, in, *and* by *to show time and place*

Showing time

AT   *at* a specific time: *at* 7:20, *at* dawn, *at* dinner

ON   *on* a specific day or date: *on* Tuesday, *on* June 4

IN   *in* a part of a 24-hour period: *in* the afternoon, *in* the daytime [but *at* night]

     in a year or month: *in* 1999, *in* July

     in a period of time: finished *in* three hours

BY   *by* a specific time or date: *by* 4:15, *by* Christmas

Showing place

AT   *at* a meeting place or location: *at* home, *at* the club

     at the edge of something: sitting *at* the desk

     at the corner of something: turning *at* the intersection

     at a target: throwing the snowball *at* Lucy

ON   *on* a surface: placed *on* the table, hanging *on* the wall

     on a street: the house *on* Spring Street

     on an electronic medium: *on* television, *on* the Internet

IN   *in* an enclosed space: *in* the garage, *in* the envelope

     in a geographic location: *in* San Diego, *in* Texas

     in a print medium: *in* a book, *in* a magazine

BY   *by* a landmark: *by* the fence, *by* the flagpole

P

Punctuation

P

Punctuation

P1

The comma

The comma was invented to help readers. Without it, sentence parts can collide into one another unexpectedly, causing misreadings.

CONFUSING   If you cook Elmer will do the dishes.

CONFUSING   While we were eating a rattlesnake approached our campsite.

Add commas in the logical places (after *cook* and *eating*), and suddenly all is clear. No longer is Elmer being cooked, the rattlesnake being eaten.

Various rules have evolved to prevent such misreadings and to speed readers along through complex grammatical structures. Those rules are detailed in this section.

> GRAMMAR CHECKERS do not offer much advice about commas. They can tell you that a comma is usually used before *which* but not before *that* (see P1-e), but they fail to flag most other missing or misused commas. For example, in an essay with ten missing commas and five misused commas, a grammar checker spotted only one missing comma (after the word *therefore*).

P1-a   Use a comma before a coordinating conjunction joining independent clauses.

When a coordinating conjunction connects two or more independent clauses—word groups that could stand alone as separate sentences—a comma must precede it. There are seven coordinating conjunctions in English: *and, but, or, nor, for, so,* and *yet.*

A comma tells readers that one independent clause has come to a close and that another is about to begin.

▶ Nearly everyone has heard of love at first sight‚ but I fell in love

at first dance.

EXCEPTION: If the two independent clauses are short and there is no danger of misreading, the comma may be omitted.

The plane took off and we were on our way.

CAUTION: Do *not* use a comma to separate compound elements that are not independent clauses. See P2-a.

▶ A good money manager controls expenses,/ and invests surplus

dollars to meet future needs.

The word group following *and* is not an independent clause; it is the second half of a compound predicate.

P1-b Use a comma after an introductory word group.

The most common introductory word groups are clauses and phrases functioning as adverbs. Such word groups usually tell when, where, how, why, or under what conditions the main action of the sentence occurred. (See B3-a, B3-b, and B3-e.)

A comma tells readers that the introductory clause or phrase has come to a close and that the main part of the sentence is about to begin.

▶ When Irwin was ready to eat, his cat jumped onto the table and
                              ^
started to purr.

▶ Near a small stream at the bottom of the canyon, we discovered
                                                ^
an abandoned shelter.

EXCEPTION: The comma may be omitted after a short adverb clause or phrase if there is no danger of misreading.

In no time we were at 2,800 feet.

Sentences also frequently begin with participial phrases describing the noun or pronoun immediately following them. The comma tells readers that they are about to learn the identity of the person or thing described; therefore, the comma is usually required even when the phrase is short. (See B3-b.)

▶ **Thinking his motorcade drive through Dallas was routine,**

President Kennedy smiled and waved at the crowds.

▶ **Buried under layers of younger rocks, the earth's oldest rocks**

contain no fossils.

NOTE: Other introductory word groups include conjunctive adverbs, transitional expressions, and absolute phrases. (See P1-f.)

P1-c Use a comma between all items in a series.

Unless you are writing for a publication that follows another convention, separate all items in a series—including the last two—with commas.

▶ **Bubbles of air, leaves, ferns, bits of wood, and insects are often**

found trapped in amber.

Although some publications omit the comma between the last two items, be aware that its omission can result in ambiguity or misreading.

▶ **My uncle willed me all of his property, houses, and warehouses.**

Did the uncle will his property *and* houses *and* warehouses—or simply his property, consisting of houses and warehouses? If the first meaning is intended, a comma is necessary to prevent ambiguity.

▶ **The activities include a search for lost treasure, dubious**

financial dealings, much discussion of ancient heresies, and

midnight orgies.

Without the comma, the people seem to be discussing orgies, not participating in them. The comma makes it clear that *midnight orgies* is a separate item in the series.

P1-d Use a comma between coordinate adjectives not joined by *and*. Do not use a comma between cumulative adjectives.

When two or more adjectives each modify a noun separately, they are *coordinate.*

> Mother has become a *strong, confident, independent* woman.

Adjectives are coordinate if they can be joined with *and* (strong *and* confident *and* independent) or if they can be scrambled (an *independent, strong, confident* woman).

Two or more adjectives that do not modify the noun separately are cumulative.

> *Three large gray* shapes moved slowly toward us.

Beginning with the adjective closest to the noun *shapes,* these modifiers lean on one another, piggyback style, with each modifying a larger word group. *Gray* modifies *shapes, large* modifies *gray shapes,* and *three* modifies *large gray shapes.* We cannot insert the word *and* between cumulative adjectives (three *and* large *and* gray shapes). Nor can we scramble them (*gray three large* shapes).

COORDINATE ADJECTIVES

▶ Robert is a warm, gentle, affectionate father.

CUMULATIVE ADJECTIVES

▶ Ira ordered a rich/ chocolate/ layer cake.

P1-e Use commas to set off nonrestrictive elements. Do not use commas to set off restrictive elements.

Word groups describing nouns or pronouns (adjective clauses, adjective phrases, and appositives) can be restrictive or nonrestrictive. A *restrictive* element defines or limits the meaning of the word it modifies and is therefore essential to the meaning of the sentence. Because it contains essential information, a restrictive element is not set off with commas.

RESTRICTIVE
For camp the children needed clothes *that were washable.*

If you remove a restrictive element from a sentence, the meaning changes significantly, becoming more general than you intended. The writer of the example sentence does not mean that the children needed clothes in general. The intended meaning is more limited: The children needed *washable* clothes.

A *nonrestrictive* element describes a noun or pronoun whose meaning has already been clearly defined or limited. Because it contains nonessential or parenthetical information, a nonrestrictive element is set off with commas.

NONRESTRICTIVE
For camp the children needed sturdy shoes, *which were expensive.*

If you remove a nonrestrictive element from a sentence, the meaning does not change dramatically. Some meaning is lost, to be sure, but the defining characteristics of the person or thing described remain the same as before. The children needed *sturdy shoes,* and these happened to be expensive.

NOTE: Often it is difficult to tell whether a word group is restrictive or nonrestrictive without seeing it in context and considering the writer's meaning. Both of the following sentences are grammatically correct, but their meanings are slightly different.

The dessert made with fresh raspberries was delicious.

The dessert, made with fresh raspberries, was delicious.

In the example without commas, the phrase *made with fresh raspberries* tells readers which of two or more desserts the writer is referring to. In the example with commas, the phrase merely adds information about the particular dessert served with the meal.

Adjective clauses

Adjective clauses are patterned like sentences, containing subjects and verbs, but they function within sentences as modifiers of nouns or pronouns. Adjective clauses begin with a relative pronoun (*who, whom, whose, which, that*) or with a relative adverb (*where, when*).

Nonrestrictive adjective clauses are set off with commas; restrictive adjective clauses are not.

NONRESTRICTIVE CLAUSE

▶ Ed's country house, which is located on thirteen acres, was
       ^   ^

completely furnished with bats in the rafters and mice in the

kitchen.

The clause *which is located on thirteen acres* does not restrict the
meaning of *Ed's country house,* so the information is nonessential.

RESTRICTIVE CLAUSE

▶ An office manager for a corporation/that had government

contracts/asked her supervisor for permission to reprimand

her co-workers for smoking.

Because the adjective clause *that had government contracts* identifies
the corporation, the information is essential.

NOTE: Use *that* only with restrictive clauses. Many writers prefer to
use *which* only with nonrestrictive clauses, but usage varies.

Phrases functioning as adjectives

Prepositional or verbal phrases functioning as adjectives may be
restrictive or nonrestrictive. Nonrestrictive phrases are set off with
commas; restrictive phrases are not.

NONRESTRICTIVE PHRASE

▶ The helicopter, with its 100,000-candlepower spotlight
              ^

illuminating the area, circled above.
                    ^

The *with* phrase is nonessential because its purpose is not to specify
which of two or more helicopters is being discussed.

RESTRICTIVE PHRASE

▶ One corner of the attic was filled with newspapers/dating from

the turn of the century.

Dating from the turn of the century restricts the meaning of *newspapers,* so the comma should be omitted.

Appositives

An appositive is a noun or noun phrase that renames a nearby noun. Nonrestrictive appositives are set off with commas; restrictive appositives are not.

NONRESTRICTIVE APPOSITIVE

▶ Darwin's most important book, *On the Origin of Species*, was the
result of many years of research.

The term *most important* restricts the meaning to one book, so the appositive *On the Origin of Species* is nonrestrictive.

RESTRICTIVE APPOSITIVE

▶ The song "Fire It Up" was blasted out of amplifiers ten feet tall.

Once they've read *song,* readers still don't know precisely which song the writer means. The appositive following *song* restricts its meaning.

P1-f Use commas to set off transitional and parenthetical expressions, absolute phrases, and contrasted elements.

Transitional expressions

Transitional expressions serve as bridges between sentences or parts of sentences. They include conjunctive adverbs such as *however, therefore,* and *moreover* and transitional phrases such as *for example, as a matter of fact,* and *in other words.* (For a more complete list, see P3-b.)

When a transitional expression appears between independent clauses in a compound sentence, it is preceded by a semicolon and is usually followed by a comma.

▶ Minh did not understand our language; moreover, he was
unfamiliar with our customs.

▶ Natural foods are not always salt free; for example, celery
contains more sodium than most people would imagine.

When a transitional expression appears at the beginning of a sentence or in the middle of an independent clause, it is usually set off with commas.

▶ As a matter of fact, American football was established by fans
  ^
  who wanted to play a more organized game of rugby.

▶ Rock and roll may be here to stay; the sad truth for some rock

  musicians, however, is that their hearing may not be.
  ^   ^

EXCEPTION: If a transitional expression blends smoothly with the rest of the sentence, calling for little or no pause in reading, it does not need to be set off with commas. Expressions such as *also, at least, certainly, consequently, indeed, of course, no doubt, perhaps, then,* and *therefore* do not always call for a pause.

Bill's bicycle is broken; *therefore* you will need to borrow Sue's.

Bill's bicycle is broken; you will *therefore* need to borrow Sue's.

Parenthetical expressions

Expressions that are distinctly parenthetical should be set off with commas. Providing supplemental comments or information, they interrupt the flow of a sentence or appear as afterthoughts.

▶ Evolution, so far as we know, doesn't work this way.
  ^   ^

▶ The bluefish weighed twelve pounds, give or take a few ounces.
  ^

Absolute phrases

Absolute phrases should be set off with commas. An absolute phrase, which modifies the whole sentence, usually consists of a noun followed by a participle or participial phrase. (See B3-d.)

▶ His tennis game at last perfected, Chris won the cup.
  ^

▶ Elvis Presley made music industry history in the 1950s, his
  ^
  records having sold more than ten million copies.

CAUTION: Do not insert a comma between the noun and participle of an absolute construction.

▶ The next day⁄being a school day, we turned down the

invitation.

Contrasted elements

Sharp contrasts beginning with words such as *not* and *unlike* are set off with commas.

▶ The Epicurean philosophers sought mental, not bodily,

pleasures.

▶ Unlike Robert, Celia loved dance contests.

P1-g Use commas to set off nouns of direct address, the words *yes* and *no,* interrogative tags, and mild interjections.

▶ Forgive us, Dr. Spock, for spanking Brian.

▶ Yes, the loan will probably be approved.

▶ The film was faithful to the book, wasn't it?

▶ Well, cases like these are difficult to decide.

P1-h Use commas with expressions such as *he said* to set off direct quotations. (See also P6-f.)

▶ Naturalist Arthur Cleveland Bent remarked, "In part the

peregrine declined unnoticed because it is not adorable."

▶ "Convictions are more dangerous foes of truth than lies," wrote

philosopher Friedrich Nietzsche.

P1-i Use commas with dates, addresses, titles, and numbers.

Dates

In dates, the year is set off from the rest of the sentence with a pair of commas.

▶ On December 12, 1890, orders were sent out for the arrest of
   Sitting Bull.

EXCEPTIONS: Commas are not needed if the date is inverted or if only the month and year are given.

The recycling plan went into effect on 15 April 1997.

January 1994 was an extremely cold month.

Addresses

The elements of an address or place name are followed by commas. A zip code, however, is not preceded by a comma.

▶ John Lennon was born in Liverpool, England, in 1940.

▶ Please send the package to Greg Tarvin at 708 Spring Street,
   Washington, Illinois 61571.

Titles

If a title follows a name, separate it from the rest of the sentence with a pair of commas.

▶ Sandra Barnes, M.D., performed the surgery.

Numbers

In numbers more than four digits long, use commas to separate the numbers into groups of three, starting from the right. In numbers four digits long, a comma is optional.

$$3,500 \; [\textit{or} \; 3500]$$
$$100,000$$
$$5,000,000$$

EXCEPTIONS: Do not use commas in street numbers, zip codes, telephone numbers, or years.

P1-j Use a comma to prevent confusion.

In certain contexts, a comma is necessary to prevent confusion. If the writer has omitted a word or phrase, for example, a comma may be needed to signal the omission.

▶ To err is human; to forgive, divine.

If two words in a row echo each other, a comma may be needed for ease of reading.

▶ All of the catastrophes that we had feared might happen,

happened.

Sometimes a comma is needed to prevent readers from grouping words in ways that do not match the writer's intention.

▶ Patients who can, walk up and down the halls several times

a day.

P2

Unnecessary commas

P2-a Do not use a comma between compound elements that are not independent clauses.

Although a comma is used before a coordinating conjunction joining independent clauses (see P1-a), this rule should not be extended to other compound word groups.

▶ Marie Curie discovered radium/ and later applied her work on

radioactivity to medicine.

And links two verbs in a compound predicate: *discovered* and *applied.*

▶ Jake still does not realize that his illness is serious/ and that he

will have to alter his diet to improve.

And connects two subordinate clauses, each beginning with *that.*

P2-b Do not use a comma to separate a verb from its subject or object.

A sentence should flow from subject to verb to object without unnecessary pauses. Commas may appear between these major sentence elements only when a specific rule calls for them.

▶ Zoos large enough to give the animals freedom to roam/ are

becoming more popular.

▶ Captain Spurlock observed/ that the vast majority of crimes in our

city are committed by repeat offenders.

The subject *Zoos* should not be separated from its verb, *are becoming.*
The verb *observed* should not be separated from its direct object, the
subordinate clause beginning with *that.*

P2-c Do not use a comma before the first or after the last item in a series.

Though commas are required between items in a series (see P1-c),
do not place them either before or after the series.

▶ Other causes of asthmatic attacks are/ stress, change in

temperature, humidity, and cold air.

▶ Ironically, this job that appears so glamorous, carefree, and easy/

carries a high degree of responsibility.

P2-d Do not use a comma between cumulative adjectives, between an adjective and a noun, or between an adverb and an adjective.

Though commas are required between coordinate adjectives (those that can be joined with *and*), they do not belong between cumulative adjectives (those that cannot be joined with *and*). (For a full discussion, see P1-d.)

▶ In the corner of the closet we found an old⁄maroon hatbox

from Sears.

A comma should never be used to separate an adjective from the noun that follows it.

▶ It was a senseless, dangerous⁄mission.

Nor should a comma be used to separate an adverb from an adjective that follows it.

▶ The Hurst Home is unsuitable as a mental facility for severely⁄

disturbed youths.

P2-c Do not use commas to set off restrictive or mildly parenthetical elements.

Restrictive elements are modifiers or appositives necessary for identifying the nouns they follow; therefore, they are essential to the meaning of the sentence and should not be set off with commas. (For a full discussion, see P1-e.)

▶ Drivers⁄who think they own the road⁄make cycling a dangerous

sport.

The *who* clause restricts the meaning of *Drivers* and is therefore essential to the meaning of the sentence. Putting commas around the *who* clause falsely suggests that all drivers think they own the road.

▶ Margaret Mead's book⟋ *Coming of Age in Samoa⟋* stirred up

considerable controversy when it was first published, but now

it is considered a classic.

Since Margaret Mead wrote more than one book, the appositive contains information essential to the meaning of the sentence.

Although commas should be used with distinctly parenthetical expressions (see P1-f), do not use them to set off elements that are only mildly parenthetical.

▶ Charisse believes that the Internet is⟋ essentially⟋ a bastion of

advertising.

P2-f Do not use a comma to set off a concluding adverb clause that is essential to the meaning of the sentence.

When adverb clauses introduce a sentence, they are nearly always followed by a comma (see P1-b). When they conclude a sentence, however, they are not set off by commas if their content is essential to the meaning of the earlier part of the sentence. Adverb clauses beginning with *after, as soon as, before, because, if, since, unless, until,* and *when* are usually essential.

▶ Don't visit Paris at the height of the tourist season⟋ unless

you have booked hotel reservations.

Without the concluding *unless* clause, the meaning of the sentence would be broader than the writer intended.

When a concluding adverb clause is nonessential, it should be preceded by a comma. Clauses beginning with *although, even though, though,* and *whereas* are usually nonessential.

▶ The lecture seemed to last only a short time‸ although the clock

said it had gone on for more than an hour.

P2-g Avoid other common misuses of the comma.

Do not use a comma in the following situations.

AFTER A COORDINATING CONJUNCTION (*AND, BUT, OR, NOR, FOR, SO, YET*)

▶ Occasionally soap operas are performed live, but╱more often they are taped.

AFTER *SUCH AS* OR *LIKE*

▶ Many shade-loving plants, such as╱begonias, impatiens, and coleus, can add color to a shady garden.

BEFORE *THAN*

▶ Touring Crete was more thrilling for us╱than visiting the Greek islands frequented by rich Europeans.

AFTER *ALTHOUGH*

▶ Although╱the air was balmy, the water was too cold for swimming.

BEFORE A PARENTHESIS

▶ At MCI Sylvia began at the bottom╱(with only three and a half walls and a swivel chair), but within five years she had been promoted to supervisor.

TO SET OFF AN INDIRECT (REPORTED) QUOTATION

▶ Samuel Goldwyn once said╱that a verbal contract isn't worth the paper it's written on.

WITH A QUESTION MARK OR AN EXCLAMATION POINT

▶ "Why don't you try it?╱" she coaxed.

P3

The semicolon

The semicolon is used to separate major sentence elements of equal grammatical rank.

> GRAMMAR CHECKERS flag some, but not all, misused semicolons (P3-d). In addition, they can alert you to some run-on sentences (G6). However, they miss more run-on sentences than they identify, and they sometimes flag correct sentences as possible run-ons. (See also the grammar checker advice in G6.)

P3-a Use a semicolon between closely related independent clauses not joined with a coordinating conjunction.

When related independent clauses appear in one sentence, they are ordinarily connected with a comma and a coordinating conjunction (*and, but, or, nor, for, so, yet*). The conjunction expresses the relation between the clauses. If the relation is clear without the conjunction, a writer may choose to connect the clauses with a semicolon instead.

> Injustice is relatively easy to bear; what stings is justice.
> —H. L. Mencken

A semicolon must be used whenever a coordinating conjunction has been omitted between independent clauses. To use merely a comma creates a kind of run-on sentence known as a comma splice. (See G6.)

▶ In 1800, a traveler needed six weeks to get from New York City to

　Chicago, in 1860, the trip by railroad took two days.

CAUTION: Do not overuse the semicolon as a means of revising comma splices. For other revision strategies, see G6.

P3-b Use a semicolon between independent clauses linked with a transitional expression.

Transitional expressions include conjunctive adverbs and transitional phrases.

CONJUNCTIVE ADVERBS

accordingly	finally	likewise	similarly
also	furthermore	meanwhile	specifically
anyway	hence	moreover	still
besides	however	nevertheless	subsequently
certainly	incidentally	next	then
consequently	indeed	nonetheless	therefore
conversely	instead	otherwise	thus

TRANSITIONAL PHRASES

after all	even so	in fact
as a matter of fact	for example	in other words
as a result	for instance	in the first place
at any rate	in addition	on the contrary
at the same time	in conclusion	on the other hand

When a transitional expression appears between independent clauses, it is preceded by a semicolon and often followed by a comma.

▶ Many corals grow very gradually ; in fact, the creation of a coral
^
reef can take centuries.

When a transitional expression appears in the middle or at the end of the second independent clause, the semicolon goes *between the clauses.*

Most singers gain fame through hard work and dedication; Evita, however, found other means.

Transitional expressions should not be confused with the coordinating conjunctions *and, but, or, nor, for, so,* and *yet,* which are preceded by a comma when they link independent clauses. (See P1-a and G6-a.)

P3-c Use a semicolon between items in a series containing internal punctuation.

▶ Classic science fiction sagas are *Star Trek,* with Mr. Spock and his

large pointed ears*;* *Battlestar Galactica,* with its Cylon Raiders*;*

and *Star Wars,* with Han Solo, Luke Skywalker, and Darth Vader.

Without the semicolons the reader must sort out the major groupings, distinguishing between important and less important pauses according to the logic of the sentence. By inserting semicolons at the major breaks, the writer does this work for the reader.

P3-d Avoid common misuses of the semicolon.

Do not use a semicolon in the following situations.

BETWEEN A SUBORDINATE CLAUSE AND THE REST OF THE SENTENCE

▶ Unless you brush your teeth within ten or fifteen minutes after

eating*,* brushing does almost no good.

BETWEEN AN APPOSITIVE AND THE WORD IT REFERS TO

▶ Another delicious dish is the chef's special*,* a roasted duck

rubbed with spices and stuffed with wild rice.

TO INTRODUCE A LIST

▶ Some of my favorite film stars have home pages on the Web*:*
John Travolta, Susan Sarandon, Leonardo DiCaprio, and
Emma Thompson.

BETWEEN INDEPENDENT CLAUSES JOINED BY *AND, BUT, OR, NOR, FOR, SO,* OR *YET*

▶ Five of the applicants had worked with spreadsheets*,* but only

one was familiar with database management.

EXCEPTIONS: If at least one of the independent clauses contains internal punctuation, you may use a semicolon even though the clauses are joined with a coordinating conjunction.

> As a vehicle [the model T] was hard-working, commonplace, and heroic; and it often seemed to transmit those qualities to the person who rode in it.
>
> —E. B. White

Although a comma would also be correct in this sentence, the semicolon is more effective, for it indicates the relative weights of the pauses.

Occasionally, a semicolon may be used to emphasize a sharp contrast or a firm distinction between clauses joined with a coordinating conjunction.

> We hate some persons because we do not know them; and we will not know them because we hate them.
>
> —Charles Caleb Colton

P4

The colon

The colon is used primarily to call attention to the words that follow it.

> There are only three seasons in this state: winter, July, and August.

GRAMMAR CHECKERS can catch some misused colons. They are less helpful at telling you when you may need a colon. For example, the programs failed to note that a colon (not a comma) belongs after the word *items* in this sentence: *Every camper should consider carrying the following items, a first-aid kit, a Swiss army knife, and a flashlight.*

P4-a   Use a colon after an independent clause to direct attention to a list, an appositive, or a quotation.

A LIST
The daily routine should include at least the following: twenty knee bends, fifty sit-ups, fifteen leg lifts, and five minutes of running in place.

AN APPOSITIVE
My roommate is guilty of two of the seven deadly sins: gluttony and sloth.

A QUOTATION
Consider the words of John F. Kennedy: "Ask not what your country can do for you; ask what you can do for your country."

For other ways of introducing quotations, see P6-f.

P4-b   Use a colon between independent clauses if the second summarizes or explains the first.

Faith is like love: It cannot be forced.

NOTE: When an independent clause follows a colon, it may begin with a lowercase or a capital letter.

P4-c   Use a colon after the salutation in a formal letter, to indicate hours and minutes, to show proportions, between a title and subtitle, and to separate city from publisher and date in bibliographic entries.

Dear Sir or Madam:

5:30 P.M. (or p.m.)

The ratio of women to men was 2:1.

The Glory of Hera: Greek Mythology and the Greek Family

Boston: Bedford, 1999

NOTE: In biblical references, a colon is ordinarily used between chapter and verse (Luke 2:14). The Modern Language Association recommends a period instead (Luke 2.14).

P4-d Avoid common misuses of the colon.

A colon must be preceded by a full independent clause. Therefore, avoid using it in the following situations.

BETWEEN A VERB AND ITS OBJECT OR COMPLEMENT

▶ Some important vitamins and minerals found in vegetables are⌀ vitamin A, thiamine, niacin, iron, potassium, folate, and vitamin C.

BETWEEN A PREPOSITION AND ITS OBJECT

▶ The heart's two pumps each consist of⌀ an upper chamber, or atrium, and a lower chamber, or ventricle.

AFTER *SUCH AS, INCLUDING,* OR *FOR EXAMPLE*

▶ The trees on our campus include many fine Japanese specimens such as⌀ black pines, ginkgos, weeping cherries, and cutleaf maples.

P5

The apostrophe

GRAMMAR CHECKERS can flag some, but not all, missing or misused apostrophes. They can catch missing apostrophes in common contractions, such as *don't*. They can also flag some problems with possessives, although they miss others. The programs usually phrase their advice cautiously, telling you that you have a "possible possessive error" in a phrase such as *a days work* or *sled dogs feet*. Therefore, you—not the grammar checker—must decide whether to add an apostrophe and, if so, whether to put it before or after the *-s*.

P5-a Use an apostrophe to indicate that a noun is possessive.

Possessive nouns usually indicate ownership, as in *Tim's hat* or *the lawyer's desk*. Frequently, however, ownership is only loosely implied: *the tree's roots, a day's work*. If you are not sure whether a noun is possessive, try turning it into an *of* phrase: *the roots of the tree, the work of a day*.

When to add -'s

If the noun does not end in -*s*, add -'*s*.

> Roy managed to climb out on the driver's side.

> Thank you for refunding the children's money.

If the noun is singular and ends in -*s*, add -'*s*.

> Lois's sister spent last year in India.

EXCEPTION: If pronunciation would be awkward with the added -'*s*, some writers use only the apostrophe. Either use is acceptable.

> Sophocles' plays are among my favorites.

When to add only an apostrophe

If the noun is plural and ends in -*s*, add only an apostrophe.

> Both diplomats' briefcases were stolen.

Joint possession

To show joint possession, use -'*s* (or -*s'*) with the last noun only; to show individual possession, make all nouns possessive.

> Have you seen Joyce and Greg's new camper?

> Hernando's and Maria's expectations of marriage couldn't have been more different.

In the first sentence, Joyce and Greg jointly own one camper. In the second sentence, Hernando and Maria individually have different expectations.

Compound nouns

If a noun is compound, use -*'s* (or -*s'*) with the last element.

> Her father-in-law's sculpture won first place.

P5-b Use an apostrophe and -*s* to indicate that an indefinite pronoun is possessive.

Indefinite pronouns are pronouns that refer to no specific person or thing: *everyone, someone, no one, something.* (See B1-b.)

> This diet will improve almost anyone's health.

P5-c Use an apostrophe to mark contractions.

In contractions the apostrophe takes the place of missing letters. In the following sentence, *It's* stands for *It is* and *can't* stands for *cannot.*

> It's a shame that Frank can't go on the tour.

The apostrophe is also used to mark the omission of the first two digits of a year (the class of '99) or years (the '60s generation).

P5-d Use an apostrophe and -*s* to pluralize numbers mentioned as numbers, letters mentioned as letters, words mentioned as words, and abbreviations.

> Peggy skated nearly perfect figure 8's.
>
> The bleachers in our section were marked with large red *J*'s.
>
> We've heard enough *maybe*'s.
>
> You must ask to see their I.D.'s.

Notice that the -*s* is not italicized when used with an italicized letter or word.

EXCEPTION: An -*s* alone is often added to the years in a decade: *the 1980s.*

NOTE: The Modern Language Association recommends no apostrophe in plurals of numbers and abbreviations: *figure 8s, VCRs.*

P5-e Avoid common misuses of the apostrophe.

Do not use an apostrophe in the following situations.

WITH NOUNS THAT ARE NOT POSSESSIVE

▶ Some ~~outpatient's~~ are given special parking permits.
   outpatients

IN THE POSSESSIVE PRONOUNS *ITS, WHOSE, HIS, HERS, OURS, YOURS,* AND *THEIRS*

▶ Each area has ~~it's~~ own conference room.
   its

It's means "it is." The possessive pronoun *its* contains no apostrophe despite the fact that it is possessive.

P6

Quotation marks

> **GRAMMAR CHECKERS** are good at telling you to put commas and periods inside quotation marks; they are also fairly good at flagging "unbalanced quotes," an opening quotation mark that is not balanced with a closing quotation mark. The programs can't tell you, however, when you should or shouldn't use quotation marks.

P6-a Use quotation marks to enclose direct quotations.

Direct quotations of a person's words, whether spoken or written, must be in quotation marks.

> "A foolish consistency is the hobgoblin of little minds," wrote Ralph Waldo Emerson.

CAUTION: Do not use quotation marks around indirect quotations. An indirect quotation reports someone's ideas without using that person's exact words.

Ralph Waldo Emerson believed that consistency for its own sake is the mark of a small mind.

NOTE: In dialogue, begin a new paragraph to mark a change in speaker.

"Mom, his name is Willie, not William. A thousand times I've told you, it's *Willie.*"

"Willie is a derivative of William, Lester. Surely his birth certificate doesn't have Willie on it, and I like calling people by their proper names."

"Yes, it does, ma'am. My mother named me Willie K. Mason."

—Gloria Naylor

If a single speaker utters more than one paragraph, introduce each paragraph with quotation marks, but do not use closing quotation marks until the end of the speech.

P6-b   Set off long quotations of prose or poetry by indenting.

When a quotation of prose runs to more than four typed lines in your paper, set it off by indenting ten spaces from the left margin. Quotation marks are not required because the indented format tells readers that the quotation is taken word for word from a source. Long quotations are ordinarily introduced by a sentence ending with a colon.

After studying the historical record, James Horan evaluates Billy the Kid like this:

The portrait that emerges of [the Kid] from the thousands of pages of affidavits, reports, trial transcripts, his letters, and his testimony is neither the mythical Robin Hood nor the stereotyped adenoidal moron and pathological killer. Rather Billy appears as a disturbed, lonely young man, honest, loyal to his friends, dedicated to his beliefs, and betrayed by our institutions and the corrupt, ambitious, and compromising politicians of his time. (158)

The number in parentheses is a citation handled according to the Modern Language Association style. (See M1.)

NOTE: When you quote two or more paragraphs from the source, indent the first line of each paragraph an additional three spaces.

When quoting more than three lines of a poem, set the quoted lines off from the text by indenting ten spaces from the left margin. Use no quotation marks unless they appear in the poem itself. (To punctuate two or three lines of poetry, see P7-h.)

```
Although many anthologizers "modernize" her punctua-
tion, Emily Dickinson relied heavily on dashes, using
them, perhaps, as a musical device. Here, for example,
is the original version of the opening stanza from
"The Snake":
          A narrow Fellow in the Grass
          Occasionally rides--
          You may have met Him--did you not
          His notice sudden is--
```

NOTE: The American Psychological Association has slightly different guidelines for setting off long quotations. See A1-c.

P6-c Use single quotation marks to enclose a quotation within a quotation.

According to Paul Eliott, Eskimo hunters "chant an ancient magic song to the seal they are after: 'Beast of the sea! Come and place yourself before me in the early morning!' "

P6-d Use quotation marks around the titles of newspaper and magazine articles, poems, short stories, songs, episodes of television and radio programs, and chapters or subdivisions of books.

Even after forty minutes of discussion, our class could not agree on an interpretation of Robert Frost's poem "The Road Not Taken."

NOTE: Titles of books, plays, Web sites, and films and names of magazines and newspapers are put in italics or underlined. (See S6-a.)

P6-e Quotation marks may be used to set off words used as words.

Although words used as words are ordinarily underlined to indicate italics (see S6-d), quotation marks are also acceptable.

> The words "accept" and "except" are frequently confused.

> The words *accept* and *except* are frequently confused.

P6-f Use punctuation with quotation marks according to convention.

This section describes the conventions used by American publishers in placing various marks of punctuation inside or outside quotation marks. It also explains how to punctuate when introducing quoted material.

Periods and commas

Always place periods and commas inside quotation marks.

> "This is a stick-up," said the well-dressed young couple. "We want all your money."

This rule applies to single quotation marks as well as double quotation marks. (See P6-c.) It also applies to all uses of quotation marks: for quoted material, for titles of works, and for words used as words.

EXCEPTION: In the Modern Language Association's style of parenthetical in-text citations (see M1), the period follows the citation in parentheses.

> James M. McPherson comments, approvingly, that the Whigs "were not averse to extending the blessings of American liberty, even to Mexicans and Indians" (48).

Colons and semicolons

Put colons and semicolons outside quotation marks.

> Harold wrote, "I regret that I am unable to attend the fundraiser for AIDS research"; his letter, however, contained a substantial contribution.

Question marks and exclamation points

Put question marks and exclamation points inside quotation marks unless they apply to the sentence as a whole.

> Contrary to tradition, bedtime at my house is marked by "Mommy, can I tell you a story now?"

> Have you heard the old proverb "Do not climb the hill until you reach it"?

In the first sentence, the question mark applies only to the quoted question. In the second sentence, the question mark applies to the whole sentence.

NOTE: MLA parenthetical citations create a special problem. According to MLA, the question mark or exclamation point should appear before the quotation mark, and a period should follow the parenthetical citation: *Rosie Thomas asks, "Is nothing in life ever straight and clear, the way children see it?" (77).*

Introducing quoted material

After a word group introducing a quotation, choose a colon, a comma, or no punctuation at all, whichever is appropriate in context.

FORMAL INTRODUCTION If a quotation has been formally introduced, a colon is appropriate. A formal introduction is a full independent clause, not just an expression such as *he said* or *she remarked*.

> Morrow views personal ads in the classifieds as an art form: "The personal ad is like a haiku of self-celebration, a brief solo played on one's own horn."

EXPRESSION SUCH AS *HE SAID* If a quotation is introduced with an expression such as *he said* or *she remarked* — or if it is followed by such an expression — a comma is needed.

> Without cracking a smile, my supervisor said, "If you want the Northeast region, it's yours."

> "You can be a little ungrammatical if you come from the right part of the country," said Robert Frost.

BLENDED QUOTATION   When a quotation is blended into the writer's own sentence, either a comma or no punctuation is appropriate, depending on the way in which the quotation fits into the sentence structure.

> The future champion could, as he put it, "float like a butterfly and sting like a bee."

> Charles Hudson noted that the prisoners escaped "by squeezing through a tiny window eighteen feet above the floor of their cell."

BEGINNING OF SENTENCE   If a quotation appears at the beginning of a sentence, set it off with a comma unless the question ends with a question mark or an exclamation point.

> "We shot them like dogs," boasted Davy Crockett, who was among Jackson's troops.

> "What is it?" I asked, bracing myself.

INTERRUPTED QUOTATION   If a quoted sentence is interrupted by explanatory words, use commas to set off the explanatory words.

> "A great many people think they are thinking," wrote William James, "when they are merely rearranging their prejudices."

If two successive quoted sentences from the same source are interrupted by explanatory words, use a comma before the explanatory words and a period after them.

> "I was a flop as a daily reporter," admitted E. B. White. "Every piece had to be a masterpiece—and before you knew it, Tuesday was Wednesday."

P6-g   Avoid common misuses of quotation marks.

Do not use quotation marks to draw attention to familiar slang, to disown trite expressions, or to justify an attempt at humor.

> ▶ Between Thanksgiving and Super Bowl Sunday, many American wives become ⁄football widows.⁊

Do not use quotation marks around indirect quotations. (See also P6-a.)

▶ After leaving the scene of the domestic quarrel, the officer said

that ⁄he was due for a coffee break.⎰

Do not use quotation marks around the title of your own essay.

P7

Other marks

> GRAMMAR CHECKERS are of little help with end punctuation and the other marks discussed in this section. Most notably, they neglect to tell you when your sentence is missing end punctuation.

P7-a The period

Use a period to end all sentences except direct questions or genuine exclamations. Also use periods in abbreviations according to convention.

To end sentences

Everyone knows that a period should be used to end most sentences. The only problems that arise concern the choice between a period and a question mark or between a period and an exclamation point.

If a sentence reports a question instead of asking it directly, it should end with a period, not a question mark.

▶ Celia asked whether the picnic would be canceled↗.
                                                    ^

If a sentence is not a genuine exclamation, it should end with a period, not an exclamation point.

▶ After years of working her way through school, Pat finally

graduated with high honors↗.
                          ^

In abbreviations

A period is conventionally used in abbreviations such as these:

Mr.	B.A.	B.C.	i.e.	A.M. (or a.m.)
Mrs.	M.A.	B.C.E.	e.g.	P.M. (or p.m.)
Ms.	Ph.D.	A.D.	etc.	
Dr.	R.N.	C.E.		

A period is not used with U.S. Postal Service abbreviations for states: MD, TX, CA.

Ordinarily a period is not used in abbreviations of organization names:

NATO	UNESCO	UCLA	PUSH	IBM
TVA	IRS	AFL-CIO	NVBA	FTC
USA (*or* U.S.A.)	NAACP	SEC	FCC	NIH

Usage varies, however. When in doubt, consult a dictionary, a style manual, or a publication by the agency in question. Even the yellow pages can help.

NOTE: If a sentence ends with a period marking an abbreviation, do not add a second period.

P7-b The question mark

Obviously a direct question should be followed by a question mark.

What is the horsepower of a 747 engine?

If a polite request is written in the form of a question, it too is usually followed by a question mark, although usage varies.

Would you please send me your catalog of lilies?

CAUTION: Do not use a question mark after an indirect question (one that is reported rather than asked directly). Use a period instead.

► He asked me who was teaching the mythology course⁄.

NOTE: Questions in a series may be followed by question marks even when they are not complete sentences.

> We wondered where Calamity had hidden this time. Under the sink? Behind the furnace? On top of the bookcase?

P7-c   The exclamation point

Use an exclamation point after a word group or sentence that expresses exceptional feeling or deserves special emphasis.

> When Gloria entered the room, I switched on the lights and we all yelled "Surprise!"

CAUTION: Do not overuse the exclamation point.

▶ In the fisherman's memory the fish lives on, increasing in length
and weight with each passing year, until at last it is big enough to
shade a fishing boat⌿.
                   ^

This sentence doesn't need to be pumped up with an exclamation point. It is emphatic enough without it.

▶ Whenever I see Steffi lunging forward to put away an overhead
smash, it might as well be me⌿. She does it just the way that I
             ^
would!

The first exclamation point should be deleted so that the second one will have more force.

P7-d   The dash

When typing, use two hyphens to form a dash (--). Do not put spaces before or after the dash. (If your word processing program has what is known as an "em-dash," you may use it instead, with no space before or after it.) Dashes are used for the following purposes.

To set off parenthetical material that deserves emphasis

> Everything that went wrong—from the peeping Tom at her window last night to my head-on collision today—was blamed on our move.

To set off appositives that contain commas

An appositive is a noun or noun phrase that renames a nearby noun. Ordinarily most appositives are set off with commas (see P1-e), but when the appositive contains commas, a pair of dashes helps readers see the relative importance of all the pauses.

> In my hometown the basic needs of people—food, clothing, and shelter—are less costly than in Los Angeles.

To prepare for a list, a restatement, an amplification, or a dramatic shift in tone or thought

> Along the wall are the bulk liquids—sesame seed oil, honey, safflower oil, maple syrup, and that half-liquid "peanuts only" peanut butter.

> Consider the amount of sugar in the average person's diet—104 pounds per year, 90 percent more than that consumed by our ancestors.

> Everywhere we looked there were little kids—a box of Cracker Jacks in one hand and mommy's or daddy's sleeve in the other.

> Kiere took a few steps back, came running full speed, kicked a mighty kick—and missed the ball.

In the first two examples, the writer could also use a colon. (See P4-a.) The colon is more formal than the dash and not quite as dramatic.

CAUTION: Unless there is a specific reason for using the dash, avoid it. Unnecessary dashes create a choppy effect.

▶ Insisting that our young people learn to use computers as

instructional tools⊬for information retrieval⊬makes good

sense. Herding them⊬sheeplike⊬into computer technology

does not.

P7-e Parentheses

Use parentheses to enclose supplemental material, minor digressions, and afterthoughts.

> After taking her temperature, pulse, and blood pressure (routine vital signs), the nurse made Becky as comfortable as possible.

> The weights James was first able to move (not lift, mind you) were measured in ounces.

Use parentheses to enclose letters or numbers labeling items in a series.

> Regulations stipulated that only the following equipment could be used on the survival mission: (1) a knife, (2) thirty feet of parachute line, (3) a book of matches, (4) two ponchos, (5) an *E* tool, and (6) a signal flare.

CAUTION: Do not overuse parentheses. Rough drafts are likely to contain more afterthoughts than necessary. As writers head into a sentence, they often think of additional details, occasionally working them in as best they can with parentheses. Usually such sentences should be revised so that the additional details no longer seem to be afterthoughts.

► Researchers have said that ~~ten million (estimates run as high as~~ *from ten to fifty million*

~~fifty million)~~ Americans have hypoglycemia.

P7-f Brackets

Use brackets to enclose any words or phrases that you have inserted into an otherwise word-for-word quotation.

> *Audubon* reports that "if there are not enough young to balance deaths, the end of the species [California condor] is inevitable."

The *Audubon* article did not contain the words *California condor* in the sentence quoted, since the context made clear what species was meant. Out of context, however, the words *California condor* are needed.

The Latin word *sic* in brackets indicates that an error in a quoted sentence appears in the original source.

> According to the review, Darci Kistler's performance was brilliant, "exceding [*sic*] the expectations of even her most loyal fans."

Do not overuse *sic,* however, since calling attention to others' mistakes can appear snobbish. The quotation above, for example, might have been handled like this instead: *According to the review, Darci Kistler's performance was so brilliant that it exceeded "the expectations of even her most loyal fans."*

P7-g The ellipsis mark

The ellipsis mark consists of three spaced periods. Use an ellipsis mark to indicate that you have deleted material from an otherwise word-for-word quotation.

> Reuben reports that "when the amount of cholesterol circulating in the blood rises over . . . 300 milligrams per 100, the chances of a heart attack increase dramatically."

MLA NOTE: MLA now recommends putting brackets around ellipsis dots, like this: [. . .]. These brackets make clear that the ellipsis dots do not appear in the original work you are quoting (see pp. 88–89). You may wish to check with your instructor before following this new MLA guideline. If you are using a citation style other than MLA (such as APA), do not follow this guideline.

If you delete a full sentence or more in the middle of a quoted passage, use a period before the three ellipsis dots.

> "Most of our efforts," writes Dave Erikson, "are directed toward saving the bald eagle's wintering habitat along the Mississippi River. . . . It's important that the wintering birds have a place to roost, where they can get out of the cold wind and be undisturbed by man."

CAUTION: Do not use the ellipsis mark at the beginning of a quotation; do not use it at the end of a quotation unless you have cut some words from the end of the final sentence quoted.

In quoted poetry, use a full line of ellipsis dots to indicate that you have dropped a line or more from the poem:

> Had we but world enough, and time,
> This coyness, lady, were no crime.
> . . . .
> But at my back I always hear
> Time's wingèd chariot hurrying near;   —Andrew Marvell

The ellipsis mark may also be used to mark a hesitation or an interruption in speech or to suggest unfinished thoughts.

> "The house next door . . . it's going up in flames!" yelled Marcia.

> Before falling into a coma, the victim whispered, "It was a man with a tattoo on his. . . ."

P7-h The slash

Use the slash to separate two or three lines of poetry that have been run in with your text. Add a space both before and after the slash.

> In the opening lines of "Jordan," George Herbert pokes gentle fun at popular poems of his time: "Who says that fictions only and false hair / Become a verse? Is there in truth no beauty?"

More than three lines of poetry should be handled as a block quotation set off from the text. (See P6-b.)

The slash may occasionally be used to separate paired terms such as *pass/fail* and *producer/director.* Do not use a space before or after the slash.

> Roger Sommers, the team's manager/owner, announced a change in the lineup.

Be sparing, however, in this use of the slash. In particular, avoid the use of *and/or, he/she,* and *his/her.*

S

Spelling and Mechanics

S

Spelling and Mechanics

S1

Spelling

You learned to spell from repeated experience with words in both reading and writing, but especially writing. Words have a look, a sound, and even a feel to them as the hand moves across the page. As you proofread, you can probably tell if a word doesn't look quite right. In such cases, the solution is obvious: Look up the word in the dictionary. (See W6-a.)

SPELL CHECKERS AND GRAMMAR CHECKERS are useful alternatives to a dictionary, but only to a point. A spell checker will not tell you how to spell words not listed in its dictionary; nor will it help you catch words commonly confused, such as *accept* and *except,* or some typographical errors, such as *own* for *won.* You will still need to proofread, and for some words you may need to turn to the dictionary.

Grammar checkers can flag commonly confused words such as *accept* and *except* or *principal* and *principle,* but they often do this when you have used the correct word. You will still need to think about the meaning you intend.

S1-a Become familiar with the major spelling rules.

i *before* e *except after* c

Use *i* before *e* except after *c* or when sounded like *ay,* as in *neighbor* and *weigh.*

I BEFORE *E* relieve, believe, sieve, niece, fierce, frieze

E BEFORE *I* receive, deceive, sleigh, freight, eight

EXCEPTIONS seize, either, weird, height, foreign, leisure

Suffixes

FINAL SILENT -*E* Generally, drop a final silent -*e* when adding a suffix that begins with a vowel. Keep the final -*e* if the suffix begins with a consonant.

combine, combination	achieve, achievement
desire, desiring	care, careful
prude, prudish	entire, entirety
remove, removable	gentle, gentleness

Words such as *changeable, judgment, argument,* and *truly* are exceptions.

FINAL -Y   When adding -*s* or -*d* to words ending in -*y,* ordinarily change -*y* to -*ie* when the -*y* is preceded by a consonant but not when it is preceded by a vowel.

comedy, comedies	monkey, monkeys
dry, dried	play, played

With proper names ending in -*y,* however, do not change the -*y* to -*ie* even if it is preceded by a consonant: *the Dougherty family, the Doughertys.*

FINAL CONSONANTS   If a final consonant is preceded by a single vowel *and* the consonant ends a one-syllable word or a stressed syllable, double the consonant when adding a suffix beginning with a vowel.

bet, betting	occur, occurrence
commit, committed	

Plurals

-S OR -ES   Add -*s* to form the plural of most nouns; add -*es* to singular nouns ending in -*s, -sh, -ch,* and -*x.*

table, tables	church, churches
paper, papers	dish, dishes

Ordinarily add -*s* to nouns ending in -*o* when the -*o* is preceded by a vowel. Add -*es* when it is preceded by a consonant.

radio, radios	hero, heroes
video, videos	tomato, tomatoes

OTHER PLURALS   To form the plural of a hyphenated compound word, add the -*s* to the chief word even if it does not appear at the end.

mother-in-law, mothers-in-law

English words derived from other languages such as Latin or French sometimes form the plural as they would in their original language.

medium, media   chateau, chateaux
criterion, criteria

ESL

Spelling may vary slightly among English-speaking countries. This can prove particularly confusing for ESL students, who may have learned British or Canadian English. Following is a list of some common words spelled differently in American and British English. Consult a dictionary for others.

AMERICAN	BRITISH
canceled, traveled	cancelled, travelled
color, humor	colour, humour
judgment	judgement
check	cheque
realize, apologize	realise, apologise
defense,	defence
anemia, anesthetic	anaemia, anaesthetic
theater, center	theatre, centre
fetus	foetus
mold, smolder	mould, smoulder
civilization	civilisation
connection, inflection	connexion, inflexion
licorice	liquorice

S1-b Discriminate between words that sound alike but have different meanings.

Words that sound alike or nearly alike but have different meanings and spellings are easy to confuse. The following sets of words are so commonly confused that a good proofreader will double-check their every use.

affect (verb: "to exert an influence")
effect (verb: "to accomplish"; noun: "result")

its (possessive pronoun: "of or belonging to it")
it's (contraction for "it is")

> loose (adjective: "free, not securely attached")
> lose (verb: "to fail to keep, to be deprived of")

> principal (adjective: "most important"; noun: "head of a school")
> principle (noun: "a general or fundamental truth")

> their (possessive pronoun: "belonging to them")
> they're (contraction for "they are")
> there (adverb: "that place or position")

> who's (contraction for "who is")
> whose (possessive form of "who")

> your (possessive form of "you")
> you're (contraction of "you are")

To check for correct use of these and other commonly confused words, consult the Glossary of Usage in this book (W1).

S2

The hyphen

GRAMMAR CHECKERS can flag some, but not all, missing or misused hyphens. For example, the programs can tell you that a hyphen is needed in fractions and compound numbers, such as *two-thirds* and *sixty-four*. They can also tell you how to spell certain compound words, such as *breakup* (not *break-up*).

S2-a Consult the dictionary to determine how to treat a compound word.

The dictionary will tell you whether to treat a compound word as a hyphenated compound (*water-repellent*), one word (*waterproof*), or two words (*water table*). If the compound word is not in the dictionary, treat it as two words.

▶ The prosecutor chose not to cross‑examine any witnesses.
                                            ^

▶ Grandma kept a small note͡book in her apron pocket.

▶ Alice walked through the looking/glass into a backward

    world.

S2-b Use a hyphen to connect two or more words functioning together as an adjective before a noun.

▶ Mrs. Douglas gave Mary a seashell and some newspaper-wrapped
    ⌄
    fish to take home to her mother.

▶ Priscilla Hood is not yet a well-known candidate.
    ⌄
    Newspaper-wrapped and *well-known* are adjectives used before the
    nouns *fish* and *candidate*.

Generally, do not use a hyphen when such compounds follow the
noun.

▶ After our television campaign, Priscilla Hood will be well/known.

Do not use a hyphen to connect *-ly* adverbs to the words they
modify.

▶ A slowly/moving truck tied up traffic.

NOTE: In a series, hyphens are suspended.

    Do you prefer first-, second-, or third-class tickets?

S2-c Hyphenate the written form of fractions and of compound numbers from twenty-one to ninety-nine.

▶ One-fourth of my salary goes toward state and federal income
    ⌄
    taxes.

S2-d   Use a hyphen with the prefixes *all-*, *ex-*, and *self-* and with the suffix *-elect*.

▶   The charity is funneling more money into self-help projects.
                                                        ^

▶   Carmen is our club's president-elect.
                                  ^

S2-e   A hyphen is used in some words to avoid ambiguity or to separate awkward double or triple letters.

Without the hyphen there would be no way to distinguish between words such as *re-creation* and *recreation*.

> Bicycling in the country is my favorite recreation.

> The film was praised for its astonishing re-creation of nineteenth-century London.

Hyphens are sometimes used to separate awkward double or triple letters in compound words (*anti-intellectual, cross-stitch*). Check a dictionary for the standard form of the word.

S2-f   If a word must be divided at the end of a line, divide it correctly.

Divide words between syllables; never divide a one-syllable word.

▶   When I returned from my travels overseas, I didn't ~~reco-~~ *recog-*
nize
~~gnize~~ one face on the magazine covers.
                                                    ^

▶   Grandfather didn't have the courage or the ~~stren-~~
strength
~~gth~~ to open the door.
^

Never divide a word so that a single letter stands alone at the end of a line or fewer than three letters begin a line.

▶ She'll bring her brother with her when she comes ~~a-~~
again.
~~gain.~~
^

▶ As audience to *The Mousetrap,* Hamlet is a ~~watch-~~
watcher
~~er~~ watching watchers.
^

When dividing a compound word at the end of a line, either make the break between the words that form the compound or put the whole word on the next line.

▶ My niece Monica is determined to become a long-~~dis-~~
distance
~~tance~~ runner when she grows up.
^

To divide a long Internet address at the end of a line, do not use a hyphen (because a hyphen could appear to be part of the address). If the address is mentioned in the text of your paper, break it at some convenient point, such as after a slash or before a period.

The Berkeley Digital Library SunSITE can be reached at <http:// sunsite.berkeley.edu>.

If the address appears in an MLA works cited entry, you must break it after a slash. See page 339.

S3

Capitalization

In addition to the following rules, a good dictionary can often tell you when to use capital letters.

GRAMMAR CHECKERS remind you that sentences should begin with capital letters and that some words, such as *Cherokee,* are proper nouns. Many words, however, should be capitalized only in certain contexts, and you must determine when to do so.

S3-a   Capitalize proper nouns and words derived from them; do not capitalize common nouns.

Proper nouns are the names of specific persons, places, and things. All other nouns are common nouns. The following types of words are usually capitalized: names for the deity, religions, religious followers, sacred books; words of family relationship used as names; particular places; nationalities and their languages, races, tribes; educational institutions, departments, degrees, particular courses; government departments, organizations, political parties; historical movements, periods, events, documents; specific electronic sources; and trade names.

PROPER NOUNS	COMMON NOUNS
God (used as a name)	a god
Book of Jeremiah	a book
Uncle Pedro	my uncle
Father (used as a name)	my father
Lake Superior	a picturesque lake
the Capital Center	a center for advanced studies
the South	a southern state
Japan, a Japanese garden	an ornamental garden
University of Wisconsin	a good university
Geology 101	geology
Environmental Protection Agency	a federal agency
Phi Kappa Psi	a fraternity
the Democratic Party	a political party
the Enlightenment	the eighteenth century
Great Depression	a recession
the Declaration of Independence	a treaty
the World Wide Web, the Web	a home page
the Internet, the Net	a computer network
Kleenex	a tissue

Months, holidays, and days of the week are treated as proper nouns; the seasons and numbers of the days of the month are not.

Our town fair begins on the first Friday in June, right after Memorial Day.

My mother's birthday is in early spring, on the fifth of April.

Names of school subjects are capitalized only if they are names of languages. Names of particular courses are capitalized.

> This semester Austin is taking math, geography, geology, French, and English.

> Professor Anderson offers Modern American Fiction 501 to graduate students.

CAUTION: Do not capitalize common nouns to make them seem important. *Our company is currently hiring computer programmers* [not *Company, Computer Programmers*].

S3-b Capitalize titles of persons when used as part of a proper name but usually not when used alone.

> Prof. Margaret Barnes; Dr. Harold Stevens; John Scott Williams, Jr.; Anne Tilton, LL.D.

> District Attorney Marshall was reprimanded for badgering the witness.

> The district attorney was elected for a two-year term.

Usage varies when the title of an important public figure is used alone. *The president* [or *President*] *vetoed the bill.*

S3-c Capitalize the first, last, and all major words in titles and subtitles of works such as books, articles, and songs.

In both titles and subtitles, major words—nouns, verbs, adjectives, and adverbs—should be capitalized. Minor words—articles, prepositions, and coordinating conjunctions—are not capitalized unless they are the first or last word of a title or subtitle. Capitalize the second part of a hyphenated term in a title if it is a major word but not if it is a minor word.

> *The Impossible Theater: A Manifesto*
> *The F-Plan Diet*
> "Fire and Ice"
> "I Want to Hold Your Hand"
> *The Canadian Green Page*

Capitalize chapter titles and the titles of other major divisions of a work following the same guidelines used for titles of complete works.

"Work and Play" in Santayana's *The Nature of Beauty*

"Size Matters" on the Web site *Discovery Channel Online*

S3-d Capitalize the first word of a sentence.

Obviously the first word of a sentence should be capitalized.

When lightning struck the house, the roof and the chimney collapsed.

When a sentence appears within parentheses, capitalize its first word unless the parentheses appear within another sentence.

Early detection of breast cancer significantly increases survival rates. (See table 2.)

Early detection of breast cancer significantly increases survival rates (see table 2).

S3-e Capitalize the first word of a quoted sentence but not a quoted phrase.

In *Time* magazine Robert Hughes writes, "There are only about sixty Watteau paintings on whose authenticity all experts agree."

Russell Baker has written that in our country sports are "the opiate of the masses."

If a quoted sentence is interrupted by explanatory words, do not capitalize the first word after the interruption.

"When we all think alike," he said, "no one is thinking."

When quoting poetry, copy the poet's capitalization exactly. Many poets capitalize the first word of every line of poetry; a few contemporary poets dismiss capitalization altogether.

When I consider everything that grows
Holds in perfection but a little moment —Shakespeare

it was the week   that
i felt the city's narrow breezes rush about
me   —Don L. Lee

S3-f Do not capitalize the first word after a colon unless it begins an independent clause, in which case capitalization is optional.

Most bar patrons can be divided into two groups: the occasional after-work socializers and the nothing-to-go-home-to regulars.

This we are forced to conclude: The [*or* the] federal government is needed to protect the rights of minorities.

S3-g Capitalize abbreviations for departments and agencies of government, other organizations, and corporations; capitalize the call letters of radio and television stations.

EPA, FBI, OPEC, IBM, WCRB, KNBC-TV

S4

Abbreviations

GRAMMAR CHECKERS can flag a few inappropriate abbreviations, such as *Xmas* and *e.g.*, but do not assume that a program will catch all problems with abbreviations.

S4-a Use standard abbreviations for titles immediately before and after proper names.

TITLES BEFORE PROPER NAMES	TITLES AFTER PROPER NAMES
Mr. Raphael Zabala	William Albert, Sr.
Ms. Nancy Linohan	Thomas Hines, Jr.
Mrs. Edward Horn	Anita Lor, Ph.D.
Dr. Margaret Simmons	Robert Simkowski, M.D.

TITLES BEFORE PROPER NAMES	TITLES AFTER PROPER NAMES
Rev. John Stone	William Lyons, M.A.
St. Joan of Arc	Margaret Chin, LL.D.
Prof. James Russo	Polly Stein, D.D.S.

Do not abbreviate a title if it is not used with a proper name.

▶ My history ~~prof.~~ was a specialist on America's use of the atomic

professor

⌃

bomb in World War II.

Avoid redundant titles such as *Dr. Susan Hassel, M.D.* Choose one title or the other: *Dr. Susan Hassel* or *Susan Hassel, M.D.*

S4-b Use abbreviations only when you are sure your readers will understand them.

Familiar abbreviations, often written without periods, are acceptable.

CIA, FBI, AFL-CIO, NAACP, IBM, UPI, CBS, USA (or U.S.A.), IOU, CD-ROM, ESL

The YMCA has opened a new gym close to my office.

NOTE: When using an unfamiliar abbreviation (such as CBE for Council of Biology Editors) throughout a document, write the full name followed by the abbreviation in parentheses at the first mention of the name. You may use the abbreviation alone from then on.

S4-c Use B.C., A.D., A.M., P.M., No., and $ only with specific dates, times, numbers, and amounts.

The abbreviation B.C. ("before Christ") follows a date, and A.D. (*"anno Domini"*) precedes a date. Alternatives are B.C.E. ("before the common era") and C.E. ("common era"), which follow dates.

40 B.C. (or 40 B.C.E.)	4:00 A.M. (or a.m.)	No. 12 (or no. 12)
A.D. 44 (or 44 C.E.)	6:00 P.M. (or p.m.)	$150

Avoid using A.M., P.M., No., or $ when not accompanied by a figure.

▶ We set off for the lake early in the ~~A.M.~~

morning.

⌃

S4-d   Be sparing in your use of Latin abbreviations.

Latin abbreviations are appropriate in bibliographic citations and in informal writing.

> cf. (Latin *confer,* "compare")
> e.g. (Latin *exempli gratia,* "for example")
> et al. (Latin *et alii,* "and others")
> etc. (Latin *et cetera,* "and so forth")
> i.e. (Latin *id est,* "that is")
> N.B. (Latin *nota bene,* "note well")
> P.S. (Latin *postscriptum,* "postscript")

> Alfred Hitchcock directed many classic thrillers (e.g., *Psycho, Rear Window,* and *Vertigo*).

> Harold Simms et al., *The Race for Space*

In formal writing use the appropriate English phrases.

▶ Many obsolete laws remain on the books, ~~e.g.,~~ *for example,* a law in Vermont

forbidding an unmarried man and woman to sit less than six

inches apart on a park bench.

S4-e   Avoid inappropriate abbreviations.

In formal writing, abbreviations for the following are not commonly accepted: personal names, units of measurement, days of the week, holidays, months, courses of study, divisions of written works, states and countries (except in addresses and except Washington, D.C.).

In company names, use abbreviated forms such as *Co., Inc.,* and *&* if they are part of the official name: *Temps & Co., Bogart Inc.* Do not abbreviate such forms if they are not part of the official name: *Dunn Photographic Associates* (not *Dunn Photo. Assoc.*). When in doubt about a company's official name, consult a business card, company letterhead stationery, or the yellow pages.

PERSONAL NAME   Charles (*not* Chas.)

UNITS OF MEASUREMENT   pound (*not* lb.)

DAYS OF THE WEEK   Monday (*not* Mon.)

HOLIDAYS Christmas (*not* Xmas)

MONTHS March (*not* Mar.)

COURSES OF STUDY political science (*not* poli. sci.)

DIVISIONS OF WRITTEN WORKS chapter, page (*not* ch., p.)

STATES AND COUNTRIES Massachusetts (*not* MA or Mass.)

PARTS OF A BUSINESS NAME Adams Lighting Company (*not* Adams Lighting Co.); Kim and Brothers, Inc. (*not* Kim and Bros., Inc.)

▶ Eliza promised to buy me one ~~lb.~~ of Godiva chocolate for my
                                      pound
               Friday.
   birthday, which was last ~~Fri.~~

S5

Numbers

> **GRAMMAR CHECKERS** can tell you to spell out certain numbers, such as *thirty-three* and numbers that begin a sentence, but they won't help you understand when it is acceptable to use figures.

S5-a Spell out numbers of one or two words or those that begin a sentence. Use figures for numbers that require more than two words to spell out.

           eight
▶ Now, some ~~8~~ years later, Muffin is still with us.

         176
▶ I counted ~~one hundred seventy-six~~ CD's on the shelves next to the

   fireplace.

If a sentence begins with a number, spell out the number or rewrite the sentence.

One hundred fifty
▶ ~~150~~ children in our program need expensive dental treatment.
   ^

Rewriting the sentence may be less awkward if the number is long: *In our program 150 children need expensive dental treatment.*

EXCEPTIONS: In technical and some business writing, figures are preferred even when spellings would be brief, but usage varies.

When several numbers appear in the same passage, many writers choose consistency rather than strict adherence to the rule.

When one number immediately follows another, spell out one and use figures for the other: *three 100-meter events, 60 four-poster beds.*

S5-b Generally, figures are acceptable for dates, addresses, percentages, fractions, decimals, scores, statistics and other numerical results, exact amounts of money, divisions of books and plays, pages, identification numbers, and the time.

DATES   July 4, 1776, 56 B.C., A.D. 30

ADDRESSES   77 Latches Lane, 519 West 42nd Street

PERCENTAGES   55 percent (or 55%)

FRACTIONS, DECIMALS   ½, 0.047

SCORES   7 to 3, 21–18

STATISTICS   average age 37, average weight 180

SURVEYS   4 out of 5

EXACT AMOUNTS OF MONEY $105.37, $106,000, $0.05

DIVISIONS OF BOOKS   volume 3, chapter 4, page 189

DIVISIONS OF PLAYS   act III, scene iii (*or* act 3, scene 3)

IDENTIFICATION NUMBERS   serial number 10988675

TIME OF DAY   4:00 P.M., 1:30 A.M.

$255,000
▶ Several doctors put up ~~two hundred fifty-five thousand dollars~~ for
   ^
the construction of a golf course.

NOTE: When not using A.M. or P.M., write out the time in words (*four o'clock in the afternoon, twelve noon, seven in the morning*).

S6

Italics (underlining)

Italics, a slanting typeface used in printed material, can be produced by most word processing programs. In handwritten or typed papers, this typeface is indicated by underlining. Some instructors prefer underlining even if their students can produce italics.

NOTE: Many e-mail systems do not allow for italics or underlining. In e-mail, you can indicate italics by preceding and ending the term with underscore marks or asterisks. Punctuation should follow the coding.

```
I am planning to write my senior thesis on _Anna
Karenina_.
```

In less formal e-mail messages, normally italicized words aren't marked at all.

```
I finally finished reading Anna Karenina--what a
masterpiece!
```

 GRAMMAR CHECKERS do not flag problems with italics or underlining. (For a general discussion of what grammar checkers can and cannot do, see pp. 20–21.)

S6-a   Underline or italicize the titles of works according to convention.

Titles of the following kinds of works should be underlined or italicized:

TITLES OF BOOKS   *The Great Gatsby, A Distant Mirror*

MAGAZINES   *Time, Scientific American*

NEWSPAPERS   the *St. Louis Post-Dispatch*

PAMPHLETS   *Common Sense, Facts about Marijuana*

LONG POEMS   *The Waste Land, Paradise Lost*

PLAYS   *King Lear, A Raisin in the Sun*

FILMS   *Casablanca, Independence Day*

TELEVISION PROGRAMS   *Friends, 60 Minutes*

RADIO PROGRAMS   *All Things Considered*

MUSICAL COMPOSITIONS   Gershwin's *Porgy and Bess*

CHOREOGRAPHIC WORKS   Twyla Tharp's *Brief Fling*

WORKS OF VISUAL ART   Rodin's *The Thinker*

COMIC STRIPS   *Dilbert*

SOFTWARE   *WordPerfect*

WEB SITES   *Barron's Online, ESPNET SportsZone*

The titles of other works, such as short stories, essays, songs, and short poems, are enclosed in quotation marks. (See P6-d.)

NOTE: Do not use underlining or italics when referring to the Bible, titles of books in the Bible (Genesis, not *Genesis*), or titles of legal documents (the Constitution, not the *Constitution*). Do not underline the title of your own paper.

S6-b   Underline or italicize the names of spacecraft, aircraft, ships, and trains.

Challenger, Spirit of St. Louis, Queen Elizabeth II, Silver Streak

▶ The success of the Soviet's <u>Sputnik</u> galvanized the U.S. space

program.

S6-c   Underline or italicize foreign words in an English sentence.

▶ Although Joe's method seemed to be successful, I decided to

establish my own <u>modus operandi</u>.

EXCEPTION: Do not underline or italicize foreign words that have become part of the English language — "laissez-faire," "fait accompli," "habeas corpus," and "per diem," for example.

S6-d Underline or italicize words, letters, and numbers mentioned as themselves.

▶ Tim assured us that the howling probably came from his bloodhound, Hill Billy, but his <u>probably</u> stuck in our minds.

▶ Sarah called her father by his given name, Johnny, but she was unable to pronounce the <u>J</u>.

▶ A big <u>3</u> was painted on the door.

NOTE: Quotation marks may be used instead of underlining to set off words mentioned as words. (See P6-e.)

S6-e Avoid excessive underlining or italics for emphasis.

Frequent underlining to emphasize words or ideas is distracting and should be used sparingly.

▶ Snowboarding is a sport that has become an addiction.

D

Document Design

D

Document Design

The term *document* is broad enough to describe anything you might write in an English class, in other classes across the curriculum, in the business world, and in everyday life. How a document is designed (formatted on the page) can affect how it is received.

Instructors have certain expectations about how a college paper should look (see D2). Employers too expect documents such as business letters and memos to be formatted in standard ways (see D3). Even peers who read your e-mail and World Wide Web pages will appreciate an effective document design (see D4).

D1

Principles of document design

Good document design promotes readability, but what this means depends on your purpose and audience and perhaps on other elements of your writing situation, such as your subject and any length restrictions. (See the checklist on pp. 4–5.) All of your design choices — word processing options and use of headings, displayed lists, and other visuals — should be made in light of your specific writing situation.

D1-a   Select appropriate format options.

Word processing programs present you with abundant format options. Before you begin typing, you should make sure that your margins, line spacing, and justification are set appropriately. If a number of fonts (typeface styles and sizes) are available, you should also determine which is most appropriate for your purposes.

Margins, line spacing, and justification

For documents printed on 8½″ × 11″ paper, you should leave a margin of between one and one and a half inches on all sides of the page. These margins prevent the text from looking too crowded, and they allow room for annotations, such as an instructor's comments or an editor's suggestions.

Most manuscripts in progress are double-spaced to allow room for editing. Final copy is often double-spaced as well, since single-spacing is less inviting to read. But at times the advantages of double-spacing are offset by other considerations. In a business memo, for example, you may single-space to fit the memo on one easily scanned page. And in a technical report, you might single-space to save paper, for both ecological and financial reasons.

Word processing programs usually give you a choice between a justified and an unjustified (ragged) right margin. When the text is justified, all of the words line up against the right margin, as they do on a typeset page like the one you are now reading. Unfortunately, text that has been justified on a word processor can be hard to read. The problem is that extra space is added between words in some lines, creating "rivers" of white that can be quite distracting. In addition, right-justified margins may create a need for excessive hyphenation at the ends of lines. Unless you have the technology to create the real look of a typeset page, you should turn off the justification feature.

Fonts

If you have a choice of fonts, you should select a normal size (10 to 12 points) and a style that is not too offbeat. Although unusual styles of type, such as those that look handwritten, may seem attractive, they slow readers down. We all read more efficiently when a text meets our usual expectations.

CAUTION: Never write a college essay or any other document in all capital letters. Research shows that readers experience much frustration when they are forced to read more than a few words in a row printed in all capital letters.

D1-b Consider using headings.

There is little need for headings in short essays, especially if the writer uses paragraphing and clear topic sentences to guide readers. In more complex documents, however, such as research papers, grant proposals, business reports, and even Web-based documents, headings can be a useful visual cue for readers.

Headings help readers see at a glance the organization of a document. If more than one level of heading is used, the headings also indicate the hierarchy of ideas—as they do in this book.

Headings serve a number of functions, depending on the needs of different readers. When readers are simply looking up information, headings will help them find it quickly. When readers are scanning, hoping to pick up the gist of things, headings will guide them. Even when readers are committed enough to read every word, headings can help. Efficient readers preview a document before they begin reading; when previewing and while reading, they are guided by any visual cues the writer provides.

CAUTION: Avoid using more headings (or more levels of headings) than you really need. Excessive use of headings can make a text choppy.

Phrasing headings

Headings should be as brief and as informative as possible. Certain styles of headings—the most common being -*ing* phrases, noun phrases, questions, and imperative sentences—work better for some purposes, audiences, and subjects than others.

Whatever style you choose, use it consistently for headings on the same level. In other words, headings on the same level of organization should be written in parallel structure (see E1), as in the following examples. The first set of headings appeared in a report written for an environmental think tank, the second in a history textbook, the third in a mutual fund brochure, and the fourth in a garden designer's newsletter.

-*ING* HEADINGS
Safeguarding the earth's atmosphere
Charting the path to sustainable energy
Conserving global forests
Triggering the technological revolution
Strengthening international institutions

NOUN PHRASE HEADINGS
The economics of slavery
The sociology of slavery
Psychological effects of slavery

QUESTIONS AS HEADINGS
How do I buy shares?
How do I redeem shares?
What is the history of the fund's performance?
What are the tax consequences of investing in the fund?

IMPERATIVE SENTENCES AS HEADINGS
Fertilize roses in the fall.
Feed them again in the spring.
Prune roses when dormant and after flowering.
Spray roses during their growing season.

Placing and highlighting headings

Headings on the same level of organization should be placed and highlighted in a consistent way. For example, you might center your first-level headings and print them in boldface; then you might place the second-level headings flush left (against the left margin) and underline them, like this:

First-level heading

Second-level heading

Headings are usually centered or placed flush left, but at times you might decide to indent them five spaces from the left margin, like a paragraph indent. Or in a business document, you might choose to place headings in a column to the left of the text.

To highlight headings, consider using boldface, italics, all capital letters, color, larger or smaller typeface than the text, a different font, or some combination of these:

boldface	color
italics	larger typeface
underlining	smaller typeface
ALL CAPITAL LETTERS	different font

On the whole, it is best to use restraint. Excessive highlighting results in a page that looks too busy, and it defeats its own purpose, since readers need to see which headings are more important than others.

Important headings can be highlighted by using a fair amount of white space around them. Less important headings can be downplayed by using less white space or even by running them in with the text.

D1-c Consider using displayed lists.

Lists are easy to read or scan when they are displayed, rather than run into your text. You might reasonably choose to display the following kinds of lists:

— steps in a process

— materials needed for a project

— parts of an object

—advice or recommendations

—items to be discussed

—criteria for evaluation (as in checklists)

Displayed lists should usually be introduced with an independent clause followed by a colon (see P4-a and the preceding list). Periods are not used after items in a list unless the items are sentences.

Lists are most readable when they are presented in parallel grammatical form (see E1). In the sample list, for instance, the items are all noun phrases. As with headings, some kinds of lists might be more appropriately presented as *-ing* phrases, as imperative sentences, or as questions.

To draw the reader's eye to a list, consider using bullets (circles or squares) or dashes. If there is some reason to number the items, use an arabic number followed by a period for each item.

Although displayed lists can be a useful visual cue, they should not be overdone. Too many of them will give a document a choppy, cluttered look. And lists that are very long (sometimes called "laundry lists") should be avoided as well. Readers can hold only so many ideas in their short-term memory, so if a list grows too long, you should find some way of making it more concise or clustering similar items.

D1-d   Consider adding visuals.

Visuals such as charts, graphs, tables, diagrams, maps, and photographs convey information concisely and vividly. In a student essay not intended for publication, you can use another person's visuals as long as you credit the borrowing (see R5-a and R5-b). And with access to computer graphics, you can create your own visuals to enhance an essay or a report.

This section suggests when charts, graphs, tables, and diagrams might be appropriate for your purposes. It also discusses where you might place such visuals.

Using charts, graphs, tables, and diagrams

In documents that help readers follow a process or make a decision, flow charts can be useful; for an example, see page 212 of this book. Pie charts are appropriate for indicating ratios or apportionment, as in the following example.

PIE CHART

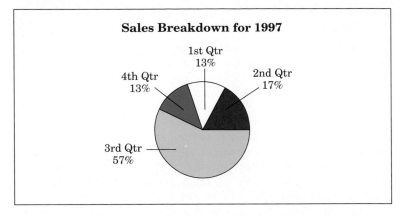

Sales Breakdown for 1997

1st Qtr 13%

2nd Qtr 17%

4th Qtr 13%

3rd Qtr 57%

Line graphs and bar graphs illustrate disparities in numerical data. Line graphs are appropriate when you want to illuminate trends over a period of time, such as trends in sales, in unemployment, or in population growth. Bar graphs can be used for the same purpose. In addition, bar graphs are useful for highlighting comparisons, such as vote totals for rival political candidates or the number of refugees entering the United States during different time periods.

Tables are not as visually interesting as line graphs or charts, but they allow for inclusion of specific numerical data, such as exact percentages. The following table presents the responses of students and faculty to one question on a campus-wide questionnaire.

TABLE

Is American education based too much on European history and values?

	PERCENT		
	NO	UNDECIDED	YES
Nonwhite students	21	25	54
White students	55	29	16
Nonwhite faculty	16	19	65
White faculty	57	27	16

LINE GRAPH

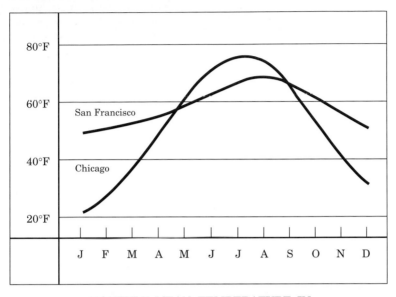

MONTHLY MEAN TEMPERATURE IN SAN FRANCISCO AND CHICAGO

BAR GRAPH

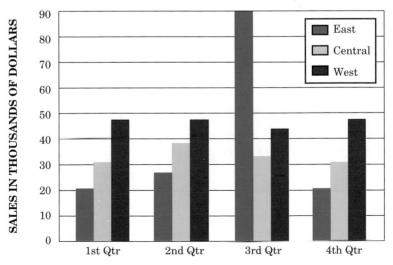

SALES BREAKDOWN BY REGION, 1997

Diagrams are useful—and sometimes indispensable—in scientific and technical writing. It is more concise, for example, to use the following diagram than it would be to explain the chemical formula in words.

DIAGRAM

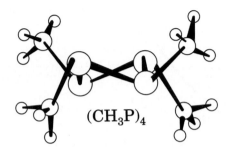

$(CH_3P)_4$

Placing visuals

A visual may be placed in the text of a document, near a discussion to which it relates, or it can be put in an appendix, labeled, and referred to in the text. In much college writing, the convention is to place visuals in an appendix; when in doubt, check with your professor.

Placing visuals in the text of a document can be tricky. Usually you will want the visual to appear close to the sentences that relate to it, but page breaks won't always allow this placement. At times you may need to insert the visual at a later point and tell readers where it can be found or, with the help of software, you may be able to make the text flow around the visual.

In newsletters and in business and technical documents, page layout is both an art and a science. The best way to learn how to lay out pages is to work with colleagues who have had experience solving the many problems that can arise.

NOTE: Guidelines for using visuals vary by academic discipline. In English and humanities classes, follow the MLA (Modern Language Association) guidelines in M4. In social science classes, follow the APA (American Psychological Association) guidelines in A1-c. For other academic disciplines, consult one of the style manuals listed in A3.

D2

Academic manuscript formats

If your instructor provides formal guidelines for formatting an essay—or a more specialized document such as a lab report, a case study, or a research paper—you should of course follow them. Otherwise, use the manuscript format that is standard for the discipline in which you are writing.

In most English and humanities classes, you will be asked to use the MLA (Modern Language Association) format. For MLA manuscript guidelines and a sample paper, see M4. If you have been asked to use APA (American Psychological Association) or *Chicago*-style manuscript guidelines, see A1-c or A2-d.

D3

Business documents

This section provides guidelines for preparing business letters, résumés, and memos. For a more detailed discussion of these and other business documents—proposals, reports, executive summaries, and so on—consult a business writing textbook or take a look at examples currently being written at the organization for which you are writing.

D3-a Business letters

In writing a business letter, be direct, clear, and courteous, but do not hesitate to be firm if necessary. State your purpose or request at the beginning of the letter and include only pertinent information in the body. By being as direct and concise as possible, you show that you value your reader's time.

A sample business letter appears on page 312. This letter is typed in what is known as "block" style. The return address at the top and the close and signature at the bottom are lined up just to the right of the center of the width of the page. The inside address,

BUSINESS LETTER IN BLOCK FORM

Return
address ———————

121 Knox Road, #6
College Park, MD 20740
March 4, 1998

Linda Hennessee, Managing Editor
World Discovery
1650 K Street, NW
Washington, DC 20036

Inside
address

Dear Ms. Hennessee: ——— Salutation

Please accept my application for the summer editorial internship listed with
the Career Development Center at the University of Maryland. Currently I
am a junior at the University of Maryland, with a double major in English
and Latin American studies.

Over the past three years I have gained considerable experience in newspaper and magazine journalism, as you will see on my enclosed résumé. I am
familiar with the basic procedures of editing and photographic development, but my primary interests lie in feature writing and landscape photography. My professional goal is to work as a photojournalist with an international focus, preferably for a major magazine. I cannot imagine a better introduction to that career than a summer at *World Discovery.*

I am available for an interview almost any time and can be reached at
301-555-2651. My e-mail address is jrichard@umdcp.edu.

I look forward to hearing from you.

Body

Close ——— Sincerely,

Signature ——— *Jeffrey Richardson*

Jeffrey Richardson

Enc.

the salutation, and the body of the letter are flush left (against the
left margin). The paragraphs are not indented.

If you choose to indent your paragraphs, you are using "semi-
block" style, which is considered less formal. If you choose to move
all elements of the letter flush left, you are using the most formal

style, "full block." This style is usually preferred when the letter is typed on letterhead stationery that gives the return address of the writer or the writer's company.

When writing to a woman, use the abbreviation *Ms.* in the salutation unless you know that the woman prefers another form of address. If you are not writing to a particular person, you can use the salutation *Dear Sir or Madam* or you can address the company itself—*Dear Solar Technology.*

Below the signature, flush left, you may include the abbreviation *Enc.* to indicate that something is being enclosed with the letter or the abbreviation *cc* followed by a colon and the name of someone who is receiving a copy of the letter.

D3-b   Résumés

An effective résumé presents relevant information in a clear and concise form. The trick is to present yourself in the best possible light without going on at length and wasting your reader's time.

A sample résumé appears on page 314. Notice that the writer has used bullets to make his résumé easy to scan. Notice too that he presents his work experience and his educational history in reverse chronological order—to highlight his most recent accomplishments.

When you send your résumé, you should include a letter that tells what position you seek and where you learned about it. The letter should also summarize your education and past experience, relating them to the job you are applying for. End the letter with a suggestion for a meeting, and tell your prospective employer when you will be available.

D3-c   Memos

Business memos (short for *memorandums*) are a form of communication used within a company or an organization. Usually brief and to the point, a memo reports information, makes a request, or recommends an action. The format of a memo, which varies from company to company, is designed for easy distribution, quick reading, and efficient filing.

Most memos display the name of the recipient, the name of the sender, the date, and the subject on separate lines at the top of the

---

Jeffrey Richardson
121 Knox Road, #6
College Park, MD 20740
301–555–2651

OBJECTIVE   To obtain an editorial internship with a magazine

EDUCATION
Fall 1995–   University of Maryland
present   • B.A. expected in June 1999
                       • Double major: English and Latin American studies
                       • GPA: 3.7 (on a 4-point scale)

EXPERIENCE
Fall 1996–   Photo editor, *The Diamondback,* college paper
present   • Shoot and print photographs
                       • Select and lay out photographs and other visuals

Summer   Intern, *The Globe,* Fairfax, Virginia
1997   • Wrote stories about local issues and personalities
                       • Interviewed political candidates
                       • Edited and proofread copy
                       • Contributed photographs
                       • Coedited "The Landscapes of Northern Virginia:
                         A Photoessay"

Summers   Tutor, Fairfax County ESL Program
1995   • Tutored Latino students in English as a Second Language
1996   • Trained new tutors

ACTIVITIES   Photographers' Workshop, Spanish Club

REFERENCES   Available upon request

---

page. Many companies have preprinted forms for memos, and some word processing programs allow you to call up a memo template that prints standard memo lines—"To," "cc" (for others receiving copies of the memo), "From," "Date," and "Subject"—at the top of the page.

Because readers of memos are busy people, you cannot assume that they will read your memo word for word. Therefore the subject

BUSINESS MEMO

Commonwealth Press

MEMORANDUM

February 27, 1998

To: Production, promotion, and editorial assistants

cc: Stephen Chapman

From: Helen Brown

Subject: New computers for staff

We will receive the new personal computers next week for the assistants in production, promotion, and editorial. In preparation, I would like you to take part in a training program and to rearrange your work areas to accommodate the new equipment.

Training Program

A computer consultant will teach in-house workshops on how to use our spreadsheet program. If you have already tried the program, be prepared to discuss any problems
you have encountered.

Workshops will be held in the training room at the following times:

- Production: Monday, March 9, 10:00 a.m. to 2:00 p.m.
- Promotion: Wednesday, March 11, 10:00 a.m. to 2:00 p.m.
- Editorial: Friday, March 13, 10:00 a.m. to 2:00 p.m.

Lunch will be provided. If you cannot attend, please let me know by March 2.

Allocation and Setup

To give everyone access to a computer, we will set up the new computers as follows: two in the assistants' workspace in production; two outside the conference
room for the promotion assistants; and two in the library for the editorial assistants.

Assistants in all three departments should see me before the end of the week to discuss preparation of the spaces for the new equipment.

---

line should describe the subject as clearly and concisely as possible,
and the introductory paragraph should get right to the point. In addition, the body of the memo should be well organized and easy to
scan. To promote scanning, use headings where possible and display any items that deserve special attention by setting them off
from the text. A sample memo with headings and a displayed list
appears on this page.

D4

Electronic documents

D4-a Follow the conventions of e-mail.

Communicating by electronic mail (or e-mail) has many benefits. Unlike conventional "snail" mail messages, e-mail messages are sent and received immediately after they are written—to and from anywhere in the world at any time. And although e-mail can be as quick as a telephone call, it provides a bit more time than conversation allows for framing ideas and thoughtful responses. As with all writing, you should keep your audience and purpose clearly in mind as you draft e-mail. But you should also be aware of the special conventions of this fast-paced form of communication.

Keeping messages brief and direct

Because the purpose of e-mail is to relay and receive information quickly, it is a courtesy to keep each message as brief as possible and to state your point early. Your message may be just one of many that your reader has to wade through. Always fill in the subject line with a clear, concise description of what your message is about (*Dec. 4 meeting agenda* is clearer than *Committee*).

If you are making a request or a recommendation, state it right away, if possible in the first few sentences (*Can you get your report to me by Monday?* or *I think we need two committees to study the impact of the proposed building*). For long, detailed messages that may fill more than two computer screens, consider providing a summary at the beginning, such as the following:

> The study on improving the work environment at DeVincent Company includes five key recommendations:
>
> 1. acquire additional space for the growing customer service division
> 2. improve lighting and reduce background noise in cubicle areas
> 3. add another break room for the third and fourth floors
> 4. purchase coffee machines and water coolers for all break rooms
> 5. move all photocopiers to a designated room

In addition to keeping your message as brief as possible, make your paragraphs relatively short. That way readers can see divisions of key ideas within the limits of a computer screen. If you indicate a new paragraph by inserting a line of white space, a paragraph indent is not necessary.

Maintaining an appropriate tone

It is appropriate for e-mail to be more informal than other types of writing; you may even alienate your reader if your tone sounds too formal. In general, maintain a tone that is friendly and conversational, yet respectful. The first-person (*I*) and second-person (*you*) points of view are standard in e-mail, and contractions are nearly always acceptable.

Though you should always try to keep messages as brief as possible, you can avoid a blunt tone by including an appropriate greeting and closing. You may also want to open with a brief personal note or include a bit of humor when communicating with friends and colleagues.

TOO FORMAL AND BLUNT
Now that the regional conference has concluded, it is my responsibility to assemble the agenda for the 1999 planning meeting. In order to do so in a timely fashion, I need your ideas about issues to cover in the meeting by October 23.

Expressions like *it is my responsibility* and *in order to do so in a timely fashion* make these sentences sound formal and stilted, and the lack of a greeting and closing give them a cold, blunt tone.

REVISED
Dear Carolyn,

I enjoyed seeing you and the other members of the steering committee at the regional conference. Now that I'm back in the office, I need to start putting together the agenda for our 1999 planning meeting. If you have any preliminary thoughts about issues to cover, could you please e-mail them to me by October 23? Thanks, Carolyn. I look forward to hearing from you.

Best,
Ada

As with all forms of writing, your tone in e-mail should suit your subject and audience. In business and academic contexts or in

E-MAIL MESSAGE

Return-Path: <dportes@umass-boston.edu>
Date: Fri, 21 Nov 1997 22:31:45-0500
To: rdayson@newhoriz.org
From: Danielle Portes <dportes@umass-boston.edu>
Subject: Telephone interview on Dec. 4
cc: Helen Tran <htran@umass-boston.edu>

Dear Ms. Dayson:

Thank you for taking the time to speak with me last week about my research project. As we agreed, I am sending some questions for you to consider before our phone interview on December 4 at 2 p.m.

QUESTIONS ABOUT GUESTS

--What symptoms of stress do guests--both women and their children--show when they first arrive at the shelter?

--What problems, in addition to the abuse itself, must guests deal with (for example, lack of support from family or friends, financial concerns, problems in dealing with police and courts)?

--Can you think of any past or current guests who might agree to an interview?

QUESTIONS ABOUT STAFFERS

--What are the main stresses that staffers face? How do they cope with these stresses?

--What do staffers see as the rewards as well as the drawbacks of the job?

--On average, how many guests does each staffer work with every day? every week?

--Can you think of any past or current staffers who might agree to an interview?

I appreciate your considering these questions and look forward to our interview.

Sincerely,
Danielle Portes
Phone: 617-555-7777

---

writing to someone you don't know well, you will probably want to use a more formal tone than you would when, say, making social plans with friends. Regardless of your subject and audience, you should always avoid harsh or flippant language in e-mail.

NOTE: Some e-mailers use emoticons (combinations of symbols that look like faces turned sideways) and acronyms such as *TIA* for "thanks in advance"). Though you may be tempted to use these shortcuts, it is usually better to convey your tone and meaning through words, especially in business and academic contexts. Readers who are unfamiliar with emoticons and e-mail abbreviations may be confused by them, and even readers who understand these shortcuts may be annoyed by them.

Following e-mail etiquette

E-mail, like other forms of communication, has its own etiquette, which varies slightly depending on your purpose and audience. Essentially, when writing and responding to others, you should take care to be prompt, clear, and courteous. Here are some principles to keep in mind:

—Check your e-mail frequently and respond to messages promptly.

—Fill in subject lines to help readers sort through their messages and set priorities.

—Include a brief greeting (such as *Hi, Gloria* or *Dear Professor Hartley*) and a brief closing (such as *Bye for now* or *Sincerely*).

—Avoid writing in all capital letters or all lowercase letters.

—Resist "flaming"—spouting off angry or insulting messages.

—Forward messages from others only when you are certain the original sender would approve.

—Restrict your use of copyrighted materials to short passages, and always name the author, title, and publication source.

Revising e-mail

Although standards for revision are not as high for fast-paced e-mail as for other forms of written communication, resist the temptation to send off a message without reading it first. Check to make sure that your tone is tactful, that your main point is clear and concise, and that your message is relatively free of errors in grammar, punctuation, spelling, and mechanics.

D4-b   Create effective Web sites.

At some point you may be asked to create a World Wide Web site as part of a school or work assignment, or you may decide to build one for your personal use. Although this book can't begin to explain all the technical aspects of creating a Web site, included here are design and organizational hints to help you make the most of this new medium. For more detailed information on creating a Web site, see *Style Guide for Online Hypertext* <http://www.w3.org/pub/WWW/Provider/Style/Introduction.html>, written by Web founder Tim Berners-Lee.

Organizing information

If you have browsed the World Wide Web, you may have noticed that the most effective sites are the simplest ones—those that give you quick and easy access to what you're looking for. The overall organization of a Web site can be found on its home page, which welcomes visitors, introduces them to the site, and gives them an overview of its contents (see the sample on p. 321).

From the home page, visitors navigate via "links," words or visual images that, at the click of the mouse, send them to other pages within the site or to other locations on the Web. In a typical Web site, the home page contains the most general information, and internal pages are more specific.

Before creating a Web site, draft an outline or a map of the information you will present: a home page linked to internal pages, which can in turn be linked to other pages in your site or on the Web. As is true in print documents, important items, such as a company name, should receive more prominence than items of lesser importance, such as a copyright date. To help you weigh the relative importance of material, think about what your readers will most likely be looking for. Why are they visiting your site in the first place? What are they expecting to find?

Breaking up text

Because the Internet is so vast, online surfers move quickly from page to page. Visitors to your page won't have the patience to scroll through long passages of text. To keep your readers' attention, present your material as concisely as possible, and break up text with headings and displayed lists (see pp. 304–07). And, where appropriate, highlight information with visuals such as clip art, photos, or even animation.

Linking to other sites

One of the most useful features of World Wide Web documents is the ability to create links to other Internet locations. You will probably decide to add some links to other sites from your Web page, but use care when doing so. Especially when creating academic or professional Web sites, keep in mind that any links you include should be relevant to your subject.

A link to another site is an implicit endorsement of that site, so you should evaluate potential sites before linking to them. As a courtesy to readers, periodically visit the sites you have links to, remove any links to sites that are outdated or nonfunctioning, and reroute links to sites that have moved.

Testing your site

When you create a Web site, you are publishing a document that represents you or your organization. Therefore, before you upload your new site to the Web, you should be certain that all your links are working and that all your text has been properly coded.

As you would in a print document, use a clear and grammatical writing style, carefully proofread your text, and give proper credit to any material you may have borrowed from other sources.

WEB PAGE

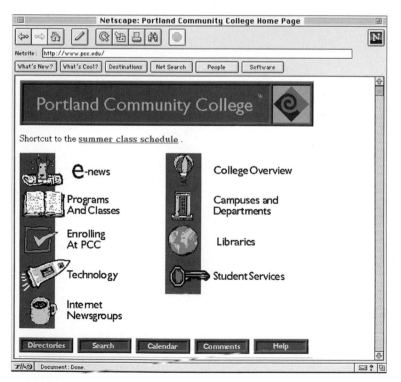

M

MLA
Documentation

M

MLA Documentation

MLA

Directory to MLA in-text citations (M1)

In academic research papers and in any other writing that borrows information from sources, the borrowed information—quotations, summaries, paraphrases, and any facts or ideas that are not common knowledge—must be clearly documented. (See also R5-a.)

The various academic disciplines use their own editorial styles for citing sources and for listing the works that have been cited. The style described in this section is that of the Modern Language Association (MLA), contained in the *MLA Handbook for Writers of Research Papers,* 5th ed. (New York: MLA, 1999), which recommends that citations be given in the text of the paper rather than in footnotes or endnotes.

If your instructor prefers the American Psychological Association (APA) style of in-text citation or the footnote or endnote system of the *Chicago Manual of Style,* flip to Alternative Styles of Documentation. That section also contains a list of style manuals.

M1

MLA in-text citations

MLA in-text citations are made with a combination of signal phrases and parenthetical references. A signal phrase indicates that something taken from a source (such as a quotation, summary, or paraphrase) is about to be used; usually the signal phrase includes the author's name. The parenthetical reference includes at least a page number (unless the work has no page numbers or is organized alphabetically).

Citations in parentheses should be as concise as possible but complete enough so that readers can find the source in the list of works cited at the end of the paper, where works are listed alphabetically by authors' last names. The following models illustrate the form for the MLA style of citation.

1. **AUTHOR NAMED IN A SIGNAL PHRASE** Ordinarily, you should introduce the material being cited with a signal phrase that includes the author's name. In addition to preparing readers for the source, the signal phrase allows you to keep the parenthetical citation brief.

> Turback claims that "regulated sport hunting has never driven any wild species into extinction" (74).

The signal phrase—"Turback claims"—provides the name of the author; the parenthetical citation gives the page number where the quoted words may be found. By looking up the author's last name in the list of works cited, readers will find complete information about the work's title, publisher, and place and date of publication.

Notice that the period follows the parenthetical citation. For the MLA technique for handling quotations that end in a question mark or an exclamation point, see page 271.

2. AUTHOR NOT NAMED IN A SIGNAL PHRASE If the signal phrase does not include the author's name (or if there is no signal phrase), the author's last name must appear in parentheses along with the page number.

> Though the number of lion attacks on humans is low, the
> rate of increase of attacks since the 1960s is cause
> for serious concern (Rychnovsky 43).

Use no punctuation between the name and the page number.

3. TWO OR MORE WORKS BY THE SAME AUTHOR If your list of works cited includes two or more works by the same author, include the title of the work either in the signal phrase or in abbreviated form in the parenthetical reference.

> In his article "California and the West," reporter
> T. Christian Miller asserts that from 1990 to 1997,
> California spent roughly $26 million on conservation
> lands "to provide habitat for exactly 2.6 mountain
> lions" (A3).

> According to T. Christian Miller, "Mountain lions, also
> called pumas or cougars, range vast territories in
> search of food, sometimes as large as 100 square miles"
> ("Cougars" 1).

The title of an article from a periodical should be put in quotation marks, as in the examples. The title of a book should be underlined or italicized.

In the rare case when both the author and a short title must be given in parentheses, the citation should appear as follows:

> The mountain lion population has been encroaching on
> human territory in California since 1972, when voters

passed a law that banned hunting of the animal (Miller, "Cougars" 1).

4. TWO OR THREE AUTHORS If your source has two or three authors, name them in the signal phrase or include them in the parenthetical reference.

Reyes and Messina report that the adult mountain lion population in California is now estimated at four to six thousand (B1).

5. FOUR OR MORE AUTHORS If your source has four or more authors, include only the first author's name followed by "et al." (Latin for "and others") in the signal phrase or in the parenthetical reference.

The study was extended for two years, and only after results were duplicated on both coasts did the authors publish their results (Doe et al. 137).

6. CORPORATE AUTHOR When the author is a corporation or organization, either name the corporate author in the signal phrase or include a shortened version in the parentheses.

The Internal Revenue Service warns businesses that deductions for "lavish and extravagant entertainment" are not allowed (43).

7. UNKNOWN AUTHOR If the author is not given, either use the complete title in a signal phrase or use a short form of the title in the parentheses.

In California, fish and game officials estimate that since 1972 lion numbers have increased from 2,400 to at least 6,000 ("Lion" A21).

8. AUTHORS WITH THE SAME LAST NAME If your list of works cited includes works by two or more authors with the same last name, include the first name of the author you are citing in the signal phrase or parenthetical reference.

At least 66,665 lions were killed between 1907 and 1978 in Canada and the United States (Kevin Hansen 58).

9. A MULTIVOLUME WORK If your paper cites more than one volume of a multivolume work, indicate in the parentheses the volume you are referring to, followed by a colon.

> Terman's studies of gifted children reveal a pattern of
> accelerated language acquisition (2: 279).

If your paper cites only one volume of a multivolume work, you will include the volume number in the list of works cited at the end of the paper and will not need to include it in the parentheses.

10. A NOVEL, A PLAY, OR A POEM In citing literary sources, include information that will enable readers to find the passage in various editions of the work. For a novel, put the page number first and then, if possible, indicate the part or chapter in which the passage can be found.

> Fitzgerald's narrator captures Gatsby in a moment of
> isolation: "A sudden emptiness seemed to flow now from
> the windows and the great doors, endowing with complete
> isolation the figure of the host" (56; ch. 3).

For a verse play, list the act, scene, and line numbers, separated by periods. Use arabic numerals unless your instructor prefers roman numerals.

> In his famous advice to the players, Shakespeare's
> Hamlet defines the purpose of theater, "whose end, both
> at the first and now, was and is, to hold, as 'twere,
> the mirror up to nature" (3.2.21-23).

For a poem, cite the part (if there are a number of parts) and the line numbers, separated by periods.

> When Homer's Odysseus comes to the hall of Circe, he
> finds his men "mild / in her soft spell, fed on her
> drug of evil" (10.209-11).

11. THE BIBLE Include the title, the book of the Bible, and chapter and verse numbers either in the signal phrase or in the parentheses.

> Consider the words of Solomon: "If your enemy be

> hungry, give him food to eat, and if he be thirsty,
> give him to drink" (New American Bible, Prov. 25.21).

12. A WORK IN AN ANTHOLOGY Put the name of the author of the work (not the editor of the anthology) in the signal phrase or in the parentheses.

> At the end of Kate Chopin's "The Story of an Hour,"
> Mrs. Mallard drops dead upon learning that her husband
> is alive. In the final irony of the story, doctors
> report that she has died of a "joy that kills" (25).

13. AN INDIRECT SOURCE When a writer's or speaker's quoted words appear in a source written by someone else, begin the citation with the abbreviation "qtd. in."

> "When lion sightings become common," says Fjelline,
> "trouble often follows" (qtd. in Robinson 30).

14. AN ENTIRE WORK To cite an entire work, use the author's name in a signal phrase or a parenthetical reference. There is of course no need to use a page number.

> Robinson succinctly describes the status of the
> mountain lion controversy in California.

15. TWO OR MORE WORKS To cite more than one source to document a particular point, separate the citations with a semicolon.

> The dangers of mountain lions to humans have been
> well documented (Rychnovsky 40; Seidensticker 114;
> Williams 30).

Multiple citations can be distracting to readers, however, so the technique should not be overused. If you want to alert readers to several sources that discuss a particular topic, consider using an information note instead (discussed in M3).

16. A WORK WITHOUT PAGE NUMBERS You may omit the page number if a work has no page numbers. Some electronic sources use paragraph numbers instead of page numbers. For such sources, use the abbreviation "par." or "pars." in the parentheses: (Smith, par. 4).

17. AN ELECTRONIC SOURCE To cite an electronic source in the text of your paper, follow the same rules as for print sources. If the source has an author and there is a page number, provide both.

> Using historical writings about leprosy as an example,
> Demaitre argues that "the difference between curability
> and treatability is not a modern invention" (29).

Electronic sources often lack page numbers. If the source uses some other numbering system, such as paragraphs or sections, specify them, using an abbreviation ("par.," "sec.") or a full word ("screen"). Otherwise, use no number at all.

> A clip of the film Demolition d'un mur demonstrates
> that "cinema is all about transformation, not mere
> movement" (Routt, sec. 1).

> Volti writes, "As with all significant innovations, the
> history of the automobile shows that technological
> advance is fueled by more than economic calculation."

If the electronic source has no known author, either use the complete title in a signal phrase or use a short form of the title in parentheses.

> According to a Web page sponsored by the Children's
> Defense Fund, fourteen American children die from
> gunfire each day ("Child").

M2

MLA list of works cited

A list of works cited, which appears at the end of your research paper, gives publication information for each of the sources you have cited in the paper. Start on a new page and title your list "Works Cited." Then list in alphabetical order all the sources that you have cited in the paper. Unless your instructor asks for them, do not include sources not actually cited in the paper, even if you read them.

Alphabetize the list by the last names of the authors (or editors); if a work has no author or editor, alphabetize by the first word of the title other than *A, An,* or *The.*

Do not indent the first line of each works cited entry, but indent any additional lines one-half inch (or five spaces). This technique highlights the names by which the list has been alphabetized (see, for example, the list of works cited at the end of the student paper on pp. 359–60).

The following models illustrate the form that the Modern Language Association (MLA) recommends for works cited entries.

Books

1. BASIC FORMAT FOR A BOOK For most books, arrange the information into three units, each followed by a period and one space: (1) the author's name, last name first; (2) the title and subtitle, underlined or italicized; and (3) the place of publication, the publisher, and the date.

Tannen, Deborah. The Argument Culture: Moving from Debate
    to Dialogue. New York: Random, 1998.

The information is taken from the title page of the book and from the reverse side of the title page (the copyright page), not from the outside cover. The complete name of the publisher (in this case Random House) need not be given. You may use a short form as long as it is easily identifiable; omit terms such as *Press, Inc.,* and *Co.* except when naming university presses (Harvard UP, for example). The date to use in your works cited entry is the most recent copyright date.

2. TWO OR THREE AUTHORS Name the authors in the order in which they are presented on the title page; reverse the name of only the first author.

Short, Kathy Gnagey, and Lois Bridges Bird. Literature as
    a Way of Knowing. York, ME: Stenhouse, 1997.

The names of three authors are separated by commas.

Rosenfeld, Louis, Joseph Janes, and Martha Vander Holk.
    The Internet Compendium: Subject Guides to Humanities
    Resources. New York: Neal, 1995.

3. FOUR OR MORE AUTHORS Cite only the first author, name reversed, followed by "et al." (Latin for "and others").

Holloway, Susan D., et al. Through My Own Eyes: Single
  Mothers and the Cultures of Poverty. Cambridge:
  Harvard UP, 1997.

4. EDITORS An entry for an editor is similar to that for an author except that the name is followed by a comma and the abbreviation "ed." for "editor." If there is more than one editor, use the abbreviation "eds." for "editors."

Kitchen, Judith, and Mary Paumier Jones, eds. In Short:
  A Collection of Brief Creative Nonfiction. New York:
  Norton, 1996.

5. AUTHOR WITH AN EDITOR Begin with the author and title, followed by the name of the editor. In this case the abbreviation "Ed." means "Edited by," so it is the same for one or multiple editors.

Wells, Ida B. The Memphis Diary. Ed. Miriam DeCosta-Willis.
  Boston: Beacon, 1995.

6. TRANSLATION List the entry under the name of the author, not the translator. After the title, write "Trans." (for "Translated by") and the name of the translator.

Mahfouz, Naguib. Arabian Nights and Days. Trans. Denys
  Johnson-Davies. New York: Doubleday, 1995.

7. CORPORATE AUTHOR List the entry under the name of the corporate author, even if it is also the name of the publisher.

Bank of Boston. Bank by Remote Control. Boston: Bank of
  Boston, 1997.

8. UNKNOWN AUTHOR Begin with the title. Alphabetize the entry by the first word of the title other than *A, An,* or *The.*

Oxford Essential World Atlas. New York: Oxford UP, 1996.

9. TWO OR MORE WORKS BY THE SAME AUTHOR If your list of works cited includes two or more works by the same author, use the author's name only for the first entry. For subsequent entries use three hyphens followed by a period. The three hyphens must stand for exactly the same name or names as in the preceding entry. List the titles in alphabetical order.

Updike, John. In the Beauty of the Lilies. New York:
    Knopf, 1996.

---. Toward the End of Time. New York: Knopf, 1997.

10. EDITION OTHER THAN THE FIRST If you are citing an edition other than the first, include the number of the edition after the title: 2nd ed., 3rd ed., and so on.

Boyce, David George. The Irish Question and British
    Politics, 1868-1996. 2nd ed. New York: St. Martin's,
    1996.

11. MULTIVOLUME WORK Include the total number of volumes before the city and publisher, using the abbreviation "vols."

Conway, Jill Ker, ed. Written by Herself. 2 vols. New
    York: Random, 1996.

If your paper cites only one of the volumes, give the volume number before the city and publisher and give the total number of volumes in the work after the date.

Conway, Jill Ker, ed. Written by Herself. Vol 2. New York:
    Random, 1996. 2 vols.

12. ENCYCLOPEDIA OR DICTIONARY Articles in well-known dictionaries and encyclopedias are handled in abbreviated form. Simply list the author of the article (if there is one), the title of the article, the title of the reference work, the edition number, if any, and the date of the edition.

"Sonata." Encyclopaedia Britannica. 15th ed. 1997.

Volume and page numbers are not necessary because the entries are arranged alphabetically and therefore are easy to locate.

If a reference work is not well known, provide full publishing information as well.

13. THE BIBLE Give the version of the Bible, underlined; the editor's name (if any); and publication information.

New American Bible. New York: Catholic Book Publishing,

    1970.

14. WORK IN AN ANTHOLOGY Present the information in this order, with each item followed by a period: author of the selection; title of the selection; title of the anthology; editor of the anthology, preceded by "Ed." (meaning "Edited by"); city, publisher, and date; page numbers on which the selection appears.

Malouf, David. "The Kyogle Line." The Oxford Book of

    Travel Stories. Ed. Patricia Craig. Oxford: Oxford

    UP, 1996. 390-96.

If an anthology gives the original publication information for a selection and if your instructor prefers that you use it, cite that information first. Follow with "Rpt. in" (for "Reprinted in"), the title, editor, and publication information for the anthology, and the page numbers in the anthology on which the selection appears.

Rodriguez, Richard. "Late Victorians." Harper's Oct. 1990:

    57-66. Rpt. in The Best American Essays 1991. Ed.

    Joyce Carol Oates. New York: Ticknor, 1991. 119-34.

15. TWO OR MORE WORKS FROM THE SAME ANTHOLOGY If you wish, you may cross-reference two or more works from the same anthology. Provide a separate entry for the anthology with complete publication information.

Craig, Patricia, ed. The Oxford Book of Travel Stories.

    Oxford: Oxford UP, 1996.

Then list each selection separately, giving the author and title of the selection followed by a cross-reference to the anthology. The cross-reference should include the last name of the editor of the anthology and the page numbers in the anthology on which the selection appears.

Desai, Anita. "Scholar and Gypsy." Craig 251-73.

Malouf, David. "The Kyogle Line." Craig 390-96.

16. FOREWORD, INTRODUCTION, PREFACE, OR AFTERWORD If in your paper you quote from one of these elements, begin with the name of the writer of that element. Then identify the element being cited, neither underlined nor in quotation marks, followed by the title of the complete book, the book's author, and the book's editor, if any. After the publication information, give the page numbers on which the foreword, introduction, preface, or afterword appears.

Kennedy, Edward M. Foreword. Make a Difference. By Henry

W. Foster, Jr., and Alice Greenwood. New York:

Scribner, 1997. 9-15.

17. BOOK WITH A TITLE WITHIN ITS TITLE   If the book title contains a title normally underlined (or italicized), neither underline (or italicize) the internal title nor place it in quotation marks.

Vanderham, Paul. James Joyce and Censorship: The Trials

of Ulysses. New York: New York UP, 1997.

If the title within the title is normally enclosed within quotation marks, retain the quotation marks and underline (or italicize) the entire title.

Faulkner, Dewey R. Twentieth Century Interpretations of

"The Pardoner's Tale." Englewood Cliffs: Spectrum-

Prentice, 1973.

18. BOOK IN A SERIES   Before the publication information, cite the series name as it appears on the title page followed by the series number, if any.

Malena, Anne. The Dynamics of Identity in Francophone

Caribbean Narrative. Francophone Cultures and

Literatures Ser. 24. New York: Lang, 1998.

19. REPUBLISHED BOOK   After the title of the book, cite the original publication date followed by the current publication information. If the republished book contains new material, such as an introduction or afterword, include that information after the original date.

McClintock, Walter. Old Indian Trails. 1926. Foreword

William Least Heat Moon. Boston: Houghton, 1992.

20. PUBLISHER'S IMPRINT   If a book was published by an imprint of a publishing company, cite the name of the imprint followed by a hyphen and the publisher's name. The name of the imprint usually precedes the publisher's name on the title page.

Coles, Robert. The Moral Intelligence of Children: How
    to Raise a Moral Child. New York: Plume-Random,
    1997.

Articles in periodicals

21. ARTICLE IN A MONTHLY MAGAZINE In addition to the author, the
title of the article, and the title of the magazine, list the month
and year and the page numbers on which the article appears. Abbreviate the names of months except May, June, and July.

Kaplan, Robert D. "History Moving North." Atlantic Monthly
    Feb. 1997: 21+.

This example uses "21+" because the article did not appear on consecutive pages. For articles appearing on consecutive pages, provide
the range of pages (for example, 50–53).

22. ARTICLE IN A WEEKLY MAGAZINE Handle articles in weekly (or bi-
weekly) magazines as you do those for monthly magazines, but give
the exact date of the issue, not just the month and year.

Pierpont, Claudia Roth. "A Society of One: Zora Neale
    Hurston, American Contrarian." New Yorker 17 Feb.
    1997: 80-86.

23. ARTICLE IN A JOURNAL PAGINATED BY VOLUME Many professional
journals continue page numbers throughout the year instead
of beginning each issue with page 1; at the end of the year, all
of the issues are collected in a volume. Interested readers need
only the volume number, the year, and the page numbers to find
an article.

Cheuse, Alan. "Narrative Painting and Pictorial Fiction."
    Antioch Review 55 (1997): 277-91.

24. ARTICLE IN A JOURNAL PAGINATED BY ISSUE If each issue of the
journal begins with page 1, you need to indicate the number of the
issue. Simply place a period after the volume number and follow it
with the issue number.

Dennis, Carl. "What Is Our Poetry to Make of Ancient
    Myths?" New England Review 18.4 (1997): 128-40.

25. ARTICLE IN A DAILY NEWSPAPER Begin with the author, if there is one, followed by the title of the article. Next give the name of the newspaper, the date, and the page number (including the section letter). Use a plus sign (+) after the page number if the article does not appear on consecutive pages.

Knox, Richard A. "Please Don't Dial and Drive, Study
    Suggests." Boston Globe 13 Feb. 1997: A1+.

If the section is marked with a number rather than a letter, handle the entry as follows:

Wilford, John Noble. "In a Golden Age of Discovery,
    Faraway Worlds Beckon." New York Times 9 Feb. 1997,
    late ed., sec. 1: 1+.

If an edition of the newspaper is specified on the masthead, name the edition after the date and before the page reference: eastern ed., late ed., natl. ed., and so on.

26. UNSIGNED ARTICLE IN A NEWSPAPER OR MAGAZINE Use the same form you would use for an article in a newspaper or a weekly or monthly magazine, but begin with the title of the article.

"Marines Charged in Assault Case." Houston Chronicle
    14 Feb. 1998: 6A.

27. EDITORIAL IN A NEWSPAPER Cite an editorial as you would an unsigned article, adding the word "Editorial" after the title.

"Health Risk on Tap." Editorial. Los Angeles Times
    11 Feb. 1998: B6.

28. LETTER TO THE EDITOR Cite the writer's name, followed by the word "Letter" and the publication information for the newspaper or magazine in which the letter appears.

Peters, Tom. Letter. New Yorker 16 Feb. 1998: 13.

29. BOOK OR FILM REVIEW Cite first the reviewer's name and the title of the review, if any, followed by the words "Rev. of" and the title and author or director of the work reviewed. Add the publication information for the publication in which the review appears.

France, Peter. "His Own Biggest Hero." Rev. of <u>Victor
    Hugo</u>, by Graham Robb. <u>New York Times Book Review</u>
    15 Jan. 1998: 7.

Taubin, Amy. "Year of the Lady." Rev. of <u>The Portrait of
    a Lady</u>, dir. Jane Campion. <u>Village Voice</u> 7 Jan. 1997:
    64.

Electronic sources

The documentation style for electronic sources presented in this
section is consistent with MLA's most recent guidelines, which can
be found at <http://www.mla.org> or in the *MLA Handbook for
Writers of Research Papers* (5th ed., 1999). If your instructor prefers
that you follow the Columbia Online Style developed by Janice
Walker and endorsed by the Alliance for Computers and Writing,
refer to <http://www.cas.usf.edu/english/walker/mla.html>.

NOTE: When an Internet address in a works cited entry must be divided at the end of a line, break it after a slash. Do not insert a
hyphen.

30. ONLINE SCHOLARLY PROJECT OR REFERENCE DATABASE For an online source accessed from within a larger scholarly project or reference database, begin with the author (if any) and title of the source,
followed by any editors or translators. Use quotation marks for
titles of short works such as poems and articles; underline or italicize book and periodical titles. Include publication information for
any print version of the source before giving the title of the online
project or database (underlined or italicized), followed by the author or editor of the project or database; the date of electronic publication (or latest update); page or paragraph numbers (if any); the
name of any institution or organization sponsoring or associated
with the site; the date of access; and the electronic address, or URL,
of the source (in angle brackets).

Dickinson, Emily. "Hope." <u>Poems by Emily Dickinson</u>. 3rd
    ser. Boston, 1896. <u>Project Bartleby Archive</u>. Ed.
    Steven van Leeuwen. Dec. 1995. Columbia U. 2 Feb.
    1998 <http.//www.columbia.edu/acis/bartleby/
    dickinson1.html#3>.

"Gog and Magog." The Encyclopedia Mythica. Ed. Micha F.
   Lindemans. 2 Jan. 1998. 31 Jan. 1998 <http://
   www.pantheon.org/mythica/articles/g/
   gog_and_magog.html>.

To refer to an entire scholarly project, begin with the title of the
project.

The Einstein Papers Project. Ed. Robert Schulmann. 9 Nov.
   1997. Boston U. 29 Jan. 1998 <http://albert.bu.edu>.

31. PERSONAL OR PROFESSIONAL WEB SITE For a citation to a personal
or professional Web site, begin with the creator of the site (if available) and continue with the title of the site (or a description such as
"Home page" if no title is available), the date of publication or of
the latest update, the name of any organization associated with the
site, the date of access, and the URL.

Spanoudis, Steve, Bob Blair, and Nelson Miller. Poets'
   Corner. 2 Feb. 1998. 4 Feb. 1998 <http://
   www.geocities.com/~spanoudi/poems>.

Blue Note Records. 19 Mar. 1998. Blue Note Records. 25
   Mar. 1998 <http://www.bluenote.com>.

32. ONLINE BOOK For citations to books available online, include all
available information required for printed books (see pp. 332–37),
followed by the date of access and the URL.

Brontë, Charlotte. Jane Eyre. 1846. 16 Mar. 1998
   <gopher://gopher.vt.edu:10010/02/50/1>.

If the online book is part of a scholarly project or reference database, follow any information about the printed book with information about the project or database (see p. 339).

Brown, William W. Narrative of William W. Brown, an
   American Slave. Written by Himself. London, 1849.
   Documenting the American South: The Southern
   Experience in Nineteenth-Century America. Ed. Natalia
   Smith. 1996. Academic Affairs Lib., U of North
   Carolina, Chapel Hill. 9 Feb. 1998 <http://
   sunsite.unc.edu/docsouth/brown/brown.html>.

Shelley, Mary. Frankenstein. An Online Library of
    Literature. Ed. Peter Galbavy. 22 Apr. 1998. 23 June
    1998 <http://www.literature.org/Works/Mary-Shelley/
    frankenstein>.

33. ARTICLE IN AN ONLINE PERIODICAL When citing online articles, follow the guidelines for printed articles (see pp. 337–39), giving whatever information is available in the online source. At the end of the citation, include the date of access and the URL.

Baucom, Ian. "Charting the Black Atlantic." Postmodern
    Culture 8.1 (1997): 28 pars. 3 Feb. 1998
    <http://www.iath.virginia.edu/pmc/current.issue/
    baucom.997.html>.

Romano, Jay. "Computers That Tend the Home." New York
    Times on the Web 14 Mar. 1998. 15 Mar. 1998
    <http://www.nytimes.com/library/tech/98/
    03/biztech/articles/15home.html>.

Coontz, Stephanie. "Family Myths, Family Realities."
    Salon 12 Dec. 1997. 3 Feb. 1998 <http://
    www.salonmagazine.com/mwt/feature/1997/12/
    23coontz.html>.

34. WORK FROM AN ONLINE SUBSCRIPTION SERVICE To cite a work from a personal subscription service such as America Online, give the information about the source followed by the name of the service, the date of access, and the keyword used to retrieve the source.

Sleek, Scott. "Blame Your Peers, Not Your Parents, Author
    Says." APA Monitor 29.1 (1998). America Online. 1
    Mar. 1999. Keyword: The Nurture Assumption.

For a source found in an online service accessed at a library, give the information about the source followed by the name of the service, the library, the date of access, and the URL of the service, if known.

Miller, Christian. "Cougars Reported in Tarzana, Woodland
    Hills." <u>Los Angeles Times</u> 25 Nov. 1997: Metro 1.
    Electric Lib. O'Neill Library, Boston College, Chest-
    nut Hill, MA. 12 Mar. 1998 <http://www.elibrary.com>.

35. ONLINE POSTING Begin with the author's name, followed by the title or subject line (in quotation marks), the words "Online posting," the posting date, the list or group name, any identifying number of the posting, the date of access, and the URL or the e-mail address of the list.

Crosby, Connie. "Literary Criticism." Online posting.
    2 Feb. 1996. Café Utne. 17 Mar. 1998
    <http://www.utne.com/motet/bin/
    show?-u4Lsul+it-1a+Literature+12>.

36. E-MAIL For correspondence received via electronic mail, include the author, the subject line (if any) in quotation marks, and the word "E-mail" followed by the recipient and the date of the message.

Schubert, Josephine. "Re: Culture Shock." E-mail to
    the author. 14 Mar. 1998.

37. SYNCHRONOUS COMMUNICATION To cite a synchronous communication posted in a MUD or a MOO, include the speaker's name (if relevant), a description and the date of the event, the title of the forum, the date of access, and the URL. If an archival version of the communication is unavailable, include the telnet address.

Kelley, Heather. Jill's Borderland Tour of DU. 14 Dec.
    1995. Borderlands MOOspace. 16 Mar. 1998 <http://
    www.cyberstation.net/~idd/v2/bordj24.htm>.

38. OTHER ONLINE SOURCES For other materials accessed online, cite them as you would otherwise, including identifying labels where necessary. End the citation with the access date and the URL.

"No More Kings." Animation. <u>America Rock</u>. Schoolhouse
    Rock. ABC. 1975. 16 Mar. 1998 <http://
    genxtvland.simplenet.com/SchoolHouseRock/
    song.hts?hi+kings>.

"City of New Orleans, LA." Map. Yahoo! Maps. Yahoo! 1998.
    4 Feb. 1998 <http://maps.yahoo.com/yahoo>.

39. CD-ROM ISSUED IN A SINGLE EDITION Some works on CD-ROM, such as dictionaries and encyclopedias, are released in single editions that are not updated periodically. Treat such sources as you would a book, but give the medium ("CD-ROM") before the publication information.

Sheehy, Donald, ed. Robert Frost: Poems, Life, Legacy.
    CD-ROM. New York: Holt, 1997.

"Picasso, Pablo." The 1997 Grolier Multimedia
    Encyclopedia. CD-ROM. Danbury: Grolier, 1997.

40. CD-ROM ISSUED PERIODICALLY CD-ROM databases that are produced periodically (monthly or quarterly, for example) may contain previously published material, such as journal or newspaper articles, or material that has not been previously published, such as reports. In either case, cite such material as you would a printed source, followed by the title of the database (underlined or italicized), the medium ("CD-ROM"), the name of the company producing the CD-ROM, and the date of electronic publication.

Bohlen, Celestine. "Albania Struggles to Contain Dissent
    over Lost Investments." New York Times 11 Feb. 1997,
    late ed.: A9. InfoTrac: General Periodicals ASAP.
    CD-ROM. Information Access. 13 Feb. 1997.

Wattenberg, Ruth. "Helping Students in the Middle."
    American Educator 19.4 (1996): 2-18. ERIC. CD-ROM.
    SilverPlatter. Sept. 1996.

Other sources

41. GOVERNMENT PUBLICATION Treat the government agency as the author, giving the name of the government followed by the name of the agency.

United States. Bureau of the Census. Statistical Abstract
    of the United States. 117th ed. Washington: GPO,
    1997.

42. PAMPHLET Cite a pamphlet as you would a book.

United States. Dept. of the Interior. Natl. Park Service.
National Design Competition for an Indian Memorial:
Little Bighorn Battlefield National Monument.
Washington: GPO, 1996.

43. PUBLISHED DISSERTATION Cite a published dissertation as you would a book, underlining (or italicizing) the title and giving the place of publication, the publisher, and the year of publication. After the title, add the word "Diss.," the name of the institution, and the year the dissertation was written.

Damberg, Cheryl L. Healthcare Reform: Distributional
Consequences of an Employer Mandate for Workers in
Small Firms. Diss. Rand Graduate School, 1995. Santa
Monica: Rand, 1996.

44. UNPUBLISHED DISSERTATION Begin with the author's name, followed by the dissertation title in quotation marks, the word "Diss.," the name of the institution, and the year the dissertation was written.

Healey, Catherine. "Joseph Conrad's Impressionism." Diss.
U of Massachusetts, 1997.

45. DISSERTATION ABSTRACT Cite as you would an unpublished dissertation. After the dissertation date, give the abbreviation *DA* or *DAI* (for *Dissertation Abstracts* or *Dissertation Abstracts International*), followed by the volume number, the date of publication, and the page number.

Chun, Maria Bow Jun. "A Study of Multicultural Activities
in Hawaii's Public Schools." Diss. U of Hawaii, 1996.
DAI 57 (1997): 2813A.

46. PUBLISHED PROCEEDINGS OF A CONFERENCE Cite published conference proceedings as you would a book, adding information about the conference after the title.

Chattel, Servant, or Citizen: Women's Status in Church,
State, and Society. Proc. of Irish Conf. of
Historians, 1993, Belfast. Belfast: Inst. of Irish
Studies, 1995.

47. WORK OF ART　Cite the artist's name, followed by the title of the artwork, usually underlined, and the institution and city in which the artwork can be found.

Constable, John. <u>Dedham Vale</u>. Victoria and Albert Museum,

    London.

48. MUSICAL COMPOSITION　Cite the composer's name, followed by the title of the work. Underline the title of an opera, a ballet, or a composition identified by name, but do not underline or use quotation marks around a composition identified by number or form.

Copland, Aaron. <u>Appalachian Spring</u>.

Shostakovich, Dmitri. Quartet no. 1 in C, op. 49.

49. PERSONAL LETTER　To cite a letter you have received, begin with the writer's name and add the phrase "Letter to the author," followed by the date.

Cipriani, Karen. Letter to the author. 25 Apr. 1998.

50. LECTURE OR PUBLIC ADDRESS　Cite the speaker's name, followed by the title of the lecture (if any) in quotation marks, the organization sponsoring the lecture, the location, and the date.

Middleton, Frank. "Louis Hayden and the Role of the

    Underground Railroad in Boston." Boston Public

    Library, Boston. 6 Feb. 1998.

51. PERSONAL INTERVIEW　To cite an interview that you conducted, begin with the name of the person interviewed. Then write "Personal interview," followed by the date of the interview.

Meeker, Dolores. Personal interview. 21 Apr. 1998.

52. PUBLISHED INTERVIEW　Name the person interviewed, followed by the title of the interview, if there is one, in quotation marks and the publication in which the interview was printed. If the interview does not have a title, include the word "Interview" after the interviewee's name.

Renoir, Jean. "Renoir at Home: Interview with Jean

    Renoir." <u>Film Quarterly</u> 50.1 (1996): 2-8.

53. RADIO OR TELEVISION INTERVIEW Name the person interviewed, followed by the word "Interview." Then give the title of the program, underlined (or italicized), and identifying information about the broadcast.

Gates, Henry Louis, Jr. Interview. Charlie Rose. PBS.
    WNET, New York. 13 Feb. 1997.

54. FILM OR VIDEOTAPE Begin with the title. For a film, cite the director and the lead actors or narrator ("Perf." or "Narr."), followed by the distributor and year. For a videotape, add the word "Videocassette" before the name of the distributor.

The English Patient. Dir. Anthony Minghella. Perf. Ralph
    Fiennes, Juliette Binoche, Willem Dafoe, and Kristin
    Scott Thomas. Miramax, 1996.

Jane Eyre. Dir. Robert Young. Perf. Samantha Morton and
    Ciaran Hinds. Videocassette. New Video Group, 1997.

55. RADIO OR TELEVISION PROGRAM List the relevant information about the program in this order: the title of the program, underlined or italicized; the writer ("By"), director ("Dir."), narrator ("Narr."), producer ("Prod."), or main actors ("Perf."), if relevant; the series, neither underlined nor in quotation marks; the network; the local station (if any) on which you heard or saw the program and the city; and the date the program was broadcast. If a television episode or radio segment has a title, place that title, in quotation marks, before the program title.

"The New Face of Africa." The Connection. Host Christopher
    Lydon. Natl. Public Radio. WBUR, Boston. 27 Mar. 1998.

Primates. Wild Discovery. Discovery Channel. Boston.
    23 Mar. 1998.

56. LIVE PERFORMANCE OF A PLAY Begin with the title of the play, followed by the author ("By"). Then include specific information about the live performance: the director ("Dir."), the major actors ("Perf."), the theater company, the theater and its location, and the date of the performance.

Six Characters in Search of an Author. By Luigi
    Pirandello. Dir. Robert Brustein. Perf. Jeremy Geidt,

David Ackroyd, Monica Koskey, and Marianne Owen.

American Repertory Theatre, Cambridge. 14 Jan. 1997.

57. SOUND RECORDING   Begin with the composer (or author, if the recording is spoken), followed by the title of the piece. Next list pertinent artists (such as performers, readers, or musicians) and the orchestra and conductor. End with the manufacturer and the date. If the recording is not on a CD, indicate the medium (such as "Audiocassette") before the manufacturer's name, followed by a period. Do not underline or italicize the name of the medium or enclose it in quotation marks.

Bizet, Georges. <u>Carmen</u>. Perf. Jennifer Larmore, Thomas

    Moser, Angela Gheorghiu, and Samuel Ramey. Bavarian

    State Orch. and Chorus. Cond. Giuseppe Sinopoli.

    Warner, 1996.

58. CARTOON   Begin with the cartoonist's name, the title of the cartoon (if it has one) in quotation marks, the word "Cartoon," and the publication information for the publication in which the cartoon appears.

Adams, Scott. "Dilbert." Cartoon. <u>Editorial Humor</u> 3 Mar.

    1998: 9.

59. MAP OR CHART   Cite a map or chart as you would a book with an unknown author. Underline the title of the map or chart and add the word "Map" or "Chart" following the title.

<u>Winery Guide to Northern and Central California</u>. Map.

    Modesto: Compass Maps, 1996.

M3

MLA information notes

Researchers who use the MLA system of parenthetical documentation (see M1) may also use information notes for one of two purposes:

1. to provide additional material that might interrupt the flow of the paper yet is important enough to include;

2. to refer readers to any sources not discussed in the paper.

Information notes may be either footnotes or endnotes. Footnotes appear at the foot of the page; endnotes appear on a separate page at the end of the paper, just before the list of works cited. For either style, the notes are numbered consecutively throughout the paper. The text of the paper contains a raised arabic numeral that corresponds to the number of the note.

TEXT

California is not alone in its concern about mountain lion attacks.[1]

NOTE

[1] For a discussion of lion attacks in other western states, see Turback 34.

M4

MLA manuscript format

In most English and humanities classes, you will be asked to use the MLA (Modern Language Association) manuscript format. The following guidelines are consistent with advice in the *MLA Handbook for Writers of Research Papers,* 5th ed. (New York: MLA, 1999). For a sample MLA research paper, see M5.

MATERIALS Use good-quality 8½″ × 11″ white paper. If the paper emerges from the printer in a continuous sheet, separate the pages, remove the feeder strips from the sides of the paper, and assemble the pages in order. Secure the pages with a paper clip. Unless your instructor suggests otherwise, do not staple the pages together or use any sort of binder.

TITLE AND IDENTIFICATION Essays written for English and humanities classes do not require a title page unless your instructor requests one. If you are not using a title page, begin the first page against the left margin about one inch from the top of the page.

Type your name, the instructor's name, the course name and number, and the date on separate lines; double-space between lines. Double-space again and center the title of the paper in the width of the page. Capitalize the first and last words of the title and all other words except articles, prepositions, and coordinating conjunctions (see S3-c). Double-space after the title and begin typing the text of the paper. (See p. 351.)

MARGINS, SPACING, AND INDENTATION Leave margins of at least one inch but no more than an inch and a half on all sides of the page.

Double-space lines and indent the first line of each paragraph one-half inch (or five spaces) from the left margin.

For a quotation longer than four typed lines of prose or three lines of verse, indent each line one inch (or ten spaces) from the left margin. Double-space between the body of the paper and the quotation, and double-space between the lines of the quotation. Quotation marks are not needed when a quotation is set off from the text by indenting. See page 355 for an example of an indented quotation; see also P6-b.

PAGINATION Put your last name followed by the page number in the upper right corner of each page, one-half inch below the top edge. (If you have a separate title page, the title page is uncounted and unnumbered.) Use arabic numerals (1, 2, 3, and so on). Do not put a period after the number and do not enclose the number in parentheses.

PUNCTUATION AND TYPING In typing the paper, leave one space after words, commas, semicolons, and colons and between dots in ellipsis marks. MLA allows either one or two spaces after periods, question marks, and exclamation points. To form a dash, type two hyphens with no space between them; do not put a space on either side of the dash.

When an Internet address mentioned in the text of your paper must be divided at the end of a line, do not insert a hyphen (a hyphen could appear to be part of the address). For advice on dividing Internet addresses in your list of works cited, see page 339.

HEADINGS MLA neither encourages nor discourages use of headings and currently provides no guidelines for their use. If you would like to use headings in a long essay or research paper, check first with your instructor. Although headings are not used as frequently in English and the humanities as in other disciplines, the trend seems to be changing.

For a full discussion of headings, including their phrasing and placement, see pages 305–06. For a sample research paper that uses headings see pages 351–60.

VISUALS MLA classifies visuals as tables and figures (figures include graphs, charts, maps, photographs, and drawings). Label each table with an arabic numeral (Table 1, Table 2, and so on) and provide a clear caption that identifies the subject; the label and caption should appear on separate lines above the table. For each figure, a label and a caption are usually placed below the figure, and they need not appear on separate lines. The word "Figure" may be abbreviated to "Fig."

Visuals should be placed in the text, as close as possible to the sentences that relate to them, unless your instructor prefers them in an appendix. See page 353 for a visual included in the text of a paper.

NOTE: See M1 for guidelines on using MLA in-text citations and M2 for preparing an MLA list of works cited.

M5

Sample research paper: MLA style

On the following pages is a research paper written by John Garcia, a student in a composition class. Garcia's paper is documented with the MLA style of in-text citations and list of works cited. Annotations in the margins of the paper draw your attention to features of special interest.

Garcia 1

John Garcia

Professor Hacker

English 101

7 April 1998

Double-spacing used throughout.

The Mountain Lion:

Once Endangered, Now a Danger

Title is centered.

On April 23, 1994, as Barbara Schoener was jogging
in the Sierra foothills of California, she was pounced
on from behind by a mountain lion. After an apparent
struggle with her attacker, Schoener was killed by
bites to her neck and head (Rychnovsky 39). In 1996,
because of Schoener's death and other highly publicized
attacks, California politicians presented voters with
Proposition 197, which contained provisions repealing
much of a 1990 law enacted to protect the lions. The
1990 law outlawed sport hunting of mountain lions and
even prevented the Department of Fish and Game from
thinning the lion population.

Summary: citation with author's name and page number in parentheses.

Proposition 197 was rejected by a large margin,
probably because the debate turned into a struggle between hunting and antihunting factions. When California
politicians revisit the mountain lion question, they
should frame the issue in a new way. A future proposition should retain the ban on sport hunting but allow
the Department of Fish and Game to control the population. Wildlife management would reduce the number of
lion attacks on humans and in the long run would also
protect the lions.

Thesis asserts writer's main point.

The once-endangered mountain lion

Headings help readers follow the organization.

To early Native Americans, mountain lions--also
known as cougars, pumas, and panthers--were objects of
reverence. The European colonists, however, did not
share the Native American view. They conducted what Ted
Williams calls an "all-out war on the species" (29).

Quotation: author named in signal phrase; page number in parentheses.

Garcia 2

The lions were eliminated from the eastern United States except for a small population that remains in the Florida Everglades.

The lions lingered on in the West, but in smaller and smaller numbers. At least 66,665 lions were killed between 1907 and 1978 in Canada and the United States (Hansen 58). As late as 1969, the country's leading authority on the big cat, Maurice Hornocker, estimated the United States population as fewer than 6,500 and probably dropping (Williams 30).

Resurgence of the mountain lion

In western states today, the mountain lion is no longer in danger of extinction. In fact, over the past thirty years, the population has rebounded dramatically. In California, fish and game officials estimate that since 1972 lion numbers have increased from 2,400 to at least 6,000 ("Lion" A21).

Similar increases are occurring outside of California. For instance, for nearly fifty years mountain lions had virtually disappeared from Yellowstone National Park, but today lion sightings are increasingly common. In 1992, Hornocker estimated that at least eighteen adults were living in the park (59). In the United States as a whole, some biologists estimate that there are as many as 50,000 mountain lions, a dramatic increase over the 1969 estimate of 6,500 (Williams 30). For the millions of Americans interested in the preservation of animal species, this is good news, but unfortunately the increase has led to a number of violent encounters between human and lion.

Increasing attacks on humans

There is no doubt that more and more humans are being attacked. A glance at figure 1, a graph of

Statistics documented with citations.

Hornocker introduced as an expert.

Short title given in parentheses because the work has no author.

A clear transition prepares readers for the next section.

Garcia 3

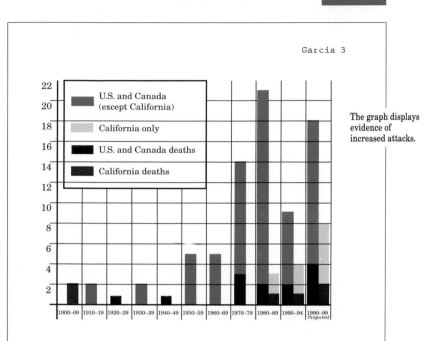

Fig. 1. Cougar attacks--a history, by Paul Beier,
Northern Arizona University; rpt. in Rychnovsky (42).

statistics compiled by mountain lion researcher Paul
Beier, confirms just how dramatically the attacks have
increased since the beginning of the century.

> The writer explains what the graph shows.

Ray Rychnovsky reports that thirteen people have
been killed and another fifty-seven have been mauled by
lions since 1890. "What's most startling," writes Rychnovsky, "is that nearly three-quarters of the attacks
[. . .] have taken place 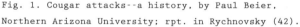 in the last twenty-five years"
(41).

> Ellipsis dots in brackets indicate words omitted from original source (see p. 88).

Particularly frightening are the attacks on children. Kevin Hansen points out that children have been
"more vulnerable than adults, making up 64 percent of
the victims" (69). This is not surprising, since children, being small and active, resemble the lion's

> Quotation intro- duced with a signal phrase.

Garcia 4

natural prey. Lion authority John Seidensticker reports that when he worked for the National Zoo in Washington, DC, he regularly observed cats stalking children who passed by the lion cages (120).

Since 1986, four children have been attacked in California ("Mountain" 7). One of these attacks was serious enough to prompt officials to place Caspers Wilderness Park off-limits to children (Tran B8). In July 1997 alone, two attacks on children, one fatal, occurred in different national parks in Colorado (McPhee A1).

In California, the state where the lion is most fully protected, 1994 was a particularly bad year. Los Angeles Times writer Tony Perry reports that two women were killed by lions in 1994 and that the year brought a dramatic increase in mountain lion sightings, "many in suburban and urban areas where the animal had previously not been spotted" (B4). With two killings in one year and an increasing number of sightings, it is not surprising that California politicians responded with Proposition 197, aimed at repealing the ban on hunting the lions.

The 1996 California referendum

The debate over Proposition 197 was inflamed by campaigns of misinformation on both sides of the issue. The pro faction included the National Rifle Association (NRA), the Safari Club, and Gun Owners of California. On the other side were animal rights groups such as the Sierra Club, the Fund for Animals, and the Mountain Lion Foundation.

The proposition itself, introduced by Republican Tim Leslie, is laced with legalese and deceptive phras-

ing. For example, in a provision aimed at amending sec-

Garcia 5

tion 4801 of the Fish and Game Code, the word <u>hunters</u>
does not appear, though the legalistic term <u>designee</u>
clearly includes hunters:

> The department may remove or take, or autho-
> rize its designee, including, but not limited
> to, an appropriate governmental agency with
> public safety responsibility, an appropriate
> governmental agency with wildlife management
> responsibility, or an owner of land, to re-
> move or take, one or more mountain lions that
> are perceived to be an imminent threat to
> public health or safety or livestock anywhere
> in the state except within the state park
> system. ("Proposition" sec. 5)

Quotation longer than four lines is indented 1″ (or ten spaces); quotation marks are omitted; no period is used after citation.

The proposition's euphemistic language, such as <u>remove
or take</u>, was echoed by the hunting factions, who spoke
much about "controlling" the lion population, avoiding
such words as <u>hunt</u> and <u>shoot</u>.

Short title given in parentheses because the work has no author.

Supporters of Proposition 197 were not above exag-
gerating the dangers posed by mountain lions, preferring lurid accounts of maulings and killings to solid
statistics. For example, writing on the Internet in an
attempt to sway voters, Terrence M. Eagan, Wayne Long,
and Steven Arroyo appeal to human fears of being eaten:
"Two small children woke up one morning without a
mother because a lion ate her." To underscore the
point, they describe a grisly discovery: "A lion prey-
ing upon neighborhood pets was found with parts of five
different puppies in its stomach."

No parenthetical citation necessary for unpaginated Internet source when author is named in signal phrase.

Whereas the pro-hunting groups used deceptive language and exaggerated the dangers posed by lions, the
pro-lion groups invoked inflammatory language and ignored the dangers. A Web page written by a coalition of
wildlife preservationists is typical. Calling Proposi-

Transition helps readers move from one topic to another.

tion 197 "a special interest trophy hunting measure,"
the coalition claims that the Gun Owners of California,
the NRA, and the Safari Club "rammed" the proposition
onto the ballot while "hiding behind a disingenuous
concern for public safety." Asserting that the mountain
lion poses a minimal threat to humans, the coalition
accuses the Department of Fish and Game of "creating a
climate of fear" so that the public will choose to re-
instate lion hunting (California Wildlife Protection
Coalition). While it is true that human encounters with
mountain lions are rare, some pro-lion publications
come close to ridiculing Californians who fear that
lion attacks on humans and pets will continue to accel-
erate unless something is done.

> **Internet source with no page number.**

Population control: A reasonable solution

 Without population control, the number of attacks
on Californians will almost certainly continue to rise,
and the lions may become even bolder. As lion authority
John Seidensticker remarks, "The boldness displayed by
mountain lions just doesn't square with the shy, retiring behavior familiar to those of us who have studied
these animals" (117). He surmises that the lions have
become emboldened because they no longer have to con-
tend with wolves and grizzly bears, which dominated
them in the past. The only conceivable predator to re-
instill that fear is the human.

> **Credentials of author mentioned in signal phrase.**

 Sadly, the only sure way to reduce lion attacks on
humans is to thin the population. One basic approach to
thinning is sport hunting, which is still legal, though
restricted in various ways, in every western state except California. A second approach involves state-
directed wildlife management, usually the hiring of
professional hunters to shoot or trap the lions.

Garcia 7

Sport hunting is a poor option--and not just because it is unpopular with Californians. First, it is difficult to control sport hunting. For instance, a number of western states have restrictions on killing a female lion with kittens, but sport hunters are rarely knowledgeable enough to tell whether a lion has kittens. Second, because some sport hunters are poor shots, they wound but don't kill the lions, causing needless suffering. Finally, certain hunting practices are anything but sport. There is a growing business in professionally led cougar hunts, as a number of ads on the World Wide Web attest. One practice is to tree a lion with radio-equipped dogs and then place a phone call to the client to come and shoot the lion. In some cases, the lion may be treed for two or more days before the client arrives to bag his trophy. Such practices are so offensive that even the California Park Rangers Association opposed Proposition 197. As a spokesperson explained, "We support managing the lions. But they shouldn't be stuck on the wall in a den" (qtd. in Perry B4).

We should entrust the thinning of the lion population to wildlife specialists guided by science, not to hunters seeking adventure or to safari clubs looking for profits. Unlike hunters, scientific wildlife managers have the long-term interests of the mountain lion at heart. An uncontrolled population leads to an ecological imbalance, with more and more lions competing for territory and a diminishing food supply. The highly territorial lions will fight to the death to defend their hunting grounds; and because the mother lion ultimately ejects her offspring from her own territory, young lions face an uncertain future. Stephani Cruickshank, a spokesperson for California Lion Awareness

Citation of indirect source: words quoted in another source.

No citation needed for "common knowledge" available in many sources.

(CLAW), explains, "The overrun of lions is biologically unsound and unfair to the lions, especially those forced to survive in marginal or clearly unnatural urban settings" (qtd. in Robinson 35).

The writer concludes with his own stand on the controversy.

In conclusion, wildlife management would benefit both Californians and the California lions. Although some have argued that California needs fewer people, not fewer lions, humans do have an obligation to protect themselves and their children, and the fears of people in lion country are real. As for the lions, they need to thrive in a natural habitat with an adequate food supply. "We simply cannot let nature take its course," writes Terry Mansfield of the Department of Fish and Game (qtd. in Perry B4). In fact, not to take action in California is as illogical as reintroducing the lions to Central Park and Boston Common, places they once also roamed.

The paper ends with the writer's own words.

Garcia 9

Works Cited

California Wildlife Protection Coalition. California
    Mountain Lion Page. 27 Mar. 1996. Sierra Club.
    24 Mar. 1998 〈http://www.sierraclub.org/chapters/
    ca/mountain-lion〉.

Eagan, Terrence M., Wayne Long, and Steven Arroyo.
    "Rebuttal to Argument against Proposition 197."
    1996 California Primary Election Server. 1996.
    California Secretary of State. 24 Mar. 1998
    〈http://primary96.ss.ca.gov/e/ballot/
    197again2.html〉.

Hansen, Kevin. Cougar: The American Lion. Flagstaff:
    Northland, 1992.

Hornocker, Maurice G. "Learning to Live with Lions."
    National Geographic July 1992: 37-65.

"Lion Attacks Prompt State to Respond." New York Times
    18 Oct. 1995, late ed.: A21.

McPhee, Mike. "Danger Grows as Lions Lose Fear." Denver
    Post 19 July 1997, 2nd ed.: A1.

"Mountain Lion Attacks on Humans." Outdoor California.
    21 Mar. 1996. State of California, Dept. of Fish
    and Game. 24 Mar. 1998 〈http://www.dfg.ca.gov/
    lion/outdoor.lion.html〉.

Perry, Tony. "Big Cat Fight." Los Angeles Times 8 Mar.
    1996, home ed.: B1+.

"Proposition 197: Text of Proposed Law." 1996
    California Primary Election Server. 1996.
    California Secretary of State. 24 Mar. 1998
    〈http://primary96.ss.ca.gov/e/ballot/197txt.html〉.

Robinson, Jerome B. "Cat in the Ballot Box." Field and
    Stream Mar. 1996: 30-35.

Rychnovsky, Ray. "Clawing into Controversy." Outdoor
    Life Jan. 1995: 38-42.

Heading centered 1″ from top of page.

List is alphabetized by authors' last names.

First line of each entry is at left margin; subsequent lines are indented ½″ (or five spaces).

Double-spacing used throughout.

Seidensticker, John. "Mountain Lions Don't Stalk
     People: True or False?" Audubon Feb. 1992:
     113-22.

Tran, Trini. "Near-Attack by Cougar Reported." Los
     Angeles Times 2 Jan. 1998: B8.

Williams, Ted. "The Lion's Silent Return." Audubon
     Nov. 1994: 28-35.

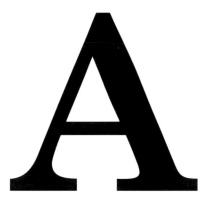

Alternative Styles of Documentation

A

Alternative Styles of Documentation

APA

Directory to APA in-text citations (A1-a)

Chicago

Directory to *Chicago*-style notes and bibliographic entries (A2-c), continued

To document sources, students in most English classes use the Modern Language Association (MLA) style of in-text citation described in M. When you are writing in other classes across the curriculum, you may be asked to use another style of documentation.

This section describes two frequently used styles: the American Psychological Association (APA) style of in-text citation, used in the social sciences, and the *Chicago Manual of Style* system of footnotes or endnotes, used in history and some humanities courses. For a list of style manuals in a variety of disciplines, see A3. Always use the style of documentation recommended by your instructor.

A useful list of sources (both print and online) and documentation models for many disciplines can be found on a Web site that accompanies this text: *Research and Documentation in the Electronic Age,* <http://www.bedfordstmartins.com/hacker/resdoc>.

A1

APA style (social sciences)

In most social sciences classes, such as psychology, sociology, anthropology, and business, you will be asked to use the APA style of in-text citations and references. The guidelines in this section are consistent with the *Publication Manual of the American Psychological Association,* 5th ed. (Washington: APA, 2001).

A1-a APA in-text citations

The American Psychological Association recommends an author-date style of in-text citations. These citations refer readers to a list of references at the end of the paper.

APA in-text citations provide at least the author's last name and the date of publication. For direct quotations, a page number is given as well.

1. BASIC FORMAT FOR A QUOTATION Ordinarily, introduce the quotation with a signal phrase that includes the author's last name followed by the date of publication in parentheses. Put the page number (preceded by "p.") in parentheses at the end of the quotation.

> According to Hart (1996), some primatologists "wondered
> if apes had learned Language, with a capital *L*"
> (p. 109).

When the author's name does not appear in the signal phrase, place
the author's name, the date, and the page number in parentheses
at the end of the quotation. Use commas between items in the
parentheses: (Hart, 1996, p. 109).

2. BASIC FORMAT FOR A SUMMARY OR A PARAPHRASE For a summary or
a paraphrase, include the author's last name and the date either in
a signal phrase or in parentheses at the end.

> According to Hart (1996), researchers took Terrace's
> conclusions seriously, and funding for language experi-
> ments soon declined.

> Researchers took Terrace's conclusions seriously, and
> funding for language experiments soon declined (Hart,
> 1996).

NOTE: A page number is not required, but provide one if it would
help your readers find a specific page in a long work.

3. A WORK WITH TWO AUTHORS Name both authors in the signal
phrase or parentheses each time you cite the work. In the parentheses, use "&" between the authors' names; in the signal phrase,
use "and."

> Patterson and Linden (1981) agreed that the gorilla
> Koko acquired language more slowly than a normal speak-
> ing child.

> Koko acquired language more slowly than a normal speak-
> ing child (Patterson & Linden, 1981).

4. A WORK WITH THREE TO FIVE AUTHORS Identify all authors in the
signal phrase or the parentheses the first time you cite the source.

> Researchers found a marked improvement in the computer
> skills of students who took part in the program (Levy,
> Bertrand, Muller, Vining, & Majors, 1997).

In subsequent citations, use the first author's name followed by "et al." (Latin for "and others") in either the signal phrase or the parentheses.

> Though school board members were skeptical at first,
> the program has now won the board's full support (Levy
> et al., 1997).

5. A WORK WITH SIX OR MORE AUTHORS Use only the first author's name followed by "et al." in the signal phrase or the parentheses.

> Better measurements of sophistication in computer use
> could be obtained through more thorough testing (Blili
> et al., 1996).

6. UNKNOWN AUTHOR If the author is not given, use the first word or two of the title in the signal phrase or the parenthetical citation.

> Massachusetts state and municipal governments have ini-
> tiated several programs to improve public safety, in-
> cluding community policing and after-school activities
> ("Innovations," 1997).

If "Anonymous" is specified as the author, treat it as if it were a real name: (Anonymous, 1996). In the bibliographic references, also use the name Anonymous as author.

7. CORPORATE AUTHOR If the author is a government agency or other corporate organization with a long name, spell out the name the first time you use it in a citation followed by an abbreviation in brackets. In later citations, simply use the abbreviation.

> **FIRST CITATION** (National Institute of Mental Health
> [NIMH], 1997)
>
> **LATER CITATIONS** (NIMH, 1997)

8. TWO OR MORE WORKS IN THE SAME PARENTHESES When your parenthetical citation names two or more works, put them in the same order that they appear in the reference list, separated by semicolons.

> Recently, researchers have investigated the degree to
> which gender affects the distribution of welfare
> (Gilbert, 1995; Leira, 1994).

9. AUTHORS WITH THE SAME LAST NAME To avoid confusion, use initials with the last names if your bibliography lists two or more authors with the same last name.

> Research by D. L. Johnson (1996) revealed that . . .

10. PERSONAL COMMUNICATION Conversations, memos, letters, e-mail, and similar unpublished person-to-person communications should be cited by initials, last name, and precise date.

> F. Moore (personal communication, January 4, 1997) has said that funding for the program will continue for at least another year.

It is not necessary to include personal communications in the bibliographic references at the end of your paper.

11. AN ELECTRONIC DOCUMENT When possible, cite an electronic document as you would any other document (using the author-date style).

> R. Fouts and D. Fouts (1999) have explained one benefit of ape language research: It has shown us how to teach children with linguistic disabilities.

When the date is unknown, APA recommends using the abbreviation "n.d." (for "no date").

> Attempts to return sign-language-using apes to the wild have had mixed results (Smith, n.d.).

When an electronic source lacks stable numbered pages, your citation should include—if possible—information that will help readers locate the particular passage being cited. When an electronic document has numbered paragraphs, use the paragraph number preceded by the symbol ¶ or by the abbreviation "para.": (Hall, 2001, ¶ 5) *or* (Hall, 2001, para. 5). If neither a page nor a paragraph number is given and the document contains headings, cite the appropriate heading and indicate which paragraph under that heading you are referring to:

> According to Kirby (1999), some critics have accused activists in the Great Ape Project of "exaggerating the supposed similarities of the apes [to humans] to stop their use in experiments" (Shared Path section, para. 6).

A1-b APA references (bibliographic entries)

In APA style, the alphabetical list of works cited is called "References." This section presents specific models to follow while preparing each entry in your list, along with the following general advice.

TITLE AND PLACEMENT OF LIST The list of references begins on a new page at the end of your paper. Center the title "References" (without quotation marks) about one inch from the top of the page. Double-space throughout. See pages 384–85 for an example.

INDENTING APA recommends using hanging indents, which make it easy for readers to scan through the list of references. To create a hanging indent, type the first line of an entry flush left and indent any additional lines one-half inch (or five spaces), as shown here.

```
Stoessinger, J. G. (1998). Why nations go to war
     (7th ed.). New York: St. Martin's Press.
```

Some instructors may prefer a paragraph-style indent, as in the following example.

```
     Stoessinger, J. G. (1998). Why nations go to war
(7th ed.). New York: St. Martin's Press.
```

ALPHABETIZING THE LIST Alphabetize your list by the last names of the authors (or editors); if there is no author or editor, alphabetize by the first word of the title other than *A, An,* or *The.*

AUTHORS' NAMES Invert *all* authors' names, and use initials instead of first names. With two or more authors, use an ampersand (&) before the last name. Separate the names with commas. Include names for the first six authors; if there are additional authors, end the list with "et al." (Latin for "and others").

DATE Place the date of publication in parentheses immediately after the last author's name.

TITLES OF BOOKS Italicize titles and subtitles of books; capitalize only the first word of the title and subtitle (as well as all proper nouns).

TITLES OF ARTICLES Do not place titles of periodical articles in quotation marks, and capitalize only the first word of the title and subtitle (and all proper nouns).

TITLES OF PERIODICALS Capitalize titles of periodicals as you would capitalize them ordinarily (see S3-c). Italicize the volume number of periodicals.

PAGE NUMBERS Use the abbreviation "p." (or "pp.") before page numbers of newspaper articles and articles in edited books, but do not use it before page numbers of articles appearing in magazines and scholarly journals.

Provide inclusive page numbers such as "pp. 203–214." If the page numbers of an article are discontinuous, provide all of them, separated by commas (for example, "A1, A5, A7").

PUBLISHERS' NAMES You may use a short form of a publisher's name as long as it is easily recognizable.

Books

1. BASIC FORMAT FOR A BOOK

Tapscott, D. (1998). *Growing up digital.* New York:
McGraw-Hill.

2. MULTIPLE AUTHORS

Hamer, D., & Copeland, P. (1998). *Living with our genes:*
Why they matter more than you think. New York:
Doubleday.

Winncott, D. W., Shepherd, R., Johns, J., & Robinson,
H. T. (1996). *Thinking about children.* Reading, MA:
Addison-Wesley.

If there are more than six authors, list the first six and "et al." (meaning "and others") to indicate that there are others.

3. CORPORATE AUTHOR When the author is an organization, the publisher is often the same organization. In such a case, give the publisher's name as "Author."

Bank of Boston. (1997). *Banking by remote control.* Boston:
Author.

4. UNKNOWN AUTHOR

Oxford essential world atlas. (1996). New York: Oxford
University Press.

5. EDITORS

Duncan, G. J., & Brooks-Gunn, J. (Eds.). (1997).
Consequences of growing up poor. New York: Russell
Sage Foundation.

6. TRANSLATION

Singer, I. B. (1998). *Shadows on the Hudson* (J. Sherman,
    Trans.). New York: Farrar, Straus and Giroux.
    (Original work published 1957)

7. EDITION OTHER THAN THE FIRST

Helfer, M. E., Kempe, R. S., & Krugman, R. D. (1997). *The*
    battered child (5th ed.). Chicago: University of
    Chicago Press.

8. ARTICLE IN AN EDITED BOOK

Fesmire, S. (1997). The social basis of character: An
    ecological humanist approach. In H. LaFollette (Ed.),
    Ethics in practice (pp. 282-292). Cambridge, MA:
    Blackwell.

9. MULTIVOLUME WORK

Wiener, P. (Ed.). (1973). *Dictionary of the history of*
    ideas (Vols. 1-4). New York: Scribner's.

10. TWO OR MORE WORKS BY THE SAME AUTHOR Use the author's
name for all entries. Arrange the entries by date, the earliest first.

Jones, J. M. (1988). Why should black undergraduate
    students major in psychology? In P. J. Woods (Ed.),
    Is psychology for them? A guide to undergraduate
    advising (pp. 178-181). Washington, DC: American
    Psychological Association.

Jones, J. M. (1996). Racism and white racial identity:
    Merging realities. In B. P. Bowser and R. G. Hunt
    (Eds.), *Impacts of racism on white Americans* (pp.
    1-23). Thousand Oaks, CA: Sage.

Articles in periodicals

11. ARTICLE IN A JOURNAL PAGINATED BY VOLUME

McLoyd, V. C. (1998). Socioeconomic disadvantage and
    child development. *American Psychologist, 53,*
    185-204.

12. ARTICLE IN A JOURNAL PAGINATED BY ISSUE

Roberts, P. (1998). The new food anxiety. *Psychology Today, 31*(2), 30-38, 74.

13. ARTICLE IN A MAGAZINE

Kadrey, R. (1998, March). Carbon copy: Meet the first human clone. *Wired, 6,* 146-150, 180, 220.

14. ARTICLE IN A NEWSPAPER

Haney, D. Q. (1998, February 20). Finding eats at mystery of appetite. *The Oregonian,* pp. A1, A17.

15. LETTER TO THE EDITOR

Westberg, L. (1997). South Bronx, New York [Letter to the editor]. *Orion, 16*(1), 4.

16. REVIEW

Ehrenhalt, A. (1997, February 10). [Review of the book *Virtuous reality*]. *The Weekly Standard,* pp. 31-34.

17. TWO OR MORE WORKS BY THE SAME AUTHOR IN THE SAME YEAR Arrange the works alphabetically by title. Add lowercase letters beginning with "a," "b," and so on, within the parentheses immediately following the year.

Chapin, W. D. (1997a). Ausländer raus? The empirical relationship between immigration and crime in Germany *Social Science Quarterly, 78,* 543-558.

Chapin, W. D. (1997b). Explaining the electoral success of the new right: The German case. *Western European Politics, 20,* 53-72.

Electronic sources

The following guidelines are based on the *Publication Manual of the American Psychological Association,* 5th ed. (2001). Any updates will be posted on the APA Web site, <http://www.apastyle.org>.

18. ARTICLE FROM AN ONLINE PERIODICAL When citing online articles, follow the guidelines for printed articles, giving whatever information is available in the online source. If the article also appears in a printed journal, a URL is not required; instead, include "Electronic version" in brackets after the title of the article.

Williams, S. L., Brakke, K. E., & Savage-Rumbaugh, E. S.
    (1977). Comprehension skills of language-competent
    and nonlanguage-competent apes [Electronic version].
    Language and Communication, 17(4), 301-317.

If there is no print version, include the date you accessed the source
and the article's URL.

Ashe, D. D., & McCutcheon, L. E. (2001, May 4). Shyness,
    loneliness, and attitude toward celebrities.
    Current Research in Social Psychology, 6(9).
    Retrieved July 3, 2001, from http://www.uiowa.edu/
    ~grpproc/crisp/crisp.6.9.htm

NOTE: When you have retrieved an article from a newspaper's
searchable Web site, give the URL for the site, not for the exact
source.

Cary, B. (2001, June 18). Mentors of the mind. *Los
    Angeles Times.* Retrieved July 5, 2001, from
    http://www.latimes.com

19. ARTICLE FROM A DATABASE

Holliday, R. E., & Hayes, B. K. (2001, January). Dissoci-
    ating automatic and intentional processes in chil-
    dren's eyewitness memory. *Journal of Experimental
    Child Psychology, 75*(1), 1-5. Retrieved May 21, 2001,
    from Expanded Academic ASAP database (A59317972).

20. NONPERIODICAL WEB DOCUMENT

Cain, A., & Burris, M. (1999, April). *Investigation of the
    use of mobile phones while driving.* Retrieved January
    15, 2000, from http://www.cutr.eng.usf.edu/its/
    mobile_phone_text.htm

NOTE: If you retrieved the source from a university program's Web
site, name the program in your retrieval statement.

Cosmides, L., & Tooby, J. (1997). *Evolutionary psychology:
    A primer.* Retrieved July 5, 2001, from the University
    of California, Santa Barbara, Center for Evolutionary
    Psychology Web site: http://www.psych.ucsb.edu/
    research/cep/primer.html

21. CHAPTER OR SECTION IN A WEB DOCUMENT

Heuer, R. J., Jr. (1999). Keeping an open mind. In
Psychology of intelligence analysis (chap. 6).
Retrieved July 7, 2001, from http://www.cia.gov/
csi/books/19104/art9.html

22. ONLINE POSTING

Eaton, S. (2001, June 12). Online transactions
[Msg 2]. Message posted to news://sci.psychology
.psychotherapy.moderated

23. E-MAIL E-mail messages are personal communications and are
not included in the list of references.

Other sources

24. DISSERTATION ABSTRACT

Hu, X. (1996). Consumption and social inequality in
urban Guangdong, China (Doctoral dissertation,
University of Hawaii, 1996). *Dissertation Abstracts
International, 57,* 3280A.

25. GOVERNMENT DOCUMENT

U.S. Bureau of the Census. (1996). *Statistical abstract of
the United States* (116th ed.). Washington, DC: U.S.
Government Printing Office.

26. CONFERENCE PROCEEDINGS

Schnase, J. L., & Cunnius, E. L. (Eds.). (1995).
*Proceedings of CSCL '95: The First International
Conference on Computer Support for Collaborative
Learning.* Mahwah, NJ: Erlbaum.

27. COMPUTER PROGRAM

Kaufmann, W. J., III, & Comins, N. F. (1998). Discovering
the universe (Version 4.1) [Computer software]. New
York: W. H. Freeman.

28. MOTION PICTURE Give the title, followed by "Motion picture" in
brackets, the country where it was made, and the name of the
studio. If the motion picture is difficult to find, include instead the
name and address of its distributor.

Soderbergh, S. (Director). (2000). *Traffic* [Motion picture]. United States: Gramercy Pictures.

Donohew, P. (Producer/Director). (1999). *Seven sisters: A Kentucky portrait* [Motion picture]. (Available from Sour Mash Films, 55 Cumberland Street, San Francisco, CA 94110)

A1-c APA manuscript format

This section presents guidelines for formatting a manuscript according to APA style. Also see the sample research paper formatted in APA style (pp. 377–85) and guidelines for preparing the reference list (pp. 369–70).

MATERIALS AND TYPEFACE Use good-quality 8½″ × 11″ white paper. For a paper typed on a computer, make sure that the print quality meets your instructor's standards. Avoid a typeface that is unusual or hard to read.

TITLE PAGE Begin a college paper with a title page. Type the page number, flush right (against the right margin), about one-half inch from the top of the page. Before the page number type a short title, consisting of the first two or three words of your title.

The APA manual does not provide guidelines for the placement of certain information necessary for college papers, but most instructors will want you to supply a title page similar to the one on page 377.

MARGINS, SPACING, AND INDENTATION Use margins of one inch on all sides of the page. If you are working on a computer, do not justify the right margin.

Double-space throughout the paper, and indent the first line of each paragraph one-half inch (or five spaces).

For quotations longer than forty words, indent each line one-half inch (or five spaces) from the left margin. Double-space between the body of the paper and the quotation, and double-space between lines in the quotation. Quotation marks are not needed when a quotation is indented. (See P6-b.)

PAGE NUMBERS AND SHORT TITLE In the upper right-hand corner of each page, about one-half inch from the top of the page, type the page number, preceded by the short title that you typed on the title page. Number all pages, including the title page.

PUNCTUATION AND TYPING   Although the APA guidelines call for one space after all punctuation, many college professors allow (or even prefer) two spaces at the end of a sentence. Use one space after all other punctuation.

To form a dash, type two hyphens with no space between them. Do not put a space on either side of the dash.

ABSTRACT   If your instructor requires one, include an abstract right after the title page. Center the word "Abstract" one inch from the top of the page; double-space the text of the abstract as you do the body of your paper.

An abstract is a 75-to-100-word paragraph that provides readers with a quick overview of your essay. It should express your thesis (or central idea) and your key points; it should also briefly suggest any implications or applications of the research you discuss in the paper.

HEADINGS   Although headings are not necessary, their use is encouraged in the social sciences. For most undergraduate papers, use no more than one or two levels of headings. Major headings should be centered, with the first letter of important words capitalized; minor words—articles, short prepositions, and coordinating conjunctions—are not capitalized unless they are the first word. Subheadings should be typed flush left (against the left margin) and italicized; the rules on capitalization are the same as for major headings. See pages 377–85 for a paper with headings.

VISUALS   The APA classifies visuals as tables and figures (figures include graphs, charts, drawings, and photographs). Keep visuals as simple as possible. Label each clearly—Table 1, Figure 3, and so on—and include a caption that concisely describes its subject. In the text of your paper, discuss the most significant features of each visual. Ask your instructor for guidelines on placement of visuals in the paper.

A1-d   Sample research paper: APA style

On the following pages is a research paper written by Karen Shaw, a student in a psychology class. Shaw's assignment was to write a "review of the literature" documented with APA-style citations and references.

In preparing her final manuscript, Shaw followed the APA guidelines in A1-a to A1-c of this book. She did not include an abstract because her instructor did not require one.

Apes and Language   1   Short title and page
                                          number for student
                                          papers.

Apes and Language: Full title, writer's
A Review of the Literature   name, name and
                                         section number of
                                         course, instructor's
                                         name, and date (all
                                         centered).

Karen Shaw

Psychology 110, Section 2
Professor Verdi
March 2, 2001

A1-d   *Sample APA research paper*

Full title, centered.

Apes and Language:

A Review of the Literature

Over the past thirty years, researchers have
demonstrated that the great apes (chimpanzees, gorillas, and orangutans) resemble humans in language abilities more than had been thought possible. Just how far
that resemblance extends, however, has been a matter of
some controversy. Researchers agree that the apes have
acquired fairly large vocabularies in American Sign
Language and in artificial languages, but they have
drawn quite different conclusions in addressing the
following questions:

The writer sets up
her organization in
the introduction.

1. How spontaneously have apes used language?

2. How creatively have apes used language?

3. Can apes create sentences?

4. What are the implications of the ape language
   studies?

This review of the literature on apes and language focuses on these four questions.

Headings, centered,
help readers follow
the organization.

How Spontaneously

Have Apes Used Language?

A signal phrase
names all four
authors and gives
date in paren-
theses.

In an influential article, Terrace, Petitto,
Sanders, and Bever (1979) argued that the apes in the
language experiments were not using language spontaneously but were merely imitating their trainers, responding to conscious or unconscious cues. Terrace and
his colleagues at Columbia University had trained a
chimpanzee, Nim, in American Sign Language, so their
skepticism about the apes' abilities received much attention. In fact, funding for ape language research was
sharply reduced following publication of their 1979 article "Can an Ape Create a Sentence?"

In retrospect, the conclusions of Terrace et al.
seem to have been premature. Although some early ape

language studies had not been rigorously controlled to
eliminate cuing, even as early as the 1970s R. A. Gardner and B. T. Gardner were conducting double-blind
experiments that prevented any possibility of cuing
(Fouts, 1997, p. 99). Since 1979, researchers have
diligently guarded against cuing. For example, Lewin
(1991) reported that instructions for bonobo (pygmy
chimpanzee) Kanzi were "delivered by someone out of his
sight," with other team members wearing earphones so
that they "could not hear the instructions and so could
not cue Kanzi, even unconsciously" (p. 51). More recently, philosopher Stuart Shanker of York University
has questioned the emphasis placed on cuing, pointing
out that since human communication relies on the ability to understand cues and gestures in a social setting, it is not surprising that apes might rely on similar signals (Johnson, 1995).

There is considerable evidence that apes have
signed to one another spontaneously, without trainers
present. Like many of the apes studied, gorillas Koko
and Michael have been observed signing to one another
(Patterson & Linden, 1981). At Central Washington University the baby chimpanzee Loulis, placed in the care
of the signing chimpanzee Washoe, mastered nearly fifty
signs in American Sign Language without help from humans. "Interestingly," wrote researcher Fouts (1997),
"Loulis did not pick up any of the seven signs that we
[humans] used around him. He learned only from Washoe
and [another chimp] Ally" (p. 244).

The extent to which chimpanzees spontaneously use
language may depend on their training. Terrace trained
Nim using the behaviorist technique of operant condi-
tioning, so it is not surprising that many of Nim's
signs were cued. Many other researchers have used a

Because the author of the work is not named in the signal phrase, his name appears in parentheses, along with the date. Citation from a long work has page number preceded by "p."

For a quotation, a page number preceded by "p." appears in parentheses.

An ampersand links the names of two authors in parentheses.

Brackets are used to indicate words not in original source.

conversational approach that parallels the process by
which human children acquire language. In an experimen-
tal study, O'Sullivan and Yeager (1989) contrasted the
two techniques, using Terrace's Nim as their subject.
They found that Nim's use of language was significantly
more spontaneous under conversational conditions.

How Creatively

Have Apes Used Language?

There is considerable evidence that apes have invented creative names. One of the earliest and most
controversial examples involved the Gardners' chimpanzee Washoe. Washoe, who knew signs for "water" and
"bird," once signed "water bird" when in the presence
of a swan. Terrace et al. (1979) suggested that there
was "no basis for concluding that Washoe was character-
izing the swan as a 'bird that inhabits water.'" Washoe
may simply have been "identifying correctly a body of
water and a bird, in that order" (p. 895).

Other examples are not so easily explained away.
The bonobo Kanzi has requested particular films by combining symbols in a creative way. For instance, to ask
for *Quest for Fire*, a film about early primates discovering fire, Kanzi began to use symbols for "campfire"
and "TV" (Eckholm, 1985). The gorilla Koko has a long
list of creative names to her credit: "elephant baby"
to describe a Pinocchio doll, "finger bracelet" to describe a ring, "bottle match" to describe a cigarette
lighter, and so on (Patterson & Linden, 1981, p. 146).
If Terrace's analysis of the "water bird" example is
applied to the examples just mentioned, it does not
hold. Surely Koko did not first see an elephant and
then a baby before signing "elephant baby"--or a bottle
and a match before signing "bottle match."

The word "and" links the names of two authors in the signal phrase.

When this article was first cited, all four authors were named. In subsequent citations of a work with three to five authors, "et al." is used after the first author's name.

The writer interprets the evidence; she doesn't just report it.

Apes and Language   5

Can Apes Create Sentences?

The early ape language studies offered little proof that apes could combine symbols into grammatically ordered sentences. Apes strung together various signs, but the sequences were often random and repetitious. Nim's series of 16 signs is a case in point: "give orange me give eat orange me eat orange give me eat orange give me you" (Terrace et al., 1979, p. 895).

More recent studies with bonobos at the Language Research Center in Atlanta have broken new ground. Kanzi, a bonobo trained by Savage-Rumbaugh, seems to understand simple grammatical rules about word order. For instance, Kanzi learned that in two-word utterances action precedes object, an ordering also used by human children at the two-word stage. In a major article reporting on their research, Greenfield and Savage-Rumbaugh (1990) wrote that Kanzi rarely "repeated himself or formed combinations that were semantically unrelated" (p. 556).

More important, Kanzi began on his own to create certain patterns that may not exist in English but can be found among deaf children and in other human languages. For example, Kanzi used his own rules when combining action symbols. Symbols that involved an invitation to play, such as "chase," would appear first; symbols that indicated what was to be done during play ("hide") would appear second. Kanzi also created his own rules when combining gestures and symbols. He would use the symbol first and then gesture, a practice often followed by young deaf children (Greenfield & Savage-Rumbaugh, 1990, p. 560).

In a later study, Kanzi's abilities were shown to be similar to those of a 2-1/2-year-old human, Alia.

> The writer draws attention to an important article.

> The writer gives a page number for this summary because the article is long.

A1-d *Sample APA research paper*

Rumbaugh (1995) reported that "Kanzi's comprehension of over 600 novel sentences of request was very comparable to Alia's; both complied with the requests without assistance on approximately 70% of the sentences" (p. 722).

> For quotations, a page number is required.

What Are the Implications of the Ape Language Studies?

Kanzi's linguistic abilities are so impressive that they may help us understand how humans came to acquire language. Pointing out that 99% of our genetic material is held in common with the chimpanzees, Greenfield and Savage-Rumbaugh (1990) have suggested that something of the "evolutionary root of human language" can be found in the "linguistic abilities of the great apes" (p. 540). Noting that apes' brains are similar to those of our human ancestors, Leakey and Lewin (1992) argued that in ape brains "the cognitive foundations on which human language could be built are already present" (p. 244).

The suggestion that there is a continuity in the linguistic abilities of apes and humans has created much controversy. Linguist Noam Chomsky has strongly asserted that language is a unique human characteristic (Booth, 1990). Terrace has continued to be skeptical of the claims made for the apes, as have Petitto and Bever, coauthors of the 1979 article that caused such skepticism earlier (Gibbons, 1991).

> The writer presents a balanced view of the philosophical controversy.

Recently, neurobiologists have made discoveries that may cause even the skeptics to take notice. On-going studies at the Language Research Center have revealed remarkable similarities in the brains of chimpanzees and humans. Through brain scans of live chimpanzees, researchers have found that, as with humans, "the language-controlling PT [*planum temporale*] is larger on the left side of the chimps' brain

Apes and Language   7

than on the right. But it is not lateralized in monkeys, which are less closely related to humans than
apes are" (Begley, 1998, p. 57).

Although the ape language studies continue to generate controversy, researchers have shown over the past
thirty years that the gap between the linguistic abilities of apes and humans is far less dramatic than was
once believed.

The tone of the
conclusion is
objective.

References

Begley, S. (1998, January 19). Aping language.
  Newsweek, 131, 56-58.

Booth, W. (1990, October 29). Monkeying with language:
  Is chimp using words or merely aping handlers? *The
  Washington Post,* p. A3.

Eckholm, E. (1985, June 25). Kanzi the chimp: A life in
  science. *The New York Times,* pp. C1, C3.

Fouts, R. (1997). *Next of kin: What chimpanzees taught
  me about who we are.* New York: William Morrow.

Gibbons, A. (1991). Déjà vu all over again:
  Chimp-language wars. *Science, 251,* 1561-1562.

Greenfield, P. M., & Savage-Rumbaugh, E. S. (1990).
  Grammatical combination in *Pan paniscus:* Processes
  of learning and invention in the evolution and
  development of language. In S. T. Parker & K. R.
  Gibson (Eds.), *"Language" and intelligence in
  monkeys and apes: Comparative developmental
  perspectives* (pp. 540-578). Cambridge: Cambridge
  University Press.

Johnson, G. (1995, June 6). Chimp talk debate: Is it
  really language? *The New York Times.* Retrieved
  February 2, 1998, from http://www.nytimes.com

Leakey, R., & Lewin, R. (1992). *Origins reconsidered:
  In search of what makes us human.* New York:
  Doubleday.

Lewin, R. (1991, April 29). Look who's talking now. *New
  Scientist, 130,* 49-52.

O'Sullivan, C., & Yeager, C. P. (1989). Communicative
  context and linguistic competence: The effect of
  social setting on a chimpanzee's conversational
  skill. In R. A. Gardner, B. T. Gardner, & T. E.
  Van Cantfort (Eds.), *Teaching sign language to
  chimpanzees* (pp. 269-279). Albany: SUNY Press.

List of references begins on a new page. Heading is centered.

List is alphabetized by authors' last names.

The first line of an entry is at left margin; subsequent lines indent ½″ (or five spaces).

Double-spacing used throughout.

Patterson, F., & Linden, E. (1981). *The education of Koko*. New York: Holt, Rinehart & Winston.

Rumbaugh, D. (1995). Primate language and cognition: Common ground. *Social Research, 62,* 711-730.

Terrace, H. S., Petitto, L. A., Sanders, R. J., & Bever, T. G. (1979). Can an ape create a sentence? *Science, 206,* 891-902.

A2

Chicago style (history and humanities)

Professors in history and the humanities often require footnotes or
endnotes based on *The Chicago Manual of Style*, 14th ed. (Chicago:
U of Chicago P, 1993). When you use *Chicago*-style notes, you will
usually be asked to include a bibliography at the end of your paper.
(See A2-b.)

A2-a   *Chicago*-style footnotes or endnotes

Notes provide complete publication information either at the bottom of the page (footnotes) or at the end of the paper (endnotes). A
raised arabic numeral in the text indicates that a quotation, summary, or paraphrase has been borrowed from a source; to find the
publication information for that source, readers consult the footnote or endnote with the corresponding number.

Individual notes are single-spaced, and the first line is indented one-half inch (or five spaces); double-spacing separates entries. Notes are numbered consecutively throughout the paper.

TEXT

Governor John Andrew was not allowed to recruit black
soldiers out of state. "Ostensibly," writes Peter Burchard, "no recruiting was done outside Massachusetts,
but it was an open secret that Andrew's agents were
working far and wide."[1]

The first time you cite a source, the note should include publication information for that work as well as the page number on
which the specific quotation, paraphrase, or summary may be
found.

NOTE

1. Peter Burchard, One Gallant Rush: Robert Gould
Shaw and His Brave Black Regiment (New York: St.
Martin's Press, 1965), 85.

For subsequent references to a source you have already cited, you may simply give the author's last name, followed by a comma and the page or pages cited.

>   2. Burchard, 31.

If you cite more than one work by the same author, include a short form of the title in subsequent citations. A short form of the title of a book is underlined or italicized; a short form of the title of an article is put in quotation marks.

>   2. Burchard, One Gallant Rush, 31.

>   4. Burchard, "Civil War," 10.

NOTE: *Chicago* style no longer requires the use of "ibid." to refer to the work cited in the previous note. The Latin abbreviations "op. cit." and "loc. cit." are no longer used.

A2-b *Chicago*-style bibliography

A bibliography, which appears at the end of your paper, lists every work you have cited in your notes; in addition, it may include works that you consulted but did not cite. For advice on constructing the list, see page 395. A sample bibliography appears on page 399.

A2-c Model notes and bibliographic entries

The following guidelines are consistent with guidelines set forth in *The Chicago Manual of Style,* 14th ed. For each type of source, a model note appears first, followed by a model bibliographic entry. The model note shows the format you should use when citing a source for the first time. For subsequent citations of a source, use shortened notes (see A2-a).

Books

1. BASIC FORMAT FOR A BOOK

>   1. Robert Service, A History of Twentieth-Century Russia (Cambridge: Harvard University Press, 1998), 314-30.

> Service, Robert. A History of Twentieth-Century Russia. Cambridge: Harvard University Press, 1998.

2. TWO OR THREE AUTHORS

2. Rudolph O. de la Garza, Z. Anthony Kruszewski, and Tomás A. Arciniega, <u>Chicanos and Native Americans: The Territorial Minorities</u> (Englewood Cliffs, N.J.: Prentice-Hall, 1973), 8.

Garza, Rudolph O. de la, Z. Anthony Kruszewski, and Tomás A. Arciniega. <u>Chicanos and Native Americans: The Territorial Minorities</u>. Englewood Cliffs, N.J.: Prentice-Hall, 1973.

3. FOUR OR MORE AUTHORS

3. Gary B. Nash et al., <u>The American People</u>, 4th ed. (New York: Addison Wesley Longman, 1998), 164.

Nash, Gary B., et al. <u>The American People</u>. 4th ed. New York: Addison Wesley Longman, 1998.

4. UNKNOWN AUTHOR

4. <u>The Men's League Handbook on Women's Suffrage</u> (London, 1912), 23.

<u>The Men's League Handbook on Women's Suffrage</u>. London, 1912.

5. EDITED WORK WITHOUT AN AUTHOR

5. Marshall Sklare, ed., <u>Understanding American Jewry</u> (New Brunswick, N.J.: Transaction Books, 1982), 49.

Sklare, Marshall, ed. <u>Understanding American Jewry</u>. New Brunswick, N.J.: Transaction Books, 1982.

6. EDITED WORK WITH AN AUTHOR

6. William L. Riordon, <u>Plunkitt of Tammany Hall</u>, ed. Terrence J. McDonald (Boston: Bedford Books, 1994), 33.

Riordon, William L. <u>Plunkitt of Tammany Hall</u>. Edited by Terrence J. McDonald. Boston: Bedford Books, 1994.

7. TRANSLATED WORK

 7. Gabriel García Márquez, News of a Kidnapping, trans. Edith Grossman. (New York: Knopf, 1997), 154-67.

García Márquez, Gabriel. News of a Kidnapping. Translated by Edith Grossman. New York: Knopf, 1997.

8. EDITION OTHER THAN THE FIRST

 8. Andrew F. Rolle, California: A History, 5th ed. (Wheeling, Ill.: Harlan Davidson, 1998), 243-46.

Rolle, Andrew F. California: A History. 5th ed. Wheeling, Ill.: Harlan Davidson, 1998.

9. UNTITLED VOLUME IN A MULTIVOLUME WORK

 9. New Cambridge Modern History (Cambridge: Cambridge University Press, 1957), 1:52-53.

New Cambridge Modern History. Vol. 1. Cambridge: Cambridge University Press, 1957.

10. TITLED VOLUME IN A MULTIVOLUME WORK

 10. Horst Boog et al., The Attack on the Soviet Union, vol. 4 of Germany and the Second World War (Cambridge: Oxford University Press, 1998), 70-72.

Boog, Horst, et al. The Attack on the Soviet Union. Vol. 4 of Germany and the Second World War. Cambridge: Oxford University Press, 1998.

11. WORK IN AN ANTHOLOGY

 11. Roland Barthes, "The Discourse of History," in The Postmodern History Reader, ed. Keith Jenkins (New York: Routledge, 1997), 121.

Barthes, Roland. "The Discourse of History." In The Postmodern History Reader, edited by Keith Jenkins. New York: Routledge, 1997.

12. WORK IN A SERIES

12. Robert M. Laughlin, <u>Of Cabbages and Kings: Tales</u> <u>from Zinacantán</u>, Smithsonian Contributions to Anthropology, vol. 23 (Washington, D.C.: Smithsonian Institution Press, 1977), 14.

Laughlin, Robert M. <u>Of Cabbages and Kings: Tales from</u> <u>Zinacantán</u>. Smithsonian Contributions to Anthropology, vol. 23. Washington, D.C.: Smithsonian Institution Press, 1977.

13. ENCYCLOPEDIA OR DICTIONARY

13. <u>Encyclopaedia Britannica</u>, 15th ed., s.v. "evolution."

NOTE: The abbreviation "s.v." is for the Latin *sub verbo* ("under the word").

Encyclopedias and dictionaries are usually not included in the bibliography.

Articles in periodicals

14. ARTICLE IN A JOURNAL PAGINATED BY VOLUME

14. Paula Findlen, "Possessing the Past: The Material World of the Italian Renaissance," <u>American Historical Review</u> 103 (1998): 86.

Findlen, Paula. "Possessing the Past: The Material World of the Italian Renaissance." <u>American Historical Review</u> 103 (1998): 83-114.

15. ARTICLE IN A JOURNAL PAGINATED BY ISSUE

15. Robert Darnton, "The Pursuit of Happiness," <u>Wilson Quarterly</u> 19, no. 4 (1995): 42.

Darnton, Robert. "The Pursuit of Happiness." <u>Wilson Quarterly</u> 19, no. 4 (1995): 42-52.

16. ARTICLE IN A MAGAZINE

    16. Andrew Weil, "The New Politics of Coca," <u>New Yorker</u>, 15 May 1995, 70.

Weil, Andrew. "The New Politics of Coca." <u>New Yorker</u>, 15 May 1995, 70.

17. ARTICLE IN A NEWSPAPER

    17. Lena H. Sun, "Chinese Feel the Strain of a New Society," <u>Washington Post</u>, 13 June 1993, sec. A.

Sun, Lena H. "Chinese Feel the Strain of a New Society." <u>Washington Post</u>, 13 June 1993, sec. A.

Electronic sources

Although *The Chicago Manual of Style,* 14th ed., does not include guidelines for documenting online sources, the University of Chicago Press recommends following the system developed by Andrew Harnack and Eugene Kleppinger in *Online! A Reference Guide to Using Internet Sources,* 1998 ed. (New York: St. Martin's, 1998). The examples of online sources given in this section are based on Harnack and Kleppinger's guidelines.

18. WORLD WIDE WEB SITE

    18. Yale Richmond and Duane Goehner, "Russian Orthodoxy," <u>Russian/American Contrasts</u>, 3 December 1997, ⟨http://www.goehner.com/russinfo.htm⟩ (15 March 1998).

Richmond, Yale, and Duane Goehner. "Russian Orthodoxy." <u>Russian/American Contrasts</u>. 3 December 1997. ⟨http://www.goehner.com/russinfo.htm⟩ (15 March 1998).

19. E-MAIL MESSAGE

    19. Eleanor Reeves, ⟨elv92@uchic.edu⟩ "Cold War," 20 March 1998, personal e-mail (20 March 1998).

Reeves, Eleanor. ⟨elv92@uchic.edu⟩ "Cold War." 20 March 1998. Personal e-mail (20 March 1998).

20. LISTSERV MESSAGE

20. Nancy Stegall, ⟨stegall@primenet.com⟩ "Web Publishing and Censorship," 2 February 1997, ⟨acw-1@ttacs6 .ttu.edu⟩ via ⟨http://www.ttu.edu/lists/acw-1⟩ (18 March 1997).

Stegall, Nancy. ⟨stegall@primenet.com⟩ "Web Publishing and Censorship." 2 February 1997. ⟨acw-1@ttacs6.ttu.edu⟩ via ⟨http://www.ttu.edu/lists/acw-1⟩ (18 March 1997).

21. NEWSGROUP MESSAGE

21. Richard J. Kennedy, ⟨rkennedy@orednet.org⟩ "Re: Shakespeare's Daughters," 18 March 1997, ⟨humanities.lit .authors.shakespeare⟩ (23 March 1997).

Kennedy, Richard J. ⟨rkennedy@orednet.org⟩ "Re: Shakespeare's Daughters." 18 March 1997. ⟨humanities .lit.authors.shakespeare⟩ (23 March 1997).

22. SYNCHRONOUS COMMUNICATION

22. Diversity University MOO, 16 March 1997, group discussion, telnet moo.du.org (16 March 1997).

Diversity University MOO. 16 March 1997. Group discussion. Telnet moo.du.org (16 March 1997).

23. ELECTRONIC DATABASE

23. Paul D. Hightower, "Censorship," in Contemporary Education (Terre Haute: Indiana State University, School of Education, winter 1995), 66, Dialog, ERIC, ED 509251.

Hightower, Paul D. "Censorship." In Contemporary Education. Terre Haute: Indiana State University, School of Education, winter 1995. 66, Dialog, ERIC, ED 509251.

Other sources

24. GOVERNMENT DOCUMENT

24. U.S. Department of State, Foreign Relations of the United States: Diplomatic Papers, 1943 (Washington, D.C.: GPO, 1965), 562.

U.S. Department of State. Foreign Relations of the United States: Diplomatic Papers, 1943. Washington, D.C.: GPO, 1965.

25. UNPUBLISHED DISSERTATION

25. Cheryl D. Hoover, "East Germany's Revolution" (Ph.D. diss., Ohio State University, 1994), 450-51.

Hoover, Cheryl D. "East Germany's Revolution." Ph.D. diss., Ohio State University, 1994.

26. PERSONAL COMMUNICATION

26. Sara Lehman, letter to author, 13 August 1996.

Personal communications are not included in the bibliography.

27. INTERVIEW

27. Jesse Jackson, interview by Marshall Frady, Frontline, Public Broadcasting System, 30 April 1996.

Jackson, Jesse. Interview by Marshall Frady. Frontline. Public Broadcasting System, 30 April 1996.

28. FILM OR VIDEOTAPE

28. North by Northwest, prod. and dir. Alfred Hitchcock, 2 hr. 17 min., MGM/UA, 1959, videocassette.

North by Northwest. Produced and directed by Alfred Hitchcock. 2 hr. 17 min. MGM/UA, 1959. Videocassette.

29. SOUND RECORDING

29. Gustav Holst, The Planets, Royal Philharmonic, André Previn, Telarc compact disc 80133.

Holst, Gustav. <u>The Planets</u>. Royal Philharmonic. André
    Previn. Telarc compact disc 80133.

A2-d *Chicago*-style manuscript format

The following guidelines on manuscript formatting are based on
The Chicago Manual of Style, 14th ed.

TITLE AND IDENTIFICATION   On the title page, include the full
title of your paper and your name. Your instructor may also want
you to include the course title, the instructor's name, and the date.
Do not type a number on the title page but count it in the manuscript; that is, the first page of text will usually be numbered page 2.
In the unusual case that your paper includes extensive preliminary
material such as a table of contents, list of illustrations, or preface,
you may be required to number that material separately. See page
396 for a sample title page.

MARGINS AND SPACING   Leave margins of at least one inch at the
top, bottom, and sides of the page. Double-space the entire manuscript, including block quotations, but single-space individual entries in notes and the bibliography.

PAGINATION   Using arabic numerals, number all pages except
the title page in the upper right corner. Depending on your instructor's preference, you may also use a short title or your last name before page numbers to help identify pages in case they come loose
from your manuscript. (See p. 397 for a sample *Chicago*-style manuscript page.)

Preparing the endnotes page

On page 398 are sample endnotes for a paper in *Chicago* style. (You
may choose to or be required to use footnotes instead.) Endnote
pages should be numbered consecutively with the rest of the manuscript, and the title "Notes" should be centered on the first page
about one inch from the top of the page. Indent only the first line of
each entry one-half inch (or five spaces) and begin the note with the
arabic numeral corresponding to the number in the text. Follow the
number with a period and one space. Do not indent any other lines
of the entry. Single-space individual notes but double-space between notes.

AUTHORS Authors' names are not inverted in notes. With two or more authors, use "and," not an ampersand (&). In notes for works with four or more authors, use the first author's name followed by "et al."

PAGE NUMBERS Page numbers are not preceded by the abbreviation "p." or "pp."

Preparing the bibliography page

Typically, the notes in *Chicago*-style papers are followed by a bibliography, an alphabetically arranged list of all of the works cited or consulted. Page 399 shows a sample bibliography in *Chicago* style.

Type the title "Bibliography," centered, about one inch from the top of the page. Number bibliography pages consecutively with the rest of the paper. Begin each entry at the left margin, and indent any additional lines one-half inch (or five spaces). Single-space individual entries but double-space between entries.

ALPHABETIZING THE LIST Alphabetize the bibliography by the last names of the authors (or editors); when a work has no author or editor, alphabetize by the first word of the title other than *A, An,* or *The.*

If your list includes two or more works by the same author, use three dashes (or three hyphens) instead of the author's name in all entries after the first. You may arrange the entries alphabetically by title or chronologically; be consistent throughout the bibliography.

AUTHORS Invert the name of the first author or editor. With two or more authors, use "and," not an ampersand (&). For works with four or more authors, use the first author's name, inverted, followed by "et al."

NOTE: The sample notes and bibliography pages show you how to type bibliographic information for *Chicago*-style papers. For more information about the exact format of notes and bibliography entries, see A2-c.

A2-e Sample pages: *Chicago* style

The following sample pages are based on guidelines set forth in *The Chicago Manual of Style,* 14th ed.

SAMPLE *CHICAGO* TITLE PAGE

Page number not
typed on title page.

The Forgotten Pioneers:

African Americans on the Western Frontier

Title page includes
full title, writer's
name, course title,
name of instructor,
and date.

Robert Diaz

History 120

Professor Marshall

3 March 1998

SAMPLE *CHICAGO* PAGE

Diaz 2

Most Americans know something of Billy the Kid, Sitting Bull, and General Custer; their lives have been featured as subjects of high school lectures as well as books, films, and TV dramas. But how many people have heard of Clara Brown, an African American who helped bring groups of her people west by wagon train, or of Bill Pickett, a black cowboy who was one of the most famous rodeo riders in the United States?[1] How many know of the Tenth Cavalry, black soldiers who rode and fought on the western plains?[2] Until recently, the role of African Americans in the settlement of the West has been largely ignored in schools and in the media. A growing body of historical research, however, has pointed out the significance of African Americans to the westward development of the United States.

From the American Revolution to the turn of the twentieth century, thousands of African Americans headed west looking for opportunity and a new start in a new land, hoping to escape slavery and racist conditions in the East. They often discovered, however, that discriminatory attitudes had preceded them. As William Lorenz Katz writes, the white pioneers who headed west "carried the virus of racism with them, as much a part of their psyche as their heralded courage and their fears."[3] In the nineteenth century, white settlers from Ohio to the Oregon Territory were quick to pass laws restricting the freedoms of black pioneers in the newly settled territories. The Oregon laws were particularly unjust. In addition to their constitutional provisions that prevented blacks from voting and serving in the militia, Oregonians passed a law in 1857 that actually excluded blacks from their territory. Black men were

Page number in upper right corner; first page after title page is page 2; writer's last name precedes page number (optional).

Raised arabic number (placed outside punctuation) indicates citation.

Thesis announces central claim of paper.

SAMPLE *CHICAGO* ENDNOTES

Notes page is numbered consecutively.

Heading "Notes" is centered 1″ from top of page.

First line of each note indented ½″ (or five spaces).

Note number is not raised and is followed by period.

Authors' names are not inverted.

Entries singlespaced; doublespacing between entries.

Last name refers to an earlier note by the same author.

Diaz 14

Notes

1. Ruth Pelz, Black Heroes of the Wild West (Seattle: Open Hand Publishing, 1990), 15-36.

2. William H. Leckie, The Buffalo Soldiers (Norman: University of Oklahoma Press, 1967), 21.

3. William Lorenz Katz, The Black West: A Pictorial History (New York: Touchstone, 1996), 307.

4. Katz, Black West, 55-56.

5. William Lorenz Katz, The Westward Movement and Abolitionism (Austin: Steck-Vaughn Publishers, Raintree, 1992), 32.

6. Scott Minerbrook, "The Forgotten Pioneers," U.S. News and World Report, 8 August 1994, 53.

7. Katz, Black West, 49.

8. Ginia Bellafante, "Wild West 101," Time, 22 February 1993, 75.

9. John Mack Faragher, "The Frontier Trail: Rethinking Turner and Reimagining the American West," American Historical Review 98 (1993): 106-7.

10. Faragher, 110.

11. Bellafante, 75.

12. Kenneth W. Porter, The Negro on the American Frontier (New York: Arno Press, 1971), 42-45.

13. Porter, 60.

14. Faragher, 107.

SAMPLE *CHICAGO* BIBLIOGRAPHY

<table>
<tr><td>

Diaz 16

Bibliography

Bellafante, Ginia. "Wild West 101." <u>Time</u>, 22 February
    1993, 75.

Crouch, Barry A. <u>The Freedmen's Bureau and Black
    Texans</u>. Austin: University of Texas Press, 1992.

Dolan, Edward F. <u>Famous Builders of California</u>. New
    York: Dodd, Mead, 1924.

Faragher, John Mack. "The Frontier Trail: Rethinking
    Turner and Reimagining the American West."
    <u>American Historical Review</u> 98 (1993): 106-17.

Katz, William Lorenz. <u>The Black West: A Pictorial
    History</u>. New York: Touchstone, 1996.

---. <u>The Westward Movement and Abolitionism</u>. Austin:
    Steck-Vaughn Publishers, Raintree, 1992.

Leckie, William H. <u>The Buffalo Soldiers</u>. Norman: Uni-
    versity of Oklahoma Press, 1967.

Minerbrook, Scott. "The Forgotten Pioneers." <u>U.S. News
    and World Report</u>, 8 August 1994, 53-55.

Pelz, Ruth. <u>Black Heroes of the Wild West</u>. Seattle:
    Open Hand Publishing, 1990.

Porter, Kenneth W. <u>The Negro on the American Frontier</u>.
    New York: Arno Press, 1971.

Wheeler, B. Gordon. <u>Black California: The History of
    African Americans in the Golden State</u>. New York:
    Hippocrene Books, 1993.

</td><td>

Bibliography page
is numbered
consecutively.

Heading "Bibliogra-
phy" is centered 1″
from top of page.

Entries are alpha-
betized by authors'
last names.

Three hyphens
indicate work by
same author as in
previous entry.

First line of entry
begins at left mar-
gin; additional lines
indent ½″ (or five
spaces).

Entries single-
spaced; double-
spacing between
entries.

</td></tr>
</table>

A3

List of style manuals

A *Writer's Reference* describes three commonly used systems of documentation: MLA, used in English and the humanities (see M); APA, used in psychology and the social sciences (see A1); and *Chicago*, used primarily in history (see A2). Following is a list of style manuals used in a variety of disciplines.

BIOLOGY

Council of Biology Editors. *Scientific Style and Format: The CBE Manual for Authors, Editors, and Publishers.* 6th ed. New York: Cambridge UP, 1994.

CHEMISTRY

Dodd, Janet S., ed. *The ACS Style Guide: A Manual for Authors and Editors.* Washington: Amer. Chemical Soc., 1986.

ENGLISH AND THE HUMANITIES (SEE M.)

Gibaldi, Joseph. *MLA Handbook for Writers of Research Papers.* 5th ed. New York: MLA, 1999.

GEOLOGY

Bates, Robert L., Rex Buchanan, and Marla Adkins-Heljeson, eds. *Geowriting: A Guide to Writing, Editing, and Printing in Earth Science.* 5th ed. Alexandria: Amer. Geological Inst., 1992.

GOVERNMENT DOCUMENTS

Garner, Diane L. *The Complete Guide to Citing Government Information Resources: A Manual for Writers and Librarians.* Rev. ed. Bethesda: Congressional Information Service, 1993.

United States Government Printing Office. *Manual of Style.* Washington: GPO, 1988.

HISTORY (SEE A2.)

The Chicago Manual of Style. 14th ed. Chicago: U of Chicago P, 1993.

JOURNALISM

Goldstein, Norm, ed. *Associated Press Stylebook and Libel Manual.* 32nd ed. New York: Associated Press, 1997.

LAW
Columbia Law Review. *A Uniform System of Citation.* 16th ed.
Cambridge: Harvard Law Rev. Assn., 1996.

LINGUISTICS
Linguistic Society of America. "LSA Style Sheet." Published annu-
ally in the December issue of the *LSA Bulletin.*

MATHEMATICS
American Mathematical Society. *The AMS Author Handbook: General Instructions for Preparing Manuscripts.* Providence: AMS,
1994.

MEDICINE
Iverson, Cheryl, et al. *American Medical Association Manual of
Style.* 8th ed. Baltimore: Williams and Wilkins, 1989.

MUSIC
Holoman, D. Kern, ed. *Writing about Music: A Style Sheet from the
Editors of* 19th-Century Music. Berkeley: U of California P,
1988.

PHYSICS
American Institute of Physics. *Style Manual: Instructions to
Authors and Volume Editors for the Preparation of AIP Book
Manuscripts.* 5th ed. New York: AIP, 1995.

POLITICAL SCIENCE
American Political Science Association. *Style Manual for Political
Science.* Rev. ed. Washington: Amer. Political Science Assn.,
1993.

PSYCHOLOGY AND THE SOCIAL SCIENCES (SEE A1.)
American Psychological Association. *Publication Manual of the
American Psychological Association.* 5th ed. Washington: APA,
2001.

SCIENCE AND TECHNICAL WRITING
*American National Standard for the Preparation of Scientific
Papers for Written or Oral Presentation.* New York: Amer.
Natl. Standards Inst., 1979.

Rubens, Philip, ed. *Science and Technical Writing: A Manual of
Style.* New York: Holt, 1992.

SOCIAL WORK
National Association of Social Workers. *Writing for NASW.* 2nd ed.
Silver Springs: Natl. Assn. of Social Workers, 1994.

B

Basic Grammar

Index

B

Basic Grammar

B1

Parts of speech

The parts of speech are a system for classifying words. There are eight parts of speech: noun, pronoun, verb, adjective, adverb, preposition, conjunction, and interjection. Many words can function as more than one part of speech. For example, depending on its use in a sentence, the word *paint* can be a noun (*The paint is wet*) or a verb (*Please paint the ceiling next*).

B1-a Nouns

A noun is the name of a person, place, thing, or an idea. Nouns are often but not always signaled by an article (*a, an, the*).

> **N**   **N**   **N**
> The cat in gloves catches no mice.

> **N**   **N**   **N**
> Repetition does not transform a lie into truth.

Nouns sometimes function as adjectives modifying other nouns.

> **N/ADJ**   **N/ADJ**
> You can't make a silk purse out of a sow's ear.

Nouns are classified for a variety of purposes. When capitalization is the issue, we speak of *proper* versus *common* nouns (see S3-a). If the problem is one of word choice, we may speak of *concrete* versus *abstract* nouns (see W5-b). Most nouns come in *singular* and *plural* forms; *collective* nouns may be either singular or plural (see G1-f and G3-a). *Possessive* nouns require an apostrophe (see P5-a).

B1-b Pronouns

A pronoun is a word used in place of a noun. Usually the pronoun substitutes for a specific noun, known as its *antecedent*.

> When the *wheel* squeaks, *it* is greased.

Although most pronouns function as substitutes for nouns, some can function as adjectives modifying nouns.

PN/ADJ
This hanging will surely be a lesson to me.

Most of the pronouns in English are listed in this section.

PERSONAL PRONOUNS Personal pronouns refer to specific persons or things.

Singular: I, me, you, she, her, he, him, it

Plural: we, us, you, they, them

POSSESSIVE PRONOUNS Possessive pronouns indicate ownership.

Singular: my, mine, your, yours, her, hers, his, its

Plural: our, ours, your, yours, their, theirs

INTENSIVE AND REFLEXIVE PRONOUNS Intensive pronouns emphasize a noun or another pronoun (The senator *herself* met us at the door). Reflexive pronouns name a receiver of an action identical with the doer of the action (Paula cut *herself*).

Singular: myself, yourself, himself, herself, itself

Plural: ourselves, yourselves, themselves

RELATIVE PRONOUNS Relative pronouns introduce subordinate clauses functioning as adjectives (The man *who robbed us* was never caught). In addition to introducing the clause, the relative pronoun, in this case *who,* points back to a noun or pronoun that the clause modifies (*man*). (See B3-e.)

who, whom, whose, which, that

DEMONSTRATIVE PRONOUNS Demonstrative pronouns identify or point to nouns. Frequently they function as adjectives (*This* chair is my favorite), but they may also function as noun equivalents (*This* is my favorite chair).

this, that, these, those

INDEFINITE PRONOUNS Indefinite pronouns refer to nonspecific persons or things. Most are always singular (*everyone, each*); some are always plural (*both, many*); a few may be singular or plural (see G1-e).

all, another, any, anybody, anyone, anything, both, each, either, everybody, everyone, everything, few, many, neither, nobody, none, no one, nothing, one, several, some, somebody, someone, something

RECIPROCAL PRONOUNS Reciprocal pronouns refer to individual parts of a plural antecedent (By turns, my wife and I helped *each other* through college).

each other, one another

NOTE: Pronouns cause a variety of problems for writers. See Pronoun-antecedent agreement (G3-a), Pronoun reference (G3-b), Distinguishing between pronouns such as *I* and *me* (G3-c), and Distinguishing between *who* and *whom* (G3-d).

B1-c Verbs

The verb of a sentence usually expresses action (*jump, think*) or being (*is, become*). It is composed of a main verb (MV) possibly preceded by one or more helping verbs (HV).

                MV
The best fish swim near the bottom.

        HV   MV
A marriage is not built in a day.

Notice that words can intervene between the helping and the main verb (*is* not *built*).

Helping verbs

Helping verbs in English include forms of *have, do,* and *be,* which may also function as main verbs; and verbs known as modals, which function only as helping verbs. The forms of *have, do,* and *be* change form to indicate tense; the modals do not.

FORMS OF *HAVE, DO,* AND *BE*
have, has, had
do, does, did
be, am, is, are, was, were, being, been

MODALS
can, could, may, might, must, shall, should, will, would, ought to

Main verbs

A main verb changes form if put into the following test sentences. When both the past-tense and past-participle forms end in *-ed,* the verb is regular; otherwise, the verb is irregular. (See G2-a.)

BASE FORM	Usually I (*walk, ride*).
PAST TENSE	Yesterday I (*walked, rode*).
PAST PARTICIPLE	I have (*walked, ridden*) many times before.
PRESENT PARTICIPLE	I am (*walking, riding*) right now.
***-S* FORM**	Usually he/she/it (*walks, rides*).

If a word doesn't change form when slipped into these test sentences, you can be certain that it is not a main verb. For example, the noun *revolution,* though it may seem to suggest an action, can never function as a main verb. Just try to make it behave like one (*Today I revolution . . . Yesterday I revolutioned . . .*) and you'll see why.

The verb *be* is highly irregular, having eight forms instead of the usual five: the base form *be;* the present-tense forms *am, is,* and *are;* the past-tense forms *was* and *were;* the present participle *being;* and the past participle *been.*

NOTE: Some verbs are followed by words that look like prepositions but are so closely associated with the verb that they are a part of its meaning. These words are known as *particles.* Common verb-particle combinations include *bring up, call off, drop off, give in, look up, run into,* and *take off.*

A lot of parents *pack up* their troubles and *send* them *off* to camp.
　　　　　　　　　　　　　　　　　　　　—Raymond Duncan

NOTE: Verbs cause many problems for writers. See Subject-verb agreement (G1); Other problems with verbs, including verb forms, tense, mood, and voice (G2); and ESL problems with verbs (T2).

B1-d Adjectives and articles

An adjective is a word used to modify, or describe, a noun or pronoun. An adjective usually answers one of these questions: Which one? What kind of? How many?

> ADJ
> the lame elephant [Which elephant?]

> ADJ   ADJ
> valuable old stamps [What kind of stamps?]

> ADJ
> sixteen candles [How many candles?]

Adjectives usually precede the words they modify. However, they may also follow linking verbs, in which case they describe the subject. (See B2-b.)

>   ADJ
> Good medicine always tastes bitter.

Articles, sometimes classified as adjectives, are used to mark nouns. There are only three: the definite article *the* and the indefinite articles *a* and *an*.

> ART   ART
> A country can be judged by the quality of its proverbs.

NOTE: Writers sometimes misuse adjectives (see G4). Speakers of English as a second language may have trouble placing adjectives correctly (see T3-e); they may also encounter difficulties with articles (see T1).

B1-e Adverbs

An adverb is a word used to modify a verb (or verbal), an adjective, or another adverb. It usually answers one of these questions: When? Where? How? Why? Under what conditions? To what degree?

>   ADV
> Pull gently at a weak rope. [Pull how?]

>   ADV
> Read the best books first. [Read when?]

Adverbs modifying adjectives or other adverbs usually intensify or limit the intensity of the word they modify.

> ADV ADV
> Be extremely good, and you will be very lonesome.

The negators *not* and *never* are classified as adverbs.

NOTE: Writers sometimes misuse adverbs (see G4). Speakers of English as a second language may have trouble placing adverbs correctly (see T3-e).

B1-f Prepositions

A preposition is a word placed before a noun or pronoun to form a phrase modifying another word in the sentence. The prepositional phrase nearly always functions as an adjective or as an adverb. (See B3-a.)

> P P
> The road *to hell* is paved *with good intentions*.

To hell functions as an adjective modifying the noun *road; with good intentions* functions as an adverb, modifying the verb *is paved*.

There are a limited number of prepositions in English. The most common are included in the following list.

about	beneath	for	out	to
above	beside	from	outside	toward
across	besides	in	over	under
after	between	inside	past	underneath
against	beyond	into	plus	unlike
along	but	like	regarding	until
among	by	near	respecting	unto
around	concerning	next	round	up
as	considering	of	since	upon
at	despite	off	than	with
before	down	on	through	within
behind	during	onto	throughout	without
below	except	opposite	till	

Some prepositions are more than a word long. *Along with, as well as, in addition to, instead of, next to,* and *up to* are common examples.

NOTE: Except for certain idiomatic uses (see W5-d), prepositions cause few problems for native speakers of English. For second-language speakers, however, prepositions can cause considerable difficulty (see T2-d and T4-b).

B1-g Conjunctions

Conjunctions join words, phrases, or clauses, and they indicate the relation between the elements joined.

COORDINATING CONJUNCTIONS Coordinating conjunctions connect grammatically equal elements. (See E1-b and E6.)

and, but, or, nor, for, so, yet

CORRELATIVE CONJUNCTIONS Correlative conjunctions are pairs of conjunctions that connect grammatically equal elements. (See E1-b.)

either . . . or, neither . . . nor, not only . . . but also, whether . . . or, both . . . and

SUBORDINATING CONJUNCTIONS Subordinating conjunctions introduce subordinate clauses and indicate their relation to the rest of the sentence. (See B3-e.)

after, although, as, as if, because, before, even though, if, in order that, rather than, since, so that, than, that, though, unless, until, when, where, whether, while

CONJUNCTIVE ADVERBS Conjunctive adverbs are adverbs used to indicate the relation between independent clauses. (See G6-b and P3-b.)

accordingly, also, anyway, besides, certainly, consequently, conversely, finally, furthermore, hence, however, incidentally, indeed, instead, likewise, meanwhile, moreover, nevertheless, next, nonetheless, otherwise, similarly, specifically, still, subsequently, then, therefore, thus

NOTE: The ability to distinguish between conjunctive adverbs and coordinating conjunctions will help you avoid run-on sentences and make punctuation decisions (see G6, P1-a, and P3-b). The ability to recognize subordinating conjunctions will help you avoid sentence fragments (see G5).

B1-h Interjections

Interjections are words used to express surprise or emotion (*Oh! Hey! Wow!*).

B2

Parts of sentences

Most English sentences flow from subject to verb to any objects or complements. *Predicate* is the grammatical term given to the verb plus its objects, complements, and modifiers.

B2-a Subjects

The subject of a sentence names who or what the sentence is about. The simple subject is always a noun or a pronoun; the complete subject consists of the simple subject (ss) and all of its modifiers.

> ┌ ss ┐
> *The purity of a revolution* usually lasts about two weeks.

> ┌ ss ┐
> *Historical books that contain no lies* are extremely tedious.

> ┌ ss ┐
> In every country, *the sun* rises in the morning.

To find the complete subject, ask Who? or What?, insert the verb, and finish the question. What usually lasts about two weeks? *The purity of a revolution.* What are extremely tedious? *Historical books that contain no lies.* What rises in the morning? *The sun* [not *In every country, the sun*].

To find the simple subject, strip away all modifiers in the complete subject. This includes single-word modifiers such as *the* and *historical,* phrases such as *of a revolution,* and subordinate clauses such as *that contain no lies.*

A sentence may have a compound subject containing two or more simple subjects joined with a coordinating conjunction such as *and* or *or.*

┌─ ss ─┐   ┌─ ss ──┐
Much industry and little conscience make us rich.

In imperative sentences, which give advice or commands, the subject is an understood *you.*

[*You*] Hitch your wagon to a star.

Although the subject ordinarily comes before the verb, occasionally it does not. When a sentence begins with *There is* or *There are* (or *There was* or *There were*), the subject follows the verb. The word *There* is an expletive in such constructions, an empty word serving merely to get the sentence started.

┌── ss ──┐
There is *no substitute for victory.*

Sometimes a writer will invert a sentence for effect.

┌─ ss ─┐
Happy is *the nation that has no history.*

In questions, the subject may appear before the verb, after the verb, or between parts of the verb.

s ┌── v ──┐
Who will take the first step?

v┌── s ──┐
Why is the first step so difficult?

HV S MV
Will you take the first step?

NOTE: The ability to recognize the subject of a sentence will help you edit for a variety of problems such as sentence fragments (G5), faulty subject-verb agreement (G1), and misuse of pronouns such as *I* and *me* (G3-c). If English is not your native language, see also T3-a and T3-b.

B2-b   Verbs, objects, and complements

Section B1-c explains how to identify verbs. A sentence's verb(s) may be classified as linking, transitive, or intransitive, depending on the kinds of objects or complements the verb can (or cannot) take.

Linking verbs and subject complements

Linking verbs (v) take subject complements (sc), words or word groups that complete the meaning of the subject (s) by either renaming it or describing it.

```
┌──────────── s ────────────┐ ┌─ v ─┐┌─ sc ─┐
The handwriting on the wall may be a forgery.
```

```
┌ s ┐ v ┌ sc ┐
Love is blind.
```

When the simple subject complement renames the subject, it is a noun or pronoun, such as *forgery;* when it describes the subject, it is an adjective, such as *blind.*

Linking verbs are usually a form of *be: be, am, is, are, was, were, being, been.* Verbs such as *appear, become, feel, grow, look, make, prove, remain, seem, smell, sound,* and *taste* are linking when they are followed by a word group that names or describes the subject.

Transitive verbs and direct objects

Transitive verbs take direct objects (DO), words or word groups that complete the meaning of the verb by naming a receiver of the action.

```
┌───── s ─────┐  v  ┌──────── DO ────────┐
The little snake studies the ways of the big serpent.
```

The simple direct object is always a noun, such as *ways,* or a pronoun.

Transitive verbs usually appear in the active voice, with the subject doing the action and a direct object receiving the action. Active-voice sentences can be transformed into the passive voice, with the subject receiving the action instead.

ACTIVE VOICE   The early bird sometimes catches the early worm.

PASSIVE VOICE   The early worm is sometimes caught by the early bird.

What was once the direct object (*the early worm*) has become the subject in the passive-voice transformation, and the original subject appears in a prepositional phrase beginning with *by.* The *by* phrase is frequently omitted in passive-voice constructions: *The early worm is sometimes caught.* (See also W3-b.)

Transitive verbs, indirect objects, and direct objects

The direct object of a transitive verb is sometimes preceded by an indirect object (IO), a noun or pronoun telling to whom or for whom the action of the sentence is done.

> ┌ S ┐┌ V ┐   IO ┌ DO ┐   S┌── V ──┐   IO   ┌── DO ──┐
> You show [to] me a hero, and I will write [for] you a tragedy.

Transitive verbs, direct objects, and object complements

The direct object of a transitive verb is sometimes followed by an object complement (OC), a word or word group that completes the direct object's meaning by renaming or describing it.

> ┌──── S ────┐ V ┌ DO ┐ ┌────────── OC ──────────┐
> Some people call a spade an agricultural implement.

> ┌ S ┐   V   ┌──── DO ────┐┌ OC ┐
> Love makes all hard hearts gentle.

When the object complement renames the direct object, it is a noun or pronoun, such as *implement.* When it describes the direct object, it is an adjective, such as *gentle.*

Intransitive verbs

Intransitive verbs take no objects or complements. They may or may not be followed by adverbial modifiers.

> S   V
> Money talks.

> S   V ⌒────────┐
> All roads lead to Rome.

Nothing receives the actions of talking and leading in these sentences, so the verbs are intransitive. Intransitive verbs are often followed by adverbial modifiers. In the second sentence, for example, *to Rome* is a prepositional phrase functioning as an adverb modifying *lead.*

NOTE: The dictionary will tell you whether a verb is transitive or intransitive. Some verbs have both transitive and intransitive functions.

> **TRANSITIVE** Sandra flew her Cessna over the canyon.
>
> **INTRANSITIVE** A bald eagle flew overhead.

In the first example, *flew* has a direct object that receives the action: *her Cessna.* In the second example, the verb is followed by an adverb (*overhead*), not by a direct object.

B3

Subordinate word groups

Subordinate word groups cannot stand alone. They function only within sentences, usually as adjectives, adverbs, or nouns.

B3-a Prepositional phrases

A prepositional phrase begins with a preposition such as *at, by, for, from, in, of, on, to,* or *with* (see B1-f) and ends with a noun or a noun equivalent called its *object.*

Prepositional phrases function as adjectives or adverbs. When functioning as an adjective, a prepositional phrase usually appears right after the noun or pronoun it modifies.

> Variety is the spice *of life.*

Adjective phrases answer one or both of the questions Which one? and What kind of? If we ask Which spice? or What kind of spice? we get a sensible answer: *the spice of life.*

Adverbial prepositional phrases modifying the verb can appear nearly anywhere in a sentence.

> Do not judge a tree *by its bark.*

> Tyranny will *in time* lead to revolution.

To the ant, a few drops of rain are a flood.

Adverb phrases usually answer one of these questions: When? Where? How? Why? Under what conditions? To what degree?

Do not judge a tree *how? By its bark.*

Tyranny will lead to revolution *when? In time.*

A few drops of rain are a flood *under what conditions? To the ant.*

B3-b Verbal phrases

A verbal is a verb form that does not function as the verb of a clause. Verbals include infinitives (the word *to* plus the base form of the verb), present participles (the *-ing* form of the verb), and past participles (the form of the verb usually ending in *-d, -ed, -n, -en,* or *-t*) (see G2-a).

Verbals can take objects, complements, and modifiers to form verbal phrases. These phrases are classified as participial, gerund, and infinitive.

Participial phrases

Participial phrases always function as adjectives. Their verbals are either present participles, always ending in *-ing,* or past participles, frequently ending in *-d, -ed, -n, -en,* or *-t* (see G2-a).

Participial phrases frequently appear right after the noun or pronoun they modify.

Truth *kept in the dark* will never save the world.

Unlike other adjectival word groups, however, participial phrases can precede the word they modify or appear at some distance from it.

Being weak, foxes are distinguished by superior tact.

History is something that never happened, *written by someone who wasn't there.*

Gerund phrases

Gerund phrases are built around present participles (verb forms ending in *-ing*), and they always function as nouns: usually as subjects, subject complements, direct objects, or objects of the preposition.

Justifying a fault doubles it.

Kleptomaniacs can't help *helping themselves.*

Infinitive phrases

Infinitive phrases, usually constructed around *to* plus the base form of the verb (*to call, to drink*), can function as adjectives, adverbs, or nouns. When functioning as a noun, an infinitive phrase usually plays the role of subject, subject complement, or direct object.

We do not have the right *to abandon the poor.*

He cut off his nose *to spite his face.*

To side with truth is noble.

B3-c Appositive phrases

Appositive phrases describe nouns or pronouns. In form they are nouns or noun equivalents.

Politicians, *acrobats at heart,* can sit on a fence and yet keep both ears to the ground.

B3-d Absolute phrases

An absolute phrase modifies a whole clause or sentence, not just one word. It consists of a noun or noun equivalent usually followed by a participial phrase.

His words dipped in honey, the senator mesmerized the crowd.

B3-e   Subordinate clauses

Subordinate clauses are patterned like sentences, having subjects and verbs and sometimes objects or complements, but they function within sentences as adjectives, adverbs, or nouns. They cannot stand alone as complete sentences.

Adjective clauses

Adjective clauses modify nouns or pronouns, usually answering the question Which one? or What kind of? They begin with a relative pronoun (*who, whom, whose, which,* or *that*) or a relative adverb (*when* or *where*).

The arrow *that has left the bow* never returns.

In addition to introducing the clause, the relative pronoun points back to the noun that the clause modifies.

The fur *that warms a monarch* once warmed a bear.

Relative pronouns are sometimes "understood."

> The things [*that*] *we know best* are the things [*that*] *we haven't been taught.*

The parts of an adjective clause are often arranged as in sentences (subject/verb/object or complement).

> S   V   DO
> We often forgive the people *who bore us.*

Frequently, however, the object or complement appears first, violating the normal order of subject/verb/object.

> DO   S   V
> We rarely forgive those *whom we bore.*

NOTE: For punctuation of adjective clauses, see P1 c and P2-e. If English is not your native language, see T3-c for a common problem with adjective clauses.

Adverb clauses

Adverb clauses modify verbs, adjectives, or other adverbs, usually answering one of these questions: When? Where? Why? How? Under what conditions? To what degree? They begin with a subordinating conjunction (*after, although, as, as if, because, before, even though, if, in order that, rather than, since, so that, than, that, though, unless, until, when, where, whether, while*).

When the well is dry, we know the worth of water.

Venice would be a fine city *if it were only drained.*

Noun clauses

Noun clauses function as subjects, objects, or complements. They usually begin with one of the following words: *how, that, which, who, whoever, whom, whomever, what, whatever, when, where, whether, whose, why.*

S
Whoever gossips to you will gossip of you.

DO
We will never forget *where we buried the hatchet.*

The word introducing the clause may or may not play a significant role in the clause. In the preceding example sentences, *Whoever* is the subject of its clause, but *where* does not perform a function in its clause.

As with adjective clauses, the parts of a noun clause may appear out of their normal order (subject/verb/object).

DO S V
Talent is *what you possess.*

The parts of a noun clause may also appear in their normal order.

S V DO
Genius is *what possesses you.*

B4

Sentence types

Sentences are classified in two ways: according to their structure (simple, compound, complex, and compound-complex) and according to their purpose (declarative, imperative, interrogative, and exclamatory).

B4-a Sentence structures

Depending on the number and types of clauses they contain, sentences are classified as simple, compound, complex, or compound-complex.

Clauses come in two varieties: independent and subordinate. An independent clause contains a subject and predicate, and it either stands alone or could stand alone. A subordinate clause also contains a subject and predicate, but it functions within a sentence as an adjective, an adverb, or a noun; it cannot stand alone.

SIMPLE SENTENCE   A simple sentence is one independent clause with no subordinate clauses.

┌─────── INDEPENDENT CLAUSE ───────┐
Without music, life would be a mistake.

COMPOUND SENTENCE   A compound sentence is composed of two or more independent clauses with no subordinate clauses. The independent clauses are usually joined with a comma and a coordinating conjunction (*and, but, or, nor, for, so, yet*) or with a semicolon.

┌─ INDEPENDENT CLAUSE ─┐   ┌─── INDEPENDENT CLAUSE ───┐
One arrow is easily broken, but you can't break a bundle of ten.

COMPLEX SENTENCE   A complex sentence is composed of one independent clause with one or more subordinate clauses.

       SUBORDINATE
┌─   CLAUSE   ─┐
If you scatter thorns, don't go barefoot.

COMPOUND-COMPLEX SENTENCE A compound-complex sentence contains at least two independent clauses and at least one subordinate clause. The following sentence contains two independent clauses, each of which contains a subordinate clause.

```
  ┌──── IND CLAUSE ────┐      ┌──────── IND CLAUSE ────────┐
      ┌ SUB CLAUSE ┐              ┌ SUB CLAUSE ┐
```
Tell me what you eat, and I will tell you what you are.

B4-b Sentence purposes

Writers use declarative sentences to make statements, imperative sentences to issue requests or commands, interrogative sentences to ask questions, and exclamatory sentences to make exclamations.

DECLARATIVE   The echo always has the last word.

IMPERATIVE   Love your neighbor.

INTERROGATIVE   Are second thoughts always wisest?

EXCLAMATORY   I want to wash the flag, not burn it!

(Continued from page vi)

Eugene Boe, from "Pioneers to Eternity: Norwegians on the Prairie," *The Immigrant Experience,* edited by Thomas C. Wheeler. ©1971 by Thomas C. Wheeler. A Dial Press Book, Doubleday & Co., Inc.

Jane Brody, from *Jane Brody's Nutrition Book.* Copyright ©1981 by Jane E. Brody. Reprinted by permission of W. W. Norton & Company, Inc., and Wendy Weil Agency, Inc.

California Mountain Lion Page from the Sierra Club Web site <http://www.sierraclub.org/chapters/ca/mountain-lion>. ©1998 by the Sierra Club.

Roger Caras, from "What's a Koala?" Copyright ©1983 by Roger Caras. First appeared in *Geo* magazine, May 1983. Reprinted by permission of Roberta Pryor, Inc.

Bruce Catton, from "Grant and Lee: A Study in Contrasts," *The American Story,* edited by Earl Schenck Miers. Copyright ©1956 U.S. Capitol Historical Society, all rights reserved.

Earl Conrad, from *Harriet Tubman.* Copyright ©1943, 1969 by Earl Conrad. Reprinted by permission of Paul S. Eriksson, Publisher.

Emily Dickinson, from "The Snake." Reprinted by permission of the publishers and the Trustees of Amherst College from *The Poems of Emily Dickinson,* edited by Thomas H. Johnson. Cambridge: The Belknap Press of Harvard University Press. Copyright ©1951, 1955, 1979, 1983 by the President and Fellows of Harvard College.

Excerpt from *The Dorling Kindersley Encyclopedia of Fishing.* Copyright ©1994 Dorling Kindersley. Reprinted with permission.

Erik Eckholm, from "Pygmy Chimp Readily Learns Language Skill." *The New York Times.* Copyright ©1985 by The New York Times Company. Reprinted by permission.

Jane Goodall, from *In the Shadow of Man.* Copyright ©1971 by Hugo and Jane van Lawick-Goodall. Published by Houghton Mifflin Company.

Stephen Jay Gould, from "Were Dinosaurs Dumb?" *The Panda's Thumb: More Reflections on Natural History.* Copyright ©1978 by Stephen Jay Gould. Reprinted by permission of W. W. Norton & Company, Inc.

Dan Gutman, from *The Way Baseball Works.* Reprinted with permission of Simon & Schuster. Copyright ©1996 by Byron Press/Richard Ballantine, Inc.

Hilary Hauser, from "Exploring a Sunken Realm in Australia." *National Geographic,* January 1984. Reprinted by permission of the National Geographic Society.

Richard Hofstadter, from *America at 1750: A Social Portrait.* Copyright ©1971 by Beatrice K. Hofstadter, executrix of the estate of Richard Hofstadter. Published by Alfred A. Knopf, Inc.

Philip Kopper, "How to Open an Oyster." Copyright ©1979 by Philip Kopper. Published by Times Books, a division of Quadrangle/The New York Times Book Co., Inc., from *The Wild Edge: Life and Lore of the Great Atlantic Beachers* by Philip Kopper.

www.lycos.com—and a search for "mountain lion" ©1998 Lycos, Inc. Lycos® is a registered trademark of Carnegie Mellon University. All rights reserved. Reprinted with permission.

Margaret Mead, from "New Superstitions for Old." *A Way of Seeing.* Published by William Morrow & Company, Inc.

Gloria Naylor, from *Linden Hills.* Copyright ©1985 by Gloria Naylor. Published by Houghton Mifflin Company.

Index

Index

S

A Writer's Online Resources

For an online version of this chart, which will be updated periodically, visit The Writer's Reference Web Site *<http://www.bedfordstmartins.com/hacker/writersref>.*

REFERENCE SITES

WWWebster Dictionary   <http://www.m-w.com/netdict.htm>

A Web of On-line Dictionaries   <http://www.bucknell.edu/~rbeard/diction1.html#special>

OneLook Dictionaries   <http://www.onelook.com>

ARTFL Project: Roget's Thesaurus Search Form   <http://humanities.uchicago.edu/forms_unrest/ROGET.html>

WRITING LABS

Online Writery   <http://www.missouri.edu/~writery>

Purdue University Online Writing Lab   <http://owl.english.purdue.edu>

The University of Michigan OWL: Online Writing and Learning   <http://www.lsa.umich.edu/ecb/OWL/owl.html>

ESL SITES

Dave's ESL Café   <http://eslcafe.com>

Topics: An Online Magazine by and for Learners of English   <http://www.rice.edu/projects/topics/Electronic/Magazine.html>

VIRTUAL LIBRARIES

The Internet Public Library   <http://www.ipl.org>

Thor+: The Libraries of Purdue University   <http://thorplus.lib.purdue.edu/index.html>

The WWW Virtual Library   <http://vlib.stanford.edu/Overview.html>

The Library of Congress   <http://lcweb.loc.gov>

The Webliography: Internet Subject Guides   <http://www.lib.lsu.edu/weblio.html>

TEXT ARCHIVES

Electronic Text Center — University of Virginia Library   <http://etext.lib.virginia.edu>

Project Bartleby Archive   <http://www.columbia.edu/acis/bartleby>

Project Gutenberg   <http://promo.net/pg>

GOVERNMENT SITES

U.S. Census Bureau:
The Official Statistics

<http://www.census.gov>

Thomas: Legislative Information
on the Internet

<http://thomas.loc.gov>

U.S. State & Local Gateway

<http://www.statelocal.gov>

NEWS SITES

The New York Times on the Web

<http://www.nytimes.com>

The Washington Post

<http://www.washingtonpost.com>

U.S. News Online

<http://www.usnews.com/usnews/
home.htm>

nationalgeographic.com

<http://www.nationalgeographic.com/
main.html>

CNN Interactive

<http://www.cnn.com>

SITES FOR EVALUATING SOURCES

"Checklist for Evaluating
Web Sites," *Canisius College*
Library & Internet

<http://www.canisius.edu/canhp/
canlib/webcrit.htm>

"Evaluating Web Sites:
Criteria and Tools,"
Olin Kroch Uris Libraries

<http://www.library.cornell.edu/okuref/
research/webeval.html>

"Evaluating Internet Information," *Internet Navigator*

<http://sol.slcc.edu/lr/navigator/
discovery/eval.html>

BEDFORD/ST. MARTIN'S SITES

Research and Documentation in
the Electronic Age

<http://www.bedfordstmartins.com/
hacker/resdoc>

Bedford Links to History Resources

<http://www.bedfordstmartins.com/
historylinks>

Bedford Links to Resources in
Literature

<http://www.bedfordstmartins.com/
litlinks>

For additional discipline-specific sites, see page 66.

ESL Menu

A complete section on major ESL problems:

ESL notes in other sections:

Revision Symbols

Numbers refer to sections of this book.

abbr	faulty abbreviation **S4**		*p*	error in punctuation
ad	misuse of adverb or adjective **G4**		*⌄*	comma **P1**
add	add needed word **E2**		*no ,*	no comma **P2**
agr	faulty agreement **G1, G3-a**		*;*	semicolon **P3**
appr	inappropriate language **W4**		*:*	colon **P4**
			⌄	apostrophe **P5**
art	article **T1**		*" "*	quotation marks **P6**
awk	awkward		*. ?*	period, question mark,
cap	capital letter **S3**		*!*	exclamation point,
case	error in case **G3-c, G3-d**		*— ( )*	dash, parentheses,
cliché	cliché **W5-e**		*[ ] ...*	brackets, ellipsis mark,
coh	coherence **C4-d**		*/*	slash **P7**
coord	faulty coordination **E6-b**		*pass*	ineffective passive **W3**
cs	comma splice **G6**		*pn agr*	pronoun agreement **G3-a**
dev	inadequate development **C4-b**		*proof*	proofreading problem **C3-c**
dm	dangling modifier **E3-e**		*ref*	error in pronoun reference **G3-b**
-ed	error in *-ed* ending **G2-d**		*run-on*	run-on sentence **G6**
emph	emphasis **W3**		*-s*	error in *-s* ending **G2-c**
ESL	ESL trouble spot **T1, T2, T3, T4**		*sexist*	sexist language **W4-e**
exact	inexact language **W5**		*shift*	distracting shift **E4**
frag	sentence fragment **G5**		*sl*	slang **W4-c**
fs	fused sentence **G6**		*sp*	misspelled word **S1**
gl/us	see Glossary of Usage **W1**		*sub*	faulty subordination **E6-c, E6-d**
hyph	error in use of hyphen **S2**		*sv agr*	subject-verb agreement **G1, G2-c**
idiom	idioms **W5-d**		*t*	error in verb tense **G2-f**
inc	incomplete construction **E2**		*trans*	transition needed **C4-d**
irreg	error in irregular verb **G2-a**		*usage*	see Glossary of Usage **W1**
ital	italics (underlining) **S6**		*v*	voice **W3**
jarg	jargon **W4-a**		*var*	sentence variety **E6-a, E6-b, E7**
lc	lowercase letter **S3**		*vb*	verb error **G2**
mix	mixed construction **E5**		*w*	wordy **W2**
mm	misplaced modifier **E3-b**		*//*	faulty parallelism **E1**
mood	error in mood **G2-g**		*^*	insert
nonst	nonstandard usage **W4-c**		*x*	obvious error
num	error in use of numbers **S5**		*#*	insert space
om	omitted word **E2**		*⌒*	close up space
¶	new paragraph **C4**			

Detailed Menu